THE BLOODLINE OF WISDOM

The Awakening of a Modern Solutionary

BY ANTHONY "TONY" BOQUET

bush
PUBLISHING
& associates

DEDICATION

This book is dedicated to Morris and Josephine who set the path for this story through loving guidance, and to all the people who make a difference in the lives of others through unselfishly offering wise solutions to their problems in an effort to relieve their suffering.

CONTENTS

PROLOGUE

"I know that I am wise, because I know that I know nothing."

SOCRATES

This book was written in a manner which will encourage you to question and think more deeply while enjoying an interesting story. It will foster ideas in your mind that will awaken and reveal concepts which have been hidden in plain sight for centuries. You will begin to form connections between our common everyday choices and the components of our natural existence.

My personal journey into this topic began with many questions.

- What is wisdom?

- Once you have wisdom, will you make all the right choices?

- Is wisdom a rare trait in today's society?

- Is there a system that pairs man-made problems to an identifiable man-made solution process?

- What attracts certain people to specific careers that focus on solving problems for others?

These are tough questions but the toughest one was:

- Why does it appear that some people make more wise choices than others?

Many people say they have wisdom, yet their choices and decisions, when viewed by others over the truth-revealing passage of time, seem to indicate otherwise. On a very personal level, I feel unworthy of delivering these lessons since I am not even close to being the wisest among us. I am, however, able to say without a doubt that I feel wiser than I did before I met my mentor, King Solomon, through the research of this material. So let me go on record by saying that this book has already made a difference in someone's life. My Own!

People often ask me, "What evidence do you have that a decision made was indeed wise?" The proof of wisdom is this: When we make a wise decision or choice, everyone involved with the outcome benefits in some way and it stands the test of time. Regrets are greatly diminished, the likelihood of positive results skyrocket, and people live a more harmonious existence with their fellow man. And yes, this is still the case. Even though there are people who may disagree, pain and suffering can sometimes accompany even the wisest decisions.

Of course, even the wisest of people will make bad decisions at times. No one is perfect, and no one can have all the knowledge needed to make the right choice in every situation. So how can we know we are making wise decisions; especially as our society grows more and more complex?

Perhaps the best place to start is with a clarifying definition:

"Knowledge obtained from experience and/or education, obtained through a trusted source of high moral and ethical character and/or through the grace of the natural discernment of divine precepts, once applied to a problem in a selfless manner as the best solution, is Wisdom."

By this definition, super intelligence is not a prerequisite for making the best decisions. Wisdom is not just education or even experience; it is knowledge transformed through its application as the best practical *solution*. That practical solution may be as simple as knowing and recognizing that you don't know enough about a problem. In order to fix that, you bring in an expert who does. This too is wisdom.

No matter what life situation we may find ourselves in, we all need wisdom, whether it is our personal wisdom, the wisdom from a wise family member or the wisdom found through a trusted advisor. When we can demonstrate the art of wise decision making, we become an important support person to those we love, those with whom we work, or as an advisor to those we do not even know.

The Awakening of a Modern Solutionary tells the story of an ordinary man with an unknown extraordinary heritage that can be traced back to the Master of Wisdom, Wise King Solomon himself. As you read this story, you too will have access to King Solomon as your own personal teacher, mentor, and important decision-making coach. And as you apply his lessons, you will find an increased opportunity to affect positive change in your life and those of whom you care about.

As you read this book, I ask that you do not make judgments on the religious overtones. Many of the people referenced are considered to be the wisest in history and have also been recognized as religious figures. The main characters are either faithful Jews or Christians whom happen to be devoted Catholics. Guided by their religious upbringing, they try to understand society's philosophies and apply them to a life full of moral, ethical, and spiritual complexities. Regardless of your religious beliefs or lack thereof, the practical insights uncovered in this book can be applied directly to your daily life, and the mysteries of the unknown will leave you with questions burning to be answered. In the same way, although this book was not written to promote a specific political or societal viewpoint, as you apply the steps of wise decision making, you might reconsider some of your own political and social beliefs. That is not the goal of this book. The ideals and concepts presented are nonspecific to religious belief (if any), political persuasion, race, sexual preference, the color of your skin, or even the color of your hair. The situations and choices that we face in our personal lives can only be improved by having a consistent *method* of reaching the right and best solutions or decisions. In other words, Truth is color blind, racially blind, and politically blind.

Throughout this reading not only will you have questions of your own, you will also be questioned as we take this journey together. Some questions will simply bring a smile to your face; others may draw concern across your brow, while others will bring tears to your eyes. For it is written, "Emotions are the fuel for the pursuit of wisdom", so get ready for a full range of emotions.

To place you firmly in the proper setting of this book, here is a thought and a couple of questions:

Before you turn to the next page; close your eyes, relax and imagine for a moment a lineage of people who have existed for over three thousand years; a race of people that all possess the wisdom of ages, the wisdom of King Solomon.

If you found out that you were an heir to this lineage, what would you do differently in your life?

How would that knowledge change your life?

Let's find out together!

1

THE JOURNEY BEGINS

"The steps of the righteous man are ordered by the Lord."

PSALM 37:23

South Louisiana, April 1982

It is a beautiful, sun-filled spring day. I woke up extra early this morning to do something I have been putting off doing for over two weeks. My twenty-year-old lean frame slides easily and silently out of bed, so as not to wake my wife sleeping beside me. As I get ready for the day, I find that my heart is heavy. I do not usually find myself overly burdened. In fact, I have always considered myself a lucky guy—an average man in almost every imaginable way, except where I believe it counts most, my ability to provide for our future children. I am happily married to Mary Melerine. We have an adorable mutt named Muffet, one alley cat called Midnight, and a tremendously large network of family and friends. We live on a five-acre tract of land which was part of a large farm owned by my family in the little town I grew up in.

One of eight children, being a closely knit family was a very important aspect of my life. As with any large family, however, the closeness came at the price of having to work together to overcome the competing personalities of ten different people at any given moment.

In addition to family, helping others has always meant a lot to me. As far back as I could remember, I have been a dreamer at heart, someone who loved the heroes that came into his life. When I was a young boy, I was often found running through the house with a towel tied around my neck, "flying" from place to place saving my older sisters' dolls from the clutches of the bad guys. Although not completely aware of what exactly I was saving them from or why it was so important to be able to save them, I instinctively knew I was good at it. With the passage of time, my heroes evolved from Superman and Captain America to the Lone Ranger, Roy Rogers, and John Wayne; real people whom, at least from my point of view, everyone could count on to be there when tough things needed to be done.

Still too young to fully understand what it meant to really be a hero to someone else, I began to develop a keen understanding of the difference between right and wrong. This set the stage for the importance of mentors in my life and the growing need inside my young heart to be a mentor to others.

Of course, my very first mentors were my parents, Jules and Josephine Morrison Jr. Thanks to my mother and father, I was taught the difference between good and evil. It was instilled in each of the kids early in life. Through this lens, my family embraced the teachings of God as guiding principles of how one should live his or her life.

From my earliest memories, both my parents were viewed as community leaders. Growing up in a small rural town, everyone knew one another and it was hard not to be active in the community. Our family would have been considered low on the middle income scale in most areas of the country; however, for southern Louisiana in the 1960s, they were more like middle to upper-middle class. Both parents had been married before, bringing together a *Yours, Mine, and Ours* family. Josephine had one son and two daughters. Jules Jr. had two sons, and through their union they had one son (Joe) and two daughters. With a family of eight children—four boys and four girls—life was never boring around our house.

But lately I have been facing some challenges. My beautiful wife Mary and I have decided to begin trying to conceive our first child. As a soon-to-be father, I want to increase my income to better provide for the family. My income isn't bad, but it is not enough to allow Mary to stay at home with the baby, which is what we both want. The machine shop I work in is primarily supported by the oilfield industry. As the shop foreman, the money is good when there is work, but in the early 1980s, the oilfield is slow and it is not uncommon to be laid off for a few weeks at a time. I have to work fifteen-hour days for eight or so weeks until the next slow period comes along.

On top of all of this, my father passed away unexpectedly three months ago, and I am still coping with the loss of my first and best hero in life. It is an outcome of this loss that has me up early today. Two weeks ago, a man dressed in a business suit, came to our door wishing to speak with Mr. Joe Morrison.

"I'm Joe Morrison."

"May I come in?" the stranger requests.

I remember sitting at the kitchen table with Mary and this unexpected guest. "What is this about?"

"Before we go any further, I must ask to see identification please. I have been instructed to speak directly with Joe Morrison."

Removing my license from my wallet, I hand it to the gentleman. The man looks the document over, nods his head, reaches into his interior jacket pocket, and hands me a plain brown envelope along with my license back. "I represent the law firm which handled your father's estate. Your father left us explicit instructions for us to deliver this to you in person two to three months after his death." The stranger who never even told me his name stood up and began to walk toward the door.

Looking down at the envelope with nothing more than my name printed across the center I ask, "What is inside here?"

Turning with one hand resting on the doorknob the man says, "I have no clue, I am just the messenger." He opened the door and was gone.

Sitting in silence at our kitchen table, Mary and I both look at the envelope resting in my shaking hands. After what seemed like an eternity but in reality was only seconds, I ease open the flap and pull out a single sheet of white paper, another sheet that may have been white a long time ago, and a single key. Laying both sheets of paper side by side on the table, I read the white page out loud.

Dear Joe,

It is with much love and equal part trepidation that I share our mysterious legacy with you. It now becomes your responsibility as to how you use what you will learn. Just as my father passed it along solely to me at his death, so I do to you. As a child, I saw a lot of your Granddad in you. I believe that was a sign to me as to which of my children should be the keeper of this family secret. Now it becomes your choice as to whom you share this knowledge with. As you will soon see, my personal fears caused me to not explore the full potential of our amazing gifts and only time will tell if that was wise or not. I trust you will do what is right, my son.

With this letter you will find a map and a key which were given to me by your Granddad right after he died. Follow the directions on the map completely and carefully to learn what your destiny holds. The key will unlock the mystery and open a door that you will find impossible to close.

May God and Solomon be with you,
Dad

With tears in our eyes, we look at one another before turning our attention to the map lying before us. I quickly recognize the destination indicated by an X. It is a piece of coastal property which the family has owned for years. As a teenager, I had earned extra money trapping furs from parts of this land. My attention is drawn to the center of the map, a faded red X placed near the center of the only island shown. The island is not a great place to visit and was one area on the map that I wasn't really familiar with. It is a breeding ground for water moccasins and alligators. I never trapped that area because even the fur bearing animals stayed away from the dangers of that God forsaken piece of land. The locals call the island by its French name, "Isle de Mauvais Choix", the Isle of Bad Choices.

And so it is that today, taking advantage of being laid off work, I kiss Mary goodbye and head off to honor Dad's wish; to learn what is the big mystery hidden away at Isle de Mauvais Choix. With the island being so remote, I pack enough food and water to last me up to two weeks. Being a person who grew up hunting, fishing, and trapping, it was not uncommon to be away for weeks at a time. With a citizen band radio in the boat as well as a base in the house, I could stay in touch with Mary. Sitting behind the wheel of my beat up truck, the heavy key from the envelope resting on my heart with a chain secured around my neck, I tow my sixteen foot skiff to the local boat launch. Once the boat is in the water, I still have a four hour boat ride before reaching the island. Plenty of time for me to imagine what I will find under that X on the island, but also to figure out what Dad meant by God and Solomon being with me.

By the time the bow of my boat slides into the short marsh grass surrounding the island, it feels much more like summer than it does spring. Though it is late morning, the sun is blazing hot, the mosquitoes are swarming like they haven't eaten in days, and the lack of wind offers no reprieve from the smell of rotten swamp mud. Easing the skiff into the slight slough indicated on the mad, I can see no evidence of anyone else being here. The small trench is deep enough to pull the boat into a slip like cove where it will be protected and completely out of sight from passing boats. As soon as my booted foot touches the soft foundation of the land, it sinks three inches into the putrid mud. The slurping sound signals danger to a four foot long cottonmouth coiled on a half exposed cypress knee by my foot. After a long hiss it slides into the murky water, putting a more comfortable distance between us.

"Don't hiss at me, I'm not wild about being here either. I remember why I disliked this place so much." Talking to the retreating snake, I thank God that I remembered to bring my machete and .22 pistol with me.

Taking the map from my shirt's chest level pocket, I once more read the handwritten directions found below the sketched picture. They are very explicit and seem to be in order to protect the person from unseen dangers. The details are so precise that they require counting your steps in some places and walking along the trunks of downed trees in others. To make the journey even slower, I have to watch my every step in order to avoid upsetting the masses of snakes found on the ground and occasionally hanging from the low lying branches. Even while following the directions, in some areas, the swamp is three feet deep, making the trek perilous through alligator rich waters. Alligators usually do not mess with uninjured adults but if you scare them or walk on them, all bets are off.

It's after 4 pm by the time I reach the last set of instructions. I didn't plan on this walk taking so long. I only brought two bottles of water and a can of Vienna sausages. I do not look forward to spending a night on this island without my supplies but walking back through the swamp at night with only a small flashlight is not an option. I know I must be fairly close to the area I am looking for. At least I am finally standing on solid ground about three feet above the water level of the nearby swamp. Above and in front of me is nothing but a wall of green. The infamous kudzu vine has taken over this part of the island. The plant is fast growing, very thick and dense, completely masking whatever lies beneath its vines. Directly to my left, just as the map indicates, is what looks to be three big downed tree trunks, stacked one on top the other, creating what looks like a wall. According to the map, I am to climb on top of that wall and walk into the heart of that kudzu mass. Do you know how many snakes could call that vine their home? The map has not led me astray yet, so let's do it. Climbing to the top of the six plus foot wall of "trees" I notice that this is not trees after all but instead is concrete cloaked to look like trees. The kudzu, however, is real and super thick and hearty. It takes me a good thirty minutes to cut through the external mass of vines. There is no way to tell how long it has been since someone did what I am doing since kudzu is such a fast growing plant. They say that it can completely cover an area in a month, and once you cut it, the growth time speeds up.

Once I made it through the outer wall of vines, I was amazed and surprised by what I find inside. Turning on my flashlight, I shined it up onto what could only be described as a roof of vines. Very little light came through the vines and leaves making up this living canopy. About thirty feet in front of me were the trunks of this colossal covering. The trunks of these mighty vines grew on each side of the concrete walkway, making an entryway to a hidden building standing above the island floor. As I walked under the entryway it was clear that this building was well hidden from the outside world. The entryway gave way to an open air cypress flooring platform that was surrounded by a wooden cypress railing. Rustic chairs surround a heavy oak table and unlit hurricane lanterns hang on wooden rungs overhead. Across the entire back side of the platform was a large metal door, sealed by a lock hidden beneath a three sided iron box. Removing the key from around my neck, the lock springs open without the least resistance. As I grasp the latch in my trembling hands, I realize I am opening a door to a large, very old, iron shipping container, not a building. As the door swings open on well greased hinges, I stand back in complete and utter silence as the beam of the flashlight reveals what reminds me of an ancient library.

2

THE DISCOVERY

"Life can only be understood backwards; but it must be lived forward."

SOREN KIERKEGAARD

Isle de Mauvais Choix

It is now after 6 pm and it is extremely dark in my own little world. I find some matches and thank my Dad for keeping the lanterns full of fuel. Once the lanterns are lit I find another pleasant surprise, a working CB radio powered by a charged 12 volt battery. I quickly try it out by contacting Mary.

"Mary, come in?"

"I'm here, Joe." As I expected, she was beginning to worry, not hearing from me since I left the boat. "Are you ok?"

"Yes, I made it to the destination and all is well."

"Well, what did you find? Will you be sleeping on the boat?"

"Well it is too soon to tell exactly what I found and no, I have shelter here and a radio, though I am not sure how strong the battery is."

"Do you know how long you will be there?"

"Not yet. I will be in touch, don't worry."

"Ok, but be careful."

"I will. Let me go, I want to try to save the battery. I will check in tomorrow morning. I love you. Good night."

"Good night, baby."

With Mary's mind at ease, I begin to search this large container. I am pleased to see that whoever designed this place did so for comfort as well as privacy. The big metal door opened outward like every shipping container but unlike all other containers, this one had a sliding wooden screen door, custom fitted along an inside track. This came in handy to keep the mosquitoes out. It also meant that I would not have to close that big metal door. The air didn't move much under the vines but at least I was not sealed in a metal box too. I was very happy to see that along one of the walls is a bed with a mosquito net covering. Near the back of that same wall was a cupboard filled with canned goods and dried meats. This brought a smile to my face since I was not in a hurry to make that journey back to the boat. To the right of the bed were another fairly large table and a single comfy looking chair. The table had a lantern perch built onto it so a lantern could be hung to the left side of the working area about a foot off the tabletop. This would allow for a well-lit reading area. On the same corner of the table were a cassette recorder and an old reel to reel recorder. The balance of the living area was covered by book filled shelves, boxes of papers, stacks of labeled cassette tapes, reels of what looks like the old audio tapes and cardboard packing tubes tightly sealed up. Many of the tubes and boxes were still sporting shipping tags stuck to them showing addresses from Egypt and Israel. I immediately realize that they must have originally belonged to my Granddad.

Looking through the soft lantern glow, the sounds of the swamp softly chirping, croaking, and buzzing through the screen inches from my head, I finally realize the responsibility to my father is now complete and I am overwhelmed by the loss of Dad. Jules Jr. had been bigger in my eyes than Superman or Captain America had ever been. He had been a very strong man, physically. He was always doing chin-ups from the door jams around the house. In fact, he had been bigger than life to all of the children. Jules Jr. worked in the oilfield until he hurt his back lifting a two-hundred-pound crate from the trunk of a car, leaving him permanently disabled. Even though he couldn't work in the oilfield anymore, he couldn't sit still or lie around the house either; he had a family to provide for.

Refusing to even consider government assistance—or welfare, as it was called back then—Jules Jr., still found a way to provide for his family. He and his wife Jo, as his mother was called by her friends, made a great team. Prior to her early death to cancer, she was a stay-at-home housewife; she raised the children, canned the fruits and vegetables that were grown on the farm, and was a very active member of the local Catholic Church. Both were considered extremely honest and to have the humblest of personalities, commanding the respect of everyone who knew them—so much so that when friends and family convinced my dad to run for the local constable position in our little town, he ran without opposition. The position did not pay much, but with him home most of the time and Jo able to hold down the farm, he was always available if someone needed the police for any reason—and in a small town of 1500 people, the reasons were light when compared to bigger cities. Whether it was a public disturbance, a drunk and disorderly complaint, or the family cat stuck in the tree, he was there to help and did so without complaint.

Now, in the silence of this remote location, I find I am very curious about what is in these old discolored boxes. Stepping to the first box I come to, I unsheathe my knife and cut through the thick, yellowed tape. It is full of what appears to be old journals standing side by side in the box. I pick one up and open it to the front inside cover; the name "Jules Morrison Sr." is written neatly inside. Just as I suspected, these journals apparently belonged not to my father, but his father, whom I have always known as Granddad. "This should be interesting." I think out loud. "After reading through these old books, I should be able to tell my future children a little about their great-grandfather."

I always wondered if Jules, Sr. was anything like my dad. Maybe now I can find out. I begin opening the other boxes.

An hour later, I sit on the bed in the tiny sealed off world surrounded by stacks of my grandfather's handwritten journals, various books—some written in foreign languages—that look very old, some legal documents, a few reeled tapes, and what appears to be ancient scrolls covered with more handwritten notes, rolled up in the tubes. I had seen documentaries about biblically dated scrolls but never imagined I would ever see them in person. Not sure of what material they are made of, I can only guess it to be of the papyrus plant.

Slowly and delicately, I unroll one of the scrolls on top of the bed. The black lettering starkly contrasts with the beige-yellow of the canvas. Directly below the words is a faint discoloration that seems to have been absorbed into the scroll itself. As my finger lightly moves intuitively from right to left, gliding over the dingy impression that underlines the ancient characters, I wonder if this trail had been left by the countless oily fingers of elders who kept their place while reading these messages throughout the centuries. Thoughts flood my mind. Who else has seen these literary treasures? It's cool to think that my grandfather was probably one of a rather small cohort able to read what they say. Never did it cross my mind what their monetary value would be or if my grandfather should even have been in possession of them.

Realizing their value at some level, I decide to carefully bring them with me when I leave and scan the scrolls into our new desktop computer. The copies of the scrolls are definitely not the best, but what's there is clear and legible and should lessen the need to handle some of the more delicate parchments.

Granddad died before I was born, so I never met him in person, and my dad said very little about him—only that he was a bit of a nutcase who was also very smart and craftily intelligent. What I did know was that he was a renowned multilingual scholar and university professor who had written numerous papers on ancient Greek, Hebrew, Coptic, and Aramaic languages, focusing on the sociology of those times.

As I skim over the journals of Jules D. Morrison, Sr., I discover that recorded in his journals were the findings of his grandfather's research on the meanings of these ancient words. Based on the dates written on the spine of some of his journals, his grandfather started his work some nineteen years before his sudden death, searching for something biblically related. My father had never seemed the least bit interested in his own father's work. By the appearance of the boxes they had been untouched in this sealed iron tomb for a long time. I find it hard to imagine that Dad never even took the time to open these boxes to try to understand their significance in his own father's life. For my part, I think it will be fun to learn more about my eccentric grandfather, whom Dad had sometimes called "the family hermit." My mechanical mind snaps into gear and begins to view this space full of archived reading material as a puzzle. I intend to determine what Granddad was working on, and who exactly he was as a person.

Piling the journals up in order and placing the oldest dates on top, I begin with the one that was clearly the oldest and first of these journals, finding the following entry.

"Being a lifelong Roman Catholic, I was raised hearing the story of Jesus' lineage as laid out in Matthew 1."

Not being one to quote scripture, I reach over to the shelf, plucking the big, old Bible from its resting place. Returning to the bunk, I flip through the pages until I find the referenced passage.

The Genealogy of Jesus
A record of the genealogy of Jesus Christ the son of David, the
*   son of Abraham:*
Abraham was the father of Isaac,
Isaac the father of Jacob,
Jacob the father of Judah and his brothers,
Judah the father of Perez and Zerah, whose mother was Tamar,
Perez the father of Hezron,
Hezron the father of Ram,
Ram the father of Amminadab,
Amminadab the father of Nahshon,
Nahshon the father of Salmon,

Salmon the father of Boaz, whose mother was Rahab,

Boaz the father of Obed, whose mother was Ruth,

Obed the father of Jesse,

and Jesse the father of King David.

David was the father of Solomon, whose mother had been Uriah's wife, Bathsheba

Solomon the father of Rehoboam,

Rehoboam the father of Abijah,

Abijah the father of Asa,

Asa the father of Jehoshaphat,

Jehoshaphat the father of Jehoram,

Jehoram the father of Uzziah,

Uzziah the father of Jotham,

Jotham the father of Ahaz,

Ahaz the father of Hezekiah,

Hezekiah the father of Manasseh,

Manasseh the father of Amon,

Amon the father of Josiah,

and Josiah the father of Jeconiaha and his brothers at the time of the exile to Babylon.

After the exile to Babylon:

Jeconiah was the father of Shealtiel,

Shealtiel the father of Zerubbabel,

Zerubbabel the father of Abiud,

Abiud the father of Eliakim,

Eliakim the father of Azor,

Azor the father of Zadok,

Zadok the father of Akim,

Akim the father of Eliud,

Eliud the father of Eleazar,

Eleazar the father of Matthan,

Matthan the father of Jacob,

and Jacob the father of Joseph, the husband of Mary, of whom was born Jesus, who is called Christ.

Thus there were fourteen generations in all from Abraham to David, fourteen from David to the exile to Babylon, and fourteen from the exile to the Christ.

Placing the Bible on the bed, I continue to read from Granddad's journal.

"It is my belief that the Sanhedrin of today and the Jewish Elders are still tracking the lineage of Jesus but they are not open to sharing their census records with me. The Sanhedrin of today does not formally exist but I have evidence to the contrary. In ancient times it was made up of a High Priest and 69 general members. These members were from the three Jewish sects, Pharisees, Sadducees and the Essenes. The public view of Judaism reveals no formal central governing body so it is difficult to find the remnants of the Levitical keepers of the Holy word. It was the chosen Levi scribes who were entrusted with the preservation of Abraham's bloodline using the census requirements of the Sanhedrin. The common Jewish surnames "Levin" and "Levine" are derived from the tribal name "Levi," but not all Levins or Levines are Levites and not all Levites have surnames that suggest the tribal affiliation. Once the Pharisee sect faded away, these chosen Levi priests, loyal to their beliefs, took their long-held practices and recordkeeping underground. I will have to use other sources but I think I am almost there. The Rabbis I have built relationships with in Jerusalem secretly admit to me that the leadership of the Jewish faith will never release this information for a number of reasons. The most important being that it would identify those living today directly related to Jesus, fearing a surge in converts to the Christian faith. Could you imagine if entire Jewish families were made aware that they were direct descendants of Jesus? How many of them would explore the Faith of their ancestor to the level of accepting Him as the world's true Messiah? How many Christian faiths would aggressively seek these families out in an effort to convert them to their Churches?"

Was the professor looking for proof that the Jewish people of modern times are still tracking the Messiah through the lineage of David, just as it is outlined in the Bible? Pictures appear in my mind's eye of Granddad stirring up such controversy. Mom always told me that I came from a long line of men who never shied away from doing what they thought was right even if it meant going against the flow. Besides, why wouldn't the Jewish people continue this practice, since the Jewish people were still waiting for the coming of their Messiah; surely they must still believe that the Messiah would be born to the House of David as prophesied by the Prophet Isaiah? If so, the Orthodox scribes of today would still practice this centuries-old form of census taking, just on a more sophisticated level. Grinning, I once more find my imagination working overtime, envisioning an elderly Jewish cleric in a musty loft surrounded by multiple massive computer banks.

Scholarly Granddad had recorded all his notes from his search through the old Jewish writings of the Sanhedrin as well as the non-Jewish secular scholars of the time, progressing forward into modern times.

"What is it you were looking for, Granddad?" I wonder aloud.

Continuing to read, I discover that Granddad did indeed find evidence that pointed to the continued census of David's family tree from antiquity to the present day (for his grandfather, the late 1940s early 1950s). Granddad had also included research on the findings of long-hidden writings—some meaningful, some not so meaningful, and some just plain insignificant from my perspective. How monotonous and time consuming it must have been for Granddad to have read over so much useless information about the rambling thoughts of long-forgotten kings of ancient times, just to find one smidgen of useful information.

Carefully turning the delicate pages, I find a well-positioned note paper clipped to the journal page. It points the reader to a numbered scroll, one I remember seeing a copy of. With not much trouble, I find the scroll and the accompanying translation clearly printed in the old journal. Apparently Granddad had found a trail of writings that seemed to have been written by the actual scribe of King Solomon himself, a man named Arif. I notice that the professor's notes on these writings are highlighted and written in bold script. Here the professor's excitement level obviously becomes elevated. He clearly believed this discovery was important and that he may have unlocked an important secret.

"Solomon discloses to Arif the secret of a previously unknown and everlasting gift to all Mankind; a gift given by the Lord of Hosts to a family from His Chosen People over three thousand years ago. It is the gift of wisdom, bestowed to a long and diverse family of people."

Reading Granddad's notes before the translation of the actual scroll, I am intrigued to learn more about this secret that my grandfather must have translated.

Very thorough as a researcher, Granddad describes the process of cross-referencing various documents, certifying that his translations were correct. Of course, I could not read nor understand the first word of the scroll's text. It was probably written in some long lost foreign language, for all I knew. However, thanks to the thoroughness of Granddad's organizational skills, I begin reading the scroll's translation.

"King Solomon, Son of David, leader of all of Israel, from this day Yahweh has granted you great wisdom to be used justly for the benefit of all people, wisdom beyond all previous belief. For all times will your children, and their children's children be blest. In their varied tribes, they in turn will enrich the lives of all they lead."

The fact that Solomon received a special gift of wisdom came as no shock or secret; almost everyone knows the story of Solomon. But I am a bit stunned for a different reason. Again I pick up the Bible, but this time I do not have to thumb through the pages to find the verse I am looking for; I turn straight to it. Sitting with the open Bible on my lap, all of a sudden I feel an extremely close kinship to my Granddad. What are the odds that a grandson, born after the death of a grandfather that he knew absolutely nothing about, would share the same interest and passion in the obscure topic of wisdom?

Once more I remember multiple conversations I had with my mom and dad as a child, questioning them about why people did bad or stupid things in their life. The answers were always the same: "They just did not make wise choices." Then one day Mom explained in detail the hurt and suffering she went through during her first marriage. This extremely strong woman bared her painful memories in the hope that her lessons would be learned by her son before he had to pay the same price. It was then that an obsession with wisdom truly took hold of my life. At the time I couldn't completely understand why someone as wise as my own mother would admit making unwise decisions that caused her and her children tremendous pain and suffering. She did not want to make bad decisions, but according to her, she still did. I remember making a vow that I would solve this mystery so others would not have to hurt as she did. With a deep breath, I compose my emotions to better focus on the words written about Solomon in the Bible:

1 Kings 3
Solomon Asks for Wisdom

Solomon made an alliance with the Pharaoh King of Egypt and married his daughter. He brought her to the City of David until he finished building his palace and the temple of the LORD, and the wall around Jerusalem. The people, however, were still sacrificing at the high places, because a temple had not yet been built for the Name of the LORD. Solomon showed his love for the LORD by walking according to the instructions given him by his father David, except that he offered sacrifices and burned incense on the high places.

The king went to Gibeon to offer sacrifices, for that was the most important high place, and Solomon offered a thousand burnt offerings on that altar. At Gibeon, the LORD appeared to Solomon during the night in a dream, and God said, "Ask for whatever you want me to give you."

Solomon answered, "You have shown great kindness to your servant, my father David, because he was faithful to you and righteous and upright in heart. You have continued this great kindness to him and have given him a son to sit on his throne this very day.

"Now, LORD my God, you have made your servant king in place of my father David. But I am but a child and do not know how to carry out my duties. Your servant is here among the people you have chosen, a great people, too numerous to count or number. So give your servant a discerning heart to govern your people and to distinguish between right and wrong. For who is able to govern this great people of yours?"

The Lord was pleased that Solomon had asked for this. So God said to him, "Since you have asked for this and not for long life or wealth for yourself, nor have you asked for the death of your enemies, but instead for discernment in administering justice and relieving the pain and suffering of others, I will do what you have asked.

But it was the writings of Arif that intrigued the professor, and now his grandson, the most, because as the scribe of the powerful King Solomon, Granddad noted that Arif must have been privy to King Solomon's personal thoughts and actions. In addition, within the writings found in Granddad's work was what could only be described as information from other sources. Granddad notes that Arif referenced other writer's thoughts or ideas, people from outside the Jewish community. Did Arif have access to other scribes of his times? A scribble found in the margin of a page of translation denoted that King Solomon was a rare king, being well educated and able to read multiple languages himself. Based on Granddad's translation of conversations between the King and Arif, Solomon enjoyed reading more than the average scholar of his time. He seemed to be interested in Greek philosophy and wanted to understand Greek scholars' thoughts of the times. It was in these translated Greek writings found with Arif's work that I first noticed the term *Solutionary*. At first glance I thought that Granddad had meant to write the word *visionary*, but it became apparent that the term defined was indeed Solutionary when I came upon the following definition:

> *Solutionary—Noun; (Sol)—ancient reference to Solomon. Greek for Sun, ancient reference to Solomon being as bright as the Sun. The Sun or Sol was an ancient Greek God of wisdom.*
>
> *Latin: root solv; to loosen. Such as to untie or loosen a complex problem.*
>
> *Suffix - (u-tion-ary)—Ancient Greek for usable as a tool; one who engages in.*
>
> *Solomon, the tool for wisdom.*

From this definition, along with the copied translated excerpts from Arif's scrolls, I learn that multiple people were referred to as Solutionaries, the first of which seemed to have been none other than the Wise King Solomon. In his notes, Granddad had circled the word "varied" and below it was written the word "diverse." The idea of diversity must have been close to heresy in the times of Solomon. The mere mention of mixing religions or cultures was taboo. As an educated Jewish leader, Solomon would have understood this, but history supports the message that Solomon may not have embraced those beliefs. Thanks to Granddad's work, it was made clear as to why this race of people, Solutionaries, were so diverse. Multiple sources found in this research showed that Solomon was said to have 700 wives.

Laughing at this bit of information, I say out loud to the bugs and the snakes, "Solomon, my friend, I am not sure that was the wisest thing a man could do,"

Based on the research found in the journals, some believed that Solomon married many of these women out of altruistic necessity. Reading the explanations of Granddad's findings, I learn that in Solomon's times, if a woman was left widowed, especially with children, they were not viewed as the marrying kind because not many men had the means to support another family. Because it was not common for women to work outside of the home, she and the children would usually starve or she would be drawn into a life of prostitution in order to feed her family. Solomon, knowing this, did the honorable thing and married many of these women, primarily the wives of soldiers fallen in battle. Most of these women were wives in name only so that they could receive royal support.

"Sure, they were," I snicker after reading what might have been considered ancient gossip.

Granddad's notes do say "most." Honorable and gentlemanly as Solomon probably was three of the referenced sources in Granddad's journal agree that Solomon still had children with 78 of his 700 wives, the majority of these being from the countries surrounding Israel—most of which were non-Jewish cultures. Granddad left a distinct note that he could not determine just how many children the Wise King sired but it was recorded to be in the hundreds. Directly below his last line of research is a handwritten note:

"If the Solutionaries referred to above are the direct descendants of Solomon, their bloodline could possibly reach every nation on earth."

Looking at my watch and rubbing my stiff aching neck, I say to the world around me, "I am one tired little puppy," Clearing the bed, I dim the lantern and call it a night.

3

THE REVELATION THROUGH AN AWAKENING

"Trust in the LORD with all thine heart; and lean not unto thine own understanding. In all thy ways acknowledge him, and he shall direct thy paths. Be not wise in thine own eyes: fear the LORD, and depart from evil."

PROVERBS 3:5-7

A noisy crow decides to caw the island inhabitants awake. I stretch in the cot, surprised to find that I was able to sleep remarkably well. Captured by the desire to learn more, I begin my personal research relationship with Granddad's work. Captivated by his gift of translating ancient words into writings that all could benefit from, I begin reading where I left off last night. Taking the journal and a wonderful can of peaches, I go outside onto the porch. The more progress I make through the journal the more I discover that the entries are a mix of notes, translations, references, and hand-drawn pictures. Some of the references direct the reader to other books, scrolls, or in what seem to be very rare instances, locations unknown to me. I do find it very helpful that either Granddad or the original author of the scrolls made the effort to include the time and place of the writing, or what I learned was called date stamping.

Jerusalem, The month of Sivan in the year 960 BC

Scroll of Solomon, scribed by Arif

Sitting in the palace as the sun begins to rise, the King is at peace with the world. Solomon treasures this time of day. The window in which he reclines is shaded by a large olive tree planted at his request. The olive tree is strong and giving. Its wood is rigid enough to give strength to the furniture the carpenters make, and the fruit brings flavor to dishes he was raised on as a boy. The breeze is light; stirring the leaves as they carry the morning smells of the market below. The aroma of fresh bread brings a smile to his lips. The city begins to come alive as the day begins for the merchants who make their livelihood providing goods and services to the residents of the city and the outlying countryside. In just a couple of hours, Solomon will be extremely busy, for this is judgment day, the day where he will hear the cases brought to him as the judge of the land. He is humbled and yet excited to have such responsibilities. Even as a small boy, his father, King David, would rely on his wisdom at times. Each day that he sits in judgment, he knows that some of the cases will be petty in nature; still it falls to him to make the final decision. In the cases of a more important nature, the weight can be heavy and bears down on his usual upbeat demeanor. As he watches the city of his Father awaken to a new day, he ponders what will be brought to his throne. What challenges will this day bring to him? Will he be able to relieve the burden from those that come before him?

As a seasoned warrior, the King was trained to hear someone approaching with caution. As the padded paws of a cat stealthily moves without a sound, so too this person must not wish to disturb the king. Turning, he sees the unmistakable profile of his trusted servant and scribe, Arif. Upon seeing his smiling face, the king pushes aside the curtain that separates his private suite from the working area he uses to do the business of the land.

"Good morning Arif!" clasping the young man's shoulder in his hand, squeezing it softly as only a friend would do.

"Good morning, your Majesty, I trust you rested well, my Lord." He bows eagerly with an even wider grin, striving to begin his day serving his Master's every need.

"Hurry Arif. Run off and grab something to break your evening fast. We have much to do this morning. I have some ideas I wish to capture in script before the day of trials begin."

"But Sir," says Arif, hesitating just slightly before pressing his king, "will you not allow me to serve you before I take care of myself?"

Once more the king smiled openly with his faithful friend, "I will be fine, young scribe. I found this fruit on my walk yesterday," he says, pointing at a sack resting near the window. "It will fill my needs until later in this day. Now off with you, but linger not in returning to me lest I will forget the purpose of our session."

Arif wasted no time in running from the room; racing down the stairs in search of the fresh bread and honey he knew would be waiting for him in the kitchen.

Immediately after scarfing down his meal, Arif returns to the king with much energy and zeal. "Arif, I would like you to write down exactly what I say to you on this most beautiful of days. The Lord of my Father has surely shined down on us this day." The two of them had moved into the garden and were now sitting in the shade of a large cypress tree near the water's edge. Arif was prepared with his blank scroll, quill and ink; awaits the rich words which the King would bestow upon his ears before all others.

"Arif, I wish to tell you about the first time I was granted the knowledge that God had special plans for me. I was but a young boy, many years before the day that Yahweh blessed me with the gift of wisdom. It was not until my anointing message from Yahweh that I understood the true meaning of The Awakening that happened to me as a small child. Have you heard the phrase, getting out of a bind?" Arif nods his head in answer to the King's question. "This day you will record its origin."

"To grow in wisdom one must overcome immaturity and impetuousness. It is only through the pains of growth that a Solutionary is groomed, but regrettably more times than not, the light of wisdom requires much pain before it shines through the clouds of Self-indulgence, Uncontrolled desires, and Self-importance."

Solomon's scroll as written by Arif

Solomon's Awakening

"I remember moving like a shadow in the background, crawling along the high stone wall which surrounds the palace. My moves were cat-like quick so that my hands and feet would not burn on the scorched bricks. Since I was not one to wear sandals, my feet were callused and tough from many hours of being exposed to the sands. My mother was always trying to get me to wear shoes, but I couldn't climb with them on, and I loved to climb. My shoes seemed to disappear as soon as I was out of her sight. After many turns and leaps, I reach my final destination; the place where the ledge meets the left gate post of the main gate. From this spot, I can see the winding road leading into the city as well as on the other side of the wall, the bustling heart of the city itself. The village was extremely busy on this hot summer afternoon; the streets thick with people, camels, mules and cows. It seemed like everyone was being driven toward someplace else but they had to first meet in the village. As a young boy, full of the energy used to fuel the mischievous streak inherent to all curious male children, I saw this exciting occurrence as an adventure. Never had I seen so many people in one place. Even in previous years when the Census was taken, the city did not seem so packed. Maybe it was the added presence of a large number of animals that added to that impression. I did not understand why so many animals were in the streets. I loved animals, especially camels. I remember imagining so many unbelievable explanations; the neighboring towns were attacked by evil serpents with glowing eyes and two heads or maybe, the sun got so hot in the neighboring villages, the sand began to melt into rivers of flowing glass. Whatever the cause that drove the crowds into our city, the merchants in the courtyard were jumping with joy with the ability to hock their wares to the masses. As a child, I wished to be a merchant. I can still picture the rug merchant directly below my perch, trying to convince this wealthy man to pay a "little" more for the added service of his expertise in perfectly matching the rugs to the furnishings of the man's home. The merchant was obviously a Master when it came to the art of selling.

From my vantage point, I could see the gates to the palace and the portico beyond the entryway. People were gathered tightly into the area usually reserved for meeting between my Father and traveling dignitaries, but today it was crammed with common people; people who I recognized as citizens of the city but also those who came from neighboring villages. Being inquisitive by nature, I swing down from the loft and sprint around the rear, not wanting to miss anything due to the crowded streets. As one running with a purpose, I know just where to climb so that I do not miss a thing.

In the old stable, now used to house of the broken chariots and wagons, I pull myself into the hay loft. Even to this day, whenever I smell hay I can see that day in my mind's eye. I quickly sprint to the front wall, finding the large loose stone. I silently slide the stone back and out into my lap. Lying on the loft floor, I have an unobstructed view of the entire por- tico to the palace entryway directly across the courtyard from my vantage point. Just as I get comfortable, my father and two of his soldiers step onto the entry step to the palace. They are greeted with reverence from the crowd gathered before them.

At once, the noise of the busy village disappears; for Father is going to speak. "My people, I know why you are here, but you need not fear. The Ammonites will be smitten down as in years past; thanks to the will of God and those chosen to protect us. We need not your offering of supplies at this time. Go home, protect your property and your children; our soldiers will send back these jackals from whence they come." Turning with a wave of his mighty arm, the Generals and their soldiers follow their King back into the palace.

Sitting back on my haunches, I realize the reason for the crowds of people and animals. All the animals were brought into the city because we are expecting to be at war for a long time and the people are offering their support for the protection of their families. Placing the stone back into its place, I rise to my feet, eager to speak to my father. The last time we fought the Ammonites, my father was my age and he went into battle, this day I was thirteen years of age, a man when it came to war. Like all male boys of that age, I had been spending four hours a day in training from the age of ten. My age would keep me from the heart of battle but I would be responsible for tending to the soldier's needs. I am both excited and scared at the same time. War is not a game and many people whom I knew could be killed or injured in the upcoming battles. I feel drawn to find Father in order to learn more. It is my place to be at his side.

Stepping into the war room, the large table in the middle of the room is completely surrounded by the captains of the military and the elders of the city. The King is in deep conversation with his first captain, the most trusted of his elite warriors. They all showed signs of distress; wet with sweat, pacing to and fro as their hands raked through their hair. I knew better than to interrupt this meeting so I found a place near the corner, where I could observe and listen without being in the way.

The hours passed and evening pushed in through the balcony windows, ringing the great room. One by one the warriors bid good night to one another until the only one left standing at the big table was the King. He looked older than he did this morning. Tears flowed down his cheeks uncontrolled by what I thought was the indescribable fear that took over his heart. The burdens brought on by the unknown of outcomes that take place in any battle must weigh heavy on a leader's heart but still I remember thinking, why was the great King so worried? Had he not defeated this foe before? Surely Father was in the right. Was I not taught that when you are in the right, you always come out on top? King David was a confident and competent leader with the Lord at his side. Everyone in the kingdom knew this to be true; then why the fear and the tears?

Moved to tears as well, I tried to silence any sniffling sound, but I was not successful. Father looked over his shoulder, seeing me as I crouched behind a shield standing in the corner. "Solomon, come here."

Running to his side, I wrap my arms around his waist. "Yes, Father." I say, drying my cheek so that his Majesty does not see evidence of my personal fears.

Hugging me against his side, he steers us to the cushions that line the low table filled with fruits and water jars. "How long have you been in hiding, my little lion?" he asks, handing me a cup of water.

With forced enthusiasm I reply, "I came in shortly after the captains, sir. How can I help Father? I want to be by your side in battle."

"I know you do, little lion, but I hope and pray that is not made to happen." Leaning back on the pillows, he lets his muscles stretch and relax for what was probably the first time that day.

I tried to voice my concerns, "Father, why are you..." I did not wanting to even say the word scared because I cannot believe in my heart that the great King could ever be scared. Like so many times before he smiles at me, knowing my thoughts before they were spoken. He was such a great reader of people.

I can close my eyes and recite the words like my father was the one speaking them. "War is not a pleasant experience and never does either army find pleasure in the act of the fight. Many people die and many more feel terrible pain, whether it is from an injury to their own body or from the loss of someone they love. With that said, war is required at times and if we must fight, we must win. By winning we remain free, free to follow our God and His commandments. As King, I am responsible for the decisions that either makes that happen or that cost us our freedom. The decisions take much thoughtful planning, prayerful consideration and careful execution. At times like this I am forced to remember that I have not always made wise decisions on behalf of those dependent upon me. I pray that I am up to the task for the sake of the entire kingdom."

All the while that the King is speaking to his son he is remembering his first battle, the battle against the Philistines. He was the exact same age as Solomon is now. In addition to the reasons given to Solomon, his tears flow because of the emotions relived from that fateful day when he took his first life in battle. It was God's will that one man, Goliath, should die in the stead of many but that it should be at the hands of a shepherd boy with a sling shot was a remarkable call to duty. As a man, in reflection upon that day, David cannot explain how or why he was drawn to stepping forward against such an imposing foe. The memory of the unjust taunting of the giant against our God and the way the Israelite soldiers feared him to the point of allowing him to continue his defiance of the Lord and disgrace to Israel enraged his personal courage. Courage or fool-hardiness, one of them should have killed David that day, but he was spared and even elevated to King. Was it for this reason, his kingship, his legacy, his people, and the children he sired, or was it for another unknown reason? He shed tears today mainly for the unknown future God continues to require of him.

Opening his eyes, Solomon smiles briefly at Arif and explains,

"Feeling better just from being able to speak with him, I find the words I had lost. I explained that I had overheard much planning today and if he would allow me, I would like to share my thoughts. I knew I was not a strategist or even a warrior but as I heard certain facts from the warriors they speared thoughts as if in a dream. Thoughts that used my architect training which I love and the fighting skills I had received. I was praying I would be able to share these ideas with this great leader and that he would take the opportunity to teach me using actual applications."

Then Solomon shifted back to describe the journey in his mind's eye.

Leaning forward with his elbows on his knees, the King smiles with sparkling eyes. "So be it, young lion. What are these ideas of yours?"

Without delay, I ran to the massive war table covered with maps of the kingdom. From what I overheard, the Ammonites will outnumber our army by 3 to one and yet we were planning to meet them in battle on the Plains beyond the river Jordan. The King nods and tells me that is the only place we will be able to use our archers effectively early in the battle. Considering this explanation, I posed another question, "What if we can use the rain and their clothing as weapons against them as well?"

I feared that I had over stepped my boundary but the Master smiled and said, "Go on my son."

With renewed zeal, I saw myself lean over the maps and point further north and east of the city to the pass the Ammonites will need to march their army through. With deep respect, my voice questioned, "Will they not come from this direction Sir?"

Father just nodded his head slightly. I explained to my Father that I heard talk of the opposing armies arriving during the peak of the rainy season. The reports from our scouts confirmed this to be true. Smiling with a twinkle in my eye, I prepare to expose the idea that formed in my mind throughout the day. The plan was to use the full combat dress of the

Ammonites and the environment against them. Father assured me that they would be covered in wooly sheep skins adorned with plates of bronze worn over a thick camel hair vests. This combination is why it is so hard to win a single killing blow against their warriors.

I feared that my strategy would sound like I had no understanding of battle strategies or of leadership in general, but the man stood and heard me out. Once I had finished with the details, I hoped he would at the very least tell me what we should do to improve it further. Instead, Father just continued to nod in agreement. He seemed to really like the idea of closing off the pass, forcing the Ammonites to travel a different route, one selected by us. By doing this, it allowed two things to happen. First, we can re-route the creek of Jasmel on the side of the closed off pass, barring the run off until the Ammonite army is entering the low lying area. And second, we can use the archers more efficiently since the heavy clothing will slow down their ability to move rapidly in the flowing water. With the additional weight of the mud and water soaking the thick woolen coat, they will surely tire quickly.

King David thought that it just might work. The King had the captain brought into the room and ordered the work to begin immediately in moving large stones to block the pass. The orders also explained that we were to make it look like it was a slide that occurred naturally so the Ammonites would not expect our hand in it. This would take many days to complete. While this is being done, Father and I go to the creek together; marking off the locations of construction needed to finish off our plan.

Surely the Lord of our fathers was on our side as the day of the battle arrived. It has been raining each day and the Ammonites have been camped just outside the plain in the exact spot Solomon expected them to be. Last night, a few of my friends and I crept to the edge of the swollen creek of Jasmel; making sure the dam was holding. With all the rain, it was no longer a flowing creek. On one side of the dam was a lake on the other a winding pathway created by the once flowing creek bed. Surely many of the Ammonite soldiers will be lulled into marching in the unobstructed pathway of the creek bed. Once the order is given and the mouth of the dam will be opened, the lake will flood directly into the rear of the field where the Ammonites will be charging. The water will not be very deep but its powerful rush will create a great diversion and distraction, slowing them down while our archers send volley after volley of arrows into their midst. They will no longer out number our army and will lose the will to fight.

I can still see my Father calling to me to join him from the rear of the palatial chariot. I was by his side for the entire battle as we executed each step of our plan. I felt like a warrior as I held on to the leather strap of the chariot, the horses bounding into motion throwing up large chunks of mud as they raced toward the hillside. The King did not go into battle but being the leader he was meant being near the front line so that he could encourage the troops and make adjustments as he sees fit. From our vantage point we are able to witness how the battle plan unfolded. The good news is that once the waters were released and the Ammonite soldiers took the brunt of several volleys of well placed arrows, they turned and retreated. Before nightfall, the leader of the Ammonites sent an emissary to the King asking for permission to gather up their dead and injured to bring them back to their home lands. The good King gave his permission and promised them safe passage home.

On the way back to the city, the chariot was filled with excited jubilation over not only winning the battle but doing so without so much as an injury to any of our soldiers. I guess that I was so distracted by the excitement that I did not pay heed to my own safety. Father was behind the reins; pushing the horses to their fastest speeds. We were laughing and enjoying the thrill of the ride, when suddenly, one of the wheels bounced over a large stone, sending me rolling along the floor of the chariot. Near the rear of the chariot was a spool of rope used for clearing large trees out of the paths. As I tossed and tumbled around on the floor, I began to get twisted in this spool of cord. Father concentrated so fully on regaining control of the bouncing rig that he did not notice me falling to the ground. With the chariot still moving at full speed, the rope twisted around my neck and arms. I quickly began rolling over in the soft field of mud, trying in desperation to free my limbs from the rope that tangled all around my body. Any second I expected the imminent pain that would come as the other end of the cord, which was securely tied to the chariot, would reach its end. Surely I would be dragged behind like a twig from a fallen tree or worse my neck would be snapped in half. Sitting up as quickly as possible once the rolling stopped, I remember watching as if in slow motion the rope being played out to its fullest extent; the chariot still rolling far too fast to stop before the rope snaps tight around my young throat. Knowing it is too late, the rope begins to lift off the ground starting at the chariot's rear and racing toward where I sit. Closing my eyes, I wait for the pain...nothing. It is like I am in a well, I hear nothing, I feel nothing, yet I know the rope is still around my neck and shoulders. Then suddenly, slack in the rope. What happened? Opening my eyes, the first thing I see is Father still moving away, both hands working the reins trying to stop the horses. How can this be? I should have been yanked to my death from my resting place. Looking down, I cannot believe what I see. The rope is still looped loosely over my shoulders but two arms lengths in front of me, lying on the ground, is a raveled end of the cord. In a panic, I jump to my feet quickly throwing the rope from my body as if at any moment the rope will stretch, taunt and end my precious life. As soon as I am free from the binds, I collapse onto my back trying to catch my breath.

"Solomon, Solomon!" Father runs to my side, leaning over my prone body. "Are you hurt?"

"I don't know father." I could only speak in a whisper.

He says, "It looks like you were able to get out of the cord before the chariot dragged you too far."

"Father, I..." No words could make clear what took place.

"What is wrong, son?" For the second time I witnessed the mighty King David struck by fear.

"It was not I who freed me from the binds of the rope, Master."

King David stood and walked to the pile of rope lying off to the side. He picked it up and began to coil it around his arm. Then he noticed something very strange. One end was waxed so that it would not fray but the other end was a complete mess, as if it was pulled to its breaking point, separating in multiple places. Bringing the rope back to me, he sits near me as he lays the tattered ends onto my lap. "What happened to you and this rope, my son?"

Shaking my head with tears flowing from my eyes, I could not answer him. From that day forward, I grew up knowing that it was the Lord's hands that freed His unworthy servant that day. My life was destined to be filled with much responsibility, but with much responsibility comes many unresolved purposes to carry out; the accomplishments of which would affect the entire world."

Immediately following this translation was a folded single loose sheet of paper written in Granddad's familiar script.

Search as I might, I could not find any other complete written record of this exact story anywhere but written fragments of reference were found leading to the oral components that have been passed down through the centuries evident through the current use of sayings referenced here. I truly believe that until now the entire story of Solomon's awakening had been lost to the ages. Accordingly, the practice of the times, stories such as these were committed to memory through countless retelling and even to this day around the world, whenever someone can, through miraculous efforts, get out of a bad situation, it is said that "… they were able to get out of a bind." I find it fascinating that this "awakening" speaks so loudly of whom these Solutionaries are; God's trusted stewards of problem solving, dedicating their lives to getting people out of binds. Who in their wildest dreams could have imagined that a little over 3,000 years ago, when this saying was first mouthed or put to script, that it would be applied to people's ability to handle tough situations? Reflect for a while that this familiar phrase was inspired by the very person that God sanctified with the gift to solve our man-made problems.

4

JOE IS MORE LIKE GRANDDAD
THAN HE THOUGHT

Apply thine heart unto instruction, and thine ears to the words of knowledge.

PROVERBS 23:12

South Louisiana, April 1982

Walking around the elevated deck under the living canopy, I lift the open journal from the table where I had last laid it down and turn the page. Folded and pressed tightly in the crease of the spine are a couple of old yellowed sheets of paper. Gently releasing the sheets from their resting place, I instantly notice they are crisp to the touch and so firmly sealed by the fold that they must have been pressed together for a very long time. The pages seem so fragile I fear they will break apart before I could get them completely opened and laid flat. After careful and tender handling, the pages are finally fully exposed to eyes other than the original author. I don't know why, but I sense that besides Granddad I may be the only person to see this long-saved memo. The pages were covered in his now-familiar scrawl of penmanship. The writing was dark and legible against the slightly yellowed paper.

Jules Morrison, March 6, 1913

The year was 1896; I was 12 years old when I had my "awakening". Though at the time, I had no idea what it meant. Yes! Whoever is reading this information will soon know that I have undeniable verification that proves that I am a descendent from the 41st generation of Solomon and by such, an heir to the Solutionary family tree.

It was October 6th of the above mentioned year, a rather warm year which probably contributed in part to the severe hurricane that struck our town head-on two days before. The storm spawned numerous tornadoes, one of which demolished the local church. Luckily, no one from the town was killed, though there were a few people with cuts and bruises and two with broken bones. Overall, a lot of property damage, but nothing that could not be replaced or rebuilt. It was during a cleanup project that something unexplainable happened to me. I am committing to paper the memories of what I remember happened that day. My father and I were working with many of the other parishioners to clean up the property where the church had been prior to being completely destroyed. It was the worst damage I had ever seen. Large whole oak trees were toppled as if they were dominos. The roof of the church was still intact, steeple and all but it now sat across the entire road about 100 yards from the original structure. The remnants of what remained of the rest of the building stood twisted and in shambles. All of the beautiful stained glass windows were gone. The hollow openings tilted in contorted rectangles. My dad and the other men of the community were lifting large beams which had come to rest across the threshold of the front of the church. The priest was eager to get inside the Church so he could begin to salvage anything worth saving, including any holy relics and the most Blessed Sacrament. The men of the parish were able to use some of the heavy lumber to pry open the massive doors of the church. I don't think anyone present was an engineer, but everyone understood that without a roof, the unfettered walls of the structure were very unpredictable and not a safe place to walk around in. There were 5 of us, including myself, selected to go into the devastated building. Looking back, I am not sure why I was picked. I thought at the time it was because I was so light in weight. The floor was tilted in multiple directions since the high water must have lifted the old building off the foundation, allowing it to drift back down on not so level footings. Once inside the doorway, I was given the task to find and take outside the altar candleholders and any other brass or gold fixtures I could safely carry. I thought that would be very easy to do since, surprisingly, the altar seemed fairly undisturbed. It would, however, take multiple trips to accomplish my assigned tasks. It was on my final trip into the church that I noticed I was completely alone in the structure. I remember looking around wondering where was everyone else. With my back to the stone topped altar, I heard someone whisper very softly in my ear, "Take a step forward". I cannot explain why, but I did as instructed without thought and suddenly was violently thrown face first onto the floor. I awoke sometime later, outside the church, lying on my side on what must have been a picnic table. The face of my father was inches from mine, a concerned or scared look in his eyes. I could see tears flowing down his dirty cheeks. I don't think I had ever seen him cry before this day. I tried to sit up, but he held my shoulder, shaking his head no. Then I started to feel the burning pain down my entire back. Someone was touching my back, but I did not know why. I remember that I started to cry, more out of fear than the burning pain. I asked my Father what happened and why does my back hurt? He answered me in his native Cajun French language that I had had an accident. Then he wanted to know if I could remember what happened.

I told him that I remembered standing in front of the altar looking up at the big cross wondering how it was still hanging in place. Then for some reason I turned to face the door. I shared with him that I thought I was all alone in the Church, but I must not have been because I remember being told to take a step forward and when I did, something or someone pushed me to the floor. The next thing I knew, I was looking at up at him.

He then asked me a very good question. "Do you know who asked you to step forward? Who did it sound like?"

I thought for a moment and then said that I didn't know. All I could remember was that the words were very softly spoken, like a whisper. It was at that time that I asked him what had happened to me.

I will forever recall his words spoken to me in French: "Jules, the large crucifix that hung behind the altar, fell forward and must have barely missed you. The top cables must have pulled out of the wall causing the top of the cross to tip toward the front; the bottom rested on the wall and is still secure. You have a scrape down your entire back where the top of the cross must have brushed against your skin. If you had not taken that step forward when you did, you would have been crushed. That cross weighs over a thousand pounds. Stay still, son, you will be fine. Sister Veronica is removing splinters and cleaning the wound so it does not get infected. "

I imagine that I was in shock but I still asked Dad who was with me when the cross fell. Who told me to take that step?"

Weeping out loud and without shame or control, Father said, "No one son. Jules, you were alone. The only One that could have spoken to you was God Himself."

Upon the initial reading of the rather short letter, tears stream down my cheeks as I mentally flip question after question through my mind. "Who knew of this "awakening" Granddad? Why did my Pa not share this with his family? Did he even know about his own father's personal thoughts and experiences as they relate to his studies of Solomon?"

Stepping into the kitchen, bedroom, library and now official office of The Modern Solutionary Society, I realize I skipped lunch.

Throwing myself down on the bed I picture Mary; sure that she will never believe what I just found out about my family. I just finished reading a letter Grandfather wrote announcing that he is a direct descendent of King Solomon and member of " The Modern Solutionary Society"—which is what I've started calling Solomon's band of Solutionaries. And what a club it is! I can't wait to share these amazing events with her. Laughing out loud, I think about shortening what I call Granddad's work to the "Society Papers." I think it is very appropriate.

The CB radio is very public and the words can break up, so speaking to Mary about this will have to wait until I get home. She would have no idea what I would be talking about anyway. I would love to bring her here so she could see this for herself but she is deathly afraid of any snakes so that will never happen.

Later that evening, after speaking to Mary and letting her know that all is well, I am once again in deep thought. The swamp is alive with nocturnal noise. The wind must be blowing at a good clip gauged by the shuffling of the vines over this resting place.

Just as my surroundings I find myself equally restless. My thoughts cannot move off of Granddad's old letter and the awakening shared by Solomon himself. Did he find proof that we are really related to King Solomon, you know, the Wise King from the Bible. If so, as a direct descendant, would I be part of this ancient race of people referred to as Solutionaries. These Solutionaries are given a share in the inheritance of the gift of Wisdom bestowed on Solomon by God Himself. If I understand the material correctly, we are entrusted to share this gift of Wisdom in the same fashion as Great-Grandfather Solomon; according to Granddad's family tree, I am in the 39th generation of Solomon's grandchildren, to be precise. Smiling as if in mock pride, I throw up my arms loudly announcing, "Solomon was my Great, Great, Great…Grandfather 39 times removed on my father's side."

I'm sure the critters right on the other side of the screen are listening intently but couldn't care less.

My playful enthusiasm subsides as memories return from a night and location much like this one. Not sure if that event should be tie to Granddad or Solomon's awakening yet, it bubbles up with rich clarity, like it was happening now. It is hard to explain because all three were different yet, each had to have left indelible marks on them. I likened it to a rite of passage or a clear message from God where by each endured a miraculous life event, making it crystal clear to that person that He has a plan for him or her. Were each chosen or marked for a unique purpose in life? From what I can gather, it seems that those who are direct descendents of King Solomon would, sometime early in their life, experience an unexplainable event that would somehow lead them to the understanding that God Himself has briefly taken control of their life or at least interrupted it. I believe in miracles but I never thought of Him truly using me.

Closing my eyes, I vividly still see a replay in my mind's eye as a television screen view of the incident that happened to me a long time ago in an equally remote swamp.

"An unjust man is an abomination to the just: and he that is upright in the way is abomination to the wicked."

PROVERBS 29:27

South Louisiana, about 70 miles southwest of New Orleans
July 1975
Even at a little before midnight, the air is extremely hot and humid. The darkness is eerily complete with no man-made lighting and no moon to brighten the landscape. The smells methane is strong from the decay of the brackish marsh hangs thick in the air. Five young teenage boys step softly and cautiously along the desolate backwater one-lane road. The silence is only broken by an occasional swamp animal scurrying through the grass growing through the shallow water that lines both sides of the gravel roadway. A casual observer might assume the boys, ranging in age from thirteen to fifteen, are simply coming home late from a hunt, considering that each carries a

shotgun and a few have ten- to twelve-inch skinning knives strapped to their belts or hidden away in a boot sheath. But a keen observer would have noticed the determination in their steps, the comfort in which they carry the weapons, and the fearless way they walk through this dangerous swamp. Not many adults who weren't raised in the swamp would have braved these surroundings in the dead of night.

Leaving the relative safety of the road for an even more perilous journey, they hop into pirogues to travel the remaining three miles to their destination. These flat-bottomed boats are either paddled or push-poled through the marsh, and with two people in one boat they become tipsy in the best of conditions. However, these boys could have done this in their sleep—even in these near-blind conditions. By 3:00 a.m. they arrive at their destination. Five miles from the closest inhabited shelter, they sit quietly in the pirogues, looking at what could best be described as a rundown old fishing or trapping camp. No bigger than a two-room shack perched six feet above the water on crooked stilts in the middle of nowhere, at first glance it appears to be an abandoned shack. Like many others in the marsh, it's damaged by the storms that plague this low-lying area. The leader of this group knows better, having visited this site during the daylight hours over the last few weeks. Upon closer examination, things didn't add up; a deserted camp would not have titanium padlocks mounted on heavy, expensive metal doors, or new, tinted windows shrouded by marsh grass, made to look as if left there by an extremely high tide. Plus, even though the pillions supporting the shack lean at a thirty-degree tilt, the floor is perfectly level. Whoever owned this camp went through a lot of trouble and expense to make it appear to be something it wasn't. That something is what brings this group of close friends here tonight.

Forty-eight miles away, a cousin of one of the five lies in a hospital bed, fighting for his life after suffering a drug overdose. An unsavory group of people new to the community had taken advantage of this mentally challenged twenty-two-year-old young man, getting him hooked on drugs and then using him to deliver their goods around the community without having to do so themselves.

The people of South Louisiana are known for their warm, Southern hospitality. Their fun-loving, good-hearted nature is shared openly with everyone they meet. In these small, remote fishing villages, family and friends are everything. If you respect their family and friends, a total stranger or not, you will be treated like one of the family. But if you disrespect the things they hold dear, or cause harm to those they care about—no matter who you are—you will be introduced to troubles you would rather not imagine. As the Louisiana natives say, "That is a Cajun recipe for disaster, and every Cajun knows how to cook."

When the leader of this band of five discovered who was responsible for the overdose, his first decision was to bring the information to the sheriff's office and let them handle it. After all, his father was a deputy. However, after a little more research, he discovered that would not be an option. You see, the sheriff was the man who owned the shack that stood only twenty yards from where they were swatting mosquitoes from their exposed skin. Once a loyal public servant, the sheriff allowed the years of unquestionable authority and the draw of big money to corrupt his very being.

These boys love to shoot their guns and each one of them an expert marksman in his own right. Sitting in the dark, far from anyone who could or would intervene, this group of heavily armed young men are about to pass judgment and send a very clear message on behalf of a family member. Each of the five has at least one box of buckshot or slugs. Once the deafening barrage begins, the swamp sounds like a warzone at the peak of battle. Fifteen minutes later, silence returns to the swamp. The shack, the illegal equipment, and any drugs that were inside are totally demolished. After the last gunshot fades away, the roof begins to collapse in on itself, and the sound of twisting, breaking wood is all that can be heard for several minutes. The five returns to the pirogues and paddle back the way they came. The marsh sounds return to normal, letting everyone know that what was damaged wasn't of great importance to world around it. It did not even belong there to begin with. However, the damage will be of great importance to the owners of what was in this shack. Will they heed the message given loudly and clearly by the people who care about the family impacted by their ill-gotten endeavors, and leave the area and never return? Will the sheriff try to find out who was responsible for destroying this operation, or will he take the hint that he and his kind are not wanted in the community?

At four in the morning, adrenaline still pumping, the five boys are kidding and talking with one another. Walking in a single line across the width of the path, they are not worried about being seen in this remote place at this time of the night. Even though the swamp and marsh still surrounds them, they feel comforted by the weapons they carry. The guns are once more fully loaded; their knives are always finely honed. They know better than to fire all of their ammunition. This area of the swamp is home to some of the biggest gators in existence, gators that can grow to over fourteen feet in length. A gator that size can seize a man and snap him in half before he knows what's happening. So even though they are at ease, they remain attentive to the dangers they know are never far away.

As they near the end of their journey, Billy, the smallest of the group, falls behind, distracted by the fact that his gun is jammed. No one else notices his change in position. As one of the five who never carries a knife, he picks up an empty soda can from the side of the road, and begins to fold it in half repeatedly to split it in two, planning to use the sharp narrow edge to dislodge the jammed round.

In the stillness of the night, the crinkling of the thin metal can is as loud as a blaring horn. Joe, the leader and self-appointed protector of the group, responds immediately as he hears the sound of what he thinks is a round being chambered right behind him and his friends. Without thinking, he spins on one foot, lifts his sawed-off shotgun from his hip, and pulls the trigger with the expectation of being fired upon. All of this happens in a fraction of a second that somehow stretches into an eternity. The squeeze of the trigger and instinctive pull from the expected recoil, which never came, is so great that he loses his balance and falls backwards.

The next thing he knows he is on his back, staring up at the circle of his friends looking down at him. "What happened, Joe?" they ask. Before he can answer, Billy, holding his crack-barrel shotgun in one hand and a bent soda can in the other, his face as pale as a ghost, leans in and whispers, "Why did it not go off?" The five always carry loaded guns with the safety off whenever they are in the swamp. Billy knows that he should have been dead; a hole the size of a watermelon where his stomach should have been. Twelve-gauge buckshot fired at a distance of ten feet would have resulted in a direct hit, and they all know it.

Joe slowly gets to his feet, gun hanging from his shaking hands. Another friend, George, reaches out and takes the gun, points it out over the marsh, and pulls the trigger, firing the deadly load without hesitation. Joe collapses in a sitting position in the middle of the road.

Current, 1982

I remember returning home in agony over almost killing someone I love like a brother. I could not understand what happened. Mentally replaying the event over and over, I turn around and see someone standing behind me with a gun. I pull the trigger on instinct, expecting the mule kick from firing buckshot out of a 10-inch barrel. The kickback never comes. "Why not? It fired fine seconds later."

Moved to tears for the umpteenth time, the answer rises up in my heart. "God has saved me from a terrible fate, one that would have surely changed my life completely. Could Granddad have just given me the long sought after answer to this nagging question?"

5

THE WISDOM FORMULA

"He that trusteth in his own heart is a fool: but whoso walketh wisely, he shall be delivered."

PROVERBS 28:26

I am beginning to enjoy poring over Granddad's work. Wishing we could have spent time together; I have a feeling that we would have had a lot of fun together.

After reading through page after page of handwritten notes in the original journals, the copies of the more delicate old scrolls and clipped articles from around the world, I notice that Granddad makes continual references to the definition of wisdom and the powerful solutions said to have been written by Solomon himself—solutions to problems he was faced with while sitting as judge and King of Israel and the Jewish people.

With now the second-oldest journal open in my hand (although the oldest looking by appearance), I look down at the actual translation, written in Granddad's cursive handwriting, of an ancient scroll. Between each set of pages of translation is a copy of what I assume to be a copy of the actual scroll. On some of these scrolls, there are handwritten notes between the original text, underlined words, and circles drawing attention to certain details.

"I think I finally figured out some of your organizational system, Granddad!" I exclaim out loud, as if I am speaking directly to the grandfather I am growing to love.

"Now tell me what our Great, Great, Great … Great Grandfather Solomon wanted to tell the world."

Solomon's Scroll scribed by Arif, 959 BC

The king looked over the garden, staring as if he were searching for someone who was speaking to him from afar.

"My trustworthy servant, pay heed to these words for they are rich with wisdom; wisdom which was bestowed upon me by the God of my father at a much younger age than most elders. Miss not a word and should you stumble in your haste, fears not to stop me, for the importance of these words is much more important than my personal feelings toward being interrupted."

Bowing his head to hide the blush raising in his cheeks at the thought of interrupting his Master the King, Arif said, "Whenever my king wishes to begin, your devoted servant will be diligent to keep up as not to make you repeat your precious words."

"First, I wish to give you the
Solution of Thoughtfulness since
it is this solution I used to perfect
the definition of wisdom.
Be it known to those wishing
to expand their profits and life's
directions, take time to think
before the day's work begins."

"It was during a time of rest that I was given these thoughts and words I share with you this day. As many times before, it seems when my mind is at rest, I can capture more messages and learn more fully the directions I should guide my path forward. I have learned many things since my youth but the one that has paid me many times more than the fruit of my toils has been the lesson that the mind is most awake when the body is at rest. This is a personal observation and should be a mandate to all who wish to make wise choices for themselves and their families."

Laughing softly to himself, he reaches down to move a twig from the grass where he intends to lay softly on his side. "If more people did this Arif, they may not need me to act as judge of their thoughtless acts against one another. What a joy and blessing that would be for all involved."

Solomon continues with his train of thought, smiling, "That recitation was part of the message I was given last night but we will now begin with the definition of wisdom. It is this definition that all Solutionaries and their disciples will need to commit to memory. It will be through the use of this definition or formula that the actual solutions will prove to be the very valuable nuggets of the wisdom they will teach and pass on to all who wish to become Solutionaries.

In my dream, the Lord's angel spoke to this unworthy one in the same manner as in Gibeon the day I received the gift of wisdom blessed upon me and all those of my bloodline. To be deemed to have wisdom one must process certain attributes or character traits which we, the Solutionary heirs will be born with and the Solutionary disciples must learn. It is God's wish, and mine as well, that any that wish to seek wisdom could find it on their own by becoming disciples of these key principles or Solutions. So be it freely given, my gift to others, I will lay out these formative characteristics so that all can grasp the key that will unlock the potential riches that wisdom can provide.

Not only riches of wealth do I speak but riches of love, joy and peace as well. As king of the land, Holder of the Almighty's gift, I make this decree on behalf of the God of all, to all of my bloodline, as well as any man or woman who desires to grow in wisdom that they become students of the following teachings. As every father cares and guides his children's steps, so I will begin with my own son, Rehoboam, and daughter, Kaila.

The reasoning of any lesson should be put forth before the student so they can find the desire to learn. So was the case just last night with Rehoboam, who asked me as to why wisdom was so important. The answer was as followed. Daily we must make decisions from choices presented to us in life's changing circumstances or problems. We can do so based on such factors as emotions, desires, or just a rash impulse. Usually, relying on these factors alone will not provide the long term and lasting solution. When we make poor decisions or select the wrong choice we normally live to regret that action and in some cases have to pay abundantly in ways that was never considered at the time of the initial decision. By pooling the resources from all three elements of the wisdom formula, Education and Experience provided by a trusted teacher with high ethical and moral character, and inherent Discernment of the Divine Precepts; the choice selection that you make will not be yours alone. You will be leaning on the lessons of all your teachers, your life's experiences, and the guidance of a higher power.

What many people never consider is that every problem and its selected solution have tentacles of outcomes, many of which take years to develop. By its very definition, a quick or poorly thought out decision or choice by the passage of time ignores the full impact on you, those you love, and those remotely affected by the action. Future problems that will surely need addressing at a later date will be said to come as a surprise and usually are not seen as being directly tied to the distance past.

The "new" problem; which is really the old problem or the tentacles related to the original solution; is commonly viewed as just bad luck resulting from being downcast, of a certain race, not smart enough, not to be given the opportunities others are given, or any of the many well warn excuses. Rarely does the person who makes repeatedly poor choices accept responsibility for their circumstances as the lack of applied wisdom. When we do not use the gifts of all three elements of wisdom, we are prone to consider self-centered views and self-serving ideas which lead to selfish acts, choices and decisions, which in turn leads to additional poor acts, choices and decisions. It becomes a self-fulfilling prophesy of negative circumstances.

As I am prone to do with all who seek my counsel, I used a past event to enforce the lesson in Rehoboam's mind. Two warm seasons ago, we went to the Oasis of Kaim to enjoy the coolness of the pool. It is a refreshing pool which is fed from a deep spring that filters over many levels of shale before falling from a height of five fully grown olive trees. Rehoboam and I climbed up the cliff to find the point where the water drained from the rock. The stream flowed from the cave, over a flat slab of shale large enough to hold an entire house. The water glistened and sparkled in the morning sun, flowing in a thin covering over the entire rock shelf to rain down the full height of the waterfall. Rehoboam, being full of energy, wanted to walk across the rock ledge in order to climb even higher since the side we were on was impassable. Without thought, the young ram started to climb out onto the slick rock. I quickly caught his arm just as his feet slipped out from under him. Had I not caught him, he would have surely fallen to his death. I continue to remind him of this event, explaining that I knew he would slide on the wet shale because I myself have walked on wet shale in a less dangerous environment as a youth and I too dropped like a rock. The difference was my pride was hurt, as all of my friends laughed at my expense but I was not harmed physically so I live to teach others of my lesson and that lesson probably saved the life of my young son. It was his youthful excitement that fueled the thoughtless actions that would have put him in serious peril, had I not been there to act quickly with my wisdom of the situation.

Arif, record these three truths that must be learned and understood from the beginning.

First, not all problems of this world can be solved to the satisfaction of man.

Second, there is certainly no problem that people cannot make worse!

Third, every problem that can carry a name created by mankind can be solved by mankind.

My Solutionaries take heart and build strength through the use of the solutions passed down through me. Apply them well to your thoughts, words, and actions so that they bring life to the solutions to the problems you will battle and without fail will you cripple them and be victorious over them. Once learned by the many, a time will come when future problems will be foreseeable and thus corrected in advance, but only if the person freely chooses to do so.

To be a Solutionary, one must first understand what wisdom is. One cannot win a race without first knowing the path on which to run. So it is with the definition of wisdom; it is the path the Solutionary must follow. It is of such importance I will repeat it slowly for you to securely position it in prominence on the scroll.

Wisdom Formula

*Knowledge obtained from
experience and education,
provided by a trusted source
of ethical and moral character
and / or through the grace
of the natural discernment
of the divine precepts,
once applied to a problem in a
selfless manner as the best solution,
is Wisdom.*

The Solutionaries of my bloodline and their Solutionary Disciples; those who study and apprentice under a trusted source of wisdom to become trusted advisors and mentors to those in need; must strive to grow in *education* from the *Past* of the very best teachers. If they feel their teacher is a disciple of a lesser teacher or they only teach to enhance their personal treasures, lofty status, or to promote a biased agenda; then the student must seek a more trusted instructor at once. The student will only be as good as the teacher they follow so to seek a lesser teacher or one of questionable character is to dishonor the role as Solutionary and the privilege that comes from the ability to serve as a Solutionary to others.

The teacher or Solutionary has responsibilities as well. They are entrusted with the development of the disciples. Here are the three areas for both intellectual development and disciple development requiring attention whether the disciple is an apprentice Solutionary, your own child, or a worker for hire; the application would be the same once the education is received:

Intellectual Development

- *Motivation* - this speaks to the motivation of the student to learn. It is the student's internal stimulation, the energy to succeed. Without this energy the student will quit at the first test to that of understanding. Difficulties are best defeated by motivation.
- *Education* - is a process of acquiring knowledge or abilities gained through personal direction or indirect means such as studying the scrolls. Our education begins in our mother's arms. At the earliest of ages we begin to receive the transfer of knowledge through the lessons of our parents and siblings. As we age, we continue this journey through the school systems. As we become elders, the lessons of life continue to teach us, usually at a price far greater than the test given us by the Rabbi. We never quit learning.

- *Training* - is defined as the process of learning how to apply the education, skills, and abilities toward a job, task or duty. Reflecting as I say this in another way, training is the process we go through in order to use our education effectively. An important aspect of effective training is that the one being trained is commonly observed and monitored during the training process by someone already proficient in the job or skill being trained on. As a disciple of wisdom, that would be the Solutionary. The disciple's intellectual development comes full circle when they are observed by the Solutionary as they demonstrate their ability to perform problem solving tasks using the education they have learned and to do so with the proper attitude of enthusiasm created through their internal motivation.

This next phase of personal growth is reflected onto the Solutionary, as they must become the student once more. To be a valued teacher, mentor, and advisor to the disciple, these three skills must be mastered so that the disciples can become a reflection of the Solutionary.

Development of Disciples

- *Mentoring* occurs when a more experienced or more knowledgeable person helps to guide a less experienced or less knowledgeable person. At times, this takes the solution of patience. The disciple will need repeated guidance until the laws and solutions are fully rooted in their minds. It is through the Solutionary's caring presence that the lessons will find healthy roots.
- *Motivating:* though the definition is the same as in the Intellectual context, the focus shifts to the Solutionary who must be able to support the disciple's desires. Encouragement is the virtue one must possess and embrace less both the disciple and the Master will fail in their endeavors. This is an

easy task with those who exceed the level of competence of the Solutionary; it is made rough when the disciple shows little promise.

- *Inspiration:* this gift gives permanency to the relationship. When the Solutionary inspires another there resides a double victory; the context of the inspiration will be impaled in the heart and mind of the disciple but so will the name of the one who planted the spike of inspiration. It will be that Solutionary who will forever be revered and remembered for this gift. Once given freely, the receiver will be bestowed with heightened levels of creativity, which in turn will lead to them inspiring others. This is truly the gift that gives in return. Every father should seek to see this flame in the eyes of their children.

With or without an *education,* some knowledge will be found through life's *experiences.* I said the word some because not all people experience the same things in life. As an example, I have never ridden an elephant. Thusly, I have no knowledge of this experience. That is why we should learn from all experiences we are given in our past and deliver it to our disciples in their *Present,* both the just and the unjust but it is only through the just that we learn and master the solutions of wisdom. The lessons learned through experiences brought about by misdeeds, unless repented upon, will prove to be shallow in nature not holding up to the just applications due to the selfish heart guiding the thoughts, words, and deeds. For is it not an enduring lesson to hear a repented thief levy the punishment of grief on his own heart through him sharing the misery he bore stealing from the family with a sick child? The most important experience is not to others in this example; it is made just and true only if the repented thief's life has been permanently reversed from the course he was on and the evidence of the repentance is made public. Should he return to his sinful ways, the lesson of repentance will prove tarnished and of little value through the lack of trust.

The final third of the formula asks nothing but internal reflection on the part of the Solutionary and our disciples. A God given gift to all souls, these *Divine Precepts* are many; so many that we will cover this in much detail on other occasions. It is well to say that without God, there can be no wisdom because of all the teachers on the earth whom one can seek out to learn from, it is God who is the most worthy of our trust. It is only through Him that we have the promise of our *Future*.

Thus I say unto thee, the first two components of the wisdom formula is a result of what has been; what is currently known and understood. Lessons already taught to us through our *Past*, experiences already learned and retold in our *Present* as education to others. The third component brings forth what is to be, our *Future*. To all who strive to understand, hear me well and take heed, it is only through hallowed divine intercession that we, the sons and daughters Adam, can discern what will be needed tomorrow. As the charioteer looks forward to make progress, the Solutionary must do the same. There is no need to question whether these lessons shared are true and so it is with the need for unity of these lessons born of the power of the trinity."

Solomon rises to his standing height and smiles down at his loyal scribe. "Are you in need of a rest Arif? I know that I have grown stiff from the time in one place."

"Thank you, your Majesty. I too must rest my fingers from the hold of the quill. I did not wish to interrupt such important points for the meager discomforts of my hands. I find your words go straight to my heart with great meaning and are thick with the substance of wisdom. I am once more honored to be your servant." He says standing up, bowing before the King.

"Very well Arif, we will start again in a short time. Take care of your needs while I enjoy a short stroll to meet with my captain of the army. I should not be long so tarry not in your relaxation. I do not wish to lose the threads of my thoughts." The two part ways for a short while and soon return to pick up where they had left off.

"Arif, we will begin our time together reflecting on the importance of being a trusted person of high moral character. I would imagine some would question their ability to label themselves thusly; however, by following these three simple principles, one may be guided appropriately."

Solomon's Principles

First, the Solutionary must always do what they deem as right in God's eyes. Be just in all dealings since trust is earned by actions not merely words or thoughts.

Second, with the understanding that the Solutionary is indeed committed to the best interest of the people they are wishing to assist they themselves, they must engage themselves fully in giving of all the talents, skills and abilities that they themselves possess. Do all that you can as well as you can.

The third measure is to be used as a gold standard, a benchmark beyond reproach. The Solutionary should, in all dealings, treat others as they wish to be treated should the sandal be on their foot.

"Your Majesty?" Arif politely interrupts.

Raising his head from the reclined position on the ground, Solomon looks to Arif with a smile. "Yes?"

"Good and wise King, this is so simple, even I could accomplish such tasks."

"True Arif, but you possess the heart of a Solutionary Disciple, even though you do not possess my blood. For anyone wishing to be an advisor, councilor, teacher, or mentor for less than honest and trustworthy reasons, they will not find these principles easy to follow nor accomplish."

I picture of the scene in my mind as I continue reading Granddad's translations of the actual scroll of King Solomon as written by Arif.

"It is my wish for my heirs, Solutionary disciples, and all people who wish to seek wise thinking that they are given a guide to assist them in their endeavors. Together, we will record and list the solutions I have been entrusted with, along with the details of their application. Be it known that all people are to follow these wise solutions to the world's trials and more importantly to problems we ourselves create. If these solutions are correctly followed, blessed will be the Kingdom and the households that abide in their ways."

Shyly interrupting his Master once more, Arif raises his quill to catch Solomon's eye. "Yes, Arif, you wish to speak?"

"For clarity, your Majesty; why would those who carry your blood be required to heed these words? Are they not born with the richness of the wisdom granted to you by Yahweh?" Arif, though a servant, is always eager to learn from one as great as Solomon. "And if I maybe so bold a repeated time, my Lord? You said any man or woman...does this opportunity truly include women and the lowly servants such as myself?"

"You are a true example of one who can benefit from these gifts, Arif. You are my servant, yet I see a future when servants will not be indentured but instead servants of choice. They will be paid abundantly to serve others. Those who serve will be the richest of people, richer than even the mightiest King, and their riches will be counted in wealth, prosperity, happiness, and with the respect of others.

"I also see no difference in man or woman. Is not my mother one of the wisest people I know? I believe that all can benefit from these lessons and I will do my part to bring these riches to the world.

"In reference to your question directed toward my heirs, you have witnessed many times that I, the gifted of God, am still called to study and practice these lessons and many areas of interest so as to stay sharp in the wisdom given to me. Does not the finest sword, though sharpened by its maker, still need to be sharpened on a regular basis? So too does the Solutionary and the disciples need to continue to sharpen the skills that can give them the edge they seek. Amen, I say to thee that of the three sources of wisdom, two are to be learned and one is a natural gift of God. Man has no say over if or when God implants His precepts of wisdom into his mind, but surely it is his responsibility to grow in the two other sources and maintain a high and unquestionable moral character."

Arif struggles to script these powerful words as the Master recites them but it is a struggle of love and respect with much purpose that makes it all good. All the while that he toils, Arif smiles broadly with the glow of one touched by greatness. He was confirmed as a just man, a man of high value and extreme worth by the one man he respects most in the world. No greater gift can be given to another.

Solomon notices that Arif has caught up in his writings so he begins to address the guidance on the source of the problems that people bring upon themselves.

"All Solutionaries and their disciples will forever be asked to solve every problem under the sun and as a reigning judge of the people, I can speak with conviction that forever that will be impossible. We can only work to solve those problems that we ourselves have created. The others we should rely on God to solve.

"Additional problems will manifest themselves through three areas of mortal weakness in our decision making process, the flaws or cracks of our Free Will are these:

Careless decision making

Destructive habits

Lack of moral judgment

"Arif, I believe I should try to explain the three areas of weakness that lead to the various problems before I present the Solutions so allow your quill to follow my words as I consider one at a time. These three weaknesses stem from a powerful gift from our Lord, the gift of free will. God allows us to choose freely our paths but too many times we do so at our own peril.

"The first weakness is the one that I see most often with the young and those free of care and responsibility. Careless decision making is usually caused by the lack of education or experience. Both can be obtained but not without the availability of precious time. When one does not have the luxury of time needed to make the required decision or choice, and they have a shortage in education or experience, they need only turn to a trusted Solutionary, advisor or mentor; however, be mindful of the deadly sin of pride. When we lack education and experience, we sometimes wish to mask this fact so we choose to not seek the council when we should.

Of the three weaknesses, destructive habits are probably the ones that cause the most pain and frustration to those wishing to fix the problems it creates. We are creature of habit and once a habit is established it causes discomfort when it is interrupted. We begin to create habits as soon as we are born. Arif, remember the discussion we had about your baby sister sucking her thumb. This is a habit that babies develop to bring them comfort. Not all habits are bad or destructive, but all habits take time to establish themselves in our lives. They also take time to destroy when we try to rid them from our lives. What makes this weakness so painful is that a single event that causes little or no problem to the person or family, can become a destructive habit and before the person is aware of the problem, the habit is firmly attached to their life. As an example, one drink of wine can be relaxing and is found to be rather tasty. I myself, enjoy a libation of the vine from time to time. However, if one turns the occasional glass of wine into an entire amphora of wine, the person will soon lose the ability to freely decide to refrain due to the strong hold of the habit and the body's craving that were created. The habit itself is not the sole problem; multiple problems can result from the behavior that the habit spawns. When one cannot control their own thoughts, words, or actions, they cannot make the wisest decisions for themselves or for others. A Solutionary must be brought in to assist in the severing of the unfavorable habit and in establishing a new more positive one as a replacement.

"I will now describe what I mean by the lack of moral judgment. Every society has a set of rules that outline the manner in which the citizens will conduct themselves. These rules of conduct go above the legal laws of the society in that they speak to the foundation of what is the right thing to do in all actions that we take. The citizens will display the morals of the society by their character. Allow me to present an example, it is said of someone with a good moral character that they are honest, so an honest person is said to be moral. To set the extreme, when one is found to be immoral they have little or no regard for what others consider to be right and just. Most people who wish to live in peace with their neighbor will not fall in this category. As an example, the majority who choose to be dishonest are led to this weakness through one of the other weaknesses we have discussed. However, should a person choose to be dishonest in order to create discord and discontent with the kingdom, they would be found to be lacking in moral character.

"With weakness, all people are drawn to them for one of two reasons, the desire to increase pleasure or decrease pain. If the person lies, it is with the belief that they will not have the pain of being exposed in whatever negative position they tried to conceal. What they do not understand is that by lying once, they must continue to lie in order to cloak the first lie. Thus telling repeated falsehoods would fall under destructive habits.

Finally, I will explain the repeated emphasis on the proper use of our thoughts, words, and actions. People will either be moved forward by their Faith or stalled by their Fear. The definition for both words is the same; "The belief of the unknown." Faith is a positive belief and fear is the negative belief of the unknown. Our positive or negative beliefs will kinder the flames of our thoughts, words, and actions. All actions begin with a thought so nothing can be accomplished without first thinking about what you wish to do. Furthermore, especially when dealing with other people, our thoughts becomes our words, either written or spoken. The words we select reflect our thoughts; thus our thoughts should be considered precious and guarded against inappropriate influences. In the same manner, our words become our actions. It is through the power of the spoken or written word that we can make the impossible possible. As a small child we have little power; not even able to communicate if we are ill and if so what exactly is not well. Once we acquire the ability to speak we are able to guide others as needed, allowing them to act on our behalf. Actions breed results but remember, those results can be either positive or negative, and they can be good or bad; results are never neutral. Solutionaries beware of your thoughts. When you are dispensing wisdom your thoughts must be centered on the just choices and the best decision. Never consider what is best for you unless it is first best for God and the ones your wisdom is serving."

Sitting back in the chair, I place the journal on my lap. Lifting my head, I stare at the lush green canopy covering my very existence in the world. Just as I am now hidden away, so has these important lessons been. Deep in thought, my mind is being bombarded by questions.

- Am I someone who could be considered of high moral character?

- Can I be a better steward of Solomon's lessons of wisdom?
- Can our society show tolerance to people without judgment and/or without acceptance?

As I sit quietly, reflecting on these three-thousand-year-old words, I can't help but think of the morally questionable issues Solomon may have been referring to.

- Abortion, the Romans were big on this practice.
- Having a baby outside of marriage
- Sexual relations between unwed people, people married to someone else, or of the same sex
- Divorce, very contemptible in his time
- Uncontrolled gambling/drinking
- Stealing or cheating

How many of these were morally debatable issues in 970 BC? I would say most if not all of them. How little have we really changed over the centuries? Even if the issue was around three thousand years ago, was it considered morally wrong then and is it still viewed as morally wrong today? It is highly likely that people of Solomon's time were split on these topics just like they are today. Probably many of these topics brought people in front of his judgment bench, but were there specific views that would consider someone of having low moral character? And would the consideration be different today? Should the definition of high moral character be different for each person based on their own views of certain issues? Should the definition of character be based on a religious view, a societal view, or both?"

Looking back through the pages that I just read, I find the words that intrigue me the most. The Wise King laid out three concepts of success in very simple terms:

- **Let your thoughts, words, and actions be just and right in God's eyes.**
- **Do all that you can, as well as you can.**

- **Treat others the way you wish to be treated. (The Golden Rule!)**

I imagine that most people would think these are simple steps to live by, but they are easy to say and not so easy to do without conscious thought and vigilant commitment. If only I could live up to these standards for every decision I make.

Getting to my feet, I stretch the stiffness out of my aching back. Looking at my watch, I am once more amazed at the lateness of the hour. "Enough for one evening," I say to myself and the nutria rat that sits twenty feet away, chewing on a root it found in the soft mud. Dimming the lantern so I can conserve the oil, I make a mental note to research other religions and cultures for these philosophies, but first it is time to check in with Mary before it gets too late.

Right before calling it a night, I take the time to look through Granddad's library of books on various cultures from around the world. I'm intrigued that Solomon just about quoted the Golden Rule word for word, and I was interested in knowing if other religions or races of people had their own Golden Rule. It seems like they do. The books all lay open on the table in front of me, revealing an interesting revelation.

The Hindus: 'Good people proceed while considering that what is best for others is best for themselves.'

Buddhism: 'Hurt not others with that which pains yourself.'

Confucianism: 'What you do not want done to yourself, do not so to others.'

Judaism, from Leviticus: 'Thou shall regard thy neighbor as thyself.'

Islam: 'No one of you is a believer until he loves for his brother what he loves for himself.'

And of course, Christianity, from Matthew: 'All things whatsoever ye would that men should do to you, do ye even so to them.'

This proves that the lessons spelled out by Solomon are not reserved for only Jewish or Christian peoples. I knew it, but this is positive proof. Solomon's teachings apply to everyone worldwide.

6

JOE'S SOLUTIONARY
CAREER CHANGE

"He that walketh with wise men shall be wise: but a companion of fools shall be destroyed."

PROVERBS 13:20

South Louisiana, September 1982

It has been 6 months since I left Granddad's hideaway on Isle de Mauvais Choix. When I spoke to Mary that last night, she told me I was called back to work. Though I was very interested in continuing to learn the mysteries found in Solomon's scrolls, they would have to wait. I sealed everything up just as I found it, packed up the garbage I created from the canned meals, selected one of the journals to bring home to share with Mary and made a list of materials I would bring out on my next visit. High on the list was a new battery for the CB and fresher groceries.

During the months that passed, I tried repeatedly to find an opportunity to return to the island. It proved to be a challenge to get away for the extended period of time that the trip would call for. Add to that, Mary and I found out we would be having a baby, so you can see why my focus shifted away from the Modern Solutionary

Society. Shortly after getting the news about the baby, I was once again temporarily laid off cinching the decision to sell the old, little Honda Civic, and buy Mary a bigger car once the baby was born. The decision seemed straightforward enough; at no time today did I or Mary actually voice or even consider the possibility that our destiny was being guided by my status as a Solutionary of the House of Solomon.

Once the ad for the car hit the newspaper, calls began to come in. One call seemed to stand out above the others.

Driving into the upper middle class neighborhood, the directions in one hand and the steering wheel of the Civic in the other, I find the appropriate street address of the home I am looking for posted on a mailbox at the entrance to a long, winding driveway. Hank and Lola Madison live in a gorgeous Antebellum home. It is a southern plantation-style mansion, really—complete with the circle drive, winding stairway opening onto a large walk-around porch, and large magnolia trees full of blossoms lining both sides of the drive. When parking at the foot of the dual stairway, I can't help but ask out loud, "What do these people want with an old Honda Civic?"

Sprinting up the stairs, I ring the bell beside the ornate oak door. A gray-haired older gentleman dressed in jeans and a well-worn shirt comes to the door, smiling warmly. "You must be Joe?" he asks. Shaking my hand, he introduces himself as Hank. After a minute or two of pleasantries, Hank asks, "Do you mind if I take your car for a drive?"

"The keys are in the ignition, sir. Take as long as you need."

"You are not coming with me?"

"No, if you don't mind, I'll just sit here on your front porch. You have a beautiful place."

Laughing softly, he replies, "Okay, make yourself comfortable. I'll be right back."

Sitting on the top step, I am able to see the beauty of the landscaping. Someone has put a lot of love into making this place special. The peacefulness was evident in this quiet neighborhood. Behind me, the door opens and out steps the woman whose love-work surrounds us. She introduces herself as Lola, Hank's wife. Standing to greet her, she takes my hand and asked if she could join me. She quickly sits on the top step, and I quickly follow her lead, sitting beside her on the stoop. "Why didn't you go with Hank while he was driving your car?" she asked.

Shrugging my shoulders, I reply, "I just wanted to enjoy your beautiful place, and I felt I could trust your husband to take good care of my car."

Lola smiles back, "You are a very warm and gentle young man. You have a gift to be able to read people well. I too have that gift of reading people's hearts. For such a young man, I feel you can be trusted and you demonstrated the intuitiveness of a man twice his age."

Blushing from the unsolicited praise of a total stranger, I try to direct the conversation to the selling of the car. Having never sold anything before, I begin to tell Lola all about our current situation and the reasons for selling the car. For some reason, I feel, even though she was not the one checking the car out physically, she would be a major player in the purchase of the vehicle.

"The car is in perfect shape. The only reason we are selling it is that I am currently laid off from my job, my wife is pregnant with our first child, and once the baby is born we hope to get a bigger car for my wife. The car has never given us a bit of trouble. It has only 80,000 miles and I change the oil every 3,000 miles. They say a Honda is not even broken in until it has 100,000 miles on it."

All the while I am speaking; Lola is smiling and nodding her head. "I'm sure that if the car drives well, we will be pleased to purchase it. Our youngest daughter will be going off to college so we are buying it for her."

Feeling good about the potential sale, I begin chatting with Lola about the yard and all the different kinds of plants and trees she has planted and cares for. Hank returns from his test drive, and before he could step out of the car, Lola tells him, "Hank, hire this young man."

Spinning toward Lola, I ask, "Hire me doing what?"

Hank laughs at my response, but he is looking into the sparkling eyes of the woman he loves and trusts more than anyone in the world. It is clear, even to a stranger, that she has been his partner in all things for a long time. In all those years she has probably never steered him wrong. I'm sure he knew and trusted her gift for understanding people.

"Selling life insurance," Hank exclaims proudly.

"Selling life insurance…you gotta be kidding. I don't want to sell insurance. I am a machinist. Hell, I can't even spell insurance."

He must have sensed my apprehension so backs off. "The car seems to be in good shape."

"It is."

"I tell you what, Joe. You come by my office tomorrow morning," Hank says, reaching into his shirt pocket for a business card, "take a sales aptitude test, and I will buy your car."

"What is a sales aptitude test?" Joe asks.

"It gauges if you would be cut out for a career in sales. Are you satisfied with your current job situation?"

"No, not really. I am temporarily laid off, but I am not a salesman, sir."

"Well, that may be true, but my wife is seldom wrong about people, and if she says I should hire you, and if the aptitude score comes back the way I think it will, we may both have more to think about. In any case, if you are drawing unemployment, you have to get three businesses a week to sign your job search booklet, so the state can verify you are actively looking for work. What do you say? It will only take you about an hour, and you will sell your car too."

"Okay, I'll take your test, but I have to be totally honest with you, I am not interested in selling life insurance. What time should I be there?"

"Is 9:45 in the morning too early?"

Smiling, I say, "Not at all sir. I run catfish lines in the morning starting at 5 AM. I will see you tomorrow morning. Thank you, Mr. Hank."

I shook Hank's hand firmly, and then turned to Lola offering her my hand; she leans in and gives him a big hug instead. "Take care,

Joe; I'm happy to have met you. Take good care of your family and tell your wife I am looking forward to meeting her soon."

Later that afternoon, Mary and I are sitting outside on the porch swing, talking about the events of the day. "Mary, I am not sure I want to take that test. I don't want to lead that man on. No matter what I score on that silly test, I am not going to sell insurance."

Mary starts to laugh at what I imagine was my off-the-cuff, steadfast decision.

"What's so darn funny?" I ask.

"I can't see you selling insurance either. Just the other day, I had to almost tie you down to talk to Mr. Caillouette about life insurance for us, and then you were rather rude to him when he tried to sell us the coverage. And by the way, I think we really need that insurance."

"I guess we might, but we do have some life insurance at work. Let's talk about something else."

Mary smiles at my obvious discomfort and says boldly, "When you are working we have the insurance. Bad things can happen when you are laid off too, you know."

I walk into the office building the following morning, and I am quickly greeted by a sweet lady who introduces herself as Stella. She gives me a job application to complete while waiting for Hank. "I'm not really applying for a position here. I am selling my car to Mr. Madison."

"Hmm, that's funny, he told me you would be taking our aptitude test."

"That's true, but only because I am unemployed."

Stella tells me, "I have been with the company for many years and can spot honesty and integrity from a mile away. I know immediately what Hank and Lola saw in you, young fellow. I can tell I will enjoy working with you. But in the meantime, if you will be taking the test for any reason, we will need this application filled out. Can you please do that for me?"

What a warm person, I think to myself. She reminds me of a sweet grandmother. How could anyone tell her no? "Sure. I just don't want to give anyone the wrong impression."

Sitting at an empty desk, I complete the form. I am soon ushered into a conference room to take the test. Once finished, Hank greets me and we finalize the purchase of the car.

"Thank you, Mr. Hank. We hope your daughter gets many more miles out of the car," I say, shaking his hand.

"I'm sure she will," he says. "Thank you for coming in and completing the aptitude test. I should have the results in a couple of days. I will give you a call then."

"That will not be necessary, Mr. Hank. I am not interested in selling insurance. Have a great day." Turning, I leave the office with a pocket full of money and a signature on his unemployment book. Not a bad morning. Before going home, I went to three other machine shops in the area to put in job applications. I am not really looking for another job, but I have to satisfy the unemployment office requirements. Work will pick up again at the shop, it always does.

The following week Hank calls as he promised. "Hello, Joe. The car made my daughter very happy. It was even the color she was looking for."

"That is very nice, Mr. Hank. What can I do for you?"

"As I promised, I got the results of your aptitude test, and just as I thought, the score was very good. When can you come by the office so we can go over the results in person?"

I am tired; it rained most of the day and the fish were not biting at all. "Thank you for buying our car and for signing my book, but I have already told you I was not interested in your job. Please leave me alone." I was way too short with the man, more so than I ever intended.

"Okay, Joe. I'm sorry to bother you, but you know where we are and I always have fresh coffee. If you ever want to talk, stop by and say hello. Have a pleasant evening. Good night."

Before hanging up the phone I already feel bad for being rude to the man. Besides, Hank was just doing his job and he seemed to truly care about me and Mary. Why was I such an ass toward him?

A month passes. I am back to work and things are really picking up. The hours are good, the pay is great with the overtime, and I am learning a new machine the company just purchased. Life is good! So why can't I get Hank out of my mind? Every day I pass Hank's office on the way to and from the shop; the memory of my rudeness to the old guy has me feeling like crap. That night, I pull an all-nighter, leaving work at 10 am the following morning. On the way home, I decide to go apologize to Hank in person. Stella greets me with a smile as soon as I walk into the reception area. "Good morning. Joe, isn't it?"

"Yes ma'am. You have a good memory, Mrs. Stella."

"I don't forget nice people, Joe."

Feeling uncomfortable. "That is kinda why I am here. Can I speak to Mr. Madison… if he is available?"

"Let me check." She steps to her phone and punches in a few numbers "Mr. Madison, Joe is here to see you. Yes, I will send him right in." Placing the receiver down, she says, "You can go right in. Have a nice day, Joe."

Shaking Hank's hand in greeting, I say, "I wanted to come in and apologize for being rude the last time you called me. I was having a bad day; I think I took it out on you and I am sorry."

Hank offers me a seat, and we both sit down side by side in matching chairs in front of his large desk. "Thank you, Joe. I truly appreciate the gesture. I was not trying to be pushy; however, I do truly think you are someone who can be extremely successful in this business. Can I show you what I am talking about?"

Looking into the caring eyes of this regal-looking gentleman, I can see a fire that burns with the passion of someone who loves what he does for a living. Slowly, I nod my head with a smile and say, "What about that cup of coffee?"

The meeting with Hank makes me feel much better. Driving home, I wonder whether or not selling insurance is a smart career move. Hank did paint a pretty favorable picture about the opportunities that he envisioned for me, but to be fair, he also gave me a number of negatives to take into consideration as well so I think he is being fair and unbiased. It's after 4:30 in the afternoon when I pull into Clark's driveway. Clark Burrow is one of my oldest and dearest friends. Our friendship started in first grade and has been close ever since. Throughout our friendship, whenever either of us was faced with a dilemma, we could always count on each other to give honest and open feedback without criticism or false support.

Knocking firmly on the front door jamb with my right hand as the other hand opens the screen door, there was no need to wait for a reply; I just walk right in. "Hey Clark, are you inside?"

"Yeah, in the living room." Clark is sitting in his favorite recliner, feet propped up and a cold beer resting on the armrest. "Get you a beer, Joe?"

"Thanks, buddy, I could use one about now."

"Me too. It was a long day."

"I know, I pulled a twenty-hour shift."

"Wow. I know that is rough, but the money will definitely come in handy with the baby on the way."

"You got that right."

"What else is new, Joe?"

"Well, I was offered a job today selling insurance…life insurance." I watch my friend's reaction but could not read if there was any. "Clark, did you hear what I said? Me selling life insurance… what do you think?"

Not even opening his eyes, Clark asks, "Do you want to sell insurance?"

"I don't know. The guy, the man who I told you bought Mary's car, said I scored very high on their sales aptitude test. He showed me the average incomes of his people, and they are making a little more than me on average, but the top 5 were making a heck of a lot more than me and the bottom 7 were starving. He said he believes that with proper training, a good work ethic, and a positive attitude, I could be making a six-figure income in two years. That would let Mary stay home with the baby. Give me your opinion, Clark—what do you think?"

Clark sits up in the chair, takes another sip of his beer, and looks at his friend. "I have an uncle that sells insurance and he has been very successful. He and Aunt Sylvie have traveled all over the world on company trips, he drives nice cars, they live in a beautiful home, and he has been with the same company for over twenty years. He says he loves his job and everyone can see why. Joe, you are smarter than he is, you are hungrier than he is, and you are better with people than he is. If he can do so well, why couldn't you?"

"Thanks, Clark. I think I will at least explore the possibility. Hank said that I'll have at least three more interviews before we would both be ready to make the final decision."

Enjoying the cool taste of the beer, I shift the discussion to the Society Papers. "Clark, I know you hate to read, but man, I think even you would enjoy reading some of Granddad's old books. It is interestingly freaky and amazing, all at the same time."

"What is freaky about it?" Smiling broadly, Clark says, "You knew I would ask about the freaky stuff first, didn't you?"

Laughing together we spend the next hour catching up on the things I have learned through Great, Great Grandfather Solomon and the notes Granddad left me. For reasons I cannot explain, I have been very leery about sharing this information with anyone, even my brothers and sisters. Clark is the only person, other than Mary, that knows anything about the existence of the Society Papers. With Clark's positive support and Hank's gracious acceptance of my apology, I return home with the hope of getting some more time in the books as soon as possible.

7

THE SOLUTIONS OF
GRATITUDE AND HUMILITY

"When pride cometh, then cometh shame: but with the lowly is wisdom."

PROVERBS 11:2

South Louisiana, November 1982

Finally, I am able to get back to Isle de Mauvais Choix. Even though this is my second trip to the secluded hideaway under the vines, it is still just as dangerous a journey as the first time. On this trip one of my questions is answered right in front my eyes. I could not understand why the map stressed the need to follow the details of the path as closely as possible. Sure, there were animal dangers to contend with, but the animals were all over this island. I don't think the track would lessen those risks. Then, it happened! As I am counting my steps through the swamp, I trip and fall into the water, splashing so loud that the entire swamp can hear my fall. The noise I make scares a large deer in front of me, making it leap twice in the air with the graceful strength of a young buck, but its third leap never occurs. It was as if the deer was tied in place, water nearly over its back. Then it hits me. Of course, quicksand; the deer is stuck in quicksand. These marshes and swamps are full of these deadly pools of muck. Depending on the depth of the pit, you could sink well below the surface of the water, never to be seen again. As I watch, unable to save the animal, the deer increases its struggle as panic sets in; the beautiful animal's fruitless efforts only acts to speed up the eventual slide under the veil of black water. All of this happened so quickly. I didn't even have time to reach for my gun to put it out of its misery. From that moment on, the map became even more precious.

This event and other things made for a much slower trip. The awful accident with the deer probably made me more cautious. The extra weight of the large battery strapped to my back and dragging an ice chest filled with food and water didn't help speed things up. Whatever the cause, the trek is almost more than I can take. I am totally exhausted by the time I climb and lift the ice chest onto the platform. I call Mary; tell her I made it safely and that I love her. I literally fall into bed and sleep like a dead man.

I wake up in the early morning, mostly because of those same damn crows. They caw so loud and almost echo in the metal walls of the container. After a good strong cup of coffee, I am ready to dive deeper into the scrolls of Solomon and the translations of Granddad. Some of the scrolls are definitely written by Arif but others seem to be written by Solomon's own hand.

***

Jerusalem, The month of Tevet in the year 960 BC, Solomon's Scrolls "Kneeling on the cold stone ground where the temple is being built late one winter night, I pray out loud, "Lord, I know that you bless me with all that I have, and I thank and praise you for such gifts. I am concerned that I am not using these gifts as I should. I need your guidance, Lord. I am questioned and accused of making decisions that benefit me or others that I favor. You, who know all, know that is not the truth Giver of All. Please release me from this burden and aid me to follow the path of righteousness." After pouring out my heart, searching for answers, I finally feel relief come over my soul so that I am once more capable to judge in accordance with my office. However, at the age of 22, when kneeling before God, in the shadow of the temple of my dead father, I still feel more is needed. I consider myself as inadequate as the burdens of king, judge, and leader weigh so very heavy on my heart. It is this need to relax that prompts me to visit the land of Egypt once more; that and the lure of the Egyptian beauty, Naamah, the Pharaoh's daughter, whom I met two years ago.

The next day I began a journey to the outer provinces of the kingdom. These areas were home to small villages with two to four hundred families scattered throughout the region. It is very enjoyable to visit the landowners and farmer. They are hardworking, God fearing people with a gracious heart, moved to deep appreciation by my attention shown toward their needs. On this trip, when we reach the kingdom's edge, we will make an excursion into some villages in the Mesopotamia region. From past experience, once the legion leaves the land of the kingdom, we will be no more than any other caravan. I will be less recognized and hopefully viewed as any other traveler. This anonymity alone brings a respite to the yoke I carry in Jerusalem.

With the pressures of the kingship pushed to the back of my mind, I am able to relax and enjoy the troops that are with me and the sites of the area. As a child, father brought me here for the first time. Memories flood back at the smells and the sights of the vistas like it was yesterday. The province was beautiful, the river majestic and powerful. As the cavalcade entered the small fishing village of Ur, the recognitions of my childhood from my long ago visits went blank. Was this the place that I hoping it was? My memories struggled to remember if this was the same town I visited as a boy. In the center of the town, just in front of the well was a stone structure where none should have been. Upon closer observation, I knew that I was in the right place because under the elaborate covering was the generous gift my father David had given to this town many years ago. On one of David's trips to Egypt, he and the legion was caught in a terrible flood stranding him and his caravan in the area for 3 months. I recalled that two of his captains were injured by the raging waters as they tried to save a drowning villager. The town's people took the entire troop of strangers into their homes, tending to their needs and healing their wounds. Even once they learned that David was the King of Jerusalem, they would not take compensation for the care and keep. Father was so moved by their kindness that he made a very generous gift to the village. While in Egypt he had purchased, at what he thought was an extreme price, a new tool recently invented by the Egyptian; he was going to bring it back to Jerusalem for mounting in his courtyard. This tool was called a sundial. When positioned as directed by the craftsman, it allows men the knowledge of predicting how the time of day would pass based on a scrolled chart. All of this was given to the village chief as a sign of gratitude to the people. Sitting with Father upon our return to the kingdom, I heard him tell everyone how much the people of Ur treasured this gift. He said the entire town would gather for hours just to watch the shadow dance across the engraved stone.

Having seen this sundial in person once as a child, I am overjoyed to be able to see the same one still in the place Father had placed it so many years ago. Even though I was a child at the time, I understood the workings of the tool from the explanation given to us by the craftsman Father purchased it from. It is for that reason that I was appalled that the chief would cover up this gift and in essence, take away its purpose. Quickly, I asked the locals to find the chief and to bring him to the dial at once. While waiting, I walked around the structure, noticing that it was a strong well-crafted and elegantly decorated structure, especially by this poor fishing village's standard. The chief arrived as soon as I entered the structure. "Greetings." came a low spoken voice. Turning, I was greeted by a very old stoop shouldered man. It soon became evident that he was the same chief that father gifted this sundial to many years ago.

"Greetings, chief", each bowing to one another. Before I could demand an explanation as to why the town had dishonored my father's gift, the Shaman knelt down in homage to the heir of David. He whispered that he knew I was David's son as soon as he laid eyes upon me. As with King David, the Shaman offered to bestow the same generous hospitality upon our nomadic party, offering food and lodging. He was indeed honored that we would travel such a long distance to visit what the villagers of Ur thought of as a shrine. Brushing aside the kindness offered, I ask, "Chief, why would you cover this dial with this building?"

Sensing the disappointment from his honored guest, the chief hurriedly says, "Good Solomon, we heard of your Father's passing to the other side, please accept our prayers for his pleasant journey in the afterlife." I was moved by the sincere wishes of this elder. The village leader continued, "Our village was truly blessed to have your father present us with such a valuable gift. The people of Ur are poor people, but we appreciate goodness that is shown toward us. We could not bear to see such a valuable treasure sitting out in the weather, day after day. To protect it, we constructed this vault as its home. It is our wish that it be an eternal reminder of your great Father."

"Chief, I appreciate your heart-felt respect and the extreme care of the gift my father bestowed upon you and your people, but without full access to the light from the sun, this rock is no more than a stone carving placed in a special way. It cannot give your people the knowledge of the progress from day to night. That is the true value of the gift not the stone of which it is made. This stone can be found all over this country."

Understanding that I was disappointed, the chief was assisted to his feet where he limped slowly forward, placing his hand on the cold stone of the sundial. "Your highness, we are a simple people. We work when the sun is in the sky and sleep when it rests. Knowing when the sun will slip beneath the hills is of little importance to us. We trust that the sun knows what to do and we cannot stop it from happening even if we wanted to. It is because of your father that, like you, we believe that God is the One who guides its path as well as the path of men. On the other hand," he pauses to look down at the gray stone dial, "This was given to us by a great man, whom we know as a mighty king. He gave it to us when we desired nothing in return for our meager gifts of shelter and food. We did deserve a gift for doing no more than helping people who needed our help. It was because of God's goodness to us, that we could share what we had at the time. To have a king give the village of Ur something that he owned for himself is like him leaving a piece of himself in our town. That endowment is more valuable to us than what this gift can do for us. It is a sign of what we did for him and for our God; what we were in his eyes. According to your God, Yahweh, is not caring for one another more important than any gold, treasure or this sundial? We cared for him, he cared for us. We protect the memory of that friendship under this roof."

I am speechless and felt privileged to be standing under this humble shelter with this wise and caring leader. The Chief, with humility of heart asked, "Did you travel here today just to eat and rest in our village?"

Solomon stared at the ancient leader with wonder, not fully understanding why such a question was asked of him.

"No sir, I came to this village to see this gift so that I could remember my father and the tales he told me as a child. He spoke fondly of your kindness and the hospitality of your people."

Smiling broadly, the chief takes his hand from the stone and places it on the shoulder of the King of the Jewish people. "We are glad you are here, Son of David. Feel the cold of the stone, feel the warmth of the memories we will share with you. Feel the respect these strangers have for the man your father was. He was not a king in our village; he was a good and honorable man; a man that left strangers knowing he was special without him telling them who he was but more importantly, he made those he met feel special too." Placing his hand from my shoulder to his own chest, the Chief looked down and turned to go.

Stepping in front of the elderly leader, I gazed deeply into his ancient, dark eyes. "Today you have given to me and my men more than I ever expected. Foolishly, I was ready to tear down this roof right before your eyes and carry away this precious tool as a punishment for what I perceived as ill treatment shown toward this gift. Instead, you taught me a greater lesson of what a gift really means to those that receive it with an open heart." Taking a knee in the presence of the men who kneel before me, I bowed to this wise and generous leader. "Thank you Chief of Ur, for giving the son of David a gift of greater measure than the one my father gave to you. May no man ever dishonor this place for as long as we all live, for in this town resides a great leader with the wisdom of God. From this point forward, I will live my life observing the solution I learned this day. It is my vow that my children will learn the importance of living their lives using the Solutions of Gratitude and Humility."

After spending a restful period of time in Ur, we continued our journey to Egypt. It was on this trip that I asked for the hand of my Egyptian wife, bringing her home to Jerusalem where we would live out the rest of our days. The events of this trip led me to ask the Lord for the gift of wisdom. He would grant that gift to me and to my heirs. How appropriate that the first "Solutions" set into my heart were based on the lessons of gratitude and humility. The birth of the Solutionary race would soon be born not because I was a great king but instead because the Wise King learned these important lessons from another wiser than he.

This trip to Ur was remarkable in many ways; some positive, some negative. It was on this trip to the land of pagans that rumors were spawned that the King of Israel was worshiping pagan gods. Some of my followers believed that my Egyptian pagan bride had such a strong influence on the King that I too would worship the gods of her ancestors. Many of my own soldiers, through their lack of understanding, would speak of the mystical powers the King possessed through the sundial's control over the sun. Some of them were afraid to even be part of the caravan that would bring one of these dials back from the land of Egypt.

Still being tired from yesterday's workout, I fight the urge to dose off. "I need another cup of coffee." The coffee is strong and the sugar will give me the extra pick me up I need. Then I feel fully awake at once, noticing Granddad's notes directly below the actual translation of the scroll I just read.

"Four non biblical sources mention Solomon's fall from Yahweh's grace as the reason supported in the Bible for Israel being divided into two after his death. Two vaguely reference the pagan grievances but all four mention the sundial as the pagan emblem. Once again the mysterious connection is made between Solomon and the Sun; remember his nickname, Sol, is the name of the Greek Sun god, their god of wisdom. If these allegations are true, how ironic would it be that the Wise King of the Jewish people would fall from the grace of his God, the God that gave him and his ancestors the gift of wisdom, over the tool of the Greek god of wisdom? Intriguing!!"

8

THE DISCERNMENT THROUGH THE POWER OF THREE

Written by the father of Solomon, King David:

"The Law of the Lord is perfect, converting the soul; the testimony of the Lord is sure, making wise the simple."

PSALMS 19:7

South Louisiana, November 1982

Sitting at the table inside the container I am glad that it is much more pleasant now that the weather is cooler. With careful precision, I insert new batteries into the cassette recorder and the reel to reel. Both seem to be in working order. I place a new cassette in the recorder, pick up the microphone and complete a satisfactory sound check. Leaning over the box of tape reels, I find and load the oldest one, pretty sure that the tape is threaded properly. I flip the switch on, and within seconds the voice of a man, whom I assume to be my Granddad, fills my ears. As if from apprehension, I immediately flick the switch off. With a deep breath, I whisper, "We are in business."

I plan to record some of my thoughts as they swirl around in his head. Thumbing the record button,

Joe Recording: "Testing one, two, testing. It is time to bring current technology and a third person to Granddad's work."

Granddad's voice: "The causes of the problems we manifest in our lives, as well as their solutions, can both be found in the Divine precepts that lead to the Grace of Wisdom. The central precept is based on the Lord's power to create and guide his people through His ability to simplify complex issues and situations using the number three. Just the thought of God taking the most complicated of issues and bringing them down to only three components, in and of itself is true brilliance. This precept was described by King Solomon this way; *"Follow the Way of the Lord. He has shown us the way through the many examples evident to all who wish to observe His lessons."* As we go through our routine daily activities, I speculate that many of us rarely, if ever, ponder exactly how three-dimensional our world actually is, yet I would like to explore just how important "The Solution of the Power of Three" is. This Solution is the power that unites, strengthens, and creates everything in our world."

Suddenly emotional, I stop the machine. I watch the reels as they stop turning while I rub the tears from my eyes. He sounds like my Dad. I lose control and weep for a number of minutes. What a treasure to be able to hear the wisdom of my late Granddad's actual voice. What did he just say? I was so focused on his voice I did not hear the actual words. I rewind the tape and hit play again, poised to listen with intent this time.

I stop the tape in what I believe to be the same place as before. With a fluid motion I key the cassette microphone in my sweating hand. I want to leave my legacy by applying the Wisdom of Three to contexts that had not yet been discovered during Solomon's time or even Granddad's time. I think Granddad would be proud.

Joe Recording: "Solomon lays a foundation of simple understanding; starting with the premise that God's laws are the same as the world's natural laws. In essence, it states that all laws have to happen.

The Law of Gravity takes place all around us every minute of every day, so does this law or solution of the Wisdom of Three. As with any natural law, you can affect a law but you cannot change a law. What do I mean? Let's walk through a simple test; say that I drop a brick from the top of a five story building. How many times will the brick fall and hit the ground? Will it even float once? Never, if we drop it from the exact same spot, it will fall straight down every single time because of the Law of Gravity."

Standing, I begin to pace on the side of the table to apply the knowledge and principles I have learned through these ancient messages to today's reality.

Joe Recording: "Now, let's assume there is a 70 mile an hour wind blowing past the building and I drop the brick. It will not drop straight down; it will veer off toward the direction the wind is blowing. So you see, outside influences can have an effect on the law, but they cannot change the law; the brick will still fall. I can't help but think of Jesus, who did not turn His back on His Jewish faith, He only enhanced it. He followed His Jewish faith, in His mind, the precepts or laws of His faith had to happen because they were God's laws. If anyone could have changed these laws, Jesus could have but he understood the importance of not changing them; He positively affected them. That is why the Torah, the Jewish Bible, the Old Testament, is still part of our Christian faith today. However, God gave us both a gift and a curse; He created us with free will which allows us the ability to turn our back on these laws. We can choose to ignore the laws God has given us. The funny thing is that even though we choose to ignore these laws, it does not mean they do not apply to us. God's Divine Discernment or The Solution of the Power of Three must be no different."

I turn one switch to off, then the other one back on.

Granddad's Voice: "With that understanding in place, Solomon introduced this law to us through a number of key examples found

103

in his writings from around 960 BC. He explained that wisdom's definition is even controlled by Solution of the Power of Three. Consider the Wisdom Formula—Knowledge is obtained through **Education and Experience** provided by a trusted source of high ethical and moral character and / or the **natural discernment of God's Precepts.** When God's Precepts and man's education and experience are applied in a selfless manner as the best solution to a problem, you have wisdom. I have determined that this formula would be applicable even to the agnostic or atheist among us. If this natural discernment is viewed as precepts addressing moral, ethical and spiritual concepts it would be all encompassing and would explain why the non-secular cultures share in the number of wise people. Still, it is clear that without the moral or ethical component, wisdom ceases to exist.

Joe Recording: "Just like in the example I gave of the Law of Gravity, we are able to affect the law but not change it, so it is with the person wishing to gather wisdom. We can all pursue more or less education and experience while following the wrong crowd or ignoring God's precepts. These choices will affect the law as it applies to us but it will not change it."

Granddad's voice: "A key part of the wisdom formula, education, is rather simple to understand and as Solomon wrote, once we are out of the formal school system, the school of hard knocks takes over in the form of Experience.

Ah, that leaves us with the most intriguing and probably most controversial piece of all, the natural discernment of divine precepts. Let's take a few minutes to discover what Solomon meant by the third component of this mysterious formula. First, he says that it is *natural*, meaning that it is normal and innate; leaving us to believe that it is readily available to everyone. *Discernment* is defined as being sensitive toward understanding and in this case, sensitive toward the understanding of God's *precepts* or principles.

In Solomon's time every unexplainable event or concept was routinely viewed as being of God. Can it be said that Solomon believed that God gave each of us the natural ability to understand the unassailable laws, rules or principles which affect each of us through the natural order of what we take for granted as physics and that some people are more or less sensitive than others to applying this understanding to the problem solving process? To anyone taking this literally that is exactly what the message is saying and I find it almost eerie that the definition of unassailable used three words; *not liable to doubt, attack, or question*. Wisdom is obtained through applying the knowledge we are given from trusted, ethical, and moral sources, either directly or indirectly through education, experience or through our natural ability to understand natures rules and these rules are usually strongly tied to the number three, thus the Solution of the Power of Three also known as the Wisdom of Three.

If people have the ability to naturally understand these laws and rules, why do people obviously do just the opposite of what these precepts would guide us to do? Well, there is one other little thing that the Bible says God gave us that interferes with our acceptance of these pesky rules; our free will. According to the Bible and the scrolls I have researched, He gave us the ability to make our own choices. In other words, He allows us to ignore what we know in our hearts to be right, just, and best."

Sliding the switch to off, my mind is once more overwhelmed by what I am studying. Who am I that I can sit here intrigued and captivated by the ability to "study" these life lessons with not only King Solomon but also with the voice of my Granddad? After a few moments of personal reflection, I re-engage the play switch.

Granddad's voice: "If Solomon is correct, the Solution of the Power of Three stands at the heart of how God implants some of the knowledge that all people need in order to develop life's satisfying wisdom. This is much bigger than the education component of the Wisdom Formula, yet without education, you might miss the lessons

He wants us to learn. It outshines experience, but, without years of experience, we might be blind to the connections made through the three components of each example of this awe-inspiring Solution. We can directly affect two of the three components of the formula, education and experience; we must rely on God for the third. After all, according to Solomon, it is God's Divine precepts. We can study and learn as much as possible or as little as we desire, and we can choose to learn or not learn from our mistakes and those of others, but we are all given this third dimension as a natural gift. The more we use all three, the wiser we will become."

Joe Recording: "From my Boy Scout years, I remember being taught that to create fire we needed three things, **Fuel, Air,** and **the Heat source.** I learned that fire needs only three components and the lesson was taught to me outside of a religious setting yet it is no less true! I am drawn to the analogy between fire and wisdom. It is said that "Wisdom burns the paths to success". The fuel is like the education we need to propel us further down the successful paths of life, the air we breathe is the experiences we draw from those around us, and the heat source is God's Divine precepts that can be sparked into our conscience just by paying attention to the world He provides us. As a child I was taught that God was everywhere that I looked, and now with the Wisdom of Three, I am seeing that revelation in a whole new light. For now I see the fire is the wisdom we achieve when all three elements are used as they were naturally intended.

Reflecting on how far the world has come in the area of education since Solomon walked the earth; we know so much more about everything, and yet we still know so little. Could these Solutions of yesterday go even further in today's world?

Whenever you hear the term, *three dimensional* or *3-D*; your mind probably immediately recites width, height, and depth or it turns directly to those cool 3-D effects that you experience when you sit in a movie theater with those stylish glasses on. Back in Granddad's time, I don't believe they had 3-D movies so this is not an example he would have used. Still, both of those examples would be correct but these examples deal only with the physical dynamic of our three dimensional existence. This powerful Solution has been there throughout our lives but no classes are taught on this integral dynamic of our life. It has been taken for granted, not connected to useful purpose or buried away from easy availability. Just how broad of an impact does these solutions have on the entire world? How many different perspectives, not just the physical one, does it impact?"

Sitting back down at the table, I quickly make a handwritten note for future consideration before flipping back to the copy of the translations of the old scrolls. I cannot help but smile and think of Granddad and all the notes he made as he tried to piece together this awesome puzzle. In clear and vivid contrast with the pale papyrus, I see the dark ink of a hand-sketched triangle, from what was probably the hand of young Arif.

Granddad's voice: "Do you know what shape, when constructed, is the strongest? You got it, the triangle. This three sided shape can bear more weight than any other shape known to man. I will not bore you by working through the mathematical formulas that prove this to be factual, but if you don't believe me consider some of the oldest structures built, which are still standing hundreds of centuries after their contractors laid the first stones, the mighty Pyramids. Even today, look out of your window wherever you are, you will see homes and buildings of every kind with the familiar triangle used to bear the weight of the roof so that the entire home does not collapse. Perfect triangles built and bound together. What makes the triangle so strong? The strength comes from each of the three components relying on the other and each of the three components supporting one another perfectly. When pressure is applied to any area of the structure, that pressure is dispersed to the other components equally. I wonder if this reliability and support system is a unique phenomenon of the triangle or does the solution the Power of Three present itself in other ways and areas of our life."

Once more, I read directly from Granddad's translation of a scroll, depicting the words likely written by King Solomon:

"I enjoy reading the words of the Book of Genesis describing the details of Yahweh creating the Land, the Seas, and the Air. To my knowledge, this was the first recorded example of the Power of Three. Our Lord, with His infinite power created this entire world with only three environments. Later in the writings we can learn that our ancestors were cursed to carry forward the indiscretion of Adam and Eve and it is through the ultimate sin of Selfishness that all tribulations spring forth. Selfishness, the root has three manifestations which are like branches, *Self-indulgence, Uncontrolled Desires,* and *Self-importance.* It is from these branches that the Seven Deadly Sins send out their tentacles to destroy peace in the world. Every problem imagined or encountered by people can be traced to the ultimate sin, the three roots and their branches. Our loving Yahweh, knowing that we were to live with this curse of Adam and Eve, placed in our eternal body the gift of the Solutions to these problems. All people who follow the Way of the Lord is shown the way through the many examples evident to all who wish to observe the lessons that He provides. We should heed and observe the multitude of demonstrations that use the Wisdom of Three. It is through this natural discernment of His precepts that His unworthy servants are given access to these nuggets of wisdom. Even I, King of the Jewish nation, am amazed by these examples of the power of three found only through His divine precepts. For it is our God that established His precepts around the number three. Amen, I say to you, no mortal man has the power to set, add to or detract from any of these universal precepts. I, King Solomon, Son of David, the first Solutionary, being immersed with the flood of wisdom bestowed by His grace, decree it to be so. Be it forever known, that the Solution of the Power of Three should be applied to all things. Its presence is an undeniable truth and so it has been since the very beginning of time. His Holy precepts offer strength that is evident and on display in all things three. As a living example to all, I decree in order to anchor the Wisdom of Three in the heart of the Solutionary's life they should be a living testament to this precept of three when establishing their personal life's priorities. God will be first in their mind, body and soul, their family will closely follow, and their work activities will take up the remainder of their time, talents and abilities, all to the service of applying wise counsel."

Joe Recording: "It was our first Solutionary, Solomon, who took the preceding gems of knowledge and recorded the first examples of wisdom passed down through the ages. I have so many questions. This all-encompassing Solution of the Power of Three must be the starting block.

It may even answer the age old question, who are we really…as a man or woman?

- How does this powerful solution manifest itself in the human race's every day existence? Does this law hold the potential of making the human body as durable as the Pyramid?

- What of the sin of Selfishness, is that truly the sole problem facing the human race?

- If we ever figured out how to overcome the sin of Selfishness what would the world be like? Can wisdom be that answer?

Still, I find myself in need of spiritual guidance. I should call Shenan for answers to these theological questions."

Shenan is one of my cousins, currently serving as an Archbishop in the Catholic Church. The more I read, the more unfathomable this whole thing becomes! Maybe it is time to use the wisdom of other experts too. Not being a scientist, I am not 100% sure, but I wonder if this Solution of the Power of Three may even be embedded into our very DNA. One of my nephews, Michael, is an outstanding genetic scientist and is someone who could bring a clearer perspective to the scientific questions being raised.

Joe Recording: "Contact my nephew, Michael to discuss his knowledge of the science of these findings. If I remember my rudimentary biology classes of high school, there are three components of every DNA molecule, Phosphate, Deoxyribose sugar, and Nitrogen base. The phosphates and deoxyribose sugars make up the sides of the familiar helix (alternating one after the other) and the nitrogen bases are the "rungs" inside the helix." I can't help but smile as I picture Mr. Audrish, my science teacher, getting so frustrated with our lack of interest in those colored swirls on the board. If I am correct, he would be very proud that I remembered these details, if I am wrong, he would be disappointed that I had not paid closer attention in his class.

To further expand this train of thought, are not all things made up of atoms, and are not these atoms made up of three basic components, Protons, Neutrons, and Electrons? There is absolutely no way that Great Great and I do mean Great Grandfather Solomon, even with his infinite wisdom, could have imagined the depth of this Solution of the Power of Three reaching the most complex problems and matters affecting the human race down to the very core of our building block molecules."

Granddad's voice: "Look at how our personal lives, our business lives, and our spiritual lives are affected by the three dimensions of the Wisdom of Three. It cannot be a coincidence that there are three lives to consider, Personal, Business, and Spiritual. In our personal lives, the family unit is the oldest basis of community on record, surviving the test of time. Is it because of this law that God made it so that only three entities were needed to create a family; a Mother, Father, and the breath of God in the form of a soul; brought together in a miraculous unity creates new life. Then we turn to the strength of any business and consider how it is gauged first by their employee but the truth be told, there are two other components that must be present for endurance and lasting success; customers and a product or service. Of course, through the centuries, both the family and the business entities were formed around a spiritual life that was firmly grounded in these basic principles."

9

JOE FINDS PERSONAL APPLICATIONS FOR THE POWER OF THREE

"Then I saw, and considered it well: I looked upon it, and received instruction."

PROVERBS 24:32

Joe's new office at Commonwealth Insurance Company, July 1983

After multiple interviews, an opportunity to spend a day shadowing Hank on a few actual sales visits, and much praying on my part, I took the job selling life insurance for Hank Madison at Commonwealth Insurance Company.

Today Hank is holding his weekly class for all employees with under two years of experience in the office. Sitting in the training session with the rest of my peers, I cannot believe what I am hearing. Hank's teachings and his somewhat astonishing business approach seems tied to other lessons I have recently been studying.

"I know that each of you have aspirations to be successful in your new career. We share your desire as well, but never confuse success or the activities that lead to success with that of monetary rewards. The money will be the byproduct of your success through the service of others. The trips you earn will be the reward for a job well done, for easing the burden of countless families. Never forget that true success will be measured by the number of people you help through the work that you do. With that in mind, there are three activities we must do each and every day when working for Commonwealth Insurance Company. These three activities are not unique to insurance sales either; they apply to any sales position or any personal business." He turns to the blackboard and begins to write.

1. You must ask three people to buy.

"That means you must explain the benefits of the specific contract and how it solves the client's problems, agree on a specific price, and ask for the payment of the first premium. If you do not do all three of these steps, you did not ask the person to buy. This level of activity will generate a minimum of one sale, feeding your family today while solving one family's insurance problem."

2. Request a minimum of nine referrals a day. (3 from each of the 3 above)

"As you have already been shown, endorsements are the most reliable source of new clients. Without prospects you are out of business. We are entrusted by others to solve their financial problems. If you are able to solve their problems, wouldn't they want you to solve the problems of those they love as well? This activity will ensure your success as a problem solver and will provide future sales to feed your family tomorrow."

3. You must complete a minimum of three fact-finding interviews a day.

"This starts the ball rolling for future closing interviews of the first activity. If you do not have enough opening interviews, you will definitely not have enough closing interviews. This activity completes the circle that allows you to do your job effectively for others. This ensures that you will always be able to feed your family."

Putting down the chalk, Hank steps to the center of the classroom. "Can each of you do these three things every single day that you work here?" He pauses and looks at each of us, waiting for either a verbal confirmation or at least a nod of the head. Once this has taken place, he shocks the entire room with his next statement.

"You can, but you won't. Life is not perfect, my friends. Some days you will not feel well. Other days it will be raining all day long and your umbrella will fly away. What I am getting at is that doing the right things is difficult and requires 100% commitment every minute of every day. Most people allow fun desires to push the work commitments to the side. For the most part, people won't fully commit every single day, but we should all strive for that lofty goal. Let me ask you another question. Can each of you do two of the three activities every day that you work for Commonwealth?"

Of course each of the students emphatically confirmed our ability to do that, since each of us had already affirmed our ability to do all three. Two would surely be doable.

"Yes, you can! Each of you can and should be able to accomplish two of these three activities every single day you are working, and the good news is that it does not matter which two you do each day. One day you might ask four people to buy and complete seven fact-finders but only get two endorsements. Feel good about yourself and go home knowing you did a good job. Another day you might have only one closing interview but get twelve referrals, and five fact-finders. Rejoice! You were successful. However, I never expect you to quit until you have accomplished at least two of these three activities. You can call it a day at noon if you have already reached your goal but I do not care what time it is if you do not have two of the three; your day is not done until you do. So plan well in advance and you will make your life so much easier. Is that clear?"

There is a unanimous "Yes, sir!" from the class.

"For your study assignment, I expect you to become very familiar with the three uses of money. As you have read in the material that we have given to you; you can only do three things with money. Does anyone remember those three uses?"

A young lady named Donna raises her hand and with a nod from Hank she replies, "**Save** it, **spend** it, and **share** it."

"That is correct. Do you happen to remember the percentages that apply to each for a healthy budget?"

"Sure, 20% to savings, 70% should be allocated for spending, and 10% should be shared."

"Very good job, Donna! As we all must be wise stewards of our own money before we can be entrusted with the financial responsibilities of others; I expect you to learn as much as you can about the Law of Budgeting. Solving people's financial problems is what we do! Dismissed."

After class my mind is whirling. Every one of us is taught these very important rules about running our own businesses. I know that is important but what resonates with me is that I am being trained to be a Solutionary. I can't believe how prominently the Power of Three applies to my new business as a life insurance salesman. The lessons from Solomon kept returning to my mind as I was listening to Hank speak. Often I wanted to yell out to everyone in the class about the ancient scrolls, Solomon, Granddad, and the Wisdom of Three but for some unknown reason I thought it best not to utter a word to anyone. I could not explain why I felt that way, but I did.

Before leaving the office, I walk into the kitchen to wash out my coffee cup only to be greeted by another surprising message. This one in the form of a recently hung motivational poster.

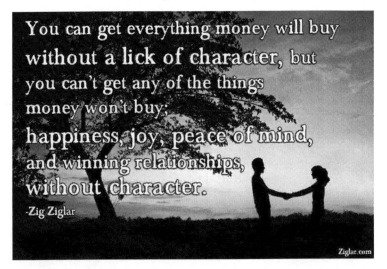

You can get everything money will buy without a lick of character, but you can't get any of the things money won't buy; happiness, joy, peace of mind, and winning relationships, without character.

-Zig Ziglar

Ziglar.com

Even after the shock of being exposed to the additional reinforcement of the lessons from the scrolls in the form of the poster, I casually thank Hank for sharing this great material with us and refrain from telling even him about just how old his material really is. I believe that my new boss would be very intrigued by what I am learning on the Isle de Mauvais Choix, but my heart is telling me it has to remain a secret for the time being. Thankfully my sales manager, Donald, and I have to leave for an appointment to visit with someone he referred to as "an old client."

Mrs. Boudreaux is a very sweet lady and after meeting her, I understand why she is an old client. She is ninety-two years old but looks considerably younger. We are visiting her to collect her premium and to discuss insurance for one of her great grandchildren. Prior to entering her home, Donald reminds me that he will be handling the interview, so I am to let him do all the talking. Sitting at her kitchen table, Donald conducts a flawless presentation and soon has Mrs. Boudreaux agreeing on the contract she is looking for. As it is a very simple presentation and being unable to participate, I find myself bored. Thankfully there is a bowl of peanuts sitting on the table, so as they speak, I snack.

Toward the end of the presentation Mrs. Boudreaux leaves the room to go find her grandson. As soon as she is out of the room, Donald turns to me with a piercing glare.

"Look at what you did!"

"What do you mean? I didn't do anything, just like you wanted."

Donald points to the empty bowl of nuts. "You ate the entire bowl of peanuts."

Looking down in shame, I say, "I'm sorry, I love peanuts."

Hearing the lady returning to the room, Donald quickly demands, "When Mrs. Boudreaux returns, I expect you to apologize and offer to buy her a bag of peanuts to replace the ones you devoured. Can you do that?"

"Yes, sir."

As soon as Mrs. Boudreaux sits in her chair, I quickly apologize for my lack of restraint. "Mrs. Boudreaux, I feel terrible for sitting here and eating all of your peanuts. It was extremely rude of me. Please allow me to buy you another bag," I say with a gracious smile.

Mrs. Boudreaux is equally gracious, smiling as she reaches over the table to pat my hand. "That will not be necessary, young man. I have already sucked all the chocolate off of them."

The rest of the interview is just a blur, but I do notice that Donald never stopped smiling.

10

THE POWER OF THREE
IN EVERYDAY LIFE

"The spirit of a man will sustain his infirmity; but a wounded spirit who can bear?"

PROVERBS 18:14

Evening, the day of Hank's class

At dinner that night, I share the information that I learned in Hank's meeting with Mary, who seemed equally amazed by the correlation. I did, however, conveniently leave out the details from the meeting with Mrs. Boudreaux, knowing that Mary would surely tell the entire family. Our daughter Tiff was cooing in the infant recliner while we finished dinner, and I must have been miles away. Normally I would have been all over the cute little thing, but instead I just played with my own fork. Sensing that I was distracted and guessing it had to do with the Modern Solutionary Society's papers that I brought back with me from my last trip to the island, Mary shoos me out of the kitchen as she does the dishes.

Sitting at the desk in my home office with the microphone in hand, eyes closed and fully relaxed, I begin to recite the thoughts I have in my mind before they are forgotten.

Joe's Recording: "Whether you believe that we were created by God in one spontaneous act or that He allowed us to evolve over time, our body is a perfect example of His use of Solution of the Power of Three. The writings of the founder of the Wise Bloodline of Solutionaries believed that we are made of a Mind, Body, and Soul. Just as a triangle supports each dimension of the structure, the elements of our being do the very same thing. Reading through Granddad's notes, I learned that many people, from many different cultures and philosophies, believe that the soul is created first as the foundation of a person's existence. Without a soul, the person cannot come to be. It is the soul that ties us to our Maker both familiarly and through ongoing communications. Some believe that our souls are recycled through reincarnation, others unique eternal spirits, and still others multiple spirits; whichever you believe, it is through these souls that our person shares the inheritance of our Creator. All cultures believe that the soul is charged with guiding the mind and the body's actions and thoughts through its connection to the Creator. Granddad used this analogy, "Have you ever felt guilty or wished you had done or said something different than you did?" I know I have. Could this be our conscience or soul speaking to us? Solomon believed that our conscience is our soul speaking to us, using divine precepts to guide us through life in a manner acceptable to our Lord."

With so much to take in, I reach for the cherry tobacco and my trusty pipe. I can't help but smile as I think of a good way of telling Mary that puffing on the pipe seems to stimulate mental activities. In May we celebrated the arrival of our daughter Tiffany. She is a very healthy baby, and even after being bedridden for the last month of her pregnancy, Mary's health is back to normal too. However, Mary, as a new momma bear, she is a bit more protective now, wanting me to give up the smoking habit all together. Even though I just puff on the pipe, the warm and inviting aroma of the cherry smoke does have a calming effect that seems to put me at ease. The sweet smell mixes well with the musty odors of the old books.

Joe's Recording: "Our body is the vessel created to protect and house the soul and the mind. This body is unique in so many ways. There are no two exactly alike, yet we all have similarities that make us all one. Could these similarities be given to us so that we can relate more easily to one another? The body is equally important to the threesome that makes up who we are. Yet, the strength of the body does not always equate to a visually and physically strong body. Unlike the soul, we can see the body, but like the soul its true strength may not be completely visible. We have all known people in wheelchairs or confined to bed because their physical body was too weak to accommodate their mobility. This can lead us to believe their body is flawed, and it may be in that aspect; however, that is not the only strength our bodies possess. The Solutionaries in Solomon's writings believe that the strength of our body will function in unison with the soul and mind until the purpose of the person is completed here on earth. Just like the body has involuntary physical functions that are controlled by the mind, they believe that the soul may also have control functions that the body is not in charge of. As Christians, we believe our body, mind, and soul is one unit that we call by our given name. It was put here for a specific reason by our Creator. That reason may not have anything to do with having a physically fit body. In contradiction to what we may like to believe, the reason may have little to do with our individuality; it is probably bigger than us. One of the oldest tenets of wisdom is that we can only grow in wisdom through the books we read or the people we meet. In this computer age, that tenet may need to be changed to reflect the additional electronic sources of knowledge. Could it be that the God-given purpose of some people is strictly to affect the opportunity for change in others? I have met many people who had a lasting impact on me personally. After meeting these people, I was permanently changed. Some of these people I did not seek out, and they did not seek me out either; so was this meeting destined to happen, and to what end? In some cases, the meeting was extremely brief yet its impact was lasting. It is my belief that our body deteriorates as our mission draws to its end here on Earth. From studying Solomon's writings he believed that the strength of each and every body is always enough to accomplish the mission assigned by our God. From a loose note in Granddad's journal, it seems that Solomon had at least one child with a less than perfect body; if that is correct I could see why he explored this train of thought. Another observation I have personally experienced is that the body declines toward life's end, the spiritual aspect of the soul expands to make up for the imbalance. Could this reflect the natural balance required by the Power of Three?"

Pausing the recording, I reflect on mysteries I have encountered of how a person with a weakened body, whether it be weakened by nature or accident, through the additional strength of mind and soul can add extraordinary value to the existence of many, and how these mysteries were made evident to me through my personal experiences. I decide to capture some of the obvious examples for future consideration by those who will one day do what I am currently doing with the notes from Granddad.

Joe's Recording: "Two people come immediately to mind: David Meador, and one of my niece's daughters, Taylor.

David was blinded in a car accident as a young adult. Prior to that life-changing accident, David had long shown a talent and passion for golf. Suddenly unable to see, he knew for a fact golf was now lost forever. With early help from his father, David was to learn his favorite sport could be played impressively well totally blind! So much so that he eventually became a four-time National Blind Golf Champion. That fact alone is impressive, but that is not what makes his life special. It is how he used his special gifts that make David a remarkable Solutionary disciple. It was the peace that he personally found on the golf course that led him to share his gift with blind children. David would go on to serve as a "celebrity" at various annual clinics put on by state schools for the blind all across the country. Though he could not see the children, he could easily see many of the kids were apprehensive and in some cases scared. Doing new things can be frightening to anyone, but to a blind child it's a gut-wrenching threat when placed in unknown surroundings. Thanks to David, each child began to see a new way forward. Through their shouts of joy and excitement, he changed their inner vision—their expectation of what can be!

When asked, "If you were able to go back in time and make a different choice the day of your accident, would you do so to avoid being blinded?" He made this astonishing pronouncement: "No. Having learned what I know today, I would choose the same path, difficult as it has been. Blindness is extremely challenging and does not get any easier over time. But let's face it. If I had not been blinded, I would not have touched the lives of so many kids in such a profound way. And if I had not been a young blind college student, I would not have met my wonderful wife Connie. As a result, I've been blessed with a lifetime of joy through love and partnership." What a remarkable gentleman.

Taylor is a preteen gifted miracle. She was diagnosed with Type 1 childhood diabetes at an early age. With a disease that can drain the life out of the strongest person, she learned to cope and even flourish under its weight. Super intelligent for a child of 9 years of age, she started questioning her parents as to why there was no cure for this dreadful disease. This quickly led to the entire family, spearheaded by Taylor, seeking out fundraising opportunities to benefit diabetes research and awareness. She does not always feel well, but that does not stop her from doing what she has to do for the cause because the cause is bigger than her."

Stopping the recording briefly, I consult the writings so I can pick up where I left off.

Joe's Recording: "Finally, we have the mind, the thought center of both the body and the soul. Our mind controls our ability to use free will. Just as with the presence of a soul, it is this free will that sets us apart from other animals. Mankind, by the use of free will, can decide whether we seek wisdom or follow blindly the paths that lead to destruction and negative results. Through the wisdom outlined by Solomon and again this morning with Hank, if we are left to our own accord, we lose focus on the things that will bring us success by directing our actions toward the selfishness inherited through original sin. The way I see it, when we hold a two-way conversation with our soul, in those moments of self-talk, it is the mind that processes the information and ultimately tries to guide the actions of the body based on our desires supported through our ability to make choices, thanks to free will. The words that we "feel" during these conversations come from the soul as a natural gift of God's Divine precepts. You could say it is the age-old battle of good versus evil, only on a more civil battlefield. I guess that is why the gift of free will can easily become a curse as well. Our mind can overrule the guidance of the soul. As an example, we all know intelligent people who have been led astray by poor decisions, which were anguished over for weeks and possibly months before the ultimate decision was actually acted upon."

Turning the recorder off, I sit up in the chair as my mind opens up to a discussion I had with a new acquaintance from the one-week insurance school I attended in Kentucky a few months ago. The acquaintance's name was Rick, and he started with the company on the same day that I did but he worked in a different region. The company paired us together in the hotel room, and due to multiple similarities in our lives, we hit it off rather quickly and started our new career together. We are about the same age (Rick being about 4 years older than me), and we are both married and at the time expecting our first child.

Even with all those similarities, we had at least one difference. I believe that cheating on your spouse is wrong, Rick, not so much. The discussion went something like this.

Returning to our room after dinner at about 9 p.m., Rick made a phone call while I jumped into the shower. When I got out of the bathroom, Rick was watching television, but he immediately said he wanted to ask a favor of me.

"Sure, Rick; what's on your mind?"

"I want you to disappear for a couple of hours. I will give you 50 bucks to go have a good time in the lounge. I'm sure there will be other people you will know from this school having nightcaps." He reaches out his hand, offering me the cash.

"Rick, I want to get up early to exercise; I think I am in for the evening," as I lay on my bed.

"Come on, dude…you're killing me. I have company coming over, and we are going to want to be alone, if you know what I mean."

"Yes, dude, I think I do know what you mean, and I am not interested in contributing to this poor decision. Besides, you told me you were happily married and your wife is pregnant. Are you totally out of your mind?"

Rick looks like he is getting upset. As a matter of fact, I think he might even take a swing at me or physically try to evict me from the hotel room. Rick stands and walks toward the phone, cursing as he goes. I do not try to overhear the conversation but I can tell it does not sound like a happy one.

When Rick finally settles down, flips off the lights, and slips into his adjacent bed, he asks me, "Why could you not just go along with the plan? My wife would have never found out."

"The main reason, Rick, is that I would not allow you—or anyone else, for that matter—to jump in front of a speeding car, so why would I allow you to do something equally as foolish? People don't always make smart decisions in the spur of the moment."

The dark silence is broken after a few moments. "I guess I should thank you, but I want you to know that it wasn't a spur of the moment decision. I have been wrestling with the idea for a long time. The opportunity presented itself this evening."

"Well, maybe you should have continued to struggle and not give in to the 'opportunity.'"

I turn over, leaving Rick to his inner struggles and drift off to a peaceful night's sleep.

Joe's Recording: "We all have to make judgment calls in our life, some of which will weigh heavy on our hearts. A mentally competent person with sound moral values should reach a just decision, but of course sometimes that will not be the case because we are not perfect.

What about when the person is not of their "right" mind, or when their mind seems defective or lacks development? This is what the Wisdom of Solomon says. "Just as with the body and soul, we may not understand the exact purpose each person is called to accomplish." In the same way as the soul, the mind cannot be visually seen. Yes, today, we do have technology that can detect brain waves, and we are getting closer to understanding new and exciting elements of our mind; still, it cannot be seen. Remarkably, with today's technology, we have learned much about how our mind works, even studying and revering the minds of people who years ago would have been labeled as dysfunctional.

A case in point is the mind of a savant. It is with the aid of Granddad's research that I have built an interest in how the mind works. Doing my own research with the aid of the internet, I learned about a Super Savant named Mr. Kim Peek, nicknamed The Rain Man. What a blessing this man is to the world. He is positive proof that we still do not fully understand the workings of our brain. How can a man who struggles to dress himself be able to do complex math equations faster than the fastest computers of his time? Many people are limited in their ability to function at the level of societal norms, yet they are able to do other mental exercises that the "normal" mind cannot even imagine. Some of these gifted people can multiply large numbers in seconds without the aid of paper and pencil or even a computer. Some can read a book once and memorize the entire content being able to recall the material at will throughout their life. Even with brilliant people studying them for years, it is still a mystery as to how they can accomplish these extraordinary tasks while not being able to brush their teeth without supervision. This is a clear example of the fact that minds thought to be damaged may not be when it comes to the person's mission on Earth."

As I move things around on my desk before calling it a night, something out of the norm catches my eye. Picking up the out of place paper, I see a handwritten note from Mary on the side of what looks like a poem.

"In support of my dear husband's interest in the phenomenon of what unique purposes each of us brings to life, I thought you would enjoy the message found in this poem. It may well have been written by a fellow Solutionary. I love you so much!" Fighting back tears of love, I read the inspired words and immediately noticed the Power of Three at work:

A Reason, a Season, or a Lifetime

People come into your life for a reason, a season, or a lifetime.
When you figure out which one it is,
you will know what to do for each person...
"When someone is in your life for a REASON,
it is usually to meet a need you have expressed.
They have come to assist you through a difficulty;
to provide you with guidance and support;
to aid you physically, emotionally or spiritually.
They may seem like a godsend, and they are.
They are there for the reason you need them to be.
Then, without any wrongdoing on your part or at an inconvenient time,
this person will say or do something to bring the relationship to an end.
Sometimes they die. Sometimes they walk away.
Sometimes they act up and force you to take a stand.
What we must realize is that our need has been met, our desire fulfilled; their work is done.
The prayer you sent up has been answered and now it is time to move on.
Some people come into your life for a SEASON,

because your turn has come to share, grow, or learn.
They bring you an experience of peace or make you laugh.
They may teach you something you have never done.
They usually give you an unbelievable amount of joy.
Believe it. It is real. But only for a season.
LIFETIME relationships teach you lifetime lessons;
things you must build upon in order to have a solid emo-
    tional foundation.
Your job is to accept the lesson, love the person,
and put what you have learned to use in all other relation-
    ships and areas of your life.
It is said that love is blind but friendship is clairvoyant.

— UNKNOWN

Smiling as I finish reading the poem for a second time, I know I will forever treasure this gift given to me by the love of my life. I decide that it should be saved with the rest of the written knowledge I have been reading. Finding the perfect spot in Granddad's journal, I place the poem and the previously loose note from Granddad directly in front of a story scribed by Solomon's own hand. Just as this poem given to me from Mary talks about the power of relationships; I remembered reading Solomon's story on the lesson of determination. The emotional strength of his son and the impact of various relation-ships in the boy's life helped him to reach his full potential.

11

THE SOLUTION OF DETERMINATION

"If thou faint in the day of adversity, thy strength is small."

PROVERBS 24:10

Solomon's Scroll, scribed by Solomon; 964 BC

There is a heartwarming family filled atmosphere inside the king's personal quarters today. The children are playing well with one another; running across the floors as an arrow shot from a bow. The mothers are gathered together, enjoying each other's company as they each share tales about their ever-growing children. Solomon strolls through the adjacent courtyard smiling in a peaceful manner as one of the neighboring children nearly knocks him down in their attempt to rush into hiding so that the seeker of the game cannot readily spot him. The king enjoys this fun-filled energy that can be felt as it pours from the children; while nearby the mothers exude an excited peacefulness knowing that the children are safe, allowing them and their friends to enjoy one another's time together. At times like these he reflects on how fast the children grow into adults. His thoughts search for ways to teach parents the importance of the solutions needed to be teachers to their children. When we are children we should be taught to make wise selections from the choices given to us by our parents. As parents we should learn to only give good choices for our children to choose from. Whichever choice they make will be acceptable to the parents and the child because it was selected from a suitable list of choices offered by a trusted and loving parent. With a sudden outburst, the King is brought back to his surroundings.

"Master!" the spell of the moment is broken by the call of one of the oldest of children. Turning toward the request for his attention, he notices that it is Jacob, one of his own children wishing his attention. Stepping to his side, he places his hand on the youth's shoulder, "Good morning, Jacob. You are growing like a weed. Your mother must be adding a special root to your food," he says, softly smiling into his sparkling eyes.

"I think she is, father. My sandals seem to tighten each time I put them on." He has his father's height and his mother's dark hair.

"What is it you wish of me, my son?"

"I did not want to bother you, father, but I noticed you were walking as if you were not being pressed into service. I wanted to speak with you about something that has been bothering me. I trust that you will lead me in the right direction."

"Of course, Jacob." Leaping slightly, he sits on a nearby ledge calling his son to sit beside him.

Jacob struggles to leap onto the ledge that is just a bit too high. Solomon acts as if he does not notice the young man's efforts. After a few minutes Jacob is successful at obtaining his perch beside his father.

"What is it you wish to discuss with me son? I bet it has to do with the young women? "The boy blushes and shakes his head vigorously.

"No, father!" His cheeks redden as he looks down at the ground a hand's width below his feet. "It is about these." He raises his deformed arms above his head.

Jacob was born with shorter than normal arms. Had he not been born of royal blood, he would have had a tremendously difficult life, likely having to resort to begging for his food. Even as the son of the King, Solomon did not treat Jacob as an invalid. Jacob was expected to pull his weight doing the chores he was given to do. Solomon and his mother were in agreement that Jacob would be an asset to the community and would live a normal life so as to not rely on his status as the King's son.

Solomon looked above the boy's outstretched hands. "About the sky?" Smiling as the boy shakes his head with a smirk.

"Father..."

"Very well, what about your arms?"

"They are nearly useless, father. I can do so little with them it causes people to stare and to treat me differently."

"Does your mother or I treat you differently? How about your brothers or sisters...Your teachers?"

"No sir, it is only those that do not know me well. It makes me uncomfortable and causes me to act differently. I get upset with myself and lose faith...faith that I will be able to find work when the time comes. I do not want to be a beggar, father."

Leaning close to his son, Solomon wraps an arm around his shoulders, hugging him against his side. "Jacob, it is understandable that you lose faith at times of struggle. Each of us is guilty of losing faith when it is easier to give up than to excel. Your arms do not give you exclusiveness to self-pity though they do make you unique. Look around Jacob; do you see anyone with arms like yours? God gave them to you for a reason. Who are we to question Yahweh? Have you ever noticed the look of a camel? Is there any other animal that has those ugly humps on its back?"

"No, father, though some have two humps and others have only one," he says, searching his father's eyes for the direction he is taking the conversation.

"That is correct my smart son but still God decided that the camel should endure the uniqueness of the hump. Should a camel be less of an animal just because it is different? If they considered themselves a lesser animal would they still be the hardest working animals on God's team? I think not.

"What I am trying to explain to you Jacob is that you must show strong determination. You must decide that you will use your unique trait as a gift, not as a hindrance," he says, whispering in his son's ear, "I will tell you a secret my son, but you must vow to never repeat it to anyone else."

Jacob looks into the king's eyes and shakes his head, affirming his silence.

"I am one of the only engineers that I know who is not good with numbers. I struggle to even add the simplest of numbers and the use of those complex formulas are like whips taken to my back."

His son leans back as if in shock. "But father, I am excellent in math. I can figure out any equation I am given. That is so simple for me!"

"I know son, I have seen your work. It is another gift you have been granted. Can I ask you another question? Do you need your arms to be great in math?"

"No father, I can still write, though it took me longer to learn how because of my...gifted arms." Smiling, he sees the path his wise father is leading him down.

"That is correct, Jacob; however, it should be considered that learning math did not take you hardly any effort, for it came very natural to you, whereby, I on the other hand still struggle in this area even in my older years."

"I will tell no one of your challenges in math, father."

"Thank you, my son." Solomon clears his throat before querying his son. "Can you tell me how you overcame your difficulties in learning to write? It may be possible I could learn from you and apply the lessons of your experiences toward my mathematical shortcomings."

"The king is asking me for advice!" he says, beaming with pride and is eager not to let his father down. He begins to explain the steps he took in learning to write. In his explanation he went into detail about how it used to hurt to bend his hand the way he needed to bend it to hold the quill firmly against the scroll. He shared that many times he had thought about giving up, but his love for math and the need to write the problem out kept him moving forward. In addition, he found joy from the praise his mother gave him when he endured. He noticed that the more he worked at it the better he got. The pain diminished with time and the messiness turned to legible penmanship. "Father, you just need to keep trying, you are so smart, I am sure you can learn to be good in math."

Solomon steps down and kisses his son on the forehead. "Jacob, through the years you have taught me so much about the Solution of Determination it is my pleasure to be your father. Thank you for the encouragement, my son."

12

JOE WANTS THE CHURCH'S ASSISTANCE

"For the LORD giveth wisdom: out of his mouth cometh knowledge and understanding."

PROVERBS 2:6

New Orleans, LA, the last week of August 1983

Taking a break from the research papers, I take one of my precious days off to travel the 70 miles to New Orleans to meet with one of my cousins, the son of one of his father's brothers, Archbishop Shenan Morrison. As soon as I arrive, I am greeted with a warm embrace then ushered through the rectory into one of the most wonderful flower gardens in the downtown area. The peacefulness of this city oasis magnifies my senses through the abundance of colorful plants, fragrant aromas, and the soft trickles of hidden waterfalls. The noise of the bustling city, only a couple of doorways removed, is locked out by the tranquility of this prayerful refuge. As we stroll side by side, I breathe in the fresh early morning air as it propels revitalizing energy into my overworked mind—a mind that continues to dwell on the mysteries around the concepts disclosed in the mass of material Granddad discovered long before Shenan and I were born.

Totally at peace with one another, the silence of the sanctuary brings joy to both our hearts in the same way that the blooming vines overhead brings protection from the rays of the rising sun. Shenan breaks the silence, "Joe, when we the last time we saw each other? I believe it was to celebrate the birth of Jenny's son."

"I think you are right, Father. That must have been two years ago, at least."

"It was, Joe. Tyler is almost three now. I am very happy to be able to visit with you again, but I believe you have something on your mind. You seemed anxious over the phone. How can I be of assistance?"

Shenan has always been a keen judge of people and even before entering the priesthood was eager to bring peace and relieve anxiety for others. Though we do not see each other often, I do know that his world is not free of worry or troubles. From past discussions, I know that his caring nature fills him with loneliness brought on by immense pressures that he cannot share with many people. As a priest who works closely with the Vatican, he is asked to deal with problems not many priests are presented with, but he sees it as an honor to be called to serve at such a high level and rightly so.

Shenan leads the way to a bench in the rear corner of the garden where he prayerfully asks God for peace, strength, and wisdom for both him and me.

Feeling safe in being able to confide completely with my most trusted friend, cousin, and confessor, I am next to break the peaceful stillness, "Shenan, before we discuss what I have come here for, can you hear my confession?"

"Of course, Joe. I even brought my stole with me just in case you would ask," Shenan replies, touching the cloth to his lips, he slips the purple stole onto his shoulders.

"Bless me Father for I have sinned; it has been two months since my last confession."

Leaning forward, resting my elbows on my knees, I confess the sins that I have committed since my last confession. "Father, I continue to struggle with my selfishness. The last time I was in the city, I was having a business lunch on Canal St., sitting at a window facing the street. A bum was walking down the sidewalk and from my table I watched as he stopped at a trash can, dug inside, selected a Styrofoam cup from the garbage, removed the lid from the cup, and drank the liquid. As he was drinking, our eyes met, Father. The man looked like Jesus. I am not kidding you; he looked like every picture I have ever seen of Christ. He finished drinking, turned and walked away. Shenan, I did not even budge from my comfortable seat inside the restaurant. I should have run outside to offer to buy him a meal and a drink but instead, I just sat there and did nothing. Now I cannot get his face out of my mind. I am so sorry, Lord. I did not show charity to one in need. For some reason, I do not consider others' needs as much as I should and I lack patience so often. In addition, I give in to the temptation of pornography, much more now that we have the internet. I am such a weak man, Father. Please help me to be a worthy brother to our Lord and forgive me of these sins and those I do not remember."

For the next half hour we spoke openly, discussing ways to limit or remove the temptations from my life. The priest and the confessor recite the Act of Contrition together before Shenan gives me my penance requirement. Laying his hand on my head, Shenan, on behalf of our Lord, absolves me of my sins.

"Thank you, Archbishop," I say, smiling at my cousin. "I feel much better. I have been trying to lead a more holy and righteous life…and that brings me in part as to why I wanted to see you. I need your help and guidance. I know you will not think I am going crazy…or at least I hope you don't."

Not wanting to interrupt, Shenan only smiles, waiting patiently. He was always a good listener.

"I am studying some ancient documents on the topic of wisdom. They cover many areas of wisdom, one in particular that I lack a full understanding of, deals with a concept called the Power or Wisdom of Three. Everything points to the fact that from the moment of creation that God used this law or precept of three to determine mankind's survival. Did you ever consider that we do not need hundreds of things to survive, we only need three: Food, Water, and Air; the perfect triangle. I have come to believe that God shows us His ultimate love and His desire for us to prosper and multiply through this same power of three when he set into motion the ability for people to procreate. The only way the human race could have even endured past the first generation was through the results of this important solution. It takes a man, a woman, and the miracle of a soul given by God to make a child; once more, a perfect three-dimensional miracle."

Taking a break to gather my thoughts, the Archbishop gets a chance to reply, "Joe, these are truly some of God's miracles, but sadly we live in a world where not everyone still believes that bringing forth a new life is a miracle of God. I personally think science may be reaching into areas that interfere with the God's Divine plan when we allow man to create life in a test tube. I can't believe that the scientific community won't come out and say that even if man can create life in a test tube, there is still no evidence that he can create a soul. Only God has that power."

"I understand what you are saying, Shenan but another viewpoint is that the scientific breakthroughs we are making are an extension of God's Divine plan because it is through God's grace that man is given the intelligence to reach these new medical frontiers. In the Society Papers..."

Shenan interrupts with a smile. "What the heck is the Society Papers?"

Returning his smile, I say, "I'm sorry, Father; that is just what Mary and I call the material I am studying. Before I go into details about the source, let's finish this topic, if you don't mind."

The Archbishop smiles and nods in agreement.

"I am learning it may be wise to consider the rule that guides all of God's Laws. We can affect the Law, but we have no power to change the Law. It is when man's ego gets so inflated that he believes he has the power of God that we as a people, get into trouble. It was one of our distant cousins, Sir Albert Einstein, who created the formula for such an ego. I can picture it in my head.

Ego = 1 / Knowledge

"More Knowledge less the Ego, Less the Knowledge more the Ego."

"Einstein was a cousin of ours? I didn't know that," the Archbishop replies, looking more inquisitive by the minute.

"That is another story." I continue on, not wanting to lose my train of thought. "The beauty of God's plan for us was so well crafted and so flawlessly laid out it baffles my mind. To be able to explain the extremely complex elements of each step of His elaborate plan, He designed this simple solution called the Power of Three. What could be simpler than three components?"

With a sparkle in his eyes, the priest responds, "Well, three obviously can be immensely daunting when placed in the Hands of God. One of the biggest mysteries the world has ever known is the paradox that attempts to explain the actual essence of God Himself as a living presence on earth, at least from the Christian perspective: the Father, Son, and Holy Spirit; The Holy Trinity.

According to your rationale, it should be so simple, but it is not. This remains a major mystery of our faith thousands of years after it was first presented to us. The Father created all things, existing always. That principle alone is amazingly difficult to grasp. Then, as the Bible says, in the fullness of time, at the time of His choosing, He sent His Son as an ambassador to walk as man, a man like every other man barring the stain of sin. When His plan on earth was fulfilled, knowing well the weaknesses of human kind, He sent us the Holy Spirit to continue His work through the hearts and hands of worthy people. How simple is that? Yet how can three separate, distinct, and dynamic entities be only one? All three the same being; God the Father is the Son and the Spirit. Without faith, this dogma would be pure fiction, but with faith, it brings a clear meaning to our life and our eventual eternal destiny. Your Power of Three so perfectly ties us to God through our shared spirits, His Holy Spirit through our eternal soul."

"Archbishop, you are becoming quite the philosopher."

"Thanks, Joe."

Opening the folder I brought with me, I remove a copy of one of Granddad's journal pages. I hand it to Shenan for him to read.

"As our creator, He knows our weaknesses and knows that we need to have a solution to the problems that threaten the salvation of our soul. Through the Power of Three, He provides lasting instructions that teach us how to preserve our Soul. Jesus, His Son, our Brother in faith, and a Solutionary by birth taught us this lesson using the Wisdom of Three. Again, it is so simple yet so difficult to do that He used the Solution given to us by Solomon to craft an easy to remember lesson: Love of God, Love of Neighbor, and Love of Self. This is the basis of our Christian faith and the clarified law that was preached by Jesus. It is also evidence that as a Solutionary, Jesus understood that Adam and Eve's sin of Selfishness had to be erased by Selflessness. When a person loves God and Neighbor in an equal measure to Self, the person will never be drawn into a sinful act. We only make poor decisions when we do not first consider God and Neighbor. The only entity considered at that moment man loses to temptation is Self. If all actions and decisions were made after thoughtful consideration of this Solution, what a beautiful world we would live in."

Mesmerized by the wisdom on this sheet of paper, Shenan reads over it twice then says, "Joe, where did you get this material? It speaks great wisdom and from an interesting theological standpoint."

"Shenan, this is part of the material I have been studying. It is our Granddad's writings. I am struggling with some of the concepts and religious applications, so I thought you would be my best resource for making sense of it. If I am right, I think these messages may bring new meaning to all of history, but they also bring mountains of questions as well. Like, did Jesus, the man, know He was a Solution-ary? Did others of His time know of the Power of Three? Did Jesus ever read the ancient scrolls of Solomon?"

"Wait, please wait!" exclaims the Archbishop. "Joe, what exactly did you find? You said Solutionary?"

"Some old boxes filled with ancient scrolls, journals, other old books, and tape reels of Granddad's thoughts and findings. It seems to be Granddad's research on Solomon as the founder of wisdom and a race of people called Solutionaries. I am led to believe that certain people have been chosen to serve others by their birthright, and others can develop an extremely high level of wisdom through applying formulas and lessons to their lives. Crazy, huh?"

Shenan seems to become tense after hearing these last comments, but I am so focused on the discussion and covering certain details I let it go.

He whispers, "Please continue, Joe."

"I am looking for spiritual guidance, I guess—as well as clarity about where this material clashes with the teachings of God, because some of Granddad's research included non-Christian sources. One key concept mentioned in multiple religions, cultures, and times is the entity referred to as our soul. Many cultures outside of Christianity have taught the belief of a soul through the centuries. They even went to the extreme of burying food and drink with the mortal body so that the body of the afterlife, the soul, could survive the long journey to paradise. It would help if you can at least point me toward in the right direction.

"I would also like you to help me to fully consider the solution that Jesus gave us in the New Testament. In numerous writings we hear Him teach the importance of loving God. This message was well accepted by everyone of His time and ever since. Even the pagans believed that it was critically important to love your God. Then He began to get a bit too radical for His times by saying that people had to love their neighbor. People were quick to ask, who were their neigh-bors? If they were the people they lived next door to, that would be fine; they were likely to be relatives that they already loved. But then He threw a wrench in the cogs. He taught them that their neighbor is anyone they may deal with on any given day, even those they do not like and may not agree with. I'm sure that went over well in old Jerusalem based on Granddad's writings. In today's culture, the people would have told Him, "Wow, you have to be kidding me! I have to love people who might wish me harm?" Yes, but only if you want to have a healthy and holy soul that finds its way into Heaven. Then He introduced the third variable in the equation: we have to love our self. To some this third factor sounds like a no-brainer and the easiest of them all; however, that is not always true. Loving our self can be defined as caring for our mind, body, and soul in all aspects and all the time, not just when our self-esteem is positive. If you truly love your body, you will probably exercise and eat right. A healthy, well-loved soul requires the avoidance of vices that could hinder spiritual growth, well-being, and the observance of the Ten Commandments. You know how hard it is for people to rid themselves of their personal vices. Also, our mind must be fed regularly if we truly love it. Not as easy as we may have first thought, but with the simple Solution of the Power of Three, He gave us the remedy that is easy to remember." I hand Shenan another page from the folder.

Matt 22:36 "Teacher, which is the greatest commandment in the Law?"

*Jesus answered vv. 37-40 "Jesus replied: "**Love the Lord your God with all your heart and with all your soul and with all your mind.**' This is the first and greatest commandment. And the second is like it: '**Love your neighbor as yourself.**' All the Law and the Prophets hang on these two commandments."*

Shenan, it cannot be just coincidence that Solomon gave us the Solution of the Wisdom of Three, and then Jesus comes along and voices the greatest commandment of all, which ties directly to the Solution that solves the problem of the original sin that plagues the entire human race. This is beyond rational happenstance!"

"I see what you mean, Joe, but I do not totally understand everything you are referring to. I can tell that you have a good grasp of the information you have read, but I am at a slight disadvantage, not having been exposed to it at the level you have. I think I will have to see more of these documents to help guide you on your journey of understanding. You have thrown a lot at me in a very short amount of time."

"I know, Shenan, I apologize for being overzealous; I am just consumed with all that I am learning and how this knowledge might answer questions that could benefit the entire world.

"I know you majored in business before going into the priesthood, so consider, how does a business thrive? It takes a Strong Company, Strong Product or Service, and Strong Personnel. The Power of Three! What are the three elements of time? Past, Present, and Future! There are so many examples of the Power of Three that it is becoming overwhelming to consider, because they all guarantee success or positive results for those who do not work against their order."

Putting his hand on Joe's shoulder, the Archbishop replies, "I see you are really into these concepts, and you seem to have many more questions than answers. Why don't we both sleep on this information and get back together in the next couple of days? I could drive to your home and have a closer look at what it is you found. How does that sound?"

"That sounds wonderful, Shenan. Mary will be very excited to see you again. We will cook you a nice dinner for your troubles, so come hungry. However, all of Granddad's work is not at our home. It is sorta in a hidden place."

"Hidden place?" Shaking his head, "Ok, enough for one day. Regardless, I will never turn down Mary's cooking."

"Good, then; I will give you a call after I speak with Mary." Standing, we slowly walk toward the outer gate. "Before I go, can I leave you some more notes that I have questions about? That way you can give me your thoughts on them next time we are together." I hand him the entire folder filled with the copies I made for him.

"Sure, Joe," he says, taking the folder from my hands. We give each other another warm hug.

"Thanks, Shenan. I appreciate your time."

Shenan returns to his office looking over the papers Joe had given him. It is a number of pages of very thorough research, some of which is from Joe, some from Jules, Sr. (Granddad), and some of which look to be copies of an actual scroll. Shenan reads a set of scribbled notes in what he believes is Joe's handwriting. Joe has questions about the writings of the person thought to be one of the Gospel writers, Matthew, who was also thought to be a relative of Jesus and thus also a Solutionary by birth.

> *"Could God have given him a clear understanding of how the Power of Three influenced the birth of the Christian Savior, Jesus? If Matthew was a Solutionary that would start to answer the question as to how the power of three appears to guide his own writings."*

In order to preserve his own thoughts and questions for their future meeting, Shenan pulls out his dictograph, starting with the time and date. Looking down at the folder of material, he begins to speak.

Dictating: "Research the significance of the three fourteen-generation eras mentioned in Matthew, 1. Based on information found in the translation of the scrolls, it may bear importance. The first era started with Abraham, our Father in Faith, the second with David, the Patriarch of the Messiah, and the final era with the Exile to Babylon, referred to in the ancient writings as the Great Scattering.

"Being a student of the human condition, I am intrigued about why the author of these aged writings worded the text the way he did. Studying the writings from a leadership perspective, a topic I have been passionate about for years, I would immediately apply leadership principles to the correlation between what happened to the Judeo-Christian faith during each period of time listed in the old documents.

"In what Jules calls the Abrahamic Era, the new faith was being born. The people were brought close together under a common belief that held indisputably strong merit regarding the general good of the people. The beliefs were well communicated by an honest and well-respected person, a common man who quickly rose to the role of leader even though he never aspired to that position.

"During the Patriarchal Era, the Faith was solid and broadly accepted, but as with any commonly shared belief, organization, or community, with the passage of time key principles and philosophies begin to lose importance in an ever-growing segment of believers. To keep the Faith strong not only in the hearts of the elders of the community but also in the hearts of the younger generations, a dynamic leader is required. This leader must possess different strengths, fresh ideas, and new skills, but more importantly must be someone viewed as powerful and fearless, someone "Beloved" by God. This was a critical need in the times of David. Not only was the Faith being attacked, so was the kingdom. It was on the battlefield that this mere boy, a shepherd who used his weapon against the wolves that threatened his sheep, not against men, proved himself worthy to be King of the Jewish people by slaying the giant of a man named Goliath. He stepped forward when the warriors were too frightened to do so. As with Abraham, he was not of royal lineage and he didn't politic for the position; instead he gravitated to the role, stepping forward when no one else would do so. What made him supremely suited to lead the Jewish race at that time in the history of the Faith was the fact that he was fearless—fearless not because he was invincible or massive in stature, but because he relied on the Lord for guidance and direction. During the Patriarchal Era, no other could have been better suited to champion the Chosen People.

"The third era is unique in many ways. First the name, the Era of the Great Scattering, quickly denotes the dispersal of the flock. The Israelites are forced into exile at the hands of another race of people. They are forced, and I do mean forced, to live in a country with different cultural, political, and religious beliefs. Even those left behind were still under the control of the Babylonian Empire. Prior to this takeover, the center of their existence was the synagogue, and the Babylonians were not a Jewish people. In addition, the Israelites find themselves with no strong leader. It has been centuries since mighty David reigned, and as with all heroes, over time his reputation of greatness begins to wane. During this era the Faith was truly shaken to the core. They became a people in need of another great leader. One who, like David, would be both fearless in battle and at the same time show mercy and compassion through the faith of their fathers.

"Three eras…that number seems to be everywhere in the writings Joe is in possession of, but here and again in many places, it is referenced in the Bible. Could this just be another coincidence? Like Joe, I too believe it goes much deeper than that. I must examine this hypothesis on the same level that the scrolls of Solomon teach. First, as with all worthy business goals, you must start with the end in mind.

"What would the Messiah bring to the Israeli people that would cause them to track the ancestry of one family over thousands of years?

A new beginning

A return to greatness

A renewed Faith.

A new beginning of what?

"The Jewish people thought the Messiah would be the greatest King of all: powerful and fearless. This king would also be the leader of their Faith, since their Faith was the center of who they were as a people. So they expected the Messiah to bring a renewed faith to the people."

Looking once more at Jules' notes circled on the page and the manner in which they were written, Shenan notices immediately the repeated presence of three:

A "reNewed" Faith!

A new religious mindset

A resurrected Church

Shenan continues his dictated notes.

Dictating: "So if the purpose of the Messiah was to bring new faith to a tired people, what would be the three components needed to renew a church body?

"You would first have to have a start, or birth. Before there can be anything, there must be conception. Whether it's the conception of an idea or a conception of a baby, without conception there can be no existence. The Abrahamic Era was the conception of the New Faith.

"Next would be the actual life, or the informative years. Whenever we bring something to life, there is a process that takes place, a need to shape it and mold it to look like what we desire. Whether it be a new company, new job, or a new child, we need to spend the years developing it so that it can be fruitful throughout its lifespan. The Patriarchal Era was the life era.

"Finally, you would have to have the death or destruction of the body. I would say there is nothing quite as destructive as the exile of an entire nation. The Era of the Great Scattering would qualify as the death of the old Faith. Then add to this that Jesus was "sacrificed" on the Feast of Passover just as the unblemished lambs were being sacrificed at the Temple. That is why He is referred to as the Pascal Lamb.

"Wow!" The Archbishop exclaims in the silence of the room, wiping his brow with the back of his hand as the realization of what he is thinking sends a shiver up his spine. "This material makes a case that Jesus can be viewed as the Resurrection of the Jewish Faith, since Christians believe He is everyone's one and only Messiah!" Eerily the author of Matthew's gospel used Solomon's solution of the Wisdom of three to illustrate that Jesus was and ever will be Jewish, while at the same time he was the head of the new church, the creator of the Catholic or Universal Church. In His own words, "It is by rising again we are made new; the old dies away to be born again new." Smiling, the priest says out loud, "The Catholic Faith is really the Jewish Faith 2.0!" trying to contain the laughter over this final notion. Feeling relieved to be finished with his review of the material, at the same time he feels uneasy about a few nagging thoughts lingering in his mind.

Dictating: "Contact the Roman Curia to inquire about the Solutionary file."

Since becoming an Archbishop, Shenan has advanced quickly in respect and position inside the church. He travels to the Vatican many times a year, working on assignments that come directly from the Big Man...not the really Big Man, but the Big Man's right-hand man, the Curia himself. He vaguely remembers seeing a wax-sealed file marked only with the Vatican's confidential markings and what he thought was the word *Solutionary* stamped in red on the front cover. He remembered it because it looked very old, and it was sitting alone on the Curia's desk on his first visit to his office. Working in that office for three months, he never saw that file again nor did he hear any mention of the term Solutionary or the file. That is why Shenan became uneasy during Joe's visit. Solutionary is a unique word. He, like Joe, is not a believer in coincidences. Could that file, his call to work in Rome, and Joe's research all be tied together in some way?

13

JOE EXPERIENCES THE IMPACT OF THE WISDOM FORMULA

"When thou goest, it shall lead thee; when thou sleepest, it shall keep thee; and when thou awakest, it shall talk with thee."

PROVERBS 6:22

South Louisiana, September 1983

It was another long, restless night; sitting at the breakfast table, I am enjoying my first cup of coffee in an attempt to wake up my mind while watching our baby girl slurp down her breakfast as I think of a future day when I will be asking her if she is ready for her math exams. Will Mary and I be ready to handle the more troubled trials of parenting? How much she has grown in just over four months? That future time will come so quickly. Over the coffee cup I send a silent prayer to the Lord, one that will become a daily request for the rest of his life.

"Lord, give me the wisdom to help solve the problems that face me and my wife, our child, the rest of our families, and all to whom you bring into our lives, while successfully doing your will. Thank you for our continued blessings. Amen."

"Good morning, honey," Mary says, as she rounds the kitchen counter to give me my morning kiss, starting the day with a smile.

"Hi, baby. Did you sleep well?"

"Yeah, but your snoring is really bad. I think you woke up the neighbor's dog, and he is a half a mile away." Smiling as she playfully pokes me in the side; Mary takes Tiff out of my arms and covers her cherub-like face with little playful kisses.

"I didn't really sleep well last night, so I am not sure I was the one snoring."

"What kept you awake?" Mary asks, as she puts the toaster pastries in the toaster.

"I had another one of those weird dreams again. You know the one where I am in a foreign land in ancient times; this time I am almost positive it was Jerusalem. You know I have never been to that area of the world, but I guess all the research I am doing with Granddad's work must be putting these stories and images in my head. I am not sure I am even myself in the dream. I can speak the language, but I hear it as English in my own head. Whoever I am in the dream, people seem to respect and seek me out because I am always busy answering people's questions. But this dream was different, this time it was like I was watching a film of the story of Jesus being found in the temple. Sit down and I will tell you all about it." Taking a breath, I begin.

"It is a spring day and the city is crowded and busy. A young boy of 12 finds himself mystified by the sights, sounds, smells, and energy as he follows his parents and cousins through the busy streets. What a different world from his "normal" life back in Nazareth. "There are so many people, James," he says to his cousin. They have been here for seven days, yet it feels like just yesterday they came through the massive gates. He remembers the tales his father and uncles told around the campfires on the journey here. How their ancestors walked these very streets; some of the more powerful ones actually built the great Temple that they prayed in. Since he was old enough to understand, he was told the stories of how his relatives were from a long line of blessed people; a people born to follow Yahweh and to lead Israel to greatness. He enjoyed hearing the stories from the family elders. He never imagined that soon he would be the main character of many stories told throughout all of history and one of them began with the rise of the sun this very morning.

"As the family's caravan crossed over the rough and rocky streets of the city, the sun was already starting to warm up the air around them. It was going to be hot as they journeyed back toward their homeland. Jesus and two of his cousins were running along the street, from the front of the line to the back, they were enjoying the freedom that would soon be over, as they crossed over from boy to man at the age of 13. They knew that once they were considered men, the free spirited play of a child would be replaced by responsibility and more important chores. Jesus enjoyed teasing his older cousin, Zakiah, who was busy keeping the small flock of sheep all together through the bustling street. Zakiah, now 16, has no time to play yet his sparkling eyes dance as he watches his younger carefree cousins throw pebbles at the birds searching from their breakfast.

"Looking ahead, the city's massive gate hangs open like a giant's door. Just to the left of the gate is the street leading to the Temple area. Jesus notices that even though the street leaving the city is packed with people and animals, the Temple way is nearly deserted. He drops the few stones still in his hands and scurries up the slight grade toward the Temple. It is not the Sabbath but still he is drawn to the structure that looms in the distance. So big in size it looks like it is not far at all, but he knows that is not the case. He is a fast runner, so leaving his cousins behind, he sprints off, knowing that he will be able to run this slight detour through the Temple courtyard and then take the western gate to catch up with his family. He will be back with the caravan before they even notice him missing. Running though the Temple portico, Jesus finds but a few scholars and their disciples clustered on the benches in small groups. The Teacher of one of the groups holds up his hand.

"Slow down, young lad." Tophus says as the boy's aggressive pace breaks the quiet morning solitude. "Why in such a hurry?"

"I beg your pardon, Rabbi. I am just passing through toward the western gate. I did not mean to interrupt your lesson."

Smiling to himself but without showing any outward sign of his amusement, "Well, having good intentions to do a task while your actions of the moment bring about the opposite result is cause for disruption. Would you not agree?"

Looking down at his shuffling feet, Jesus knows the Teacher is being kind and considerate in the reprimand of his behavior in the holy place. "You are right Teacher. Please forgive me."

Tophus pats the lanky youth on the head. "You are forgiven boy. I have not seen you here before, have I? What is your name?"

"My name is Jesus." Bowing in respect, "We came from Nazareth to celebrate Passover."

Always the student, Jesus continues, "Teacher, May I ask you questions about the lesson you just quoted me?"

Tophus had a good feeling about this lad. "Come; sit with my disciples so they can learn as well."

Reflecting as he sits with the four other students, all of which are a good bit older than he, "I can take a little time with this man of God and still beat the caravan to the main road outside the city's western gate. Father would not want me to walk away, insulting the Rabbi as he takes the time to teach me an important lesson."

Bowing to the Teacher, he says, "May I speak, Master?" The Rabbi smiles with the slightest of nods. "Is it not taught to us that one's actions begin with an idea or thought? Does not a good thought lead to good actions and unclean intentions lead to bad actions or behaviors? If this is so, how can the best laid plans of God fearing men result in sinful results? I am a faithful servant of Yahweh, Teacher. I would never intentionally do anything to bring shame to myself or my family."

Looking down at this mere parcel of a man, Tophus is struck by the eagerness of this boy to learn and the level of understanding he already processes. He thinks like a man of many years. The other students, all men with more years of experience whom are now themselves beginning to teach in their own Temples and schools, are looking at Jesus with wonder.

"Thoughtful questions, young Jesus. We are truly blessed that you stumbled into our midst. Let us take each question in turn and learn more about what the Law tells us. You are correct that every good intention can and should lead to a positive and beneficial action. Just as correct, in the actions of the sinner, one will find the root in the thoughts and plans of the ill doer."

"May I be so bold as to question you in this thought as well, Teacher?" Not waiting for permission, "A thief, when stealing, would clearly fall into this pattern; however, he does not steal each hour of each day. As an example, if he comes to the aid of his neighbor and plans these good deeds prior to the actions, would that not cause the Law to be incorrect? Should not your lesson of the sinner be stated thusly; "the actions of the sinner, when their intent goes against the Law, will surely find that their thoughts led the way to the path of the sin."

"Where did you learn such lessons?" Tophus asks Jesus.

"My parents Master; they make sure that I know the Law and the difference between right and wrong. They allow me to question them and listen to my thoughts as well."

This discussion leads to other discussions and the other Teachers and students come together as one large group. The positive energy is palatable by everyone there. Who is this student who challenges with thoughtful respect and whose lessons teach the Teachers? The Law of the time stated that once a sinner always a sinner. That is why they were outcast from the community. This thought of forgiving ones actions or even considering doing so was unheard of and definitely not discussed in a public forum or temple.

Evening descends on the caravan as the people prepare to make camp in the wilderness. There are 16 families comprising the pilgrimage. They are still two or three days from home, but they have all they need to make the journey safely. They have traveled this way many times through the years. Mary and Joseph are tired after they finally sit down to rest; they will have another long day tomorrow. The kids of the caravan are all family; it is not uncommon for them to find shelter with whomever they have been playing with. That is why Mary and Joseph are not aware that Jesus is not with the group. They will learn he is missing when they walk through the camp in the morning. For now, they are bone tired, and assume he is still with the group.

Early in the morning, it becomes clear to Mary that Jesus is not with the caravan. She and Joseph quickly arrange for their return to Jerusalem. Though they traveled only one day outside the city, they are unaware as to where Jesus could have left the family. He could have been hurt anywhere along the way so they take their time; shouting his name as they walk along the rough road.

It has been three days since the caravan left the city. Joseph is beginning to lose heart that they will find their son safe. He believes Mary feels the same way, especially when she tells him she wants to go to the temple. He believes she is seeking solace in her loss. As they walk into the temple portico, they are overjoyed to find Jesus sitting on a Teacher's bench circled by a large group of scholars and other church goers. When Jesus sees them, he jumps up with tears in his eyes and runs into the arms of Mary. She gives him a generous squeeze and praises God for bringing him safely back to her.

Then she holds him out at arm's reach saying, "Why have you put your Father and me through such hardship and worry? We thought we had lost you. What are you doing here?"

Jesus looked sorrowfully at the ground, not wishing to cause anyone harm or pain, "Did you not know I would be about my Father's work?" Mary assumed Jesus meant, that as he was about to turn 13, he was beginning his role as a man and a true student of the Law. Many years later Mary would remember that statement and it would take on a much deeper meaning. While Mary was mothering over her found child, Tophus walked up to Joseph and pulled him aside.

"He was kept under my roof since you left. He thought you would return for him so he did not seem ill at ease. You have a remarkable young man. He has a deep wisdom for one so young in age."

"Thank you Rabbi, for taking care of my son. Can I pay you for his keep?" Joseph offers.

"I will not hear of it. He has paid me back 100 fold just by the discussions we have had. He has given my eyes a new vision. Please bring him back to me whenever possible."

Bowing to the Teacher, Joseph gathers up Mary and Jesus; making their way home."

For the first time since I started the story, I raise my eyes to look at my wife. "Mary, it was like I was there with the Holy Family. Somehow I was able to pick out details of this experience that seem remarkable for a number of reasons. Regardless, if you do believe that Jesus is God, you must admit that he definitely made a tremendous impact on the world. Also, if He is God and man, as God, He would not have needed wisdom, yet as a man, it was wisdom he sought even from a young age, first from his family then from the scholars. It felt like the Temple was the place to learn like a school and was where the scholars could be found. Isn't it interesting that the Temple was where his parents went for answers, too? I could sense that Mary and Joseph were wise people; they obviously taught their child what he needed to know. Whether Jesus was there in the Temple as God or just a man, Jesus did not come across as all knowing. He questioned things and listened to the answers."

Placing my head in my hands, I ask, "Am I going crazy, Mary?"

"You are not going crazy, Joe. I cannot explain what you are going through, but it does not seem too dangerous or even disturbing for that matter, other than you not getting enough restful sleep. Maybe your work with Granddad's journals is becoming too much. You do spend a lot of time with those old books."

"They are interesting, Mary. I can't help myself. The more I read the stuff, the more questions I have—and to make matters worse, after this dream I have even more questions. For example, through the centuries countless discussions have taken place about the wisdom of Jesus and whether that wisdom was Divine, achieved through education, or earned through life's lessons. How important was his upbringing compared to the God-nature of his being? I'm sure that a child's upbringing is a central question each parent thinks about while raising their children. Did Mary and Joseph have it made as parents raising Jesus, or was he an average child facing the same issues that faced every child of his day? Like, did he get mouthy as a teenager? Was he an exceptional child? If you have an exceptional child, how do your lessons impact their development? If you have an unexceptional child, can the lessons you teach them make a substantial difference in their lives? You see what I mean? I know this will sound like I am a nut case, but I think this dream was an example of one of Grandfather Solomon's Solutions, and it revealed to me another example of how Jesus was tied to the bloodline of Solomon and the Wisdom of Three."

Mary, obviously sensing my desire to expand on this dream, sits at the table listening patiently as I continue to explain my thoughts.

"Baby, Solomon is all about solutions to problems. It felt like Jesus needed to solve a problem in His mind and in the mind of Tophus, the Rabbi, using the first two components of the Wisdom Formula, Education and Experience. What was really weird was it seemed like I was in school as well, learning along with the other elders listening to Jesus and Tophus. I remember all the times in the New Testament verses where the older Jesus quoted scripture then interpreted it differently than the written words. He was doing the exact same thing as a boy, only with much more respect than He would eventually show to the Sadducees and the Pharisees. I know that in some of today's churches He is the only one that could get away with not taking scripture literally. If some of the Christian pastors of today would try to teach that method of scripture study they would lose their job in a heartbeat. With that said, I felt that was the way all Jews were taught to read the Torah. It was also obvious that He was taught to be a good communicator from a very young age. I can't explain why, but I needed this lesson personally, and I came away a different man because of it. Also, my mind was drawn to the

Divine Precept of the Power of Three again, in a way that I feel I would have never discovered alone."

With closed eyes, my mind goes back to the vision of the city of Jerusalem as my heart and mind recalls the emotions and the intense thoughts I experienced in the dream. Taking a deep breath I begin to relax, speaking in a voice lower than normal, I attempt to relate to Mary the key points now etched in my soul from this experience.

"Jesus would visit this very temple many more times in the next 20 years and in exactly 20 years to the day he would be greeted to shouts of Hosanna in the Highest as He rides an ass into this peaceful Temple area."

Opening my tear filled eyes looking deeply into Mary's. "None of the other people in this "dream" could have known that some of these same priests, Rabbis, and scribes who sat around listening as Jesus, the child, was teaching with Rabbi Tophus, would also be praising his name in exultation on that Wednesday morning procession as he enters the city being hailed as their Messiah. Shortly thereafter they would weep bitterly as they would witness His bruised and beaten body, along with their lost hopes and dreams of His Messianic reign as the bloody nails are driven through His flesh into the hard wood of the cross on Friday. Not one of these learned men will envision His resurrection on that Sunday morning, but all who were touched by His words on the steps of the Temple twenty years before will have experienced personal growth through that unplanned indelible incident with a remarkable child. Mary, How can I put this into words for others to understand? They were first changed by the experience with the wise child, and as word spreads of His resurrection, their change becomes complete, leading the way for them to be among the early converts, continuing to tell the story of the young Jesus, once lost from His family, found in the Temple teaching the Jewish faith with a whole different view. One filled with the wisdom of forgiveness and understanding. Their retelling will emphasize the immense faith of this boy turned man over twenty years of loyal devotion to the Law, but dear, it was more than that. For twenty years these strangers to Jesus, the child, were annually reminded, by His return to Temple in Jerusalem. Reminded of the way they were individually touched through a single experience through one remarkable event! How many of us are similarly touched by a single opportunity to attend a presentation where a speaker's message makes a huge difference in our life, or a talented musician's music reaches the depths of our soul to the point that we have to hear it over and over again? Now imagine a similar experience multiplied sevenfold when you witness a young man you see once a year, possibly twice a year, who continues to enrich your life each year for twenty years by His non-threatening, non-imposing message of love, peace, and kindness. It was a very human perspective of a familiar Bible story that I have never heard preached or spoken of in this manner. I bet that most people have never considered it from this viewpoint. Yet it is one that I lived in a dream as real as I am sitting here with you now. I could tell He needed to be in the Temple at the turn of His adulthood. Possibly in order to lock in the memory of this special boy in the minds of the teachers of the Law. They all would have retained individual memories of the things He taught to them, and then they lived their unique experiences over the next twenty years based on those lessons that He taught, which they in turn used in their own personal wisdom formula. What a gift these people were given.

"Oh, and Mary, I could not miss the reference to the Wisdom and Power of Three. Mary and Joseph suffered greatly during the loss of Jesus for three long days. I saw a loving mother and a toughened father both weep bitterly on the long road back to Jerusalem; as each day passed, their heartache increased accordingly. Then the joy returned to their hearts as Jesus was reunited with His Mom and Dad after those three days. Their family was made whole again after three days. Then, twenty years from that day, He would once more be ripped from his family's arms for three days, and would return to make His entire family whole again. Only this time His family would include the entire human race."

With tears streaming from both of our eyes, we smile at each other and nod our heads in silence. Quietly we ponder the lessons each of us learned from this special dream. Mary brushes the last of my tears from my cheek and softly says, "Joe, just relax and try to leave Great-Grandfather Solomon's papers alone for a couple of days. You need a break, baby. Now, finish your breakfast and get to work. I love you."

14

JOE BECOMES A
SOLUTIONARY

"He that refuseth instruction despiseth his own soul: but he that heareth reproof getteth understanding."

PROVERBS 15:32

Clark and Sherry Burrows' home, an evening in early October 1983

My practice is growing fairly well. I have already qualified for my first sales incentive trip with the company. I am getting much better at my interviewing techniques, and through the college studies at The American College, I feel much more confident in my level of technical knowledge about insurance and finance, which in turn seems to be resulting in much bigger paychecks. So then why do I feel like something is missing?

Little did I know that the puzzle piece would soon fall into place.

I begin my day with the usual Friday routine: a 10 a.m. meeting at the office, lunch with a coworker, finishing my paperwork by 4:30 p.m., and then off to Clark's home for our weekly beer together. Every Friday, Clark gets home from work by 4 pm and I arrive before 5 pm. Together we celebrate the end of another week with a cold beer or two. Now this Friday was a bit special in that Clark and his new wife, Sherry, has just returned from their honeymoon. What Clark and Sherry didn't know was that I planned on speaking to the newly-weds about the additional life insurance now that they were husband and wife. When I began my insurance career, the very first person I sold insurance to was Clark. A single man with no debt, Clark first purchased a $10,000 life policy, but now that he was married and would soon be starting a family, they needed much more coverage. I have been casually planting the seeds through various hints and playful suggestions about buying more coverage, but today I would make it a formal interview. This was business.

Pulling into their driveway, I am pleased to see both cars are there, but I wonder who is parked on the side of the road in the black sedan. I hope they don't have company. That would definitely ruin the chance of me speaking to them in private. I ring the doorbell, waiting patiently with a big smile on my lips as the sedan slowly drives away. Clark opens the door, smiling as he fills the doorframe with his 6' 5" physique.

"What is that?" Clark asks, pointing to the briefcase in my hand.

"It's a briefcase, Clark; don't you remember, I sell insurance. Oh, and this is the scroll you wanted to see," I laugh with my buddy, handing him the long cardboard tube.

"Yeah, I remember. You can come in and have a beer, but the briefcase stays on the porch," Clark says, trying to remain stern without cracking a bigger smile.

Sliding past him to give Sherry a big hug, "That is not going to happen tonight, Clark. We need to talk business."

We eat dinner together, drink way too many beers, and share dozens of stories with Sherry from our childhood growing up together. We all have a great time; however, I'm failing miserably in getting Clark and Sherry to purchase the coverage they so desperately needed. I could tell that Sherry was in total agreement, but each time I would try to close the sale and slide the application across the table to Clark for his signature, Clark would slide it right back, saying the exact same thing: "Joe, I am 24 years old, in perfect health, and have a lot of time to make this decision. Have another beer."

It was around 5:30 in the afternoon when I arrived at their home, and Sherry drove me the one mile home at about 1 AM Saturday morning.

The world changed for so many people at about 11 AM that same Saturday morning. I receive the call from Clark's sister at about 11:30 AM. Clark was killed in an accident in his own front yard. A car left the road and struck him while he was cutting the grass. The rest of the weekend is nothing more than a blur of those well-trained actions required to handle "the business" of Clark's final arrangements.

On Tuesday afternoon, things start to get real. Mary and I drive to the funeral home together. We walk up to the casket where we are greeted by Sherry, who hugs me tightly around the shoulders as if she needs something solid to hold on to. We all cry in each other's arms at the unexpected loss of a dear loved one. Still wrapped in the embrace, Sherry leans in close to my ear and whispers the words that would burn into my soul for the rest of my life. These words would cause me continued pain, unimaginable drive, and tremendous success for me and those I would serve. "He was going to buy the policy on Monday; he was only kidding around with you."

CRASH!! My heart feels like a molten mess inside his chest. I swear it stopped. Mary and Sherry have to almost drag me to a chair to keep me from collapsing onto the floor. The rest of the day is a blur of pain and suffering from both the loss of my best friend and the internal struggle brought on by the belief that I neglected my duty to offer sound financial advice to protect Sherry with the required insurance on her husband, punctuated by the glimpses of joy of reliving so many good memories with the friends and loved ones gathered to honor an all-around great guy.

When we finally return home for the evening, I aimlessly walk into our bedroom and ball up on the mattress and cry like a baby. Soon I feel the pressure of Mary lying beside me, brushing her fingers through my hair.

"Shhh, I know it hurts baby, but it will be alright."

Finding some composure and say, "I know, baby, but it hurts so bad. I let down Clark when he needed me the most."

"Don't say that, you know that is not true!"

"But it is Mary!" I slam my fist into the mattress. "I took the entire interview way too lightly. I just wanted to have fun and didn't care about whether or not Clark and Sherry solved their problems with my services. What good am I as an advisor if I do not truly believe in the solutions I offer to my clients, much less to my friends and family? I let everyone down without even thinking about the possible outcomes."

"Joe, I was not there but I know you very well. I know you did your very best."

"That's just it, Mary," I shout into my clenched fists, "I didn't!! And I didn't when it mattered the most." Through a gasping breath, "I am not a Solutionary...not even close."

I fall asleep with tears dripping down my cheeks, the one I love holding me tight and a decision weighing heavy on my heart.

I walk into Hank's office bright and early the following day. "Mr. Hank, I quit!" I exclaim, placing my office key and all of the books on the table near the desk chair.

Never one to overreact, Hank looks at me over his half-glasses on the tip of his nose. "Please have a seat, Joe."

Getting up from his desk chair, he walks to the door and softly closes it. Taking the chair next to his, Hank asks, "Why are you quitting?"

I tell him the details of the last couple of days. We both shed some tears as I vividly relive the nightmare of losing my best friend and the fact that I was not much of a salesman, since I could not sell Clark a policy that he definitely could afford and certainly needed.

Finishing my narrative, I stand to leave but not before I feel a hand on my arm. Hank whispers, "Sit."

"You are one of the best advisors I have ever worked with in my 30-plus years of managing people. You are a natural and are very gifted in your ability to communicate on a deeper level than using just words. People can feel that you care about them. Mark my words and I know you will not agree with me now, but this will turn out to be a blessing to you, your clients, and future clients."

"You are right about one thing, Mr. Hank," I say, shaking my head in disbelief. "I do not see this as a blessing. I could not even close a ridiculously small premium on someone who trusted me like no one else. Thank you for everything." Reaching the door, I turn back to Hank. "I would appreciate it if you would let me deliver the proceeds check to Sherry when it comes in."

Smiling softly, Hank says, "Of course you will deliver the check. It is your client. I know that today you think you are quitting, but I do not think that will happen. I will be happy to hold your books and keys for a week or so if it makes you feel better, but I know you cannot walk away from your destiny. This is what you are meant to do."

Hank stands up and walks to my side, placing a hand on my shoulder. "Though you received your insurance licenses about 2 years ago, it wasn't until today that you could say that you are now in the insurance business. You now know the true meaning of the work that you do for others."

It took only two weeks for the $30,000 check to come from the home office and only another day for me to garner enough gumption to make the appointment with Sherry to deliver the check. Sitting in the living room of Clark and Sherry's home, I kept waiting for Clark to walk through the front door. That experience turned out to be the most emotional rollercoaster ride of my life. On one hand I was very sad for our loss of a wonderful husband and friend, and on the other hand I was sure that Clark was at peace in Heaven. Clark was a God-fearing Christian man. I was also relieved by the fact that Sherry would be able to use this money to go back to college and complete her nursing degree. Clark's mom and dad had another policy with me that they used to pay the final arrangements, and the home Clark and Sherry lived in was fully paid for since it was bequeathed to Clark by his aunt. In addition, the big fear and the real reason I was hoping to sell Clark the additional protection would not be happening. Two weeks ago they thought Sherry was pregnant; it turns out she wasn't.

As Sherry and I sit together on the sofa, both wiping the tears from our eyes, I blurt out, "Sherry, I quit my job, so if you need anything else, please let Mr. Madison know, and I'm sure he will be able to assist you. It is clear to me that I am not cut out to do this job."

Looking at me, tears still streaming down her cheeks, she begins to laugh uncontrollably causing me to laugh as well. "What is so damn funny? I am unemployed, and you think it's funny?"

Still laughing, she answers, "No, that is not what I find funny. It's funny that you think you can just up and walk away from what you obviously were put here to do. Let me tell you what happened when you left here the other night. You left here that night at about 1 o'clock, and you were probably home by 1:10 and sound asleep by 1:20 at the very latest, right?"

Nodding my head in agreement, she continues, "I, on the other hand, did not get to sleep until after 3 AM. Clark loved you so much and was so wired about pulling your chain about the insurance. He just lay in bed laughing about making you wait until Monday to sell him that policy. He kept telling me that if there was an insurance Hall of Fame, you would be in it in record time. He was extremely proud of what you were doing in your business. He said you were the wisest man he ever knew. Clark would not want you to end your promising career over what he thought was the ultimate prank. He did not know he would be dying the next day, and I am pretty sure you didn't know that either. Besides, I still need that insurance you presented to us, and I am not going to buy it from anyone else. Can we take care of that paperwork today?"

Crying in each other's arms, I tell her, "No, I can't; I turned in my books and forms to the office manager. I guess I will have to go back and beg for my job."

"Yes, you will, Joe, but I don't think you will need to do much begging."

"I don't think so either. Mr. Madison told me pretty much the same thing you did and with a lot of the same confidence, that I was not going to quit."

At that point in my career, the world began to change yet again. Hank was correct; Clark's death did become a blessing of an enduring manner. Every time a prospective client would tell me, "I would like to think about it," or "I am healthy and don't think I need this insurance at this time," I would tell them the story of Clark, adding one final comment, usually fighting back tears of remembrance: "If you even THINK you may need this insurance, you will sign this application and pay me the initial premium now; then you can think all you want to. You see, I am not wise enough to know who needs my services or at what time in their lives we need to meet, but there is a power much greater than us that I trust is handling those issues."

A couple of months later, we were visiting with Sherry when the topic of Clark's death comes up again. "What is the latest on the investigation of Clark's hit and run?"

"The police still have nothing. They have checked all the body shops and they have questioned everyone in the neighborhood, but still nothing. It is like the car just disappeared."

"So it was a car that hit him? Did someone see who did it?"

Shaking her head, she says, "No one saw it happen, but the detectives believe it was a car based on Clark's injuries and the paint chips left on the lawnmower. They are looking for a recent model Chevy sedan."

Snapping my head up. "A dark-colored sedan?"

Sherry notices my reaction with surprise. "Yes, Joe, why? Do you know something?"

"I am not sure, but the evening I arrived at your home I saw a dark sedan parked on the side of the road in front of your house. I remember thinking you may have had visitors. But the car drove away while I stood at your door. I didn't see anyone in the car because I remember the windows being darkly tinted. Sherry, I never thought that there would have been a connection. I think I should at least talk to the detective about it."

"Please Joe, any additional information you can shed on this mystery would be appreciated. I really want whoever killed Clark to be punished."

The following day, at the police station, the detective handling the case speaks with me, but I am unable to give them any more information than what they already have. The detective did ask if I knew of anyone who would have wanted to see Clark dead. My quick reply was; "Clark was a good man with no enemies, I cannot think of anyone." The detective discloses that was the prevailing sentiment from everyone they interviewed so far.

"Detective, do you believe Clark was murdered? I thought his death was an accident."

The detective replies, "We are looking into all possibilities, Mr. Morrison. Thank you for coming in."

That would be the first and last discussion that Joe would have with the detective. Clark's case would be closed as an accidental death, and no one would be charged in the accident.

15

THE SOLUTION OF THE MESSENGER

"That I might make thee know the certainty of the words of truth; that thou mightest answer the words of truth to them that send unto thee?"

PROVERBS 22:21

Isle de Mauvais Choix, December 1984, the night before Shenan's visit

It is turning cold outside, and I love it. It is mostly unbearably hot and humid in South Louisiana, so whenever the temperature drops even slightly, it is an enjoyable occurrence. It is after nine in the evening. I just spoke to Mary and Tiffany over the CB, telling them both how much I love them. Mary told me she has already started preparing the meal she will be cooking for the good Archbishop tomorrow night. She said I needed to get home as early as possible tomorrow so I can give her a hand. I promised I would and told her I was all packed so when I wake up all I have to do is lock up. I told my two loves good night and signed off. It was not only Mary that had preparations to make before Shenan's visit. I open Granddad's journal to the interesting topic from the translated scrolls.

*Partial remains of Solomon's scroll
scribed by Solomon,
The Solution of the Messenger, 964 BC*

*"Each Solutionary or Solutionary Disciple
will be asked to bring forth a message to
whom those they serve either personally or
through the use of another chosen as their
messenger. Therefore it is of importance
that they be aware of the three character
traits of the worthy messenger.*

- *Trustworthiness*

- *Goal Oriented, for delivery of the
message is their primary goal*

- *Truthfulness, for the message must be
given truthfully and without bias"*

For the first time, I have encountered an incomplete or partially missing scroll. The message ended without Solomon's usual flair of a detailed explanation, but thanks to the translation and Granddad's tape reel I have the opportunity to hear Jules Sr.'s thought process and research abilities in the discernment of what Solomon was trying to pass along.

Granddad's voice: "My personal note on The Solution of the Messenger.

In Solomon's time, men would brave the elements and sometimes even enemy lines to get information from one person to another. It is nothing like today, where information can be shared from across the globe between the two people or even a group of people completely anonymously thanks to the telegraph. No longer does it take months, weeks, or even hours; the messages can be sent, received, and replied back to all in a matter of seconds. Solomon would be impressed… or would he?"

Joe Recorded: "With the advent of the Internet, information can be traded and made available to almost any one with a computer and an Internet connection. Some see this information as knowledge, and it most definitely can be; however, information is just data until you know it came from and why it is important, and then it becomes knowledge. Once it is knowledge, it can become usefully applied. For it to be viewed as useful depends on the needs of the recipient. For this useful knowledge to be deemed education, it must be truthful and factual. How silly would it be to get an education in false knowledge? Once this knowledge rises to the level of education, there remains only one hurdle barring it from reaching the doorstep of wisdom: it must be delivered by a trusted and unquestionable source as the best solution to a problem. The source is the Messenger, the Solutionary.

"The way I see it, our readiness to believe untrusted sources of data has become a problem of epidemic proportions and will likely only get worse. We live in a world filled with information that is readily available literally at our fingertips. That in and of itself is not bad; the problem is that very little of this information is from reliable sources—"reliable" meaning from a moral, ethical, and respected source; a source of high moral and ethical character. This untrusted information, once believed and widely spread, feeds the emotions and biases of groups of well-meaning people. They want so badly to believe what they feel is an important message, but they do not think to question the source. It is said, "When an idea or concept causes emotions to rise to a high level of agitation, the will to believe differently disappears." To make matters worse, today's biggest source of untrusted information is being peddled by our own government through a massive bureaucracy it has built and continues to build. Bureaucrats constantly have to justify their existence or cease to exist. The only way to do so is through fabricated and/or self-serving means supported by a media machine that finds itself equally in peril of extinction with the advent of the Internet. I do not mean to say that all reporters intend to mislead the public, because they too are human and are prone to the same emotions as those who receive the information secondhand. Many who issue and pass along the messages do not take the time to quantify the information as truthful before reporting on it. To do so takes work. And of course, the Internet can and does spread even more untrusted information to millions of people, many of whom are children who cannot rationalize or who choose not to take the time to distinguish true knowledge from misleading lies and partial truths.

"This may shock some, but the world we live in today has a tendency to be self-centered, egotistical, or a bit of a "know-it-all" society. A relatively small mass of people, when viewed against the entire populace, come across as believing that what they do and/or say is their business and no one else's. They act as if they live in their own little world. Though this group is considered small, they leverage great influence on the lives of the majority because the majority chooses to remain silent in order to not be branded as a racist, radical, or another socially unacceptable moniker. It is true, everyone is entitled to an opinion, but that is all it is, an opinion, until it is proven to be factual. If we choose to not heed the history of other countries

(Experience being one of the tenets of Wisdom), it will repeat itself on our own shores, causing major problems not easily reversed (by the tentacles of Problems not solved properly).

"This might begin to prove the point that Solomon toiled with since 970 BC. He believed that we needed to have a wise society. If the majority of society supports wise decisions and laws, it is less likely that individuals will be drawn into making less than wise choices in their moments of weakness, and believe it or not, we all have moments of weakness. Our parents, grandparents, and great-grandparents understood this principle. This loss of our understanding of moral and ethical truths slowly grew due to our enthusiasm over the benefits of widespread, globally available, untrustworthy information.

There are a number of reasons for this shift in culture, but lack of wisdom stands as the main reason, followed by popular culture rewarding and praising the wrong people in the eyes of our children. Should we return to holding public figures and celebrities to a higher moral and ethical standard? In Granddad's era, elevating anyone to a position of role model on a public pedestal was a status reserved for the honorable, the noble, and the morally sound.

"Are people getting tired of the popular culture dictating their farfetched beliefs to our children with the help of a less-than-fact-based widespread media that share those unfounded beliefs?

"Do the well-meaning parents of today struggle to raise their kids with morals based on honorable values and ethical behavior?

"Is the truth no longer considered important in our schools, in our businesses, or in our government? Is that why we have to endure so many years of controversy over all the major issues in Congress, while never reaching a truth-based solution? In the United States, we have been told for over 10 years that Social Security will need to be fixed. Every expert agrees that, based on unquestionable facts, unless something is done soon, it will go broke. Yet, neither side is interested in applying the real truth; they only want what best serves their constituents and their personal interests. I wonder if my children will see this solution in their life time. We no longer have debates where people come together with the intent to listen and learn as well as to speak. I cannot remember the last time you heard a CEO of a major corporation say, "We changed our mind about this issue or that product?" What about after a political debate; have you ever heard a candidate say, "I was wrong and will be changing my stance on that matter?" Very rarely if not ever!!

"Solomon was passionate about teaching people how to solve their own problems, thus avoiding the need for leaders to do so for them. This process would likely expand to our ability to solve more of the world's problems and in doing so spread the moral and ethical ideals that would be best for our children. Today, we have to add the complication of the exposure to the so called truths of the day. This should not be an issue but it is. When the world lost these scrolls of Solomon and the teaching they possess, it allowed us to walk away from the permanency that Wisdom provided. Could the reappearance of this information spur a resurgence of this moral way of thinking?

"Let me use a modern metaphorical approach to summarize these thoughts. Our minds are like a blank hard drive from birth. As we go through life our mind absorbs information that becomes data, not all of which is positive or even accurate. The mind cannot distinguish the difference between truths or lies.

"The wise who have walked before us understood that unsavory leaders, whether political, business, or spiritual, can and do take advantage of our inability to determine truths from lies. By doing so unhindered, they can control the judgment of an entire generation without them being aware it is happening."

I turn off the microphone; sit back in my chair drained from the mental challenges set before me. Humbly amazed by how quickly and completely the Lord uses His Solutionaries once they openly pursue educational opportunities, consciously deciding to absorb life's experiences and allowing His Divine Precepts to become our guide in the counseling of others. It's like taking a journey in Solomon's sandals. It was God that put me into Hank and Clark's life and Hank and Clark into mine. I now realize that I will never know where I will be needed, who the Lord will select as my teammate in carrying out His plans, and when the fullness of His gifts is to be revealed. Solutionaries must live their lives for others. No warning will be given, no extra preparation time is provided. When the time arrives the lesson will be made in the form of one of His Solutionaries or their Disciples; delivering the right and just results through the application of the Wisdom Formula given to them by King Solomon all those years ago. The scrolls clearly reveal that the Divine Precepts, the third component of the Wisdom Formula, are God's guides to all the people of the Earth. It is the wise Solutionary who uses them to help steer those in need to the places that He wants them to be, not where they are today.

Could this be the reason I am keeping all of this information a secret?

Would the world misuse this knowledge, this wisdom, should it fall in the wrong hands?

Is that why this material has been lost through antiquity, in an attempt to protect it?

I make a handwritten note to contact Michael tomorrow once I get home.

16

SHENAN REVEALS MORE THAN EXPECTED

"When the righteous are in authority, the people rejoice: but when the wicked beareth rule, the people mourn."

PROVERBS 29:2

Joe and Mary's home, December 1984

The morning is clear and the air is crisp; a beautiful morning to be alive. I arrive home around 10 AM so that I could help Mary with the last-minute details for the dinner party tonight. Shenan said he would arrive around 3 PM so that they could spend time with Granddad's work before they share a meal together. As soon I showered the stench of the swamp from my body, knowing that my nephew Michael would be at work, I strike this off my to-do list by dialing Michael's work number.

"Good morning, Michael. It's your poor Uncle Joe. Do you have a minute to speak?"

"Hey, Uncle Joe; what a wonderful surprise to hear your voice; of course I do. What can I do for you?"

"I have a few questions that I thought you could provide answers to. They are scientific in nature—more precisely, genetic in nature, so I thought of you."

"Wow, my dad told me you recently changed careers, but he said it was insurance related, not genetic. Why the interest in this field?"

Laughing with him, I reply, "I assure you the questions will probably be very menial to you since I know so little about the topic. And it has nothing to do with work; you could say I have a new hobby. I found some of your Great-Granddad's research papers, and the more I read through them, the more questions they are generating. I thought you could help me with a few."

"Sure! Shoot."

"First, is it true that our DNA is made up of only three chemical compounds?"

"Yes—Phosphate, Deoxyribose sugar, and Nitrogen. Why was that important to Great Granddad? I thought he was a literary professor."

"It probably wasn't important to him because they didn't even understand DNA when he was alive. Michael, could genetics identify someone who is of a certain bloodline of descendants? In other words, could you tell if I was related to my Great-Great-Great;Grandfather?"

"Well, the quick answer, Uncle Joe, is yes; if we had the DNA of the original person, your DNA markers would show familial similarities."

There is a hanging silence as I think about the information being provided by my nephew. "Uncle Joe…are you still on the line?"

"Yeah, I'm here, just thinking. Michael, are you still into science fiction?"

"You know it, Uncle Joe—which is why I do what I do."

"Let's play a little science fiction 'what if.' What if there was a lineage of people, who were the only people to be given a gift from God, a special power. Do you think that gift could be transferred genetically and possibly be detectable through an identifiable gene?"

"Hmmm." Now it is my turn to sit in silence as Michael thinks the question over.

"That is a good question, and without knowing specifics, I cannot be absolutely sure. But knowing what I know about gene mapping, I would say yes—the "power," if genetic based, would provide a marker. What exactly are you working on, Joe?"

"Nothing much, Michael—just some old writings my Granddad translated. It is probably nothing. Thanks for your help; you are one smart cookie. Please tell your mom and dad we said hello. I hope you are able to make the family Christmas party this year."

"I should be there."

"Good, we will see you then. Take care and don't work too hard."

"No problem, see you soon. Bye."

"Bye, Michael, and thanks again."

Sitting at the desk, looking at the notes I took while speaking to Michael, it dawns on me that once more I am being evasive about the Society Papers and do not have a clear understanding about why. Shaking these thoughts from my head, I rush to help Mary. Shenan will be here very soon.

Prompt as always, Shenan arrives right at 3 PM, bearing gifts of pralines for Mary, a bottle of wine to accompany the meal, and a leather satchel. After an appropriate amount of time spent on pleasantries, the gentlemen excuse themselves to slip into the office to discuss what really brought the Archbishop here this evening.

I have arranged two chairs in front of the desk, equidistance from one another, facing the computer monitor that sits toward the rear of the desktop. A desk lamp glows warmly to the left. In front of the keyboard that sits in front of the monitor rests a stack of Granddad's first two journals and another stack of loose pages, representations of the copied scrolls. Beside the desk, leaning against the wall, are six plastic-capped cardboard tubes, the current repositories of the actual ancient scrolls. Shenan wastes no time as he places his satchel at his feet and claims a chair to begin flipping through the pages of Granddad's journals. Not wanting to interrupt, I sit on the bed, answering the sparse questions as they arise.

It doesn't take the Archbishop long to begin taking notes on his notepad. Once Shenan finished his cursory inspection of the books, he reached into his satchel and removed a plain manila folder. Placing the folder on top of the journals, he sits back and stretches, glancing at his watch; he has been sitting for over an hour and a half. I hand the priest a glass of water, procured while he was deep in study.

"Thank you, Joe." He smiled in a reserved manner. "Mary will think we are being very rude."

"Not at all, Shenan. She sneaked a peek in the room a few times already, but you didn't even notice. Besides, she shares the value of your insight. Your thoughts, Archbishop: in your opinion, are these really the scrolls of Solomon?"

With a silent prayer still in his mind, the priest nods his head affirmatively. "I believe they are, Joe. Their intrinsic value alone is priceless, but adding to that the value of the lessons we can learn from the writings, no dollar amount can be reached. I can see why Mary said you have been spending so much time with this material. It is fascinating!"

Mary is once again standing by the door. I pat the bed beside me as she adds, "Shenan, I feel there is something you are not telling us. I can see you are excited, but you are also very reserved, too much so if this is indeed what we think it is."

"You were always very intuitive, Mary. I need to share something with you that I found after our last visit at the rectory. When you were with me last, you shared much, but the one thing I picked up on above all else was the term found in these documents, the word Solutionary. Before finding these documents, have either of you heard that word before?"

We both shake our heads no.

"I had." We are both surprised by the revelation. "That is why I did some research of my own since we last met."

Opening his folder, he removes notes that were obviously jotted down at different times based on the differences in ink color and the progressive dates by each entry.

"Joe, you know I have been assigned to a position at the Vatican, and in that position I had access to the office of a high-ranking leader of the Church. The first time I saw the word Solutionary was in that office on a sealed folder marked Confidential. I have tried, though inconspicuously, to find that file; I have never seen it again. In addition, I cannot find any formal record that it even exists, but I know that I saw it. I remembered it because before that day, I too had never heard that word used, seen, or said."

"I noticed you said no formal record. What did you mean, Shenan?" Mary asks softly.

"I was able to ask around, to a few people I know well and trust with their promised silence, and was told some off-the-record kind of gossip. I heard that in the early 1900s a researcher did find what was thought to be the original scrolls of Solomon. These scrolls were very protected by the Jewish people and were thought to be lost or destroyed sometime around 49 BC. It is thought that a sect of Greek Jews took possession of the scrolls in order to protect them. The Greeks have always been well known as thought leaders, and because of the value they placed on learning and ethics, they would have protected them whatever the cost. No one knew where the researcher found them, but it was likely in the Greek Isles. The source who shared this information with me also said that it is believed that the researcher lost the scrolls again when he was killed trying to protect them from falling in the wrong hands. I think the researcher was our Granddad. As to the file, I would speculate that the Vatican found out about the find and started a file on the subject. I have no way of knowing what is in the file or if this information is correct."

I sit with my hands in my lap, looking solemn. "I thought our Granddad died in an accident." Looking at Mary, fear creeps into my mind. "Shenan, are we safe holding on to this stuff? I can't have anything put Mary or Tiffany in danger. Should we turn all of this material over to the Church?"

Shenan quietly ponders the answer before speaking. "My thoughts are that the Vatican would be solid protectors of the find and may even turn everything back over to Israel for safe keeping…"

"I detect a 'but' in there somewhere." I say, smiling for the first time since this discussion started.

"I cannot explain what I have experienced since I learned of your find. For reasons I cannot fully understand, I feel that it all has to stay hidden for the time being. It has obviously been hidden somewhere safe for a very long time; it is probably long forgotten by whoever was looking for it."

I stand and begin pacing in the tiny room like a caged animal. "What if Dad did not die in an accident either?"

Pivoting to the desk, I reach for the journal on the bottom of the stack, the last of Granddad's journals. My fingers shuffle through the pages in search of a certain date, the year that he died. In the months I have been researching Granddad's work, never have I considered jumping around to the end of my grandfather's research. It was the OCD family trait that prevented me from "spoiling" the journey, but with this mystery possibly turning sinister, I feel compelled to flip to the very last handwritten note by our Granddad. Slowly, I read the words out loud.

> *"To the family member in possession of these journals: do not tell anyone—I repeat, ANYONE—of your relationship to King Solomon! They will want to control you, but wise people cannot be easily controlled. They will want to silence you, but wise people MUST speak the truth."*

The three of us look at each other in shock.

"Who are 'they?'" Mary asks in alarm.

I say without thinking, "I don't know, I am just the messenger." Then as soon as the words escape my lips, a cold shiver runs down my spine. My mind vividly displays the image of the messenger standing at my front door about three years ago mouthing the exact words.

Suddenly the messenger is replaced by the dark sedan pulling away from in front of Clark's house the day before he died. "I have a feeling we're going to find out."

bush
PUBLISHING
& associates

BushPublishing.com

41404702R00104

Made in the USA
Middletown, DE
11 March 2017

Ryker

A Kings of Korruption MC Novel

Book One

By

Geri Glenn

Ryker

©Geri Glenn, 2015

Ryker is a work of fiction. All characters, organizations and events portrayed in this novel are either products of the author's imagination or used fictitiously.

Dedication

This book is dedicated to my daughters, Avery and Maryn. Even though you are still far too young to read it, this book is for you. You were there for every struggle and watched me pour every bit of myself into this project. Let it show you that there's no limit to what you can achieve, as long as you're willing to put forth the effort. Don't ever let anything stand between you and your dreams.

Love you girls

xoxoxo

Contents

Chapter One

Charlotte

"There isn't much new to report since you were in yesterday. There's a new patient in room 239. He just got here this morning, and he likely won't be with us long. His file's there for you to read over. Fifty-eight year old man in the end stages of lung cancer."

I look up at Ellen as she finishes her shift change report. I've only been working at the nursing home for about a month now, and have settled right into their palliative care ward. The home itself is clean and basic; not at all fancy. This is not a home for rich people. Someone had once made an attempt to make it homier, but that attempt was an epic fail. It still looks drab and institutional. The corridors are long, with beige walls and dull, beige tile flooring. Depressing, really. There are paintings along the walls and fake potted plants dotting different areas of the floor. The air inside smells of disinfectant and cheap lemon cleaner. The staff here are nice though, and the job itself is exactly what I've been looking for. There's something rewarding about making the last few days of someone's life more comfortable for everyone involved.

Nodding, I pick up the file she's talking about, and flip through the pages. Harold Harvey, fifty eight years old, stage four lung cancer. He's still so young. I'm looking it all over and familiarizing myself with his plan of care when Ellen speaks again.

"There's one other thing."

I glance up from the file. "What's that?"

She leans toward me and lowers her voice to a whisper. "He's a member of a biker gang." My back stiffens with a jolt of fear. "Ever hear of the Kings of Korruption?"

I shake my head while a ball of dread forms in my stomach. Bikers? This is *not* good news. My sister had been involved with a biker gang just before we moved here. It was *why* we'd moved in the first place – so she could break ties with them. They scare the shit out of me. The good news is, the gang I'd helped my sister run from was *not* the Kings of Korruption.

"They're a pretty big gang." She tilts her head slightly, a frown creasing her forehead. "Or should I say motorcycle club?" She waves her hand dismissively. "Whatever. Anyways, there's a chapter here in town, but they tend to keep to themselves."

Her face breaks out into a grin. "Mind you, after seeing some of Mr. Harvey's visitors, I wish they wouldn't." She wags her perfectly shaped eyebrows at me. "There's a whole lotta hot biker down that hall lady! Enjoy your shift." With those parting words and a wink in my direction, Ellen grabs her stuff and leaves.

I look over at the other two girls working this afternoon, but they aren't paying attention. They're both leaning over the counter, peering down the hall towards room 239, trying to get a glimpse of the previously mentioned, hot bikers.

Rolling my eyes, I head off down the hall and start my rounds. Checking in on my first three patients, I find all of them doing well and resting comfortably. Taking my time, I wander to each room, dealing with each patient. My dread grows as I get closer to the room where our new patient lays. *I can do this. They aren't the Devils. There's no way they'll know who I am. Will they?*

My fear of all men on motorcycles is one I'd developed when my sister got herself tangled up with the Devil's Rejects MC in Toronto. My sister, Anna, has always liked her men bad, and the Devils are about as bad as it gets. After meeting a few of them at the bar one night, she started hanging around their clubhouse on a regular basis, and became what I believe is called, a club whore.

They'd used her up and passed her around, with Anna loving every minute of it. She'd been in a rough place in her life and had allowed them to treat her like shit. This went on for about a year, then something happened with them and she still won't tell me what that something was. All I know is, she stopped going around and the Devils started showing up everywhere we went. The store, our home, my job. We never went to the police because Anna was worried they'd retaliate even worse. Apparently bikers don't like rats.

One day Anna came home with a broken arm, two black eyes and a bloody lip. Again, she wouldn't tell me what had happened but I knew then, it was time to get the hell out of there. We packed up whatever we could fit in my beat up old Toyota Echo, and got the hell out of town. I'd found this job online and that's what led us here, to Ottawa. We're a five hour drive from the Devils, and I can only pray that it's far enough. We'd been here just over a month, and so far there's no sign that the Devils are even looking for us. I'm taking this as a good sign.

I continue my rounds, checking on my next patient. He needs his catheter emptied and another blanket and I happily do this for him, deliberately stalling.

When I get to Mrs. Evans' room, I take a deep breath, then open the door. Mrs. Evans is a thirty year old mother of two young children, dying of cervical cancer. Every time I come into her room, she greets me with a smile. She never complains or gets upset. Her bravery and acceptance of her impending death humbles me.

Her husband never leaves her side and her children come in each day to visit. Watching this family, knowing their mother is about to leave them, makes my heart bleed. I've been that kid – watching my mother die. I know how devastating and scary it is. I was older than the Evans children when my mom passed away but losing a mom at any age is traumatic. This is especially true when you have to watch them wither away in a slow death that steals them from you day by day, right in front of your eyes.

They don't notice me when I first enter the room. Mr. Evans lays comfortably beside his wife, reading a novel out loud. She has her eyes closed, smiling with a peaceful look on her face. I clear my throat softly. Mr. Evans stops reading, marks the page with his thumb and looks up at me. Mrs. Evans opens her eyes and smiles in my direction. Her face is serene – peaceful.

"Well, hello there." I approach the bed with a smile of my own. "Just wanted to let you know that I'm on shift now, and will be your nurse for the evening. Lucky you!" I wink at them both.

"Lucky us indeed." Mrs. Evans' smile widens. She holds her arm out for me to place the blood pressure cuff on her so I can take her vitals. "Jeff was just reading to me." She uses her free hand to lace her fingers with her husbands. Her voice is weak and husky with fatigue. "I have a to-read list a mile long, but I can't seem to keep my eyes open long enough to read anymore. You should stick around for when he gets to the sexy parts." She winks at me again. "His face turns red as a tomato."

"Now that I would like to see." I chuckle with her. Mr. Evans is blushing furiously – already looking like a tomato. "Ah. There it is." I look to her and can't help it when my face breaks out in a wide smile. For a mountain of a man, he is quite adorable. "I see what you mean." I don't know how it's possible, but his blush deepens and Mrs. Evans grins at him. "Is there anything I can do for you folks at the moment?"

"Nope. We're going to lay here and read some more of this book, then I think I may take a little nap." She yawns the last three words, turning to snuggle back into her husband. They are such a sweet couple. My heart clenches in sympathy for them. The love they share is obvious and beautiful. I wonder what it's like to have someone love you like that.

"Sounds like you might need that nap." I reach down and squeeze her hand, then turn to leave. "Push the call button if you need anything at all. I'm at your service." Smiling at them again, I leave the room.

I'm only a few steps down the hall when a giant man comes barreling out of room 239. My heart stops. This man is terrifying – exactly the type of biker that stars in my nightmares. He's huge, hairy and covered in tattoos. The leather cut he wears tells me that he's a member of the Kings of Korruption. His dark hair hangs just past his shoulders, a long beard hiding most of his face.

I quickly look to the floor as I pass, not missing the scowl he has aimed in my direction. "Hey." His voice is gruff and gravelly, like he has been smoking a pack of cigarettes a day since he was born. "Hey!" *Oh God. He's talking to me.* "You Smokey's nurse?"

I look up at him but quickly avert my eyes. He's staring at me, intense blue eyes trying to bore into mine. "Smokey?" My voice sounds shaky and unsure to my own ears.

"Yeah. Smokey. Room 239. You his nurse?"

The annoyance in his voice causes my face to flush and my heart to pound erratically in my chest. I clear my throat, attempting to sound more in control. "I am. I'm just headed that way now."

He gives me a quick nod of his head. "Good. He's … just … take care of my brother." His order is gruff and sharp, startling me. It takes an astounding amount of control to stay put, and not run screaming down the hall like a lunatic.

"I will definitely do that, sir," I manage.

He stares at me a moment, nods again before stalking off down the hall. I stare after him and wait for my racing heart to slow. That was intense. I don't know many bikers but the ones I've had the horror of meeting terrified me. If that man was any indication of who was in room 239, my worst fears were about to be tested. *Something to look forward to.* Taking a calming breath, I mentally beat back my panic attack and continue down the hall to finish my rounds.

The next two patients are settled and don't need anything. This left only our newest patient to check in on. I stand outside the door, taking a deep breath in an attempt to collect my courage. *Let's just get this over with.*

Giving the door a quick knock, I push it open and enter the room. A sigh of relief escapes me when I see only the patient, who is asleep, and one visitor in the room. When the visitor looks up, my sigh catches in my throat becoming a silent gasp. *Holy. Shit. He is breathtaking.*

He's sitting in a chair at the side of the room, cell phone in hand. Even though he's sitting, I can tell he's huge. He's wearing a leather cut over a white t-shirt, but it does nothing to hide the fact that he's ripped. His chest muscles strain the white cotton t-shirt and his heavily muscled, tattooed arms bulge out from under the sleeves.

I drag my eyes from his impressive body up to his face, my cheeks flaming when we make eye contact. He smirks, clearly noting the thorough eye fucking I just gave him, but I still can't seem to tear my eyes away.

His hair is dark and in need of a cut, curling a little at the nape of his neck and around his ears. An unruly lock falls across his forehead, into his eyes. Those eyes are incredible; deep blue with long dark lashes. His nose and chin are chiseled, as if made from granite, and his jaw is covered in stubble. He's gorgeous. Rugged and masculine.

I blink quickly, praying that I'm not drooling while I remind myself that not only am I working, but also that this man is a biker. A dangerous, likely criminal biker, who's here because his biker buddy is lying in *my* palliative care unit, dying of lung cancer. Giving my head a quick shake, I force a polite smile onto my face.

"Hi. I'm Charlotte. I will be Mr. Harvey's nurse this afternoon."

"Smokey." His voice is gruff and his eyes are boring into mine, causing my heart to skip a beat.

"Pardon?" God. That voice.

"Smokey. Mr. Harvey likes to be called Smokey. He'll tell you that himself, once he wakes up." He gives me a small smile, and I see a hint of a dimple on his stubbled cheek.

"Okay then." I nod. "Smokey it is." I walk up to the bed, look down at the patient in question and begin taking his vitals. While I'm working, he continues to speak.

"My name's Ryker. If you're curious." I look up and see him smirking at me again. Oh yeah, he'd definitely noticed the eye fucking. Once again, I find myself blushing, and this just won't do. I have no business getting flustered over this guy.

"Well Ryker, how is Mr. Har – I mean Smokey feeling today?"

"Much better now that he's here." He frowns. "Smokey's been suffering a long time with this. The pain was getting to be too much and he doesn't have an old lady at home to take care of him. We told him, at least here, they have good drugs and hot nurses." He looks me up and down, making it obvious that he means me. "Nice to see we were right on both counts."

My breath catches in my throat and my eyes shoot to his. He's smiling now. And there's that dimple I'd seen a hint of earlier. It's deep, and if at all possible, just adds to his beauty.

"Right. Well ... his vitals are good, and he seems comfortable, so I'll be back later to check on him again. If he needs anything, just push that button over there to page me to the room." I say these words in a rush, then turn on my heel, hurrying out of the room. Bikers scare me, but this one in particular scares me on a whole other level. *This is not good.*

***

Ryker

I'm sitting in a chair, thinking about the hot as fuck nurse that just took my breath away when Smokey wakes up. Shaking off those thoughts, I lean over and pat his skinny arm. "Hey brother."

"Hey." He raises his hands and rubs the heels of them into his eyes, trying to wake himself up. He's been sleeping a lot lately but this past week, his sleep has been troubled. That's what made us decide to bring him here. Everybody deserves the right to die at home, but there's only so much pain that can be cured with weed and Tylenol. The man was in desperate need of prescription medicine and professional care. "You been here long?"

"Nah. 'Bout an hour. Just happy you can finally sleep brother. Be thankful you're awake now though. You should see your nurse, man. She's fuckin' fine."

Smokey snorts and smirks at me. In the last couple weeks, he's really gone downhill fast. His skin is pale and pasty. His eyes, sunken and dark. I barely recognize him as the man he once was. He's fading away right before my eyes. I know he doesn't care about any hot nurses, or anything else for that matter, but fucked if I know what to talk to him about. The man is dying. This is *not* something I know how to deal with. I'm far from my comfort zone, but I volunteered to sit here with him because he's the closest thing to a father I've ever had. I'm going to miss the crazy son of a bitch.

His breathing is ragged and labored. Smokey hasn't spoken a whole lot lately because talking takes air, and he doesn't have much access to that anymore. "Ryk, if there's one thing I've learned while this fuckin' cancer has eaten away at my lungs, it's that life's short." He lifts his tired eyes to meet mine. "I don't have a whole lot of regrets, but one I do have is, I fucked around my whole life and never settled down." He coughs, his lungs wheezing as he tries to catch his breath. "Never had an old lady. Dying alone fuckin' sucks, man." He clears his throat, wiping his mouth with the back of his hand. "Pussy is fun. Bein' bikers, we don't even have to work for it, but thinkin' back, I wish I hadda found me a classy lady and tied myself to her. Someone to love, who loves me back, ya know?"

His words hit me. I know what he's saying and it's something that's crossed my mind before, but I've shoved that shit down deep. I've seen what happens when someone in our world hooks himself to another person. An old lady just complicates things and I don't do complicated.

"Holy fuck, Smoke. Those meds they put you on earlier make you grow a fuckin' vagina or somethin'? That was some deep shit. Since when do you do deep shit?"

Smokey laughs softly, which abruptly turns into a cough and shortness of breath. I instantly regret my attempt at humor, but I'd needed to change the subject to something less heavy.

Once he catches his breath, he throws a small grin my way. "Nah, no vagina. Just reflectin' on life now that my time's getting' closer. Seriously, Ryk." He puts a hand to his chest and winces. "You're a good kid. You deserve a hot woman, warmin' your bed and lovin' you 'til your last breath." He pauses again, attempting to fill his lungs. The pain on his face is like a knife in my gut. "I

16

may sound like a pussy, but I want to be sure you don't die with the same regrets I am."

I swallow down the lump that'd formed in my throat while he was talking and nod my head. "Yeah man. I hear ya."

Smokey just winks at me. "Good. Now, enough of that shit. Let's get this sexy nurse in here and see if I can't get her to give me a sponge bath."

Crazy son of a bitch.

Chapter Two

Ryker

It's been two days since Smokey was admitted into this life-sucking building of death. He gets weaker every day, but his pain is moderated now. The catheter they gave him makes it so he doesn't have to get up to take a piss, and that's a blessing in itself. Poor fucker would get winded just taking a leak before we came here.

Smokey's been asleep for about an hour when Nurse Charlotte walks in the room. *Fuck me, she's gorgeous.* Her hair is a dark, chocolate brown with hints of red throughout it, which she keeps in a messy bun high up at the back of her head. I would give anything to pull out that elastic and see what it looks like down. I can tell that it's curlym and maybe even a little wild. She has a round face with rosy cheeks, and a pert little nose that has a patch of freckles fanning across it. Her eyes are a deep brown; large and bright, framed with thick long lashes. She doesn't appear to wear makeup, but then she doesn't need it. She's average height, about five foot five, has great fucking tits a slim waist, and from what I can tell her ass is smoking hot too.

I smirk when I see what she's wearing tonight. Fucking kittens. All over her scrub top are bunches of little kittens playing with balls of yarn and chasing butterflies. Ridiculous, but cute as hell.

She looks hesitant as she enters, but when she sees it's just me and Smoke there, she relaxes. She seems almost frightened when the other guys are around and I won't lie, it gives me some kind of fucked up thrill to know that she's only relaxed around me.

"Hey." Her smile is small but it lights up her whole fucking face, and my chest tightens every time I see it. She's so beautiful. I've been with a lot of women. I'm not being cocky when I say that - just stating fact. Women love me and I love women. Not one of those women had a smile like hers though – I'd remember. "How's Smokey doing tonight?"

God, I'm a dick. Smokey's lying in bed, dying, and here I am getting a hard on for his sexy as fuck nurse. I shake my head and try to sound cool. "Good. He's tired but not in any pain."

Charlotte just nods. "Ok. Well, let me know if he needs anything. I'll be back in a while to check on him." She smiles again before leaving the room. It's quiet in here and I wish she could have stayed, but what the fuck would I talk to her about. She's a nurse and I'm a criminal – not exactly a whole lot in common. Regardless, I'm drawn to her; I want to know her.

Smokey continues his nap and I continue reading the thriller novel I've been reading on my phone. About an hour later, Smokey's breathing becomes more labored, his breaths coming out in a scary combination of strangled wheezes and gasps.

I jump up and hurry to the bed. "Smoke? Brother? You cool?" His face is turning a strange shade of red and he's staring at me with panic in his eyes. He shakes his head violently, indicating that no, he is *not* cool. My heart pounds in my chest. *He can't breathe. He's gonna fucking die! Like, right now, he is going to fucking die! I'm not ready for this shit.*

Reaching over Smokey's shoulder, I quickly stab at the call button, praying to whatever God will listen that the nurse is an Olympic athlete and will be here in a flash. I'm relieved when Charlotte runs into the room just seconds later.

She takes one look at Smokey and rushes over. Automatically, she pushes the button on his IV, causing more morphine to run into his drip. Then she grabs his hand, leans in real close and starts to whisper to him.

"Shhhhh. Smokey? I need you to settle down, honey." She grips his huge hand in her tiny one, smoothing his sweaty hair back from his forehead. "Ryker and I are right here with you. I need you to take a deep breath for me, ok?" Her voice has a soothing quality to it, which not only instantly calms Smokey, but works wonders to calm me too. She continues talking in that soft, calming voice as Smokey's breathing returns to normal. His eyes drift closed, then he's asleep once again.

Still stroking his head and holding his hand, Charlotte turns her eyes on me. "How about you? You ok, Ryker?"

I'm not, but fuck me if I'm going to admit that to her. I just nod and stare at Smoke, unable to tear my eyes away from the slight rise and fall of his chest.

"It can be really scary watching that." She nods her head at the man who was like a father to me. "He had a panic attack. Once they lose their breath, even a little, some people tend to panic, and that throws their breathing right off. It's very scary for them too." She smiles at me with sympathy in those deep brown eyes of hers.

"Well ..." I clear my throat, stalling to think of something to say. My brain is still paused on the scene of my buddy turning fucking red, gasping desperately for breath. "Thanks for calming him down, Charlie. I didn't know what the fuck to do." I feel like a god damned pussy.

I hear her quick intake of breath when I call her "Charlie," and watch her standing there, wide eyes on me before her expression clears and she gives a small shake of her head, as if clearing it. Her cheeks flush a beautiful shade of pink before she smiles again. "Press the button if you need me." She turns to leave but then stops. "Oh and Ryker?" Her hand lands hesitantly on my shoulder. "You did great." And with those parting words, she was gone.

I stand by Smokey's bed, staring at the door she'd just exited from, trying to figure out what this feeling is that I just can't seem to shake. *Jesus.* She's so fucking sweet. She genuinely seemed to care about how I was feeling, and her "you did great" was not something I'd ever heard from anybody but Smoke. Somehow, those words are different coming from a beautiful nurse with deep brown eyes.

I shake my head. I can't believe I'd called her Charlie. I'd been doing it in my mind, but never before had I said it out loud. I need to pull my head out of my ass. Thinking about her all the time is doing me no favors. Charlie's a civilian. Getting involved with me and the MC isn't in her best interest. It's something that I've seen happen before and I'll be damned if I let it happen to someone like her. Charlie is not for me.

***

Charlotte

Throughout the night, I've been in and out of Smokey's room. He'd spent most of that time sleeping and Ryker stayed quiet, letting his friend sleep. I've struggled to avoid eye contact with him at all times, but the couple of times I do risk a glance, his eyes are always pinned in my direction, causing my heart to pound erratically in my chest .

He'd called me Charlie. Nobody had ever called me Charlie and gotten away with it. I've always hated that name, but when it came from Ryker's mouth, voice full of such gruff affection, my brain had pretty much turned to mush. It'd taken a great amount of effort to not show him how much I liked hearing him call me that name. To not tackle the poor guy to the ground and screw the ass right off him. Charlie is my new favorite name.

My shift almost over, I'm just finishing up my final rounds and have only one patient left to check. Knocking softly on the door to room 239, I quietly enter the room. Smokey and Ryker are sound asleep. This is the perfect opportunity to get a closer look at the man that seems to be consuming my every thought lately.

His leather cut lays on the back of a chair, at the other side of the room. Without it, Ryker looks a lot less menacing. He's slumped down, right ankle resting casually on his knee, head against the back of the chair. My chest tightens as I take a step closer. He looks so peaceful in sleep, his face relaxed. That lock of dark hair lays across his forehead, my hand itching to reach out and smooth it back. Absolutely gorgeous.

What the hell is it with this guy? I can't remember ever being so affected by anyone before, let alone a stranger – and a biker at that. Shaking my head, I turn towards Smokey. He's lying there, eyes on me, quietly watching me while I check out his friend. The blush on my face is instant and he lets out a small chuckle. "Don't worry, honey. You're not the first girl to look at him like that. Likely the first nice girl though, and that may mean somethin' to Ryk."

I frown, trying to hide my embarrassment and step up to the bed to take his vitals. "You feeling any pain at the moment?"

"No, darlin'. I'm good. Just tired." He gives me a weary smile. "You scared of my boy over there?"

My eyes widen at his bluntness. "Um ... well ... honestly? A little. I don't have many good experiences with bad boys, if you know what I mean." My blush deepens and I aim a shy smile in his direction before turning to leave the room.

"Honey." Turning back to Smokey, I focus on him. I know it's difficult for him to be saying so much right now. "He ain't nearly as bad as he's gonna want you to think he is."

Flustered, I just nod, pat his hand and bid him a good night. Risking one last glance at Ryker, I leave the room.

Chapter Three

Charlotte

The next evening, I find Smokey alone in his room. He's asleep, but I can't stand the thought of him waking and nobody being there. After finishing my rounds, I grab my stack of patient files and head back down the hall to Smokey's room.

Grabbing a chair, I pull it over to the chair beside his bed, where Ryker usually sits each night. After placing my files on one chair, I sit back in the other and start my paperwork. Smokey's breathing has become more labored since he was admitted. His meds seem to be keeping him free from pain, but I can tell that breathing is even more of a struggle for him. *Where's his family? Or Ryker for that matter?* He's always here at this time.

I'm halfway through my reports when the door opens. I look up with a smile on my face, expecting to see Ryker, but the smile wavers when I see it's not him. Standing before me is the scary biker from the hall, the day Smokey was admitted. He steps into the room and closes the door. My heart races, realizing that I'm closed inside a room with this guy. He glances at Smokey and then spears me in place with narrowed, angry eyes.

"What the hell are you sittin' in here for?" His voice is rough and accusatory. Completely caught off guard, words fail me and I sit there staring at him with wide eyes, my mouth opening and closing like a fish out of water. *What the hell does he think I'm doing in here?*

"I … I just." I clear my throat and try again. "I'm just keeping Smokey company. Nobody was here, so I thought I'd sit with him in case he wakes up." I stand and quickly begin gathering my things. "But you're here now, so I will leave you to your visit." I fumble while gathering up my files and they fall to the ground, papers scattering across the floor.

"Why's he breathin' so rough? Can't you give him somethin' to help him breathe?" He takes a menacing step towards me while I kneel on the floor, once again collecting my folders. My hands are shaking, my heart threatening to leap out of my chest entirely. "We brought the poor fucker here so he could be at peace. This doesn't look too fuckin' peaceful."

As he takes another step, getting far too close for my comfort, I jump to my feet. "He …" My throat won't cooperate with me at all and I just can't get out the words. Struggling to swallow back my fear, I take a step back from the giant monster in front of me.

Just as I'm about to try another attempt at explaining, the door opens again and Ryker fills the doorway. Relief floods my entire body. He steps inside, his eyes flicking from the angry monster to me. I watch his face darken, his jaw tightening.

"What the fuck, Reaper?" So monster man's name is Reaper? I shiver. *Charming.* "What'd you do to Charlie?" My eyes snap from one man to the other.

Ryker storms past his buddy, shoulder slamming into him as he passes. He heads directly towards me, and now my pulse is racing for an entirely different reason. It's not fear, but I don't have time to figure out what it is before he reaches me.

"Jesus Christ, baby girl. You're shaking like a leaf!" He places his giant hands on my upper arms, rubbing them gently up and down, then turns his head to glare at Reaper once more. "Why the fuck is she so pale? What'd you do to her?"

Reaper opens his mouth to respond, but I beat him to it. I just want to get the hell out of this room. "Mr … Reaper didn't do anything to me, Ryker." I place my hand on his arm. Touching him skin on skin sends a jolt of electricity straight through me, causing the hair on the back of my neck to stand on end.

Leaning over so I can see around Ryker, I look directly at his friend, feeling bolder now with him here – touching me. I feel safe. "Smokey *is* on medication. His pain is mostly gone. Unfortunately, with lung cancer, his breathing is going to get more and more difficult as it progresses. Aside from pain medications and oxygen, there isn't much we can do for him."

Reaper just continues to glare at me, not saying a word. "I know that seeing it isn't easy, but be assured we're doing everything we can to make him comfortable." I glance back at Ryker and give him my most reassuring smile. He doesn't look reassured. He looks pissed.

Kneeling down once again, I collect the last of my files from the floor and stand. "Now, if you'll both excuse me, I have rounds to do." I quickly step past Ryker, my chest brushing his as I do. Ignoring the butterflies that suddenly go wild from the contact, I take a wide step around Reaper and rush from the room.

In the hallway, I breathe a sigh of relief as I close the door behind me. That was intense and scary, but mostly I'm confused by the emotions Ryker caused me to feel. Squaring my shoulders, I decide to think about it later, when I'm not on shift and caring for dying people with many more important problems than my butterfly attacks.

As I approach the nurse's desk, the call bell for Mrs. Evans' room chimes. I plunk down my files and hurry down the hall. Mrs. Evans had taken a turn for the worst over the last couple of days. The doctor had informed her husband that it was only a matter of time, and advised that her family be called in to say their final goodbyes. Since then, there's been a steady flow of visitors to her room and her husband hasn't left her side. She's been in a comatose state for almost twenty four hours now.

I've been giving them privacy to be with each other in her final moments, just checking in discreetly and keeping the coffee pot full. Mr. Evans is standing in the doorway, looking up the hall as I approach. His eyes are filled with tears and his voice shakes with sadness. "She's gone." All thoughts of scary biker men and butterflies vanish.

I enter the room and find Mrs. Evans is indeed gone. My heart is lodged in my throat. Life is just so unfair sometimes. She was so young, and her children are now going to grow up without a mother. She was such a kind lady and so full of love – I fucking hate cancer.

Slowly, I approach Mr. Evans who stands before me, looking lost. I place my hand on his arm gently. "I am so very sorry for your loss." My voice quivers with grief for this family. Normally, I'm able to say the right things to grieving families, but looking into the eyes of this broken man, I'm at a complete loss for words.

"I will give you some time with her. The doctor will be in momentarily." The grief clogs my throat and tears threaten to pour from my eyes. After gently squeezing his arm, I leave the room.

***

Ryker

I haven't seen Charlie again since I walked in on whatever the fuck was going on between her and Reaper earlier. *Cocksucker.* When I came into that room, seeing her pale and clearly terrified, I wanted to rip that fucker's throat out for scaring her. That thought alone is messed right the fuck up. Reaper is my brother. We stand together – always. So why did I want to kill him for scaring Charlie?

Reaper'd told me what had happened and I believed him. He can be a scary bastard, but Charlie's reaction was extreme. She was petrified. It was eating at me, and I need to know why she'd been so afraid. I'd warned Reaper to stay the fuck away from her. He'd agreed, but not before cracking a joke about her having me by the balls. *Asshole.*

Smokey's sound asleep. I need a smoke, and a break from this depressing as fuck room of death. Quietly slipping out of the room, I wander down the hall and out into the chilly night air. Snagging a cigarette out of my pack, I put it to my lips and light it. The first inhale works wonders to relieve some of the tension that's been weighing on my shoulders and my mind for months, even if that relief is only temporary.

Waiting for your buddy to die fuckin' sucks. My old man had been a dick. I hated the son of a bitch. Smokey'd been there for me since I was just a little kid, filling in that father role. Dad had been the president of the Kings of Korruption. He didn't give a shit about anyone or anything but his club, and making money however he could. My mom had died when I was only six years old, so since then it'd been just me and my old man.

My dad lived and breathed the MC. We lived at the clubhouse, where I had my own room. I was raised by club whores and the old ladies of other members. I'd seen more sex, drugs and drunken disputes by the age of ten than most people had seen in their entire lives. By the time I was fifteen, I had experience with all of the above. My old man rarely spoke to me, unless I did something to piss him off. He knocked me around a lot. His hatred was evident every time he looked at me. In the end, I found that if I just avoided him, he wouldn't even know I was around. He was killed by a rival club when I was seventeen years old, and I hadn't missed him one day since.

Taking another deep haul off of my smoke, I look out into the night. Hearing a noise that sounds an awful lot like crying, I look towards a bench that's cast in shadows. I can't see over there at all, but the sounds are obviously coming from a woman. Crying women freak me right the fuck out. I'm about to look away, when a car turns into the parking lot, the headlights briefly passing over the crying figure.

An unfamiliar tightness forms in my chest when I see that it's Charlie sitting on that bench, crying all alone in the dark. This woman has been driving me fucking insane for days. I can't seem to get her out of my head. If I'm not thinking about her tits, or her ass, or what it would be like to be inside her, I'm thinking about something she'd said or that sexy shade of red she turns when I say something suggestive. It's been a couple of weeks since I've gotten laid. I need to find some random chick, get me some and move the fuck on.

Knowing she's upset about something, I have the overwhelming urge to go to her and make whatever's wrong, right. Slowly, I make my way toward her, mentally cursing myself for being so weak. I need to leave her to cry. She's not mine to take care of. Ignoring my own advice, I approach her, unsure what to do but needing to do something. I need to know what's wrong with her.

Maybe I'm too quiet as I approach because I'm pretty sure I scare the shit out of her when I speak. "Charlie?" She makes a little squeak and jumps in her seat. Her head lifts in my direction, her face is cast in shadows. "You ok?"

She quickly wipes her face with the sleeves of her long grey sweater. "Ryker! Yeah ... um ... I'm good. Just getting a little air." Her voice quivers, and I can still hear the tears in her words.

"Ah. I see." *Now what?* I'm completely out of my element here. "Mind if I sit?" I gesture towards the seat on the bench beside her.

"Oh ... yeah ... I was actually just heading back in anyways. My fifteen minute break is just about over." She's attempting to be nonchalant and act like everything's fine, but the thought of her upset about something causes my fucking guts to churn and I want to do something ... anything. As long as it makes her not cry anymore.

Sitting on the bench, I turn my body towards her, and before I can stop myself, reach out to grasp her chin. A small gasp escapes her as I gently tilt her face to mine so I can look into her eyes. Now that I'm closer, I can see her clearly in the moonlight. The shadows dance across her face, doing nothing to hide her watery eyes and the tear stains on her rounded cheeks. "Why were you crying?"

I hear her breath hitch and she stiffens under my fingertips. "I wasn't crying Ryker. Like I said, I was just getting some air." She waves her hand in the air, changing the subject. "I'd love to sit and talk, but I really do have to be getting back in." She smiles tightly and moves to stand. I grasp her clasped hands and press them down gently, indicating for her to stay put.

"Bullshit, Charlie." My words are harsh but said in a whisper, hopefully not conveying anger but concern. "I can't help you if I don't know what's wrong."

She gives me a sad, shy smile. "I don't need help. I just get a little emotional sometimes." She takes a deep breath. "One of my patients just passed away, and there are times when that makes my job a little ... difficult."

My heart clenches in sympathy. The feeling is completely foreign. I hate that she's hurting and don't know what the fuck I can do to make her feel better. This woman should never cry, and I want to be the one to fix it for her. *Fuck. Why can't I just leave her alone?* I shouldn't be doing this with her.

"Why do you do it?" I know I shouldn't ask, but I genuinely want to know. I'd wondered more than once since Smokey had been moved to palliative care. Why would someone like her want to work in a hospital like this and be around dying people all the time?

"Do what? My job?" I nod my head to indicate that yes – that is what I'm asking. She takes a deep breath and I hear her swallow hard. "I love my job. It gives my life purpose."

"I have to admit baby, I don't understand." Her eyes shoot to mine at the word baby. I don't know why I called her that, but right now, I don't care. It just came out.

The expression on her face is vulnerable – maybe even a little unsure. "It's a long story."

"I've got time."

She smiles again. "Well, unfortunately, I don't. I really do have to get back in a few minutes. Long story short, these people are dying." She sends me an apologetic smile. "My job is to make their final days comfortable. Allow them to tie up loose ends, laugh and cry with their loved ones. And allow them to say goodbye."

Her eyes fill with tears again. "Being able to do that for them … for their loved ones, it's an honor. I don't take it lightly. It can be hard not to get attached to some of them, and when they pass, it breaks my heart. Every time."

I nod. That makes sense. She's so different from any other woman I have known. She's sweet and kind and she cares about people - even complete strangers. She's pure. I haven't spent a lot of time among civilians, having spent most of my life surrounded by the club, but I know that she's not like most women. Even civilian women. She's in a class all of her own. It reminds me, once again, just how different we really are, and that she doesn't fit in my world.

A slight breeze in the air causes a stray lock to escape the mass of hair she has piled at the back of her head, only to blow across her cheek. I clench my fists, resisting the urge to sweep it behind her ear. She takes another deep breath, wiping her eyes with the sleeves of her sweater and smiles at me.

If I wasn't already sitting, I would have been knocked on my ass. *Fuck me.* Her beauty gets me every time. Even in the dark, her chocolate brown eyes are glistening and filled with kindness. Her dark curly hair is unruly and pulled away from her face in her trademark messy bun. "I'm sorry, Ryker." Every time she says my name, a jolt goes right through me. This is unfamiliar territory and I'm not sure how to deal with it. "You're here for Smokey. You don't need to be listening to his crazy nurse crying alone in the darkness."

"Baby, don't worry about that. I like hanging out in the darkness with you." I bend forward slightly and catch her eyes with mine, giving her my most charming smile. *What am I doing?*

She chuckles softly and stands. "Well, I better be getting back to my rounds. Thanks for listening, Ryker."

My mind racing, I just nod, toss my cigarette and watch as she turns and walks back inside. I'm not sure what to do with what I'm feeling. Charlie is unlike anyone I've ever encountered before and I'm drawn to her like a moth to a flame. I can't *not* flirt with her – it's impossible.

One thing I know for certain is that she's just too pure for someone like me. Listening to her describe her job only proves it. She's the light and I'm the dark. My dark would eat every ounce of her beautiful light, leaving her tarnished and dimmed. It's going to take some effort, but I need to keep my distance from now on.

Chapter Four

Charlotte

My little meeting in the garden with Ryker has my head spinning. On one hand, he represents everything I've feared for years. Danger, criminals and instability. On the other hand, he makes me feel completely safe and that isn't something I've felt in a very long time – ever really. He's attentive and sweet. I wasn't prepared for that.

Over the last few days, Smokey's had several visitors and all of them had been wearing a leather cut with the Kings emblem sewn onto the back of it. Each and every one of those men scared the crap out of me. Some of them were perfectly polite, though a couple of them had openly leered at me, but every one of them had a dangerous vibe that was all too familiar. Ryker had that vibe too, but somehow, he also intrigued me. It just doesn't make sense.

At eleven o'clock, finished with my shift for the day, I walk the six blocks to the small two bedroom apartment I share with my sister. It's dark tonight, and the moon's glow has been muted by dark clouds in the night sky. As I approach the block that my building's on, I get the feeling that someone's watching me. An icy shiver runs down my back, goosebumps race across my entire body and I'm completely creeped out. Looking around quickly, I hurry to my building, thankful for the security locks on the front doors.

I dash up the stairs and when approaching my apartment I come to an abrupt halt, seeing the door cracked open. Something isn't right. My heart beats frantically in my chest while I fumble around my purse for the pepper spray I'd bought a few months ago. I'd gotten my sister one too, making her promise me she'd carry it at all times. She thought I was paranoid.

I look again at the open door, trying to calm my racing thoughts. *Should I call the police? Should I go in? What if someone is still in there? What if Anna is in there? What if she's hurt?* My mind races, trying to decide what the hell to do. I don't own a cell phone and it's late. I don't want to bother a neighbor for their phone, only to find out that Anna is alright and that I *am* completely paranoid. But Anna could be in there, and she could be hurt. The longer I stand out here trying to form a complete thought, the longer she could be in danger.

Steeling my nerves, I cautiously approach the door to what is supposed to be my safe place. I place a hand on it and slowly push it open, the hinges squeaking loudly. My heart beats a staccato rhythm in my chest as my eyes flick rapidly around the room, looking for any signs of an intruder.

"Anna?" My voice is quiet, coming out in a squeak. I need to know if she's home. Maybe she'd left the door open by accident. Maybe she just hadn't latched it completely when she left. Just in case, I call out again, louder this time. "Anna? Are you in here?"

Silence greets me. Another quick glance around the room shows that nobody's hiding in there and nothing seems to be missing. Slowly, I go from room to room, checking for any signs of a burglar … or something worse. My bedroom is the last room to be checked. So far, my search has shown nothing wrong or suspicious, but I still open the door with caution.

My room is my sanctuary. The furniture's old, but well maintained, the wood stained a dark brown. A white and green ceramic vase holds a place of honor on top of my nightstand, filled with fresh flowers, which I replace every Friday. I love the smell of fresh flowers, the smell reminding me of my mother. The vase had been my mothers, and her mother's before that. It was one of my most prized possessions.

The double, four poster bed has a handmade quilt in white and mint green, neatly lying on the immaculately made bed. Or at least, it had been immaculate. I tend to be a bit of a neat freak. Instead of being neatly made, the bed has a clear rumpled quality on one side, in the shape of a body. A very tall body. It's obvious that someone had been lying on my bed ... but who? My skin crawls and I have to concentrate on my breathing to avoid hyperventilating.

Relieved that Anna's not home, therefore hopefully not in apparent danger, I call her cell phone. It goes directly to voicemail. "Anna? Hi … um ... we have a bit of an issue here. Can you call me as soon as you get this? Thanks. Oh, and Anna? Be safe." I know my voice is shaking, but I'm completely freaked out.

With that said, I hang up the phone and go to the door to lock it. Maybe I'm overreacting. I tend to do that. Nobody is here, nothing seems to be missing, and it's highly doubtful that anyone had broken in to my apartment just to sleep in my bed. Anna must have been preoccupied and just forgot to latch it. But even if that's the case, who *had* lain on my bed?

Clutching my pepper spray like a lifeline, I sit on the couch, pulling my knees up to my chest. Fear threatens to overwhelm me. Eyes on the door, I pray the next person to walk through it is my sister.

***

Ryker

I don't know what's worse, someone you love dying instantly or having the time to come to grips with their death, while getting a chance to say goodbye. I've lost people the first way, but now, with Smokey about to go out the second way, I'm not sure which is easier. I've been preparing myself for his death for months. All of his affairs are settled. He's said goodbye to everybody that ever mattered to him. All that's left is for him to just die. He's ready. Tired of fighting to live, Smokey has accepted his fate and isn't afraid anymore. It's me that's not ready. I need that fat bastard, and I'm not sure how I'll live in a world where he doesn't exist.

It's around noon when I get the call that Smoke has taken a turn for the worst. It's time. I usually head in around three o'clock and stay with him until morning. After calling a few of our brothers, I rush to the nursing home, hoping that I'm not too late to say goodbye.

Seeing him lying in that bed, even more withered than when I'd left that morning, sends pain and panic through my body. *This is really fucking happening. What the fuck am I gonna do without Smokey?*

Ellen is the nurse on duty. We've met a few times before when she was on shift and I liked her. She was good to Smoke. I ignore the flash of disappointment when Charlie isn't the one that walks through the door. I may just need a little of her light to get through this, and that thought throws me. Ellen explains that Smokey's no longer conscious, but that he isn't in any pain and can still hear us.

A few of our brothers come and go, getting in one final goodbye to a good friend. I stay for all of it, and between visits I carry on a one way conversation with him. I'm only there a couple hours before his breathing is coming faster and shallower. Ellen tells me that it won't be long now.

It's scary as fuck watching my buddy laying there, about to die. She gives us our privacy and I'm left alone with him once again. Placing my hand on his shoulder, I attempt to say my final goodbye, praying that he will go quickly now. I can't bear to watch the poor bastard suffer any longer.

"Brother, you've been a good fuckin' friend." I clear my throat to get rid of the lump that'd formed there when I'd gotten the phone call this afternoon. Damned thing seems to keep growing back every time I clear it. "You and me both know that my old man was a dick. You weren't a dick though. You got me through a lot of rough shit. I am who I am because you gave a fuck, and for that, I thank you, man. You've been like a father to me. I just wanted you to know that."

After pouring my fucking heart out to what was left of my buddy, I just sit beside him with my hand on his forearm – waiting. Tears keep welling up in the corners of my eyes. I won't let those fuckers fall though. I will *not* cry. My father taught me early in life that only fucking pussies cry, and I'm no pussy.

After a few minutes, Smokey lets out one last rattley, deep breath and then goes silent. I can only sit there and stare at him. He's gone. Like really fucking gone. Shaking my head, I quickly wipe away a tear that escapes from one eye. Taking a deep breath, I stand and whisper, "Goodbye, brother". With that, I turn and walk out of the room without looking back.

As I walk by the nurse's station, Ellen looks up with a question on her face. I give a curt shake of my head and keep walking, right out the door. I don't make it far. My entire body is shaking, and I feel lightheaded. There's no way I can drive in this condition. I need to calm my nerves. I walk over and sit down on the bench Charlie had been on the other night. After lighting a smoke, I sit and think about absolutely nothing. My mind is blank. Numb.

"Ryker?" I don't know how long I've been sitting here before her voice brings me back from the edge of wherever the fuck I'd just been. Charlie. A light amidst all of this darkness. "You ok?" She sounds hesitant and a little concerned.

41

I look up at her just as she sits down on the bench beside me, then attempt once more to clear my throat. "I ... uh ..." I can't even form a complete fucking sentence in my mind, let alone speak one.

She nods in understanding. "It's not easy to lose someone you love." Her eyes fill with tears and she smiles sadly. I can tell that she's speaking from experience. *Who did Charlie lose?* "Smokey seemed like a good person. I didn't know him before he was sick, but you generally get a feel for a person when they're at their weakest. He was a good guy. And he seemed to really love you." She reaches out tentatively, like she's not sure if I will bite, and gently takes my hand, giving it a squeeze before she lifts her eyes to meet mine. "I'm sorry that you lost him, Ryker."

I have to look away, hiding another fucking tear as it runs down my cheek. *Fucking pussy.* Swallowing that damn lump, I pull my hand free and use the heel of both hands to grind into my eyes. I lean forward and place my elbows on my knees. Burying my face in my hands, I take a deep breath. I don't respond; I have no words.

Charlie moves closer and places a hand on my back, rubbing in slow, soothing circles. It feels good – comforting. Just what I need. I want to curl up in a ball on her lap and have her soothe me like she did to Smokey. I want to wrap my arms around her and just hang on until all of this awful shit just goes away. Instead, I sit there and try to get a grip on my emotions.

After a few minutes of silence, she stops rubbing my back and bends forward to look me in the eyes. I hitch my mouth up on one side in a sorry attempt at a smile. She smiles sadly back at me, then lifts her hand as if to touch my face, but pauses, eyes searching mine.

I don't move – I can't. I just continue to stare into the deep brown eyes that are locked on mine. My heart loses it's steady rhythm and pounds furiously in my chest. Slowly, her hand moves forward and gently lifts a lock of hair that'd fallen across my forehead, smoothing it back into place. The action itself is sweet, but the wave of need that washes over me is not. It's intense. I need her right then. I need her comfort. I need her compassion. I need her joy and her laughter, but most of all, I need her love. Charlie makes me feel actually connected to another human being somehow. I've never felt that before, with anyone.

The need is so strong, I forget to breathe for a few seconds. Closing my eyes, I take a deep breath. I have to get a handle on myself. I'm a dude for fuck sakes. Dudes don't get all breathless just because some chick touches their hair. They don't feel connections with their dead buddy's nurses and dudes, especially this dude, do not want or need that connection. Charlie doesn't need that connection.

Grasping her wrist, I pull her hand from my hair and place it gently but firmly in her lap, then I stand quickly and turn to look down at her. "Thanks, Charlotte. You were great to Smoke. I appreciate what you've done for him. You're a good nurse." I smile tightly at her. She stares at me and nods. Nodding back, I turn and stride over to my bike. Driving away, I see her standing there watching me, her brow furrowed in confusion. I pretend not to notice and get the fuck out of there.

Chapter Five

Charlotte

Watching Ryker drive away, while I stood alone on the sidewalk the other night had confused the hell out of me. There had been several times since I'd met him, when he'd look at me and I almost believed our connection was mutual. I could feel his attraction to me, but it went farther than that – deeper somehow. Then he'd driven away. I knew in that moment that we'd likely never see each other again. So what do I know? I'm not exactly experienced when it comes to men. I'd never had any real relationships, aside from a brief one when I was seventeen. To be honest, my social skills kind of suck.

As a young girl, I'd never had a lot of friends. I spent all of my free time at home, doing anything I could to help my mom out. She was a single mom who worked constantly to keep a roof over our heads and food in our bellies. For as long as I could remember, I'd made it my mission to make her life a little easier. I cooked meals, made lunches, did laundry and cleaned the house. My sister was the one who had all the fun and all the friends. She was a wild child who did what she wanted, when she wanted. She invited me along with them sometimes, but I suspect this was mostly out of pity, and I'd never accepted so eventually she just stopped asking.

My mom was diagnosed with cancer when I was fifteen years old. After that, I threw myself into taking care of her while she had treatments, working an after school job to help pay the bills. The first year had been hard on her body. The second year had been harder.

I started dating a boy from school when I was seventeen. His name was James. He was a nice guy, not to mention handsome. No boy had ever paid attention to me before, and I was kind of flattered that he even liked me. We were dating for about a month and went out on a handful of dates before we'd had sex for the first time. It had been awkward and painful. Not at all the romantic, loving experience I'd always imagined. Still, I thought I loved him so I'd had no regrets. We had sex two more times and although it was less painful, it was nothing like I'd seen in the movies.

About six months into our relationship, my mom's cancer treatments were failing. The chemo treatments hadn't worked and we learned that she was going to die. I took some time off school to take care of her. All of my free time was taken up with work and caring for my dying mother. Anna was rarely home and James had gotten tired of never having any time with me. He hooked up with another girl from school and broke up with me in a text message. At the time, I was too overwhelmed to even care.

My heart had been shattered the day Mom passed away. I found myself at a loss for what to do with myself. For months, my life had been devoted to her care and suddenly I found myself with nobody but Anna to care for. I went back to school and worked full time in the evenings. When I graduated high school, I immediately went to college to get my nursing degree. I had to work all through college to pay my tuition and bills. Anna rarely worked at all so I found myself responsible for taking care of her too. With all of this, there'd never been time for me to have a social life so I never did.

After I got my degree, I'd gotten a good job as a nurse and slowly started making friends at work, but it was never the same. They weren't people I ever spent time with outside of my job. I'd been asked out a few times by different guys, but there was no attraction on my end so I'd always politely declined.

All of this made it so that at the age of twenty six, I'd never had a close friend, had only ever had one somewhat serious boyfriend, and the only person left in my life that truly cared about me was Anna. There were times when I wondered just how much she cared though. Anna was selfish and spoiled and always made everything about her. Sometimes I felt that she only cared as long as I kept the bills paid.

Losing my Mom meant that I'd lost the only person that had ever truly loved me. Watching Ryker with Smokey, I felt their bond, and with my experience, I got the impression that's how it was for them too. He'd sat with Smokey the same way I'd sat with Mom, and he'd been heartbroken when I last saw him. My heart ached for him. I know all too well what it's like to be alone. I wish more than anything that I could be there for him to help him through his grief.

I give my head a shake, chastising myself. Ryker likely has tons of people to help him through that grief. I'd seen all the bikers that were in and out of Smokey's room before he'd died.

They may not be warm and fuzzy, but they'd been there for each other through it all. Not only that but let's face it; Ryker is kind and gorgeous and likely has beautiful women throwing themselves at him to help him "grieve." *Who am I to compete with them? And, why does it bother me that I can't?*

As I complete that depressing thought, I look up to see that I'd pondered my life all the way home and am now standing outside my apartment building. I glance around, paranoid as always now, that someone is lurking around the corner. Nobody's there. After letting myself in the building, I approach my door, relieved to see that it's locked up tight, just the way I'd left it when I'd left for work that afternoon.

This feeling of paranoia had grown considerably since the other night, when I'd found the rumpled outline of a body on my bed. I'd seen my share of horror movies. I have a vivid imagination and I'd come up with all kinds of colorful and terrifying explanations. When Anna had come home that night, I'd still been sitting on the couch, clutching my pepper spray like my life depended on it. After telling her about my feeling of being watched, and showing her my bed, she looked panicked for a moment before her face had smoothed out. She'd brushed it off, saying that I mustn't have made my bed up as perfect as usual. She and I both knew that wasn't even a possibility. I was a nut when it came to a properly made bed.

Since then, there have been no further incidents so I'm trying to let it go. Trying would be the key word. My mind still wanders over various theories and each one gives me goosebumps. Every noise I hear in the night makes my heart pound so hard, I'm sure an intruder would hear it from the other room. This means my nights have been mostly sleepless, and I now go to bed with my pepper spray close at hand, just in case.

I enter my apartment and do a cursory look around, reassuring myself that I'm alone. I'm exhausted. Grabbing a quick snack, I get ready for bed, crawl beneath the blankets and curl up on my side. Between my fear of someone being in my home and my nearly constant thoughts of Ryker, I know that I won't be getting much sleep tonight either. My heart clutches when I think of Ryker. Even though I barely know him, I miss him.

***

Ryker

I'm sitting at the clubhouse bar, downing whiskey like water, surrounded by my brothers and a bunch of club whores; all of them drinking and having a good time. The air is thick with smoke and the booze are flowing freely tonight. It's a celebration. Today we'd laid Smokey to rest.

Smokey's funeral had been one of the hardest things I'd ever done. How do you say goodbye to the only person who ever really cared about you? Brothers from all over the country had shown up for the event. The parade of motorcycles following the hearse had been at least three hundred bikes long.

The service itself had been quick and informal. Jase had said a few words about him and he'd done a good job. He'd told stories about Smokey, adding a few memories that had all of us chuckling. He was going to be missed by many.

Afterwards, we'd all come here to the clubhouse for a celebration of his life. The party is wild and crazy – just like Smokey liked them. I'm on my fifth whiskey in less than an hour and the buzz is settling in nice, working it's magic to numb my pain.

Just then, Jase approaches the bar, beer in hand, and slides onto the stool next to mine. "Hey, fucker."

I smirk. "Hey." I take another swig, finishing off my whiskey and motion to the prospect at the bar for another one. Turning slightly, I face him. "You did a good job today, Jase. Smokey would have loved that speech. Especially that story you told about the three girls on the pool table."

Jase and I both chuckle. "Yeah. He always did like to be the center of attention. I'm gonna miss that fat fuck."

Nodding my head in agreement, I grab my fresh whiskey off the counter. Jase and I had both grown up in the clubhouse and had been best friends since we were six. Jase's dad was a brother, although he wasn't as active in the club anymore. He'd been away a lot back then, and Smokey had been a big part of Jase's life too. I know he'd loved him almost as much as I had.

"So I went to the home today to get the last of Smoke's things." I turn my head to look at him, waiting for him to continue. "Wasn't much there, but I put it on your bed here for you to have a look through."

I pull in a deep breath through my nose. I can't even think of going through Smokey's things right now. I just nod. "Thanks man."

"No problem." He takes a swig of his beer and looks around the room. Swinging back to me, a wide grin splits his face. "Gonna miss seein' some of them hot fuckin' nurses every day, I must admit."

My chest tightens. *Charlie.* Am I ever going to get that girl out of my head?

Jase keeps talking. "You see that tall one with the short blonde hair? Ellen? Fuck me. Girl has the tightest ass I've ever seen." He laughs, shaking his head. "Or better yet, you see the one with the dark, curly hair? Charlotte, I think her name was?"

I nod my head, praying that he'll shut the fuck up. He's not helping me not think about Charlie. He doesn't shut up though. He keeps talking. "Now she's fucking hot. The tits on her?" He pulls his lip in between his teeth. "Mmm. Fuck. She can be my naughty nurse any day. She was busy when I left, but I'm thinkin' 'bout goin' back tomorrow and askin' her out. I'd break my no datin' rule for a chance at tappin' a bitch like that."

I'm trying so hard to ignore him. Trying not to go ballistic on him for even noticing Charlie's tits. He's just Jase and Jase is a dog. He talks shit about women all the time and he fucks a new one almost every night. I'm surprised the fucker's dick hasn't fallen off yet. But when he talks about tappin' Charlie, I can't take it anymore. Maybe it's the booze, but I can't help it when I spear his eyes with mine and growl, "Charlie's *mine*."

Jase's eyebrows raise high in surprise. "Yours? Since when is she yours? You claimin' that bitch?"

I hold his shocked eyes with my glare and keep growling. "Since now. She's mine. Off limits. Got me?"

Jase's face breaks out into an ear to ear grin. "Well fuck me sideways. I never thought I'd see the day when little Ryker Cole would meet himself a nice girl and become a family man."

I keep scowling at him which causes him to burst out laughing. "Ok. Ok man. I hear ya. She's yours. I'll go ask out the blonde one instead." He wags his eyebrows at me and then stands. "Gotta take a leak."

I watch him walk away, my mind running back over the conversation we just had. Jase had called me a family man. I'm no family man. *Why the fuck had I called her mine?* I have no intentions of ever seeing her again, but there's no way I'm letting that slutty fuck anywhere near her. She's a nice girl, just like Jase had said, and nice girls didn't belong to guys like me ... or him.

All my life, I'd stayed away from people that weren't related to the MC. This included women. I slept with a lot of them, but they were all club whores or friends of the MC, looking for a good time. From a young age, I'd promised myself that I wouldn't be responsible for ruining the lives of decent people by involving them in our chaos. It was something I'd seen happen before and I'd be damned if I was going to live through that shit again.

My mother had been a civilian. She'd met my father at a bar and they'd had a one night stand. That one night had turned into many nights and once she found out she was pregnant with me, he moved in with her. He never settled down though. He never married her. He continued to fuck any woman that looked in his direction and left my mom at home, alone, to raise me.

She was a good mother – great even. I can remember many little things about my time with her. I remember her reading me stories at bedtime and singing silly songs with me while giving me a bath. I remember her taking me to the park and out for ice cream. I also remember them fighting. It would wake me up in the middle of the night. It was always him screaming at her, her crying and the sounds of objects being hurled across the room. The next morning, he would be gone and she would be full of smiles, acting like nothing had happened, but even as a kid, I could see the sadness in her eyes and the bruises on her body.

One night, when I was six years old, three men had broken into our house and dragged me from the bed by my feet. When I cried out in shock and fear, one of them had drove his fist into my temple, causing my head to swim and my belly to hurl up everything I'd eaten that night.

They dragged me down the stairs to the living room where my mom was tied up on the floor. She was crying and saying something to me, but I couldn't understand her through the gag tied across her mouth. The three men had demanded to know where my father was, but neither of us knew. We hadn't seen him in over a week, which wasn't uncommon.

One of the men, the biggest one of the three, had pulled out a gun and pointed it at my mother's head. He screamed at her about his wife, saying something about how my father had taken her from him. I was too young to understand what he was talking about at the time, but now that I'm older, I know he was pissed because my father had banged his old lady. She'd cleaned out a substantial amount of money from their bank accounts and left him, taking off with my old man, and now he wanted to make him pay.

I'd watched, eyes wide with fear, as my mother cried and pleaded with her eyes. I knew all hope was lost when he placed the gun at her temple and she squeezed her eyes shut. He pulled the trigger.

Watching my mother being shot in the head is an image I see in my nightmares almost every night. I'd been a little kid and helpless at the time. Now, in my dreams, I'm a grown man and I fight back. I fight with everything I have in me, but I never save her. She always gets her brains blown all over the carpet.

My mother dead, the man turns to me and places the gun under my chin. "You tell your old man that we're even now." Then they left. I'd lain on the floor for a long time, staring at my mother. After what felt like hours, I went to the phone and dialed the only number I knew. Smokey.

That's why I don't get involved with civilians. My mother had been a good, ordinary person. Just like Charlie. She'd met my father and her life had gone to hell. She'd been brutally murdered because of him. That's the way it goes in my world, and that's why I can't claim Charlie as my own. No matter how bad I want to, I need to leave her to live her life free from that shit.

Chapter Six

Charlotte

Only one week after Smokey had died, life has gone back to business as usual. I haven't seen a single biker since that day I'd found Ryker shouldering his grief in the garden. I'm not exactly sure why, but that thought makes me anxious. I wonder how he's doing and how Smokey's funeral went, wishing that I could have said goodbye to him too. I don't like how we'd left things. Something feels ... incomplete somehow. I keep reminding myself that I was just his friend's nurse, but there's no doubt in my mind that we'd made a connection, and now that connection has been severed.

Walking home from yet another evening shift, I feel those eyes on me again. Fumbling my pepper spray out of my oversized purse, I hurry to my building, dropping the keys on my first attempt to unlock the front door. My heart beats frantically, panic clawing its way up my throat as I look around, convinced that someone is coming up behind me. Nobody's there. I feel foolish. My imagination is running away from me again.

Once the door is unlocked, I dash inside and push the security door closed, effectively locking myself in from the outside world. My chest heaves and my head feels light as I turn and rush to my apartment, locking the door once I get inside.

Relief washes over me as I lean my back against the barrier between me and whatever threat may be, but likely isn't, out there. After my breathing returns to normal, I push myself off the door and remove my shoes and jacket, placing them in the front closet. Sticking with my normal routine does little to calm my nerves. I'm shaking like a leaf and my nerves are shot.

Anna's at work and won't be home for a few more hours. About a month ago, she took a job at a local bar as a waitress. It's not the best job, but it pays the bills and she seems to enjoy it. I just hope that she doesn't fall back to her old ways, getting involved with more dangerous men. They are exactly her type and I fear she will get herself into even more trouble. She may be my older sister, but it seems like I'm the one that's always looking out for her, and it's been that way ever since I was old enough to talk.

After double checking that the door's locked, I head to my bedroom and change from my scrubs to a pair of cute and lacey pajamas. The pale blue tank top has a fringe of lace along the hem and around the chest. The tiny matching shorts are a bit darker, and covered in white and light green polka dots.

As I enter the bathroom to brush my teeth, I hear a click from the living room. *What the hell was that?* It sounded like the lock on the front door, but the only other person with a key to this place is Anna and she has about 4 more hours until her shift is over.

I stand in the bathroom, toothbrush in my mouth, frozen. My heart pounds frantically, causing the blood to rush behind my ears. I listen in petrified silence for any other noises. My mind goes back to that night a couple weeks ago, when I found the body outline on my rumpled bed. I don't know what to do. *Do I lock myself in the bathroom and wait for whoever it is to take what they want and go? Do I rush to my bedroom, lock the door and call the cops? Do I rush out and see who the fuck dares to enter my apartment without permission, scaring the shit out of me in the process?* My mind races to come up with a plan, while I stand there like a deer caught in the headlights. That's when I hear it.

The sound is so quiet, I almost miss it. A floorboard squeaking. The floorboards in the hallway squeak all the time when you step on them. Someone is out there, and I am in the first room of that short hall with the door wide open. My phone's in my bedroom, and the lock on the bathroom door is useless; anyone could break it down with little trouble. I need to get to my bedroom, which is at the end of the hall, not even ten feet from where I am standing. *I can do this.*

Quietly putting down my toothbrush, I face the door and clench my jaw in determination. My heart is pounding in my chest as I lean forward to peek around the corner to the living room. A jolt of fear shocks my body when I see him standing there, looking directly at me. Krueger. A Devil's Reject notorious for cutting people up with his favorite knife when they pissed him off or got in his way. He had always been the one that scared me the most. I never did like the way he always stared at me – like I was a piece of meat that he couldn't wait to take a bite out of with those nasty crooked teeth he had.

A yelp of surprise and fear escapes my throat as I dash towards my bedroom. My only thought is that I have to get to a phone and call for help. I haven't even made it halfway when his arms wrap around me, crushing me back into his chest. One hand covers my mouth and the other squeezes the breath right out of my lungs. I kick my legs frantically, struggling to break his hold, my screams muffled behind his giant meaty hand.

His chuckle is evil and vicious as he gives my body a shake. "Shut the fuck up, bitch!" He shakes me again and uses his hand to cover my nose and my mouth at the same time, cutting off my air supply. Panicking, I struggle harder, managing to kick his shin with my heel. "Fuck! Fucking cunt! Calm the fuck down."

Taking a couple steps forward, he presses my front into the wall, his body pinning me from behind. The hand over my mouth and nose changes position, allowing me to breathe again but still muffling my screams. He reaches down in front of me and grabs onto my crotch roughly, digging his fingers painfully into my most private place. I squeeze my eyes closed, crying out into his hand. He grinds his hips into my ass, his erection rubbing me through his jeans and my tiny shorts. Bile rises in my throat. "Keep struggling, honey. It turns me right the fuck on."

My body stills, fear causing my muscles to stay tense and my mind alert. His breath comes out rapidly, puffing across my cheek with each exhale. The stench is unbearable and I hold my breath to avoid taking it in. "That's a good girl. I ain't gonna hurt ya, but you and me need to have a little chat." He continues to cover my mouth and wraps his other arm around my chest, pinning my back to his front as he turns and walks us right into my bedroom.

"Now, I'm gonna remove my hand. We're gonna talk, and if you scream, I'll shut you up by cramming my cock down your fuckin throat. Got me?"

Fear and despair courses through me, and tears stream down my cheeks as I nod frantically, letting him know that I did indeed "get him." There's not a doubt in my mind he'll do exactly as he threatened. Slowly, he removes his hands and spins me around to face him before pushing me down into a sitting position on my bed. My whole body trembles violently, my mind racing to come up with some way to escape him. He says he just wants to talk, but I don't believe him for a second. The Devil's Rejects are known for being violent and vicious, and I know that no matter what he says, I may not survive this conversation.

He stands in front of me, leering with a cocky smirk on his face. I'd only met him a couple of times before, when I'd gone to the Devil's clubhouse to pick up Anna. Krueger had shown an interest in me both times. The problem with that was, his interest came out as crude come-ons and openly groping at me whenever he got close enough to touch. He made my skin crawl.

His hair is short and greasy, dandruff showing at his temples, proving his hygiene habits to be severely lacking. His eyes are beady and dark, his nose hooked and narrow like a beak. His nose and cheeks are covered in pockmarks and his lips are so thin they're virtually invisible. He only stands about three inches taller than my five and a half feet, his body thin and sinewy like a snake. It takes everything I have not to show my disgust. I'm in no position to piss him off.

"Fuck, you are one gorgeous bitch." He lifts his hand, rubbing the heel of it up and down over his erection. I stifle a gag, desperately trying to keep down the bile that keeps rising higher and higher in my throat. "I can see your nipples through that thin little shirt of yours."

His words cause my trembling to increase, and I quickly raise my arms, crossing them over my chest. He chuckles again and drops his hand. "Where's your fuckin sister? That bitch owes me money, and we had an arrangement. She didn't pay up, so I'm here to collect."

My mind races. Anna hasn't told me much about what went on with the Devils, but I know it was bad, and I know that she's completely terrified of them – Krueger especially. I need to tell him something to get him to leave, but there's no way in hell I'm giving up my sister. "I ... I ... I don't know. I haven't seen Anna in months." My fear causes my voice to stutter, and I pray he believes me and moves on.

His backhand knocks me back on the bed, clutching my busted lip, my nose dripping blood down the front of my shirt. The pain is excruciating and unexpected – I've never been hit before.

"Fucking LIES! I know that bitch lives here with you. I saw her shit in the other room when I was here a couple weeks ago. Now where. The. Fuck. IS SHE?" He roars, bending down to get directly in my face.

It makes sense now. It had been Krueger here that night. Krueger that had lain in my bed, doing God knows what.

Revulsion, anger and fear battle for first place in my mind, while I try to keep the tears at bay. Fuck him. He isn't getting his hands on Anna. Removing my hand from my bloody lip, an eerie calm washes over me. Anger courses through my veins.

"Fuck you! I won't tell you where she is. I don't care what you do. Leave my sister alone, you fucking psycho." The words rip from my throat before I can stop them, but I don't care. I meant every word – no way am I telling this bastard where my sister is. I brace myself, knowing that he's going to hurt me; I can take anything he does to me, if it means keeping my sister safe. *I hope.*

His face twists into a sinister sneer as he leans even farther into my space. "Oh honey. I love your filthy mouth. You really should have just told me where the bitch was, because now I'm gonna take my time with you. Your sister gave you to me fair and square, and if she isn't gonna pay up, I'm takin what's owed to me."

He lunges at me so fast, I don't have time to roll out of the way. His body pins me to the bed, the smell of cigarettes and body odor filling my nostrils. His infamous knife in his hand, the light glinting off the steel blade. I know he's not going to let me live through this, so I fight. I fight with everything I have. I scream and claw and kick and bite at any part of him I can connect with.

"Fuckin BITCH!" Krueger rears his arm back, punching his fist right into my temple. The room spins, my vision blurring. Nausea roils through my belly. My body stills as I try to keep from throwing up. His hands are all over me, squeezing my breasts and pulling on my shorts, yanking at them in a terrifying attempt to get them off. He presses his dry, chapped lips to mine and I break out of the daze his punch had caused. Opening my mouth, I bite down on his lip, drawing blood.

He screams. "FUCKIN CUNT!" He delivers another blow, to my cheek this time, and claws at my shirt. I buck and scream and flail my arms and legs, doing anything I can to get him off me. My heart is pounding and my breathing comes out fast and labored. Light headed, I feel like I'm going to pass out.

Krueger grinds his cock down onto my pubic bone, one hand squeezing my breast like a vice while the other embeds itself in my hair, effectively holding my head still. Flailing wildly, my hand catches the vase on the nightstand. It's still filled with the flowers I'd bought myself the other day. Reaching a little farther, my fingers catch the mouth, scrabbling to get a grip on it. The second I do, I lift it from the stand. Krueger is so caught up trying get my shorts off, he doesn't notice when I lift it as high as I can, above our heads. This vase is an heirloom; it's ceramic and heavy. If I hit him just right, I may just be able to get away.

Using every ounce of strength I have, I slam the vase down onto the side of his head. I know it won't knock him out, but it should knock him off me. Flowers and water spray us both as it shatters against his temple. He goes flying off me, landing on his back beside the bed, clutching his head and screaming obscenities at me. I scramble to my feet and turn to run, but I see him struggling to get up. Turning back to him, I use every ounce of strength I have and kick him right between the legs. I hope I knocked his balls right up into his nostrils. *Fucker.*

Turning again, I run from the room, getting the hell out of there.

***

Ryker

I don't know what the fuck is wrong, but this bitch just isn't doing it for me. It's been three days since we laid Smoke to rest, and seven days since I'd walked away from Charlie. My head is all kinds of fucked up, and I don't know what to do. I miss Smokey; it kills me inside that I won't ever see the crazy bastard again. There's some comfort in knowing that he went peacefully, and that he was prepared for his death. As for Charlie ... fuck. I feel empty; like I made the wrong choice turning away from her. That girl stars in almost every thought I have lately, and I want nothing more than to just show up at the nursing home, throw her over my shoulder like a caveman and claim her. But I can't do that. Not if I don't want her to end up like my mother.

I'm at The Pig's Ear tavern with a bunch of my brothers, knocking back a few pints to unwind after a shit week. The waitress had been rubbing her tits all over me, offering herself up on a silver platter. Normally, I would just fuck her and be done with it. I've had several offers this past week to get laid, but I can't get Charlie out of my mind.

This bitch though ... at first, she'd had potential. With her long, dark curly hair and big brown eyes, she looks enough like Charlie to make my dick stir in my pants. My thought was, I could fuck her, pretend she was Charlie and work that damn woman out of my system once and for all. It's not working though. She smells like cigarettes and cheap perfume, and she's moaning into my mouth like a porn star. It's not sexy at all. It's fucking annoying.

Earlier, when she'd called out that she was taking a break, grabbed my hand and dragged me back here to the staff room, I went willingly. Now, I'm just trying to ignore the stupid bitch, and imagine Charlie in her place – it's not working. Her hand's in my pants, jerking my cock and I'm not even hard. My hand's up her shirt, but it's doing nothing for me. Her tits are too small. Charlie's are bigger, fuller ... perfect. Just as I'm about to push her away and go back out to my beer, the door to the staff room flies open, slamming against the wall.

Our heads whip in that direction and I freeze when I see her. *What. The. Actual. Fuck?* Charlie is standing in the doorway, tearstains on her cheeks. Her nose is obviously broken, her eyes already starting to bruise. Her lip's busted and looks like it needs a couple of stitches. There's a large bruise at her temple and her hair's wild and falling from the ponytail that it'd once been in. She's wearing pajamas – tiny ones that would usually turn me right the fuck on, if it weren't for the fact that the strap on her tank top is torn and there's blood all over her shirt. I can see scratch marks on her chest and shoulders, and more bruises appearing on her upper arms. Her feet are bare and I can see scrapes on her toes from walking outside without shoes.

She stands there staring at us, her expression shocked and likely mirroring my own. That's when I realize that the waitress I was trying to lay the nuts too still has her hand down my pants, and I still have my palm wrapped around her tiny little tit. I jerk away like I've been burned, hurriedly fastening my pants.

The waitress recovers from her shock quickly and rushes over to Charlie, placing her hands on her upper arms. "Oh my God! Charlotte? What the hell happened to you? Are you ok?"

Charlie is still staring past her, eyes locked on mine. Anger fills her face before she swallows, giving her head a quick shake. "Anna. We need to talk. Now." Peeling her eyes off me, she looks to the waitress. "In private."

It's not until the waitress nods and moves to pull her out of the room that I pull my head out of my ass. "Charlie? Baby, what the fuck happened to you?"

Charlie ignores me, avoiding my eyes as she tugs on the waitress's arm. The waitress has a different idea. She looks pissed, standing beside the doorway, glaring at me. "Baby? Did you just call her baby?" She rips her arm out of Charlie's grasp and turns on her, hands resting on her scrawny hips. "What the fuck, Charlotte?"

Charlie's eyes fill with tears and she opens her mouth to reply, but I cut her off. Clearly this bitch needs a lesson. Charlie is standing here bleeding and crying, and she's pissed that I called her baby? Who the fuck is she?

"Charlie! Answer me." What I meant to be a demand came out more as a plea and her eyes shoot to me. The tears start falling freely down her cheeks and the thought of my Charlie being hurt almost brings me to my knees. I rush to her, ignoring the fuming waitress, and take her in my arms. At first, she resists so I lean in closer to whisper in her ear. "Babe. It's ok. You're safe now."

Her body relaxes slightly while she clutches me like I'm a lifeline. Her hands clutch the back of my shirt while she buries her face deep into my chest. The sobs that escape leave her gasping for air, and she trembles as I hold her tighter. Smoothing her hair back, I try my best to soothe her but I'm desperate to find out how she ended up beaten and bloodied, standing in the door to the staff room of a seedy bar. Her arms are cold, and I realize that her trembling may not be entirely from fear.

Without a thought, I whip off my leather cut and remove the long sleeved shirt I'm wearing. Pulling it over her head, I cover her before yanking my cut back on, over my bare chest. That done, I pull her back into my chest and hold her while she cries.

The waitress wisely takes a step back, glaring at us while I try to calm my girl down. When Charlie sniffs a couple more times and slowly pulls away, wiping the tears from her cheeks, the waitress pounces. "Charlotte Elizabeth Daniels! You mind telling me why you're here, crying all over this guy five seconds after I had my fucking hand wrapped around his cock?"

She flinches and her face pales as her eyes shoot from me to the waitress once again. Shaking her head quickly, she takes a couple steps back from me, putting too much distance between us.

"Anna, it doesn't matter. Ryker's just someone I met at work. What does matter is that we need to talk. I have a message for you."

Anna's face goes from annoyed to instantly terrified. "They found me?"

Charlie nods. "Oh no. Oh no oh no oh no oh no." Anna is backing farther away, hands over her mouth, freaking right the fuck out. I'm still stuck on why Charlie looks like she's been in a brawl and what the fuck she means about me being just a guy she met at work. I mean I am, but fuck ... I'm more than that, and she knows it.

"Enough!" My command makes both women yelp and turn their frightened faces towards me. "Charlie, you're gonna tell me what the fuck happened to you. Now."

She sighs, tears forming in her eyes again. "Ryker, I ..." She pauses and takes a deep breath. "I appreciate your concern, but this is between me and my sister." She motions towards Anna, who is still in the corner of the room, having what appears to be a full blown panic attack. My mind flashes back a few moments, to the part where she said this bitch is her sister. *Not good.*

"Bullshit. Baby you're standing here in front of me, after crying in my arms, looking like someone went at you with a god damned baseball bat. That automatically makes me involved. Now what the fuck happened?" My fists are clenched tightly and it takes everything I have in me not to wrap her in my arms again and make those tears go away.

"I'm fine, Ryker. Anna and I just have to talk, and then we'll be leaving. I appreciate your concern, but I'm ok." She attempts to smile but quickly changes her mind when she remembers her swollen, busted lip. Wincing, she covers it with her hand, but holds my eyes with a determined look on her face.

"My concern? Again, woman, you in front of me, half-dressed and bleeding is definitely my concern. Now, I'm not gonna fucking ask you again. Tell me what happened."

She sighs, her shoulders slumping in defeat. Looking around the room, she moves to close the door, shutting herself, her sister and me into the drab, little staff room. She then looks over to the small couch Anna and I were making out on, wrinkles her nose in disgust and moves over to the chair in the corner. Anna moves and sits on the couch. There's no way in hell I'm going to sit next to that bitch so I stand, arms folded over my chest and wait.

I wait some more while Charlie sits there, staring at her bare feet. Finally, I can't take it anymore. I need to know what happened to her and who hurt her. The anger I felt when I first saw her battered appearance is growing to a full on rage. I take the couple steps between us and kneel directly in front of her, lifting her chin until she meets my eyes, making an attempt to keep my voice calm and soothing. "Baby. I know somethin' bad has happened, but you really need to tell me what it was, and then I need to get you cleaned up and into some warmer clothes."

She nods before looking over at her sister. "I got off work tonight and walked home. I felt like I was being watched again." Her words cause me to still and my rage grows. *What the fuck does she mean "again"? Someone's been watching her?* "When I got home, nobody was there, but when I was in the bathroom, I heard someone in the apartment." Charlie fists her hands tightly in her lap.

"I tried to get to my room so I could lock myself in and call the police, but he caught me before I could." She pauses, then looks to her sister. "Anna? It was Krueger."

"No!" My back is to her, but I can hear the fear in Anna's voice. Krueger? I only know of one Krueger, and the guy is a fucking nightmare, worthy of his name. I'd met him on more than one trip to Toronto, and he gave even me the creeps. He's fucked in the head and had raped more than a few club whores that had been stupid enough to wander into his path. One of whom, he'd enjoyed taking his knife to. *But he's a Devil. There's no way my Charlie's messed up with the Devil's Rejects. Is there?*

Charlie nods her head slowly at her sister. "It was, honey. He grabbed me, roughed me up a little and demanded to know where you were." My eyes still locked on her, I can hear her sister's gasp of fear from behind me, and Charlie hurries to finish her story. Balling up my fists, I remain silent, waiting for the rest of it. "I didn't tell him. I didn't. That's what pissed him off. He was so angry." She inhales a shaky breath. "He said you owed him money, and that you had a deal he was here to collect on." Her voice softens to a whisper. "That's when he tried to rape me."

I spring to my feet and drive my fist into the wall. That fucker had tried to rape her? Had dared to lay a greasy finger on her? I'm gonna rip his fucking balls off and feed them to him.

My entire body shakes with rage. Anna is crying behind me, but now Charlie's looking at me. Trying to soothe me. Suddenly, Charlie's reaction to Reaper last week makes a whole lot more sense. She's had issues with the Devils.

"He didn't though. I managed to get ahold of a vase in my bedroom and hit him over the head with it. It knocked him to the floor and then I kicked him in the balls and ran. He didn't rape me. I'm ok." Her words don't help.

She grabs my hand and stands in front of me, placing her free hand on my cheek while I attempt to lock down the anger. "Ryker. I'm ok. Really. Now Anna and I need to talk, and figure out what we're gonna do because this guy will be back, and there's no way he's getting his hands on my sister." She stares up at me confidently. The look would be reassuring if it weren't for the bloody nose, black eyes and split lip.

I grab her shoulders, looking directly into her eyes. "Charlie, you and Anna aren't going anywhere. This guy ain't coming back, 'cause I'm gonna fucking find him, and then, I'm gonna kill him."

Chapter Seven

Charlotte

Shit! This whole night just keeps getting worse. I'd come to the tavern to get my sister, so we could come up with a plan to keep her safe. Walking in on her and Ryker ... my heart clenches just thinking about it. *How long have they been sleeping together? I have no right to feel this way. Ryker was never mine but ... God.* Watching Anna pull her hand out of his pants, while I stood there staring at them in shock, had made my already racing heart shatter into a million little pieces. Jealousy is a new feeling for me. I'm going to have to work hard at not reacting to the pain I'd felt when I found them about to make love.

While I was telling Anna and Ryker what happened, he'd been pissed – worried even. He was likely freaking out that there was a maniac out there, looking for Anna. He'd growled at us both that he would be right back and to stay put. Storming out of the room, he closed the door behind him, finally giving my sister and me a much needed moment of privacy.

"Anna." She's still sitting on the couch, fear her only expression. Her hands are pressed over her mouth, while she rocks back and forth. "Anna! Look at me. Honey, we need to go. We need to get our stuff and go!"

Letting out a keening moan, her face crumples and she sobs. "Oh Char. I am so sorry. I didn't think they would ever find us, but now …" She takes a deep breath and jumps to her feet. "You're right. We need to go. We need to be separate though. They'll keep tracking me down, and I can't ask you to keep uprooting your life."

"Honey, you're my sister. We're in this together. Now, let's get the hell out of here before it's too late." I grab her hand and we start for the door, just as it swings open.

"Going somewhere?" Ryker stands in the open doorway, arms crossed on his chest, two of his "brothers" standing behind him, looking angry and, quite frankly, terrifying. One of them is Reaper. The other one I'd seen around the nursing home visiting Smokey. It was hard not to notice him. He's almost as beautiful as Ryker.

"Ryker, we really need to get out of here. I –"

"You're not fuckin' going anywhere, Charlie." He steps into the room, followed by his two buddies. Reaper turns, closing the door behind them. "This here is Reaper and Jase. Reaper's a trained medic and he's gonna look you over."

My eyes widen in shock and fear. *Reaper's not looking at shit as far as I'm concerned!* I open my mouth to tell him as much, when he shoots me a leveling glare. "No arguments. You need medical attention. While he's takin' care of you, we're all gonna have a little chat about this Krueger guy, and why he's lookin' for you."

Anna's face crumples, and again, she bursts into tears. She flops back onto the couch, burying her face in her hands. "Oh

God. I am so sorry Char. So sorry. I never, ever thought he would find us."

Ryker moves to stand in front of her. "Who? Krueger?"

Anna yelps and nods her head quickly.

He squats in front of her and pulls her hands from her face, looking into her eyes. "How the fuck do you ladies know Krueger?"

Reaper distracts me by grabbing my arm and sitting me down in the chair. He opens a small first aid kit, pulling out gauze and band aids, littering them across the table beside me. He's surprisingly gentle and maybe slightly less terrifying than I'd previously thought. He tends my wounds while I watch the scene in front of me unfold.

Anna continues to cry and looks at Ryker. Her sobs cause her words to come out in gasps. "A couple months before we left, I borrowed money from him. I borrowed some from a couple of the other guys too. When I couldn't pay them back from the money I expected to get from Mom's inheritance, I avoided them. They found me, and that's when they broke my arm and beat the shit out of me." She takes a deep breath and looks to me. "That's when I made them a deal."

"What deal?" Ryker growls. I'm glad he did because I want to know too. What did she borrow money from an MC for? And why would she think she'd get an inheritance after Mom died? What the hell was going on in her head?

"I ... I promised them ..." She chokes on another sob and squeezes her eyes closed in defeat.

"Damnit, woman! What did you promise them?" Ryker's pissed. He's visibly trying to suppress his rage, but his voice rumbles with fury.

Anna yelps before rushing to answer. "Charlotte. I promised them Charlotte." She slaps her hands back over her mouth in fear, her eyes darting around the room.

Everyone in the room is frozen in shock. My body goes stiff when I register what my crazy, stupid sister had just said. *She'd promised them me? What does that even mean?* Jase is still standing by the door, but he's standing like a statue, a shocked, angry look on his face. Even Reaper has stopped wiping the blood from under my nose, his hand still hovering in the air with the disinfectant covered cotton ball between his fingers.

Anna is frozen solid, fearful eyes glued to the man standing in front of her. Ryker is frozen in place, eyes wide. His body is vibrating and rage engulfs his features. "What the fuck do you mean you promised them Charlotte?"

"Krueger told me he'd forgive all my debts if he could have my sister. He wants her ... to own her. He's been obsessed since he first saw her." She shoots her eyes to me and whispers, "Oh Char. I'm so sorry." Tears fall down her cheeks. I can't bring myself to care. She'd intended to just give me to that ... psychopath?

"I was never gonna let him have you, Char. I just wanted him to leave me alone. They were gonna kill me! I just – "

"Enough!" The roar breaks the shocked vibe in the room and causes both me and Anna to jump. Ryker spins towards me and stalks over. Reaper has gone back to working on my battered face, so he kneels to the side, looking me in the eye. "That fucker is not getting anywhere near you, Charlie. I'm gonna deal with him. Ok?" I'm mesmerized by those blue eyes. They're looking at me, full of determination and anger, mixed with tenderness and something else I can't put my finger on. I nod my head slightly, not wanting to hinder Reaper's work as he applies some sort of greasy ointment to my cut lip. I'm in shock, my mind numb. *She was going to give me to Krueger? What kind of person sells out her sister for a few dollars?*

Ryker stands and looks to Jase. "Head over to Charlie's place. Make sure that son of a bitch is gone. I'm gonna bring her by later to grab some things and I don't want him makin' another play for her. Take Mouse with ya."

Jase nods and looks to me. "What's your address, sweetheart?"

I rattle off the address, my head spinning from everything that's happened tonight. Jase turns and leaves. Ryker opens the door, calling out to him. "Send Bone in here. He's takin' Anna to the clubhouse." Coming back into the room, he shuts the door, then spins to face us.

"Alright ladies, this is how it's gonna happen. Anna, you're goin' with Bone. He'll take you to the clubhouse, set you up in a room and keep an eye on you. No phones, no leaving. Got me?" Anna just nods her head, clearly not about to argue with a pissed off, determined Ryker. Even though the jealousy I've been feeling flares again, I'm glad my sister has him to take care of her. This is one mess I just can't save her from.

"Charlie." My eyes shoot to him. "You're comin' with me. We're gonna get your shit from your place once Jase clears it, then we're headin' to my house where I can keep an eye on you." He doesn't wait for a reply, and right then, there's a knock on the door.

His house? Why would he send Anna to the clubhouse with this Bone guy and take me to his house?

Before I know it, Anna is gone with Bone, Reaper has patched me up, and Ryker is pulling me out of the tavern towards a very large, very scary looking motorcycle.

He reaches behind the bike and grabs a helmet, plunks it on my head, then reaches out to do up the strap, while I stand there unmoving. When he's done, he places a finger under my chin and lifts my face to meet his eyes. "Baby. It's gonna be ok. I'm not gonna let anything happen to you, and that fucker is gonna pay for hurtin' you."

Tears fill my eyes as I look into his and nod my head. He grins at me, clearing some of the fog that's been swirling around my mind. *Mmmmm. Dimple.*

After swinging his leg over the bike and turning on the motor, he looks to me. "Hop on, baby."

Approaching the death machine, I pray that I don't make an ass of myself and send us both falling to the ground. I've never been graceful, and I'm worried the size of my ass is going to make the bike groan in protest when I sit on it. Ryker watches me while I send up a silent prayer before swinging my leg up and over the seat behind him.

"Hang on, baby girl." He has to yell to be heard over the sound of the bike's motor. I grab onto the sides of his leather cut and close my eyes tightly, glad that my place isn't too far. I've never been on a motorcycle before, it's not something I thought I'd ever do. Grabbing my hands, he jerks them around his waist, pulling me up against his back. "I said hang on."

I do. I hang on for dear life as he lifts his feet, and then, we're roaring out of the parking lot. I'm barely aware of how fast we're moving, my fear temporarily forgotten when I realize I'm pressed up against Ryker's muscled body. He smells of leather, and deodorant, and man. It's intoxicating.

I'm still shoeless, only wearing his long sleeved shirt over my torn pajamas. I'm freezing my ass off, so I do my best to ignore the flutter in my belly as I try to press as much of myself as possible up against his hard, warm body. My hands are pressed flat against his bare belly, under his cut. Knowing that my hands are resting against his perfectly formed six pack causes my belly to flutter. He turns, giving me a wink over his shoulder before placing a warm hand on my arm around his waist, giving it a squeeze. I pray that he can't feel my heart pounding against his back.

Before I know it, we pull up to my building, where Jase, and who I assume is Mouse, are waiting beside their bikes. Jase walks over and offers me his hand, helping me off the bike. His smile is warm and appealing, and I find myself smiling back as I send him a quick "Thanks." His grin widens and he continues to hold my hand, rubbing his thumb along the back of it in slow strokes.

Ryker is suddenly there, grabbing my hand from him, taking it into his own. He glares at Jase, who smirks and puts his hands up in a surrendering motion. "Apartment's clear. Nobody's there. The one bedroom's a mess, obvious signs of a struggle." He looks at me and smiles. "I gotta say though girl, Krueger is a fuckin' maniac. I'm impressed that you were able to get away with as little damage as you did. You're one tough little lady."

I don't know what to say to that, so I stay silent. Ryker places his arm around my shoulder, squeezing tightly. "Come on baby. You gotta be freezin' your ass off out here. Let's get you into some warm clothes." Turning, he leads me off to my apartment.

***

Ryker

I can tell Charlie is scared shitless to go back into her place. Her body trembles, and I know it's not just the cold causing it. I keep my arm wrapped tight around her, leading her inside. She looks around the living room, clearly expecting someone to jump out at her.

Placing my hands on her shoulders, I turn her towards me. "Baby, nobody's here. You're safe with me and you're gonna stay that way." The fear in her face relaxes a bit before she nods and smiles softly. The fact that I've calmed her fears makes me feel like the king of the fucking world. This woman trusts me and feels safe with me and that blows me away; especially after everything she's been through.

"Grab your shit. Not too much. Only as much as we can carry on my bike. Try to get enough stuff for a few days though." Nodding, she starts for the short hallway. Once in her room she freezes. I come up behind her and instantly see why. Her eyes are on a broken vase and flowers scattered across her bed and floor. Blood spatters the white and green quilt and the bed itself looks like it had been used as a fucking trampoline. Placing my hands on her shoulders once again, I give them a slight squeeze. "Babe. Grab your shit."

She nods absently, still looking at her fucked up bed, then moves to the closet where she pulls out an oversized sweater and a pair of yoga pants. Turning to me, then looking back to her clothes, she looks uncertain. I continue to stare at her, wondering what the fuck is taking so long when she finally speaks.

"Um, Ryker could you ..." She trails off, chewing on her lower lip. She winces when she accidently nibbles on the place where it's split. I raise my brows in question as she takes a deep breath before continuing. "Could you turn your back?" She holds up the clothes in her hands. "I don't want to be alone, but I really need to change."

Like the gentleman I am, I nod curtly and turn my back, giving her some privacy. She doesn't get any though – not when I realize I can still see her through the mirror hanging above the dresser.

She stares at my back for a moment before turning slightly and pulling off her shirt. Next she removes her tattered tank top. *Fuck. Me.*

Charlie's naked body makes my mouth run dry. I can't peel my eyes away from her. Her tits are fucking perfect. Big, but not huge, perky, and tipped with the tightest dusky pink nipples I've ever seen. I may be a total dick for watching her without her knowing, but I can't fucking help myself. She's fucking gorgeous.

My cock roars to attention as she pulls on her oversized University of Toronto hoodie, then shimmies out of her tiny little polka dot pajama shorts. I lose the battle with my rock hard cock when I get a glimpse of her in that tiny little white thong. Perfection. Her waist is slim, and from the angle of her ass that I can see, it's round and firm. Her legs are muscular and long, just the perfect length for wrapping around my hips … or shoulders. Reaching down, I readjust my straining erection just as she pulls her tight as fuck yoga pants up and over those trim hips.

"All done." I turn as she tosses me my shirt, then moves back to the closet. Grabbing a backpack, she begins stuffing it with clothes and toiletries. I stay silent, willing my cock to go back to sleep when I notice her folding up her scrubs to put into the bag.

"No need for those, baby." Her eyes shoot to mine, a frown creasing her brow as I continue. "You won't be going to work for a while. At least not until I can make sure Krueger is history."

She places her hands on her hips. "I need to work, Ryker."

"Sorry, babe. Not gonna happen. That dumb fuck knows where you live and where you work. He's been watching you. Said so yourself. Until we can get him dealt with, you're on vacation."

Now her frown goes from one of confusion to one of anger. "Ryker ... I appreciate you helping Anna and I out, and protecting us from the Devils, but I can't just not work because of them. My job's important to me. I can't just end my career because some psycho tried to ..." She chokes up, not able to say the words. Watching her struggle because of what that fucker did pisses me off even more.

"Rape you?" I growl the words angrily, arching my eyebrow in a challenging look. "Charlie, that fucker came into your home and tried to rape you. He hurt you." My chest burns with rage, the burn getting stronger as I look around the room and picture him putting his hands on her, knowing that she had to defend herself with a vase of fucking *flowers.* "You're *not* going to work until we find him. I won't argue on this. Not even an hour ago, you were ready to skip town altogether, so what does it matter? People die all the time, Charlie. We'll find you another job when this blows over."

A tear rolls down her cheek, dripping from her chin. She stares at me, her eyes blank – empty. Watching her, I swear to myself that for every tear she cries over Krueger, that sick fuck will meet his own blade. One slice per tear. Every fucking one.

Finally she nods, throws the scrubs on the rumpled bed and continues to fill her bag. Once she's done, she moves to stand in front of me. Reaching out, I take her bag and grab her hand in mine. Leading her out of the apartment, we walk hand in hand to my waiting bike.

Chapter Eight

Charlotte

Ow. I pull in a shaky breath and try to force my eyes open. My head is pounding. My nostrils are full of a familiar, welcoming smell. *What is that?* I finally win the battle with my eyelids and peel them open. *Where the fuck am I?* I lay there for a minute, looking around the unfamiliar room and try to figure out what the hell is going on. The room is small and contains only a bed, nightstand and dresser for furniture. Other than a lamp and blinds, there's no décor in this room at all. I lay in a large rumpled bed that contains a smell I recognize instantly. Ryker.

The events of last night come back to me in a rush. Sitting up quickly, I gasp for air, trying to control my rapidly conflicting emotions. Krueger, my bedroom, smashing my favorite vase on his head, Ryker and Anna groping each other in the staff room, and then, Ryker whisking us both off to safety. My head throbs, causing stabbing pains to my nose and cheekbones. Slowly, I lift a shaky hand to my face and gasp. My nose is swollen, which explains the need to breathe through my mouth. My cheek feels puffy and tight.

I don't remember much from last night, after we left my apartment. I vaguely remember Ryker pulling up to a tiny white house in the middle of nowhere, and leading me inside. He'd tossed me one of his t-shirts and told me to get ready for bed. I'd been like a zombie, just going through the motions. I pulled on the shirt, crawled into his bed without argument and was dead to the world within seconds.

A glance at the clock, sitting on the battered old nightstand, tells me that it's almost eleven o'clock in the morning. Figuring I'll find Ryker asleep on the couch, I pull on my yoga pants, quickly run my fingers through my hair and leave the bedroom in search of him. The house isn't very big and the living room is just down a short hallway so I find it quickly. The couch is older and worn, but comfortable looking. I notice that just like his bedroom, the living room has very little furniture and no decorations or personal effects at all. Nothing to hint about the person who lives here. I also notice that Ryker is not in here, so I wander into the kitchen.

Again, no personal touches at all – just a sparse kitchen, with a small table and four chairs in the corner. The place is clean and tidy. It's also empty. *Where is he?* I look outside and see a motorcycle. Moving to the front door, I slowly push it open. The screen door squeaks on it's hinges. Outside, a very large man in a leather cut stands from where he was sitting on the front step. Yelping loudly, I stop mid-step.

Taking a step back inside, I pull the screen door half closed and look through it. He's about six feet tall, in his early twenties and covered in brightly colored tattoos. I notice right away that his cut represents the Kings and not the Devils so I relax a fraction. When my eyes meet his, my relaxation fades and fear fills me again. His eyes are dark and cold. He's an attractive man, but the hard expression he wears makes him look intimidating and menacing.

His jaw is covered with several days of dark stubble and there's a deep scar slashing across his right cheek. He stares back at me, and the longer I stare at him, my mouth open in fear, the angrier he looks.

"Like what you see?" Anger and sarcasm drip from his voice.

Realizing too late that he thinks I'm staring at his scar, I close my mouth and try to find my voice. "Sorry. I – I – I'm just looking for Ryker?" I try to smile at him politely, but I know it looks phony. I'm scared out of my mind.

"He ain't here." He turns away then and sits down on the step once again, his back to me. From the back, I take in his muscled frame and the back of, what even I have to admit, is an extremely sexy fauxhawk.

"Do – do- um … you don't happen to know when he'll be back, do you?" I'm trying so hard to sound natural but I'm stuttering like a fool.

He doesn't even turn around to look at me. "No," is all he says, telling me that I've been dismissed.

"Okay. Um … thanks." I stare at his back for another moment, trying to figure out what the hell to do now, before I turn and close the door behind me. I make sure to lock it.

Now what? I don't even know where I am. Taking another look around at Ryker's small house, I swallow the bubble of panic rising in my chest. I need to talk to my sister. Ryker is probably with her. He's said he was having her taken to the "clubhouse," so

I assume that's where he went. I'm amazed at the jealousy I feel over their relationship. Ryker isn't mine to be possessive of, and he seems like a good person, biker status aside. I should be happy that my sister finally has someone good in her life. *Shouldn't I?*

Sighing sadly, I go back to the bedroom, grab my stuff and go to the bathroom to take a shower. I might as well get ready for the day. When Ryker comes home, he will take me to Anna, and then we can figure out what's next.

***

Ryker

I finally roll back into my driveway in the middle of the night. Tease is already mounting his bike as I pull to a stop. With a quick nod, he speeds down the drive and out onto the road. Tease is a prospect, and a man of few words. He got his name after beating the shit out of one of the biggest sons of bitches I've ever seen, after the guy had the balls to make fun of his scar. He's not a fan of being teased. He doesn't talk much, and has absolutely zero sense of humor, but he's loyal and one tough motherfucker. I'd felt safe leaving him to protect Charlie today.

It'd been a long ass day, and I want nothing more than to crawl into bed, where Charlie lays, warm and sleeping. After she'd passed out the night before, I'd stripped down to my boxer briefs and crawled in beside her. She'd smelled so fucking good. My erection had started before I'd even gotten into bed with her, but the moonlight on her face revealed the bruises and steri-strips holding her cheek together. Rage once again took over, quickly deflating my overeager cock.

I'd woken up early and set off to find Krueger. I wanted that fucker dead. He didn't know it yet, but hurting Charlie was the biggest mistake of his life. It felt like a personal attack, even though he didn't know she knew me. The possession I feel towards her is overwhelming and I can't figure it out. *What is it about her that makes me want to kill any son of a bitch that even looks at her?* I don't want an old lady, and there's no way there can ever be anything between us, but knowing that doesn't make me want her any less. It also doesn't mean that I'm not going to do everything I can to bring that psycho bastard down, so he can't lay a finger on her ever again.

For the second night in a row, I look down at my bed to see Charlie sleeping peacefully. Her dark hair is spread out in a fan across my pillows, and I can smell her fresh, floral scent from where I stand. The room is dark so I can't make out the severity of her bruising, but I can see places on her face that are darker than they should be. Anger churns in my gut. Swallowing it down, I once again strip down to my boxer briefs and crawl into bed beside her. She lays on her side with her back towards me so I curl up behind her, needing to be close to her – reassuring myself that she's still safe.

Draping my arm around her middle, I pull her back into me, curling myself into her. When her warm body hits mine, I have to think ugly thoughts to will my cock into submission. I lose when she squirms her round little ass into me. *Fuuuuck. She fits me perfectly.* She's so fucking sexy and I know she doesn't even know it.

Feeling her close to me, I can't help myself. Tilting my head, I shove my nose into the crook of her neck and inhale her sweet scent. It calms my rage, if not my hard on. I lay there holding her tight to me, inhaling her smell, when she takes in a deep breath, yawning.

Turning her head slightly, she looks back at me. "Ryker? Where have you been?" Sleep and confusion cloud her voice as she tries to sit up, but my hold on her is solid. "Why are you – " She struggles against me, trying to sit up again. I let her go instantly when I feel her panic. The reminder of what she'd been through the night before fuels my ever present anger. Sitting up quickly, she whips around to face me.

"Where have you been? I woke up and you were gone! The scary guy at the door just said you weren't here, but wouldn't tell me anything. I don't even know where the fuck I am! Did you see Anna? Is she ok? When can I see her? When can I go home? Why did you –" The questions pour from her mouth in a rush. She's had all day to stew, likely going crazy with worry and boredom, but I've had a shit day and I'm exhausted.

"Shhhh, baby girl. I promise, I will tell you everything, but right now, I just want to curl up in this bed and pass the fuck out. Can we save the game of twenty questions for morning? Please."

She must hear the exhaustion in my voice because she's quiet. Her body relaxes before she replies, "Okay. I'll just go sleep on the couch. Let you have your bed back."

I wrap my arm around her waist before she can escape, and drag her back into me until we're spooning again. "Like fuck you will. You're stayin' right here, woman. Now, sleep."

She lays stiff in my arms. A moment passes before I hear her swallow thickly. "Um … Ryker?"

I groan. "Babe. Just chill the fuck out and sleep."

"Um ... I will. I just … why do you want me to stay here? I'm not comfortable sleeping all cuddled up to my sis –"

"Seriously. Babe. I'm tired as fuck. You're tired. I just want to lay here with you and sleep, feelin' you beside me so I know you're fuckin safe. It's the only way I'll get any sleep so just lay there, shut it and go the fuck to sleep. Ok?"

"K," she whispers. *So fucking cute.* After a couple minutes, her body relaxes and I pull her closer. It doesn't take long before her breathing evens out and I know she's asleep. I plan on telling her everything I know, but the truth is, right now, I don't know much at all and that pisses me off. Krueger's in the wind, and I don't know where to even begin to look for him, but I'm positive that he's still around. He wouldn't give up that easy. Truth is, Charlie getting the better of him last night would have just pissed him off even more.

I want to kill her crazy fucking sister for practically handing her to him. I have no clue how I'm going to get her out of this mess, but I will stop at nothing to save her. Pressing my nose into the crook of her neck once again, I let her sweet, feminine scent lull me into a deep sleep of my own.

Chapter Nine

Charlotte

It's been three days since Krueger assaulted me in my apartment. Three nights of sleeping in Ryker's bed, with Ryker in it. Likewise, it's been three mornings that I've woken up to an empty bed and an empty house, with the exception of the angry ogre on the front step. The only thing I've learned in those three days is that the ogre's name is Tease. *Strange.*

To say I'm angry is putting it mildly. I'm pissed. One minute I'm coming home from work, the next, I have a psychopathic biker trying to claw his way into my panties. I finally free myself from that situation, only to be whisked away to God knows where, and left on my own. Ryker's gone each morning when I wake up and doesn't come home until long after I'm asleep. He still hasn't answered any of my questions, and I've had enough.

I've searched this house high and low, looking for a phone but there isn't one. I can't call a cab without it, and I know that I'm not close enough to the city to just walk home. There's no way that Tease will let me leave either. I'm a prisoner. Tonight, my plan is to stay awake and confront Ryker as soon as he walks through that door. I will not go another night without getting the answers I need.

I've spent the day cleaning Ryker's already clean house, and reading the only book that I could find. The Outsiders. *Good thing it's one of my favorites.* It's nearing midnight, and I'm struggling to stay awake when I hear the roar of a motorcycle coming up the driveway. Running to the window, I see Ryker pulling up in front of the house and Tease walking to his own bike. The two exchange a couple of words, then Tease is leaving and Ryker is walking up the front steps.

I position my body a few feet in front of the front door, hands on my hips. There's no way in hell he's avoiding me tonight.

He enters quietly but stills when he sees me. A grin spreads across his face. *Fucking stupid, gorgeous dimple.* "Hey, baby girl." Coming the rest of the way into the house, he turns to close the door. Turning back to me, he takes a few steps in my direction. "I'm surprised you're still awake."

I'm beyond pissed. I know that I've gone along with everything Ryker's told me to do up to this point, but I was in shock then – I'm not in shock anymore. Now I'm just angry at being practically kidnapped, then ignored entirely. "Oh, I'm awake. Wide awake. I'm not waiting anymore Ryker. Tell me what the fuck is going on. Everything." Anger colors my voice.

His grin gets wider, which only makes him even more beautiful. His stupid, sexy grin isn't going to distract me though. "You pissed at me Charlie?"

His apparent amusement at my anger throws me a little. *What a dick!* "Yes! I'm very pissed at you, Ryker. And my name is Charlotte. Not baby, not baby girl, and especially not Charlie. Nobody calls me Charlie."

"I call you Charlie." He takes another step, putting himself directly into my space. "Now *Charlie*, why are you so pissed at me?"

His sexy grin, and the closeness of his body, cause my heart to pound in my chest. My brain forgets everything I'd rehearsed saying to him while I sat and stewed all day. "I – I'm pissed because ... well because you practically kidnapped me, dropped me here, have told me not one thing about what is going on, and I don't know where my sister is, *and* you told me that you'd tell me, but you've conveniently been gone since we had that conversation." I'm out of breath after that run on sentence, and my chest heaves while I glare into his amused eyes.

"That's a long list, baby girl." His eyes dance with laughter as he takes in my glare. "Should I address your issues in order, or was one more important than the other?"

"I don't give a fuck Ryker, as long as you finally fucking address them!"

He chuckles. "Ok. First of all, I did not kidnap you. I brought you to my *home,* so that I could ensure your safety. I'm sorry that I haven't told you anything, but to be honest, until today there wasn't a whole lot to tell. Your sister's still at the compound. I haven't seen her, but Bone assures me she's scared but fine. Lastly, I've been gone because I've been trying to get a lock on Krueger, which today, I finally made some progress."

I stand there staring at him, waiting for him to continue. "We gonna stand by the front door for this conversation, or do you wanna sit down?"

I blink, then turn and move to the couch, turning my body so I'm facing him. Sitting beside me, he angles himself in my direction. "The first couple of days, Krueger was in the wind. No sign of him in the area. We have a shaky relationship with the Devils. For years, our two clubs were not friendly, but since our old Prez died and we got a new one, we've slowly mended fences. It took until today to finally get ahold of one of them. I explained the situation, and told them that you and your sister were under our protection. They were pissed. They agreed to back off you, but they still want the money your sister owes them."

"I don't understand why she borrowed money from them in the first place." I have been over and over this in my mind, and I just can't figure it out. What did Anna need that money for? We may not have had everything our heart's desired growing up, but we made it work. *What did she need that was so important that she'd trade me to get it?*

"I don't know either, but she owes them almost fifteen thousand."

I gasp. Fifteen thousand? Why the hell would she borrow fifteen thousand dollars from a biker gang?

Ryker reaches out and grasps my hand. "Here's the thing. Because our relationship with the Devils is shaky, we have to tread lightly. We're going to help your sister stay hidden until she can come up with the fifteen grand, and they've assured us that they'll call Krueger off you. I don't know that I trust them completely, so we're gonna keep a man on you until we can sort this shit out. You'll stay here with me in the meantime, but you can go back to work, if that's what you wanna do."

I stare at him in surprise. "What do you mean stay with you?"

"I don't want you goin' back to your place until I know for certain that bastard's gone. Anna made it seem like he's got a hard on for you, so I don't trust him to back off that easily. Especially after you kicked a field goal with his testicles."

At his mention of hard on, my mind flashes back to the night Krueger assaulted me, rubbing his erection through his pants. I shiver in revulsion.

Ryker reaches out and gently cups my cheek, his thumb drifting along my cheekbone. "He's not gonna get near you again, Charlie. Do you trust me?"

I'm shocked to realize that I do. Ryker has done nothing but try to protect me, and I trust him with my life. Looking up to meet his eyes, I nod.

He smiles. "Good girl."

My return smile is a little shaky, but my rage is gone, and I'm relieved to know that Anna's protected and Ryker is dealing with Krueger. I'm also happy to know I can return to work. I'll have to call them and come up with a good story to explain my absence the other night, but the last two nights were my days off so technically, I've only missed one shift.

"Let's get you to bed. I need a shower, and then I'm gonna crash." He stands and holds out his hand. When I take it, he leads me to the bedroom. Leaning in, he places a soft kiss on the top of my head. "Sleep, baby girl."

When he turns and leaves the room, he's not even aware that he'd just caused my heart rate to double with that sweet kiss.

***

Ryker

Leaving Charlie in my room, I quickly shower and tug on a clean pair of boxer shorts. I prefer to sleep naked, but she may not be quite so cool with that.

Crawling into bed, I'm surprised to see she's still awake. She rolls over, facing me in the dark. "Ryker?"

Hearing her whisper my name, while lying in my bed is a total mind fuck. I shouldn't be here with her. I need to get out of this bed. I need to move to the couch. I need to stay here and just be close to her. I need to kiss her sweet lips. I need to touch her.

Reaching out, I lay my hand on her cheek, stroking her cheekbone with my thumb. "Hmmmm?"

"Why are you helping me?" I blink in surprise, but before I can answer, she rushes on. "I mean, I know that you and Anna are … are whatever you are so, I get why you'd help her, but why me?"

I can't contain the chuckle that escapes my throat. "Anna and I? Babe, Anna and I are nothing."

"But … but you … she –"

"Your sisters a skank baby girl." Her body stiffens, but I continue. "Just a warm body that'll spread her legs for anyone." I shake my head. "I'd never even met your sister before the other night, and I gotta say Charlie, I do *not* like her at all."

She props herself up on her elbow, and I can see her cocked eyebrow in the moonlight. "Don't like her?" Her voice is laced with disbelief. "You sure seemed to like her when she had her hand down your pants!"

Holding her gaze, I shake my head. "Nope. Not even then. I only followed her into that room because, honest to God Charlie, she looked a fuck of a lot like you." I hear her surprised intake of breath. "I'm helping you because Krueger is a sick fuck, and I'll be damned if I'm gonna just step aside and let him have you. I'm helping Anna because she's important to you, not to me. I just want to make sure you're safe."

In the dim light streaming through the window, I watch her nose scrunch up in confusion. "But I thought ... you and Anna? I thought you were together?"

"You thought wrong, baby girl. I didn't even know her name 'til you stormed in." I give her cheek another stroke, bringing my face closer to hers. "You're the reason I'm doing this. Not her."

She swallows thickly. "Oh."

I grin. She's so goddamned cute.

She continues to whisper, "Do you really think he'll leave me alone?"

Moving my hand to the back of her head, I pull her into me and press my lips to her forehead. "I'll make sure of it, baby girl."

She nods and looks up at me. Our faces are so fucking close. Her breaths fan across my lips, smelling like the mint toothpaste from my bathroom. Lowering my eyes, I stare at her full pouty lips just as her little pink tongue darts out to moisten them. I can easily imagine them wrapped around my cock. Her eyes are locked on *my* lips, her breaths coming more rapidly.

"Fuck it." Using the hand at the back of her neck, I yank her face to mine, claiming her mouth with my own. She gasps. My body hums with electricity and my tongue darts forward, tasting her. Her floral scent surrounds me and my cock jumps to attention. Sliding her tongue along mine, she lets out a sexy little growl. She wraps her arms around my neck, pulling my body into hers.

Tilting my head, I deepen our kiss and wrap my arm around her tiny waist, bringing our bodies even closer. Hitching her leg up over my hip, she uses her foot to pull me into her. Bodies locked together, hearts pounding, we kiss like our lives depend on it. I swear it's this moment that I become hers. My chest burns with an unfamiliar emotion. Sex for me has never been about emotion, but this … this is different. I feel something intense for her, and if my dick wasn't screaming for attention, I would take the time to figure out what that something is.

I can't stop. I need to feel her. Every single part of her. Running my hand down her back, I cup her tight, round ass. She moans into my mouth, grinding her hips into mine. I can't contain the moan that escapes me. My heart pounds out of control as I grind my hips back against her. Reaching down with both hands, she grabs onto my ass, pulls me into her and rubs that sweet pussy over my boxer clad erection.

Fuck me. I feel like a fifteen year old boy. I'm so close to coming just from dry humping this girl, but I don't even care – it feels so fucking good. I've fucked a lot of women over the years, all of them were too easy. They all begged for it but I always knew if I said no, they'd just go and find someone else's cock to ride. Charlie's different. I can almost taste her innocence. She's nothing like the other women I'd been with.

Her hands roam up and down my back as she continues to grind against me. She's wearing nothing but a pair of cotton panties and my old AC/DC t-shirt. Those panties are soaked, her wetness coming right through the material of my boxers, driving me fucking crazy. Reaching my hand up her shirt, I palm her tit, rubbing my thumb quickly back and forth over the hard peak of her nipple. My other hand on her hip, I guide her body as we continue to grind against one another. Breathing heavily, she lets out a moan from deep in her throat. I know she's about to come. *Fuck.* I'm close too. I pinch her nipple, hard. Her breath catches in her throat, and she's done for. She screams out my name, her body shaking with her release. *So fucking hot.*

Her hips still, then she's reaching down the front of my shorts, grasping my aching cock. My breath hitches and her eyes pierce mine as she runs her thumb over the tip, collecting the little bead of pre-come sitting there. I can't tear my eyes from hers. Just when I think she's going to stroke me, she pulls her hand away. I growl in protest, but she stops me before I can move. Looking me right in the eye, she pulls her thumb deep into her mouth. Sucking it slowly, she closes her eyes and moans. Watching her, it takes everything I have not to come in my pants. "Fucking Christ, baby." Charlie is a naughty girl after all.

Opening her eyes, she looks into mine once again, running her tongue along her lower lip. She reaches back into my pants and slowly strokes my cock. It's my turn to close my eyes. *Fucking heaven.* She only strokes me about five times before I feel the familiar tightening in my spine. White hot pleasure builds in my groin. My orgasm takes over and I call out her name, pumping roughly into her hand. "Jesus fuck."

Fifteen year old boy or not, that was one of the hottest fucking things that's ever happened to me. A hand job from this woman beats the hell out of every threesome and foursome I'd ever participated in. Charlie removes her hand and smiles at me. Her smile causes my heart to stutter in my chest. Smiling back at her, I lean in and kiss her sweet mouth. Pulling back, I look into her eyes, and flooded with emotion, I lean in again, giving her a peck on the nose.

"Let's get you cleaned up, baby." Climbing out of bed, I go to the bathroom to get a wet cloth.

Chapter Ten

Charlotte

I wake up wrapped in the familiar smell of Ryker. Opening my eyes, my vision fills with a muscular chest and tattoos. My head rests on his shoulder, our legs tangled together under the blankets. *Oh. My. God.* The memory of last night comes flooding back to me. Ryker and I making out, my uncharacteristically bold move of licking the come from the end of my thumb. My cheeks heat when I remember his delicious, salty taste. I don't know what had come over me. I've never been so bold. I'm not a virgin, but my sexual encounters have all been with one man, and I can count them on one hand. Last night blew those few encounters out of the water.

Ryker sets me on fire. He's undeniably the sexiest man I've ever met – not to mention talented. The man could kiss. I tilt my head and look at his perfect lips. His jaw is covered in dark stubble, his lips pink and full. The familiar heat of arousal begins in my belly as I stare at him. No man has ever turned me on like Ryker. He makes me feel beautiful – sexy even. No man has ever made me feel that way before.

Just then, his eyes open and he peers down at me through sleep clouded eyes. Giving me a gentle squeeze, he smiles sleepily at me. "Mornin', baby girl."

I smile shyly back at him. "Mornin'."

His hand travels down my back, then back up until his fingers are tangled in my hair. Pulling my head towards his, he leans in to kiss me. When his lips touch mine, I give him a quick peck before pulling away. He frowns deeply, giving me a questioning look.

Covering my mouth, I smile sheepishly at him. "Morning breath."

"Fuck that," he growls before his mouth crashes into mine. His kiss takes my breath away and I cling to him, kissing him back just as hard, morning breath be damned. Rolling me to my back, he settles his hips in the cradle of my legs. I'm positive he can feel my heart pounding through my chest.

Reaching up with both hands, I twist my fingers into his messy hair giving it a gentle, but firm tug. He growls into my mouth and grinds his hips into mine, his cock hitting me in just the right spot. Pleasure spikes through me. "Ryker," I breathe.

Breaking the kiss, he runs his lips across my cheekbone then settles at the lobe of my ear. He pulls it between his lips, giving it a gentle nip. I reach down and grab onto his ass with both hands, attempting to rub him against me once again.

"Need to fuck you, baby girl." His hoarse voice is right in my ear, causing goosebumps to break out across my skin. I can only whimper and nod my head.

"Need the words, Charlie."

Need fills me, my pussy clenching tight. "Fuck me, Ryker." I bend forward and place my teeth around his nipple, flicking it with my tongue. "Please."

The sound that rips from his throat is one of pure need. I feel like the sexiest woman alive. Grabbing the hem of my shirt, he drags it up and off my body in the blink of an eye. And then he's on me. His lips. His teeth. His tongue. His hands. All worshipping my body. My breasts feel heavy and full. Swollen. My nipples have never felt so sensitive. He focuses all of his attention on my tits, his free hand at the top of my panties. Lifting my hips, I allow him to drag them off to join my shirt on the floor.

His mouth releases my nipple and he pulls back a little, looking down the length of me. I suddenly feel exposed; shy even. Raising my hands, I try to cover myself, but he grabs my wrists and lifts them high above my head, holding them there with one hand.

"Don't ever hide yourself from me." His intense blue eyes bore into mine as the rumble in his voice settles over me. "You're the sexiest fuckin' woman I've ever seen in my life. I wanna spend every fuckin' second looking at you, touching your body." He leans down and laves his tongue across my nipple before looking up at me. I let out a moan, ready to combust just from that.

Still holding my wrists above my head, he leans forward, taking my mouth in another hot, hungry kiss. Stars shoot behind my closed eyelids, heat building low in my belly.

Once again, he pulls back and looks me up and down. "Spread for me, baby."

Feeling self-conscious, I spread my legs – just a little. "Let me see your pussy, Charlie. I wanna look at it, then I wanna fill it up and fuck it until you forget every other man but me."

God. I spread my legs wider, showing him everything I have. He releases my wrists, but growls down at me, his control hanging on by a thread. "Leave 'em up there." Breathing heavily, I stare into his eyes and nod, pulling my lower lip between my teeth. I'm so fucking turned on. The heat of my orgasm is building behind my clit and he hasn't even touched me yet.

Looking at my lips, he groans and sits back, kneeling between my legs. He places his finger on my pubic bone before drawing it through my wetness. I lay there, arms above my head, legs spread wide for him. I can't stop myself from moaning, rotating my hips slightly at his slow, calculated touch.

A wicked grin spread across his face, he moves to lay between my legs. My heart races and I try to sit up. I know what he's going to do and it overwhelms me. Nobody's ever done this to me before. I don't know if I will even like it; the intimacy of the act is too much. His eyes shoot to mine and he says firmly, "Lay down."

I immediately obey, arms going back above my head, legs spread wide.

"God, baby. You're soaked. I've barely touched you and I can see it dripping down your legs." My cheeks flame. *Is that a bad thing?* I don't know what to say, so I just look at him, eyes wide.

Running his finger through my wetness once again, he looks into my eyes. "Gonna taste you now, Charlie."

I take a deep breath and nod. Then I feel his tongue. *Sweet. Baby. Jesus.* I've never felt anything like it before in my life! Pleasure shoots through me, causing me to lift my hips as I cry out. He places his hands on my hips, pushing them back on the bed.

"Fuckin' sweetest pussy I've ever tasted." He runs his tongue from my hole to my clit once more, then pulls up to look at me again. "Watch me, baby. Watch me fuck you with my mouth."

I stare down at him, all embarrassment gone. He sticks his tongue out, flicking my clit. I cry out, but keep watching. He growls, closes his eyes, then he buries his face deep into my folds. He licks and sucks and nips at my clit like a starving man at an all you can eat buffet. Squirming, I scream his name but he holds me in place with an arm across my hips.

My orgasm rips through me when he plunges two fingers deep inside my pussy, hooking them at just the right angle. Eyes rolling back in my head, I scream without words while he continues to pull every ounce of pleasure from me.

When my body stops shaking, he kisses his way up my belly and over my breasts, stopping at each one to place a tender kiss on each nipple. His lips trail a path to my neck, nuzzling me just behind my ear before finally placing his mouth on mine.

Something about tasting myself mixed with the taste of him drives me wild. I pull my hands from above my head and grab onto his head, deepening our kiss. My tongue slides against his, savoring the flavor of "us." Groaning, he kisses me back with just as much passion.

Planting a foot in the bed, I use it to push up and over, rolling him onto his back. He allows this move, never breaking our kiss. Swinging my leg over him, I sit astride his lap. Looking down at him, my breath catches in my throat. His dark hair is messy from my fingers, blue eyes hooded. His cheeks have a ruddy pink flush to them and his full lips are swollen from our kisses. It hits me then that he's looking at *me* like that. *I* am the object of his desire and *I* put that sexy flush on his chiseled cheeks.

This knowledge makes every ounce of apprehension and self-doubt float away. I suddenly feel bolder and more brazen, wanting to do anything I can to keep that look on his face.

"You gonna stare at me all day, or you gonna fuck me?" His voice is husky but has a hint of amusement in it.

I hold his eyes for a moment before my face breaks out in a wide grin. Sliding my booty down his legs, I use my hips to spread them as I go. His head comes up off the pillow, watching me with lust filled eyes. It's his turn to bite his lip. I watch, intrigued, as he pulls it between his teeth.

I look down at his cock, tongue flicking out to moisten my lips. I've never done this before either. I hadn't ever wanted to before. In fact, the idea of it, in my past relationship anyways, had always kind of grossed me out. Now my mouth waters with the thought of Ryker's cock in my mouth. I want to taste him.

Bending forward slightly, I run my tongue along the underside of his cock from base to tip. I hear his breath catch and look up from beneath my lashes as I swirl my tongue around the thick, round tip. His head is still lifted, brows drawn low over his eyes as he watches me. Shooting his hand out, he gathers my hair in his fist and holds it gently at the nape of my neck. "I've never done this before," I whisper.

Surprise registers on his face before being replaced with a naughty smirk. "No way you can do it wrong, baby girl. I could come just watching you look at my dick like that. Adding your tongue just makes it that much better."

I look back down, wrap my fist around his erection and stroke him. His hips slowly pump into my hand as he groans again. Placing my tongue on the underside of his tip, I lick him slowly, like a lollipop, swirling my tongue around the slit. *Delicious.* He lets out a quiet hiss and tightens his fist in my hair.

Placing my lips around his dick, I continue to stroke with my hand as I wrap my lips around him and suck. Bobbing my head up and down, I take him farther and farther into my mouth with each stroke. A couple of times, he hits the back of my throat and I almost gag, but I learn quickly that if I keep him there and swallow, he lets out a groan of pleasure.

He pumps his hips harder into my mouth until he's fucking my face. I increase the suction and tighten my hand as I stroke his cock. Cupping his balls with my free hand, I roll them around in my palm. Suddenly, his dick is ripped out of my mouth and I'm airborne.

"Comin' in your pussy, not in your mouth."

My pussy agrees as it pulses with excitement. Kneeling between my legs, he leans over to the nightstand, fumbling around for something. He sits up, placing a condom wrapper between his teeth. Holding my eyes, he tears it open and reaches down to roll it over his massive, hard cock. *Is that even going to fit?* I barely finish that thought before he surges forward, filling me, stretching me. Completing me. I yell out with pleasure.

He slides in all the way to the hilt and pauses. "Fuuuuck. You're so fuckin' tight, baby. Fuckin' heaven."

Placing my hands on his shoulder blades, I roll my hips, urging him to move. He does. The feeling of Ryker inside me is earth shattering. The pleasure overwhelms me, causing my head to swim. He glides in and out, silently panting. I'm not so silent. I moan with each thrust, dragging my fingernails down his back. When I reach his ass, I dig them into each globe, squeezing and pulling him into me harder.

Suddenly, he pulls out and once again, I'm airborne. My hands and knees hit the mattress, Ryker's arm around my waist, pulling my ass up high in the air. Before I even register the move, he slams into me from behind. I don't know who groans louder. I rear back into him, amazed at how deep he is in this position. His hand comes around my front, finger finding my clit. *"Oh God."*

"Spread your knees wider, baby."

I spread my knees as wide as I can, Ryker slamming into me from behind, finger still strumming my clit. The sounds and screams coming from my throat are loud and unintelligible. My head swims with pleasure, my mind lost to Ryker. My orgasm comes over me slow, but hard. Ryker slows his hips, continuing to glide in and out, my pussy clenching him like a vise. I'm still coming when his cock gets impossibly bigger and his body tightens behind me. Growling, his hips stutter before he calls out my name in a raspy groan. "Charlotte. Fuckin' Christ." He stills, burying his face in my neck.

I whimper when he pulls out, not wanting it to end. He lays down beside me, gathering me to his chest, hands back in my hair. Squeezing me tight, he kisses the top of my head, both of us trying to catch our breath. I look up at him, a grin spread across my face. "So I take it you don't mind my morning breath?"

His face breaks out into the most beautiful smile I've ever seen, that amazing dimple making an appearance before he answers. "Yeah, baby girl. I don't mind your morning breath. Not at all."

My smile widens and I press my face into his chest, emotions overwhelming me. He's almost too good to be true. He takes away all of my inhibitions and fears, making me feel like the only woman in the world.

Looking up at him again, I find him staring down at me. He places a kiss on the tip of my nose before pulling back slightly to look in my eyes. Then he's kissing me again, the fire in my belly building once more.

After a few minutes he tears his lips away from mine, stopping to place another kiss on the tip of my nose. Butterflies dance in my belly. That's the third time he's done that now. I think those three kisses are my favorite kisses of all.

"Alright woman. Enough molesting me. We got shit to do today." He grins at me, knocking the wind out of me with his dimple once again.

I just stare at him stupidly, my brain still wrapped up in our kiss, my body wanting more. He chuckles, kisses my nose and climbs out of bed. "I'm gonna shower, then it's your turn."

I nod and he chuckles again. "So fuckin' cute," he mutters, shaking his head as he walks out of the room.

I lay there and smile, my body still recovering from the most amazing sex I'd ever had. My mind wanders lazily, until I find myself thinking about my sister. I try to wrap my head around what I'd learned the night before. Ryker and the Kings had called the Devils off me, but they still want their fifteen thousand from my sister. The Kings are going to hide her until she can come up with the money. What did he mean by hide her? And, I would be staying with Ryker, but able to go to work as long as there was a "man on me." I guess I would have to get Ryker to elaborate because I was still a little confused about what all of that meant.

After just a few minutes, Ryker comes striding back into the room wearing nothing but a towel. My mouth goes dry. *Good God.* Beads of water cling to his arms and torso. His hair is wet and messy. Tattoos cover his arms and chest and I want to trace each and every one individually with my tongue. "You're up, baby girl."

I pull myself together and manage a nod. Climbing out of bed, I grab my backpack and head for the shower. As I pass, Ryker reaches out and grabs my hand, pulling me into him. His wet chest presses against my t-shirt clad one, my nipples hardening on contact. Staring down at me for a moment, his eyes search mine. Not sure what he's looking for, I can only blink at him. He smirks and shakes his head before leaning in and touching his lips to mine.

He releases me then and I stumble out of the room, dazed by his affection. I swear I hear him chuckle, but I'm too busy grinning to care.

***

Ryker

Waking up with Charlie in my arms was new for me. I've never actually slept with a woman before her. I'd had sex – a lot of it – but when it was over, they left. End of encounter. Waking up, seeing her looking at me like she wanted to climb me like a tree was sexy as fuck. This was getting complicated. I can't have a relationship with her – I won't. But I can't seem to stop myself. She is amazing. Being with her just feels right somehow. Those sexy noises she makes when I'm fucking her don't hurt either.

After her shower, Charlie calls her work and tells them some bullshit story about a car accident. That will make explaining her cuts and bruises much easier. They seem to buy it and she has to be to work by three this afternoon. She exhales after she gets off the phone, like a giant weight had been lifted. I'm glad for her. Charlie is good at her job – if it brings her happiness, she needs to be there.

I'd explained to her that we were going to see her sister next, and that it was likely the last time she'd see her for a while. We need to get her out of town, and fast. The Devils don't fuck around when they're looking for you. She's being sent to stay with another chapter of our club, in Quebec. She's going to work for them in their bar, earning money so she could pay off her debt and be rid of the Devils once and for all. In the meantime, we're going to ensure they couldn't find her and collect in blood.

Charlie climbs on the back of my bike like she belongs there. Her arms around me, chest pressed to my back, feels so fucking good that I have to remind myself not to grin while I drive. I'm a badass biker. I have a rep to maintain.

It's almost noon by the time we pull into the clubhouse parking lot. A few of my brothers are outside smoking or working on their bikes. I give them all a chin left, grab Charlie's hand and head into the building.

Walking into the common room, the first person we see is Lucy. Fucking figures. Lucy's a club whore and a pain in my ass. I'd hit that shit multiple times. Lucy's wild and likes it any way she can get it. She's a whore though and aside from fucking, I didn't have much to do with her. Lately, she'd been clingy as fuck, so I'd been sure to stay away from her. No way was I getting caught up in her shit.

The seductive smile she puts on when she sees me falters a bit when her eyes land on Charlie. She recovers quickly though, turning it back on. She smiles directly at me, ignoring Charlie completely. "Hi Ryker. Where've you been, baby? I've missed you."

Missed me? What the fuck is this bitch playing at? I haven't talked to her in weeks, and even then it was just to tell her to find another cock to ride because I wasn't interested. I nod in her direction, pulling Charlie along as I mumble my greeting. "Lucy."

She glares at Charlie as we pass, but I ignore her and her bullshit, continuing on until we come to the door of the room Anna's been staying in. I haven't seen her since that night – I don't care to see her now. This stupid bitch almost got Charlie raped to save her own skin. I don't care who she is. Sister or not, she doesn't deserve to even be in Charlie's breathing space.

I knock once on the door. When I hear Anna call out, I push it open and look down at Charlie. "I got shit to do. Visit with her for a bit. She's leaving this afternoon, and I don't know how long she'll be gone."

Charlie looks me in the eye then nods, her lip quivering a bit. I plant a kiss on the tip of her nose, leaving her to visit with her skanky sister.

Chapter Eleven

Charlotte

Walking into the dingy room my sister occupies, I'm surprised to see her looking happy and well. In my mind, I'd pictured her falling apart – it's just the way she is. She falls apart, and I hold her together while I go about fixing everything. That role had fallen on me at an early age and I've never questioned it. This time though, she had made a mess I could not fix. It's reassuring to see her in control of herself.

"Char! Hi!" She smiles at me, wrapping me in a hug before holding me out at arm's length to look at my healing face. Her smile falls away, eyes filling with tears. "Oh, sweetie. I can't tell you how sorry I am."

I smile tightly. "I know. I'm ok."

Nodding, she moves to the bed where she sits on the edge, looking at me with concern showing in her deep brown eyes.

"Anna? I need to know. Why did you borrow all that money from the Devils?" I have to ask. There's no way to ease into this conversation. I need to know and, I'm tired of everybody keeping me in the dark.

Anna's eyes go to the floor in front of her feet. She sighs and doesn't speak for a few seconds, searching for the right words.

"It's so stupid. I never meant for it to go so far. I got a couple of credit cards using Mom's name." She swallows thickly. "She was pretty sick at the time and didn't even know about them. After she died, nobody else knew about them either ... so I just kept using them. I kept buying more and more shit; clothes and jewelry and stuff. Those couple of trips I took to Vegas were all put on those credit cards. They were maxed, they cut them off and were about to send them to collections. I knew if that happened, I'd be in a lot of shit for using a dead woman's credit cards, so I borrowed the money to pay them off."

I stare at her. *All this shit is happening because she wanted dangly earrings and tube tops? What an idiot!* "So what you're telling me is, you stole from Mom, even indirectly before she died and continued to do it afterwards ... so you could buy clothes and trips to Vegas?

She looks at her feet and nods her head. I'm still confused though. "Why on earth did the Devils even lend you that money? I mean, it's not like they're a friendly group of guys looking to help a woman in need."

She looks up at me, tears falling down her cheeks. "I guess it's 'cause I was kind of their favorite. I'm ... I don't know. Flexible? The couple of guys I was sleeping with were the ones to lend it to me."

Revulsion washes over me. "Ew! Even Krueger?"

She nods her head and continues to cry silently. I can't even hide my shiver. *Disgusting.* I force myself to push that horrible mental image to the back of my mind and decide to let it all go for now. Anna has always been greedy, so that part's no surprise. I figure that will never change either. Anna's leaving tonight and I don't want to fight with her. Especially when I don't know when I'll see her again.

"So now you're off to Montreal?" She nods again. "Well, Ryker tells me you're leaving soon, so let's get you packed up."

Meeting my eyes, she gives me a soft, relieved smile before nodding her head.

***

Ryker

I glance at my watch one more time. This church meeting is taking way longer than I expected. I need to get Charlie home to get her shit, then get her to work for three o'clock. All of my brothers are sitting around the long wooden table that sits as the centerpiece of our club's meeting room.

"Well, now that we got that settled, there's one last order of business to see to." Gunner's voice breaks through my thoughts. Snapping back to attention, I see his gaze on me. As the president of the Kings of Korruption, Gunner Munroe is a force to be reckoned with. He's not a man whose attention you want aimed in your direction.

I stare back at him, waiting to hear what he has to say. I don't have to wait long.

"Some crazy shit went down the other night, Ryker." I nod. Crazy shit did go down. "Some of our brothers helped you deal with that shit. That's cool – that's what brothers are for." I nod again, waiting to see where he's going with this. "What I wanna know now is, you want more help dealing with this shit, to protect a couple of civilian bitches that have no affiliation with this club. You claiming one of these bitches as your own?"

"No." My answer's immediate. Memories of this morning flash through my mind. Charlie moaning sweet for me, coming on my tongue, and then again around my cock. Charlie smiling her mega-watt smile at me, causing the breath to catch in my chest. I want nothing more than to claim her as my own, but that shit just can't happen. Gunner cocks his eyebrow at me. "I don't know." I stab my fingers through my hair. "I just … fuck. I'm not claimin' her. I don't want an old lady, and Charlie's not going to get involved in our world."

"Seems to me she's already involved," Tease drawls.

I glare over at him. "She is. Her sister's a fuckin' cunt. The type of cunt who'd sell her own sister to fuckin' Krueger, of all people, to use as a goddamned sex slave. All over a few thousand fucking dollars." I glare around the room, looking each one of them in the eye. "Charlie's a good person. She was good to

Smokey before he died." I stand my ground as they all stare at me, each one looking skeptical. I decide to pull out the big guns. "Smokey liked her. He would have wanted us to protect her."

Ten sets of eyes lower to the table, looking thoughtful. "Look. I just can't let him take them. We have the resources to fuckin' help these women. Krueger's been a pain in our ass for as long as I can remember. He's been raping our whores for years, and last year he cut that one bitch up so bad, she was in the hospital for fuckin' weeks. Maybe this whole situation will allow us to get rid of him once and for all." Silence fills the room.

My chest grows heavy as the tension in the room builds. Regardless of what these fuckers say, I'm going to take care of Charlie. That cocksucker Krueger, is not getting his hands on her.

"I'm in." This comes from across the table. Jase. That crazy son of a bitch always has my back. I nod at him in appreciation.

"Me too." This comes from Tease. Tease is just a prospect and his vote doesn't count for shit, but he's one tough son of a bitch. Having him at my back will be a definite advantage. I give him a chin lift.

"Alright, let's put it to a vote," Gunner says. "All in favor of helping Ryker protect his pretty little nurse and her cunt sister, and hopefully getting our hands on Krueger in the process, say aye."

The room resounds with a unanimous round of "aye's." Relief washes over me. I would've protected the Daniels sisters no matter what, but with my brothers helping me, it won't be nearly as difficult.

"It's unanimous. Ryker, you've got the club's help when you need it. I will say though, somethin' else comes up that needs our attention, the club comes first and those bitches will be left on their own. We clear?"

I nod my head, not about to argue. I've got the club's help and that's all I can ask for. Hopefully nothing else comes up, but if it does, I will cross that bridge when I come to it. Gunner bangs his gavel, adjourning our meeting. *Fucking finally.*

I stand, moving to follow my brothers out of the room when someone places a hand on my arm. Turning, I see Reaper standing there, not looking happy.

"Ryk. We need to have a word."

I really need to get out of here and get shit done, but the seriousness of his tone has me curious. Nodding my head, I turn back to the room, waiting silently as everyone clears out. When the room's empty, I look to him again. "What's up?"

"I want to talk to you about these women." My body stills as I wait for him to continue. "I got a bad feelin' about this shit, brother. It's not gonna end well for you. You say you're not claimin' her, but you're swingin' all our asses out there to protect them. And for what?"

Anger flashes through me. "What do you mean, for what? You want to leave two defenseless women to Krueger, so he can do whatever the fuck he wants to them? That shit's fucked, Reap. Even for you."

"You seem to be gettin' awful attached to that pretty little nurse of yours, but I gotta say it." He leans in, putting his face directly in mine. "She ain't from our world, Ryker. Gettin' attached to a bitch like that is fuckin' insane, and you know it."

He's not saying anything I haven't thought myself already, but having someone else voice it out loud is like a physical punch to the gut. "You think I don't fuckin' know that?" My face twists with anger. "If we don't fuckin' help them, Krueger is gonna use her like a goddamned sex slave. Can you live with that? With knowing that he's raping her every goddamned night? We have the power to stop him, and I'm going to. No way in hell am I stepping aside."

I glare at him, a clear challenge to argue with me. I'm wound so tight, I know that if he does, I'll snap. He glares back at me. "See what I mean? Fuck, Ryker. You're willin' to take me on right here and now for even suggestin' we don't help them. You're too fuckin' attached to her." He sighs, running his hand through his hair in frustration. "I'm not tryin' to be a heartless dick, but you need to see the big picture here. You're our VP. You're next in line to be the fuckin' president of this MC. Gunner's leavin' soon and we need you. Not a doubt in my mind, you're gonna be the best prez we've had, but bein' with a bitch like that makes you vulnerable. In your position, bein' vulnerable is a fuckin' liability. You should know that better than anybody."

My heart clenches. *Fuck. My mom.* Reaper's right. I can't get involved with Charlie. I should never have touched her last night, and I definitely shouldn't have fucked her this morning. I'd fucked up royally, but it's not too late. I know I can still protect

Charlie and Anna, but I need to do it while maintaining my distance from them both.

"I'll help you out. Take her to my place. Protect her myself." His words snap me out of my thoughts. No way in hell is he taking Charlie to his place. Not only is she fucking terrified of him, but the thought of Charlie sleeping in Reaper's bed instead of mine has me wanting to take a swing at the son of a bitch.

I try to maintain my cool. "Not happenin'. I got this. Shit stays as is. Charlie will stay with me, and Anna is out of here tonight. We'll get that fucker, then life can go back to business as usual."

Reaper just stares at me. I know he doesn't believe my act. Is my affection for Charlie that clear by the look on my face? *Fuck. Charlie. My liability.*

Chapter Twelve

Charlotte

Before taking me to work, Ryker takes me to my apartment to get my scrubs and anything else I may need in the days to follow. I don't need much, but I make sure to grab a few books and my iPod. Pulling up to the nursing home on the back of Ryker's motorcycle, I don't miss the stares coming from my fellow co-workers as they arrive to start their shifts.

Climbing off the bike, I turn to say goodbye to Ryker. I'm a little unsure of what to say. *Do I kiss him? Do we do that now?* Before I can make up my mind, he reaches into his saddlebag and pulls out a sleek iPhone.

"I noticed you don't have a phone. Every woman needs one." His voice is deep and rich, reawakening the butterflies in my belly. I would listen to him recite the phonebook if I could. He holds it out to me and as I take it, I notice he isn't making eye contact, his face cold and blank.

I want to protest but the look on his face stops me in my tracks.

Right away, I notice that it still has the plastic sheet over the screen. It's brand new. "Thank you. I've never had a cell phone before. It just wasn't something I could ever afford."

"Well you have one now." His voice is gruff and terse, causing confusion to flood my mine. "I already programmed in my number. Use it. I want you to text me when you leave here, and again when you get home." A shiver runs up my spine when he uses the word "home". "Tease will be right out here all night, and Jase is coming to get you at eleven."

I nod, frowning a little in confusion. "Jase? But where will you be?"

He smirks. "Charlie. I'm a busy man, not your personal chauffeur."

I nod again, embarrassed. "Ok. See you tonight."

"Don't wait up. I have some shit I gotta do, and don't know when I'll be home. Text me when you get there though."

Just then, Dr. Anders comes walking up the sidewalk. Dr. Anders had been working at the nursing home just a little longer than I had. We'd bonded a bit over being the new kids on the block – I always enjoyed working with him. He's about thirty years old and extremely handsome. I'd known right away that he was interested in me, but I tried not to encourage it. Yes, he's attractive and I consider him a good friend, but I don't think it's wise to date someone in the workplace.

I smile at him as he approaches and his lips tilt up when we make eye contact. The smile falls from his face before it's even fully formed. Coming to a stop in front of me, he reaches out to gently grasp my chin between his thumb and forefinger.

"Charlotte! What happened?" He turns my face from side to side, assessing the damage.

I feel bad lying to him, but I need to stick to my story that I'd given to save my job. "Just a little car accident. I'm fine, really. It looks much worse than it is."

He continues to hold my chin, concern blanketing his features. Suddenly, I feel Ryker beside me. He'd gotten off his bike, moved to me and was glaring daggers at my friend. Clearing his throat, he places his hand on my arm.

Dr. Anders looks up then, noticing Ryker for possibly the first time. I don't know why it feels so awkward, but it does. Not knowing what else to do, I clear my throat. "Ryker, this is Dr. Jeremy Anders. Jeremy, this is my –." *My what?* "My friend, Ryker." The two men each give a slight nod and continue to glare at each other. I paste on a smile and turn to Ryker. "I better be getting in now."

His eyes flick from Jeremy to me, a small frown creasing his forehead. Finally he nods, leaning in to whisper in my ear, "Don't forget to text me."

Smiling, I nod, heart fluttering from his proximity.

Always the gentleman, Jeremy offers me his arm. I politely take it, following his lead up the walkway. When we get to the door, Jeremy opens it for me, placing his hand on my lower back to guide me in ahead of him. I glance back at Ryker, seeing him still standing beside his bike, glaring at us.

It excites me a little that he seems jealous. He has nothing to worry about from Jeremy, but it warms me from the inside out that he appears to be possessive of me. My feelings for Ryker are growing fast and that scares me. He seems almost too good to be true. I just know that the other shoe could drop at any time, and I need to be prepared. My heart may not survive him.

***

Ryker

I drive away from the nursing home pissed right the fuck off. *Who the fuck was that ass clown?* Charlie and him had seemed awfully friendly. My jealousy unnerves me. I feel possessive of Charlie and that shit just can't happen. Losing my mom was something I was still dealing with over twenty years later – losing Charlie the same way would ruin me.

She deserves a good life. White picket fence, two and a half children and a husband without a criminal record. I'm not that guy for her – I can never be that guy. I don't know how many times I have to remind myself that this is for the best, but I would do it a million times if it meant I got her out of my fucking head.

Regardless, when he grasped her chin and moved into her space, I was off my bike and beside her before I even knew what I was doing. That fucker had eyeballed me too. She'd introduced us and he'd just stood there and eyeballed me. It took everything I had not to rip the son of a bitch a new asshole. Then he'd offered her his arm like he was some kind of fucking prince. *Fuck.*

I need to get a handle on myself. Charlie's a grown ass woman, and she certainly doesn't belong to me. If she wants to be with some stick up his ass doctor, there's nothing I can do about it. I should never have taken things so far. I can't quite bring myself to regret it though. It had been the most amazing sex I'd ever had.

It doesn't help matters that she's cute as hell and makes me laugh. Charlie is smart, beautiful and sexy. She won't be on the market for long. I know that she's going to go her own way one day soon. To get some distance from her, I need to break off whatever it is we have and make it known that we can never be anything but friends. *Friends? Like that's going to happen.* As much as it kills me to think about, as soon as I can find Krueger and ensure her safety, Charlie has to go.

I have to physically stay away from her. No way in hell can I go home tonight. Seeing her, asleep in my bed, hair spread out on my pillow will break down my resolve. Tease is going to be pissed, but it looks like he's spending an all-nighter on my front porch.

Chapter Thirteen

Charlotte

At eleven o'clock, my shift ends and I walk out of the building to see Jase leaning up against his bike, looking like every woman's dream man. He's breathtaking. His blond hair is a little scruffy and his muscles are bunched up where his arms cross his chest.

Jeremy walks out behind me. "Friend of yours?" He nods to Jase and looks at me, confused. I know why. I'm a good girl. It's completely outside my normal routine to hang out with bikers.

Smiling, I try to act like this is normal and say, "Yeah. He's my ride."

Jeremy grasps my elbow gently, turning me to face him. "Charlie, if you ever need a ride, you know I'll give you one, right?"

I smile up at him and nod. "Sure. Thanks Jer. I'll keep that in mind." I turn towards Jase, but don't miss the frown on Jeremy's face.

Jase stands as I approach, and I can't help but grin. He's the only King besides Ryker that does *not* scare the shit out of me. He always has a sexy smile on his face that makes my panties melt just a little bit. "Hi Jase."

"Charles," he drawls.

I wrinkle my nose. "Charles?" That's a new one for me, but he says it with such affection, I instantly decide I kind of like it.

He nods, his grin getting wider, his eyes dancing with amusement. "Yup."

"Charles it is then," I say on a laugh. Jase climbs onto his bike. I approach and take the helmet he's holding out to me. "So, where to, handsome?"

"Handsome?" Laughter laces his voice, but he maintains a straight face. Grinning at him, I nod. "I like it. You will call me this from now on." He winks at me before continuing. "You're going to Ryker's house. Tease is going to meet us there and stay with you 'til Ryk gets home."

I nod but I'm a little confused. "Why isn't Tease just taking me home then? He's been here my entire shift."

"Awe, Charles. I'm hurt. You'd rather ride with Tease? You crushin' on my boy?"

I pause in my struggle with the helmet strap, my eyes widening even though I know he's joking. "Um, no. Honestly? Tease scares the shit out of me." I giggle, sounding nervous to my own ears. Truthfully though, Tease and I have developed a kind of comfortable silence. He's still scary as hell, but there have been a few times now, where I've caught him almost smiling when I handed him a cup of coffee, or brought him out something to eat.

129

He spent a lot of time just sitting around waiting for me. It's the least I can do.

Jase chuckles. "Yeah, Tease ain't real friendly. You're ridin' with me 'cause I'm way more bad ass than him. Nobody would dare fuck with you while you're with me. *And* I provide the eye candy you need at the end of a long night."

"Ah. I see," I deadpan. "I'm not sure about the badass thing though. His muscles are much bigger than yours." I struggle to keep a straight face.

"The fuck you say?" He reaches out to tighten the strap on my helmet. "Women have killed each other to touch these guns. Tease is a fuckin' pussy."

I laugh, grabbing his wide shoulders to steady myself as I climb onto his bike. "Whatever you say, handsome."

Jase grunts then tears off out of the parking lot. We arrive at Ryker's house before I know it, finding Tease already sitting on the front step. Jase looks back and forth between the two of us, wagging his eyebrows suggestively. Rolling my eyes, I chuckle softly.

"Thanks for the ride, Jase."

"Anytime, Charles." He gives me a wink. "Sleep well, lady." With that, he drives off.

I climb the stairs, smiling politely at Tease as I pass. In return, he gives me a chin lift then looks away.

After making myself a sandwich and washing it down with a glass of milk, I remember to text Ryker.

Me: I'm home.

A few minutes later, with still no reply, I ready myself for bed. Just as I climb between the sheets, my phone chimes with an incoming text.

Ryker: K

Hmmmm. Not very chatty. I send him another.

Me: This phone is great. I love it.

I fall asleep waiting for his reply.

***

Ryker

I read Charlie's text for what has to be the fifteenth time, trying to remind myself why I can't answer her. I can't stop thinking about her. Reaper was right though; being with her would make me vulnerable, and that's not a risk myself, or my brothers, can afford to take, not to mention, it will put her in danger.

As a member of the Kings, I have a lot of enemies. Charlie would provide the perfect target to ruin me. It makes matters worse when I remember back to this morning, when I was balls deep inside that tight as fuck pussy of hers. Ignoring her now is a total dick move, but it's the only thing I can do.

Stuffing the phone into my pocket, I turn and take another swig of beer. Lucy appears out of nowhere, standing beside me. "Hi, Ryker."

I swallow down my beer, and my annoyance. It's not Lucy's fault I'm in a shit mood. I look around me and take in the clubhouse. I'm sitting at the polished, but beaten wood bar, on a red, fake leather bar stool. The room holds several similarly beaten wood tables with mismatched chairs, along with a few tattered leather couches. There are three pool tables, and a few dart boards along the far side of the room, where several of my brothers are drinking, laughing and having a good time. There are other whores scattered throughout the room, hanging onto some of the guys, looking to get laid. Lucy is just playing her part, but tonight, I'm not in the mood.

"Not tonight, Luce."

This isn't the first time I've blown her off, but she never seems to get the message. She smiles, her thick makeup cracking a little around the corners of her eyes. Moving forward, she presses her tits into my arm. "Oh, poor Ryker. You need a little cheering up, baby?" She moves to caress my hair, but I stop her before she touches me, grasping her wrist tightly.

"Bitch, go! I said not tonight!" She narrows her eyes, looking pissed, but she doesn't argue. Pulling away, she yanks her wrist out of my grip with a glare.

"Whatever." She turns and stalks away, stopping at Reaper and dragging her finger down his chest. *Skank.*

Just then, Jase comes through the door, a wicked grin on his face. He smirks when he sees me, coming to sit on the stool next to mine. He orders a beer from the prospect working the bar before he turns to me.

"Charlie's at your place." I nod and take another swig of my beer. "She's a nice girl." I nod again, but don't look at him. "Ya know, anytime you want me to drive her anywhere, just let me know." My eyes shoot to his, only to see him grinning from ear to ear. "What?" He chuckles. "I never turn down the opportunity to have a gorgeous woman press her tits into my back."

My eyes narrow and I turn to him, staying silent. Hearing him talk about Charlie's tits is testing what little patience I have. He's not done. "When you're done with her, mind if I give her a go?"

"You'll stay the fuck away from her." The words are out of my mouth before I can stop them, my voice shaking with anger. I know he's teasing me, but the thought of Jase fucking Charlie makes me want to beat the fuck out of him.

Jase laughs. "Fuckin' Ryker, never did want to share your toys. Charles is cool shit. If you don't want her, leave her to me. I'd love a shot at a bitch like her."

I leap off of my stool and get in his face, wrapping my hand around his throat and squeezing tightly. "Leave her. The. Fuck. Alone. Charlie is not for you." It takes everything I have not to punch the smirking bastard in the face.

Jase's face loses his smirk when I grab his throat, but he doesn't move. He glares right back at me, eyes full of challenge. "You wanna back the fuck off me, brother?"

"Just stay away from Charlie." I give his throat one last squeeze before releasing him and taking a step back.

"You need to calm your fucking tits, man. I was just bustin' your balls. What the fuck's your problem anyway?" If Jase wasn't my best friend, I wouldn't see the hurt in his eyes, but I am, so I know that my anger wounded him. Jase grew up in the MC right along with me, and we'd been through a lot together. We'd never had an argument before this shit started. I'd feel kind of bad for fighting with him, but that fucker was talking about taking a shot at Charlie, and that wasn't fucking cool.

I sigh and sit back down on my bar stool, taking a long pull from my beer. "Look, just stay away from her. Once this shit with the Devils is finished, she'll go back to her life, and we need to let her do that without adding our own shit to the pile."

Jase shakes his head. "I don't get it. You fuckin' like her. I mean, you must. You just tried to choke me out because I talked about her tits. Why don't you just take a shot at her yourself?"

I look at him and smirk. "Since when are you Dr. fucking Phil? My reasons are my own and none of your concern. End of story. Now, you need a pap smear, or do you want another fucking beer?"

Jase grins and grabs one from the prospect. "All I'm sayin' is that Charlie's cool shit. She'd be good for you." I narrow my eyes at him and he holds his hands up in surrender. "That's all. Now drink your fuckin' beer and let's go play a round of pool."

Chapter Fourteen

Charlotte

I'd woken up this morning to an empty bed. Ryker hadn't come home last night, and he still hadn't texted me back at all. My stomach's in knots, worrying about what's going on. We'd connected yesterday, in an amazing and intimate way that shook me to my very core, but now I get the feeling that he's pulling away and I don't know why.

I like Ryker. A lot. I don't know what a relationship with a biker looks like, but I like him enough to want to find out. He's gorgeous, kind, very bossy (in an annoying, yet sexy way) and most of all, I feel comfortable and safe with him. I've never felt that way with anybody else before. He may be a biker, but maybe all bikers aren't all bad.

I spend the day puttering around the house and reading one of the books I'd brought with me, but Ryker never does come home. I have to admit, that hurts. I just don't understand what's happening. For him to ignore me now, after everything we'd been through, makes me believe that I was just another conquest for him. Used.

At noon, I make myself a sandwich and throw some chips on the plate. Glancing outside, I see Tease sitting on the front step, in his usual spot. I make a plate for him as well, grabbing two cans of Pepsi from the fridge.

When I come out the front door, Tease turns his head to look at me. I give him a small smile and hold up the plates I hold in each hand. "Thought you might be hungry."

He turns back around and grunts out, "Not hungry."

I push onward. There's no way the man's not hungry. He's been sitting out here for hours. The least I could do is feed him lunch. Moving forward, I tentatively settle beside him and offer him a plate.

"Well, might as well eat it so it doesn't go to waste." I don't look at him, but I do an inner victory dance when he takes it from my hand.

"Thanks." He sounds annoyed, but I don't care. I just don't want to be alone.

Nodding, I stay silent. Tease is a man of few words and I don't want to piss him off – I know it wouldn't be hard to do. Instead, I just pass him a Pepsi and bite into my sandwich.

We sit silently, side by side, eating our lunches. I don't know what he's thinking about, but I'm just trying to choke down my lunch and stop fretting over what's going on with Ryker. Tease finishes before me, sitting quietly while I finish mine.

When I'm done, he hands me his plate, not saying a word. As I move to stand, Tease reaches out and gently places his hand on my arm. Shocked at the gesture, my eyes shoot to his.

He maintains eye contact when he says, "Thanks, Charlotte."

I can't help myself. I smile brightly at him. "You're welcome."

I know better than to ask Tease where Ryker is. He may not scare me so much anymore, but I know we won't be having a conversation anytime soon. I've never heard the man say more than three words at a time. Leaving him to brood on the step, I go inside to do some brooding of my own.

Finally, at two o'clock, I give up waiting for Ryker and ready myself for work. I ride with Tease, who drives me right to the entrance before turning his bike around and going to sit and wait in the shade across the parking lot for me to finish my eight hour shift. I feel kind of bad that he has to just sit there, but Ryker had assured me that this was part of his job, and that he'd had worse gigs.

About an hour into my shift, I look up to see Jeremy approaching, one hand held behind his back. He smiles at me, flashing his perfect white teeth. He really is very good looking and he's a great guy. Any woman would be lucky to have him – I just know I can't be that woman.

"Charlotte. You're looking lovely as usual." He approaches the nursing desk, coming around to stand beside me.

I turn to him and smile back. Smiles haven't been coming easily to me tonight, and I've really had to work at being cheerful. Ryker's silence is making me nauseous. I just want this shift to end, so I can talk to him and see if he's ok – if we're ok. If he had just used me for sex, my heart would be broken. I shrug off that thought and concentrate on my friend, forcing myself to sound cheerful. "Hey Jeremy. How are you?"

"I'm great!" He pulls his hand out from behind his back, revealing a large bouquet of mixed flowers. They're gorgeous. My stomach drops. I don't handle these situations well. I like Jeremy, but not in the way that he likes me, and I don't know how to let him down without hurting his feelings. "I got you these." He grins, holding them out to me. I see a ribbon woven into the bouquet saying "Get Well".

I relax just a little, realizing that he'd gotten these because of my "car accident", not because he was attempting to be romantic. At least I hope that's the case. Taking them from him, I force my most cheerful smile.

"Oh, Jer! Thank you so much! You didn't have to do that!" I look up at him and he winks.

"I know. I just wanted you to know I was thinking of you. Now ..." He looks down at his watch. "I have to go see a patient. See you later, Charlotte."

"Bye Jer," I say to his retreating back. He throws another smile over his shoulder and then he's gone.

The flowers are beautiful. I love fresh flowers. Every pay day, I go to the florist and get a fresh bouquet for my bedroom. I wouldn't be doing that again until I get a new vase though. The reminder causes my smile to fall. Ryker hasn't mentioned anything else about Krueger. I can only pray that he's right and I have nothing else to worry about. Remembering that horrible night feels like a nightmare. It was easily the scariest moment of my life.

I finish out my shift, gathering my coat and flowers on my way out the door. Expecting to see Tease, I'm surprised to see Ryker sitting on his bike at the end of the walkway. Relief washes over me. Grinning, I walk out of the building towards him. He sits up when he sees me, reaching back to grab the helmet. He does *not* smile back.

"Hey," I breathe when I approach him. He just nods, handing me the helmet. I see the moment that he notices my flowers.

His eyes shoot to mine. "Nice flowers." His voice is so deep, causing me to shiver, realizing just how much I've missed hearing it.

"Yeah! Jeremy got them for me." His jaw tightens and I see him clench his fists. I hurry on with my explanation. "Because of my "car accident". They're just "get well" flowers." I force myself to continue smiling at him, hoping for even a ghost of a smile in return, but his eyes are narrowed at something across the parking lot.

Looking over to where he's glaring, I see Jeremy walking to his car. His head is turned, watching Ryker and I. Ryker revs the motor and growls at me. "Get on." I jump a little at his command. "Now!"

My hands shaking, I hurriedly put on my helmet and jump onto the back of his bike. He's so angry. Grasping onto Ryker, I can feel the tension in his body. My heart drops. I know now for sure that something is very wrong, and I also know beyond a shadow of a doubt, that I *won't* be escaping this night with my heart still intact.

***

Ryker

It takes me the entire twenty minute drive home to compose myself. When I'd seen that bouquet of fucking pansy ass flowers in Charlie's hand, I knew right away they'd come from that fucking douche, Jeremy. Then he'd fucking eyeballed me again. *Fucker.*

The worst part was, Charlie had looked so goddamned beautiful standing there holding a bouquet of flowers that some other man had given her. She deserves that shit – flowers. She obviously loves them. This serves as yet another reminder that I can't be the man for her. I don't buy flowers. Ever.

We walk into the house, and after placing her flowers in a milk pitcher she found in the kitchen, she moves towards the bedroom to get ready for bed. She hasn't spoken to me once, and I know that she's feeling the tension that must be rolling off me in waves. I need to talk to her now and just get this shit over and done with. Put us both out of our misery.

"Charlotte?" She stops, her back to me, shoulders tensed. Slowly she turns around, apprehension clear on her face. "We gotta talk."

She nods, so I gesture to the couch. I sit on one end, right at the edge, elbows to my knees. She positions herself at the far end of the couch, feet up, wrapping her arms around her knees. My heart clenches when I see her in that self-protective position ... because of me. I don't look at her as I speak.

"What happened the other morning with us was a mistake." I hear her soft gasp and have to force myself to keep going. "It was great, but it can't happen again. I don't have room in my life for an old lady, and you are definitely *not* old lady material." Her body jerks as if I'd struck her. "You deserve a good life, with a good man, Charlie. Someone like Dr. whatever the fuck his name is." I glance over at her again. She's staring down at her fingernails, eyes filled with tears. She doesn't speak. "I have a lot of shit going on in my life, and it would just complicate things to – "

"Don't I get a say in what I deserve? What I want?" Her voice trembles with anger. I look up to see her glaring right at me. Our eyes lock. I want to grab her, crush her to me, and never let her go, but I can't. I have to finish this shit before we get in any deeper.

"It doesn't matter what you want." I hold her gaze, ignoring the flinch my words caused. "We're done. In fact, we never started. We fucked. Big deal. Like I said, it won't happen again.

You'll stay here until Krueger is gone for sure, then you can go back to your life. Without me."

Her body trembles. I almost take it all back. I can't stand the thought that *I've* done this to her. *Me.* Tears spill over onto her cheeks, and she quickly dashes them away before taking a deep breath. "I ... I just ..." She shakes her head and clenches her fists. "You know what? Fuck you, Ryker."

She stands and walks back to the bedroom, shoulders squared and her head held high. My heart cracks. I want to chase her down and apologize – kiss away all of those tears I'd just caused. I feel like such a dick. The thought of her hating me makes me want to claw my own eyes out. I know it will get better in time, but I need to find Krueger fast so I can get her the hell out of here, and get back to living my life. A life without Charlie.

I want nothing more than to go back to the clubhouse and pound back a few thousand beers, but Tease needs a night off, and I won't leave her here unprotected. Grabbing the throw blanket off the chair in the corner, I curl up on the couch.

I can hear her sobs coming from down the hall. Laying there, on my shitty couch, in my tiny house, I curse myself for being the one to make her cry – for not being the man she needs. I'm still laying there long after the sounds of her crying end and the sun is rising. Sleep never does come to me.

Chapter Fifteen

Charlotte

Crushed. Smashed. Shattered. I don't know which word best describes the way my heart feels right now. Last night, when Ryker had told me that he didn't want me, that I wasn't good enough for him, I didn't even argue. What was the point? When he'd called me a mistake and said that I was just a fuck to him, my heart bled.

I knew our worlds were different, and I'd been so lost in the amazing way he made me feel, that I'd never stopped to think I wasn't right for him – that he didn't feel the same for me. At first, I'd been scared by his club and his way of life, but Ryker had done nothing but make me feel safe. I'd let myself get swept away by that. *What an idiot.*

I'm also angry. Ryker had played my heart and my body. I wasn't just some woman he could fuck when he wanted then push to the side when he was done. I will never let myself be that woman – not for anyone. When James had broken up with me, all those years ago, I'd been sad, but it was nothing compared to the heartache I felt when Ryker called, what had been the most amazing morning of my life, a mistake. I'd been a fool to think we'd connected on a deeper level.

After gathering up my bruised and battered pride and telling Ryker to go fuck himself, I'd proceeded to the bedroom, where I had cried until there weren't any tears left to shed. I would've left, but I had no car here, and no way home. I knew if I'd called a cab, he'd refuse to let me leave because for some strange reason, he still wants to keep me safe – to keep his conscience clear, most likely.

I hadn't slept well and I'd stayed in bed until almost noon to avoid Ryker. It wouldn't have mattered though because when I came out to use the washroom, he'd been gone. Tease had been in his usual spot, smoking a cigarette on the front step. After a cup of coffee and some toast, which was all my roiling stomach would allow, I went into the bathroom to get ready for work.

I looked like complete crap. It wasn't hard to tell I'd spent the entire night crying. I made an attempt to fix my puffy eyes, then yanked my mass of dark curls into a messy bun before putting on my scrubs. When I'd come out of the house, Tease had frowned a little at my appearance, then shook his head before climbing onto his bike. Accepting the coffee and toast I'd given him, he'd taken me to work. He then dropped me off without a word, but the way he looked at me appeared almost concerned. I'd forced a smile at him before going into the building.

This brings me to now. I'd had an off day since I'd gotten here. I'd mixed up several charts and fumbled the pills a few times, even going so far as to drop an entire bottle of morphine on the floor. It had taken me almost five minutes to find all of them and put them back into the bottle. Several patients had asked if I was ok when I forgot something or had to keep retaking their blood pressure. My mind was on Ryker and my wounded heart. Finally, after scolding myself for the hundredth time, I decided that Ryker didn't deserve any more of my head space. I had an important job to do, and I needed to be mentally present for it.

So far, I'm doing well at this, even though my guts are churning and my heart is sad. It's helped that Jeremy is off today because I don't think I could handle his kindness. I know he wants to be more than friends and at the moment, I want absolutely nothing to do with any man, including him.

Ten minutes before my shift ends, I get a text from an unknown number.

Unknown: It's Tease. Got a meeting at the club right after 11. I have to be there. I'll take you, then Ryk takes you home.

So many emotions from that one text flow through me. Anger. Ryker had given Tease my number because he was so done with me that he couldn't even be bothered to give me that information? Nervousness. Ryker is taking me home? I don't know if I can ride on his bike with him again. I don't even want to see him, let alone wrap my body around his for the ride home. More anger. I'm done staying at Ryker's house. I know he's trying to protect me, but I just can't be around him anymore. He'd told me that Krueger was gone so why can't I just go home?

I don't bother replying to the text. Like a good little girl, I climb onto the back of a noticeably worried Tease's bike and accept the ride to the King's clubhouse. Tease deposits me on a barstool and wordlessly gets me a cold beer before disappearing into another room. I can hear the sounds of a group of men coming from in there, so I figure that's where the meeting is happening. I can't hear what they're talking about and I can't say I even care. I nurse my beer and sit, lost in thought about how I can get out of going back to Ryker's place tonight.

"You still fuckin' here?" Those words said in such a nasty tone cause me to jump. I spin around looking for who spoke them. The club whore from the other day is standing three feet behind me, sneering in my direction. I frown at her, confused.

She takes a few steps and comes right up beside me, pulling the beer from my hand and taking a swig. "Ryker said two nights ago that he was gettin' rid of you."

Shocked, I stare at her. *Getting rid of me?* I knew Ryker didn't want to be with me, but knowing that he'd said that he was getting rid of me to *this* woman felt like a punch to the gut. And two nights ago was the same day we'd had sex.

She takes another long swig from my beer, grinning when she pulls the bottle from her lips. "Don't look so surprised. He was balls deep in my pussy two nights ago. That man knows how to fuck like a stallion." I mustn't be successful in hiding my shock because she looks at me with a vicious smirk on her face. "You really think he'd want a fuckin' uptight bitch like you, when he has me to fuck him the way I know he likes it?"

I can't breathe. *Ryker had sex with her two nights ago?* I'd spent that night waiting for him to text me back, stupidly thinking we had something special, and he'd been here the whole time fucking Lucy. *I'm such an idiot.* I swallow thickly, trying to fight the tears back before answering. "Yeah, well … don't worry. I'll be gone soon. He made it clear we're not together."

She smirks and finishes off my beer, slamming it down on the counter. "Fuckin' right he did. That's 'cause he has me." She stabs her long, phony thumbnail towards her chest. "He always comes back to me. Keep your fucking hands off my man, bitch." She puts her face right in mine, her finger positioned right next to my eye. "Or I'll claw those filthy doe eyes right outta your head. Got me?"

I move to get off the stool, ready to rip this bitch's fingernails off and shove them up her ass, when Jase comes strolling in. He sees Lucy in my space and scowls. "Luce. Back the fuck off of Charles before I throw your skanky ass out on the street."

Lucy returns his scowl, but steps away. Looking back at me one last time, the warning clear on her face, she walks to the other side of the huge room. I glare back, fists balled at my side, anger burning in my chest.

Jase approaches, an easy smile on his gorgeous face. "Hey, Charles. Don't let that whore bother you. You just gotta put bitches like her in their place so they'll leave you alone." He pauses, looking at me more closely and leans towards me. "You ok, honey?"

I peel my eyes from the back of Lucy's bleached out head, forcing a smile I know looks as phony as it is and nod. "Peachy." My voice is hoarse. The emotions tumble round and round in my mind like wet clothes in a dryer. I feel like I'm about to throw up.

Jase frowns and wraps an arm around my shoulders. "Talk to me."

Before I can respond, Ryker and a few other guys come stalking out of the meeting room. "Charlotte! Let's go!" Jase glares at him, his frown deepening at the way Ryker had barked at me.

I look up at him, forcing another smile, trying my best to reassure him. "Looks like I'm outta here." I place my hand on his cheek. "Don't worry about me, handsome. I'll be ok." I give him a wink and move towards Ryker, who stands glaring at us by the front entrance.

**

Ryker

Charlie climbs onto my bike without a word and I take her home. I do my best to ignore how good it feels to have her arms wrapped around me, thighs hugging my hips. The tension between us is like a physical force, laying heavy on my chest. Before getting on the bike, I'd looked into her eyes and what I saw there made it hard to breathe.

Charlie's usually bright, brown eyes are dull and sad. She averts her gaze immediately, doing everything she can to avoid eye contact. The silence guts me. I couldn't handle it if she hated me and it crushes me to see her look so wounded. I'd done that to her.

She's been through so much in the last few days and my actions have only added to that. Her indifference to me is the hardest to take. I can't imagine being around her while we search for Krueger, and have her look right through me like that; it will kill what little bit of heart I have left. I've distanced myself for good reason, but that doesn't mean she has to hate me. *I need to fix this.*

After she's gone to bed, I approach the room, knocking quietly on the door. My ears strain to hear any sign of her from behind it. After a second, she calls out, her voice hoarse. "Yes?"

Pushing the door open slowly, I see Charlie sitting in my bed, wearing a pink tank top and covered to her waist with blankets. The only light in the room comes from the table on her side of the bed. *Her side?* Funny how quickly we'd developed sides.

"Can we talk?" She looks at me, uncertainty and anger swimming in her eyes before she nods. I move to her, sitting on the edge of the bed beside her feet. "Look, I know you're pissed at me." She snorts and rolls her eyes before looking back at me, eyebrow arched.

Fuck. This sucks. My mind races, looking for something to say that'll take that pained look from her face. "Charlie, I'm just not good with this shit." I open my mouth to continue, but she cuts me off.

"And what shit would that be, Ryker?" She says my name, sarcasm dripping from her voice. I squeeze my eyes closed, taking a deep breath. It wasn't even three days ago, she was saying my name in ecstasy; now she says it like a curse.

"Just ... I don't know." I spear my fingers through my hair. *I'm such a dick.* "I don't want you to hate me." She snorts again, but holds my gaze. "It would kill me if you hated me." I sigh. "Baby girl, I – "

"Don't you call me that! Don't you *ever* call me that," she grinds out in anger. I can only nod. *Fair enough. I did this.*

"Charlie, I want you to be safe." I clench my fist and place it over my heart. "I need to make *sure* of it. In the meantime, I would like it if we could be ... I don't know ... friends?"

Sitting up straighter, she cries, "You want to be *friends*?"

"I think we could be friends if we tried." *I sound like a fucking pussy right now.*

Another snort from her. "Sure, Ryker. Let's be pals. What do you want to do now, *buddy*?"

I ignore her sarcasm. "I don't know. I guess we could just talk. Maybe tell each other about our day or somethin'?" I'm nervous. I've never been so nervous, but I need Charlie to stop hating me.

She sighs, shoulders slumping in defeat. "Ryker, you don't want to hear about my day. It was a shit day anyways, and I'm so fucking glad it's over."

I agree with her. It was a shit day for me too. "Mine too." She snorts again. This isn't going well. I need to change the subject; get her talking. "I heard from a buddy in Montreal today."

Her eyes shoot to mine and she watches me silently, waiting to hear more. "He said your sister is a real piece of work." I give her a half-hearted smile; she doesn't return it. "They set her up workin' as an office manager for their garage. Said she had a lot to learn, but the customers like her better than the old lady they had workin' there before."

She smiles then; soft and wistful. "I needed to hear that. Believe it or not, Anna is a good person, and she deserves to be happy." She picks at some invisible lint on the blanket. "She got herself a little lost along the way, but I know that given the chance, she can turn things around."

I've been wondering about their story since the minute I met Anna. She's so different from Charlie, it's hard to believe they share the same parents. "What's her story anyways? I mean, you turned out great but she ..." I search for the right words, not wanting to offend her now that she's finally talking to me. "She's kind of a mess."

Charlie pulls a deep breath in through her nose. "It's a long story."

"I've got all kinds of time, bab –" She looks at me then, anger reappearing on her features, but I press on. "I've got time."

Her eyes narrow, the anger still on her face. "Maybe I don't want to share it with you."

Ouch. "Even if I say please?"

She sighs and flops back against the pillows. "Why do you even care? I thought I was a mistake? Just some bitch you fucked."

My jaw clenches. *Does she really believe that shit?* I lean forward, grasping her wrist and growl, "Don't say that."

"Why not? You did." She leans into me, eyebrows raised. "What did you call my sister again? A warm body that will spread her legs for anyone? You, Ryker, are a dick."

Fuck. I can't believe she'd been in this bed with me the other day, and didn't know in her heart that it was different for us. "I never said that shit about you, Charlie. Never about you."

She watches me for a moment, eyes narrowed. "Anna's a good person you know. If you only knew ..." She trails off and looks at me before nodding, apparently coming to a decision. "She's three years older than me, but somehow, it's always been me taking care of her. About six months after I was born, my dad took off. We never heard from him again. My mom was good to us; maybe too good. Anna got away with murder." She chuckles softly, caught up in the memory, while I watch her, anxiously waiting for her to tell me more.

"My mom worked hard to keep us fed. She worked two full time jobs just to pay the bills. We never had much left for fun stuff, but that was ok with me; it was never ok with Anna. She wanted everything and resented my mom for not giving her all the things her friends had." Pausing, she shakes her head. I wait silently for her to continue. I don't know much about her past, but suddenly, I want to know everything about her.

"While Anna was out with her friends and going to the mall, I stayed back to help my mom with housework and chores. I did everything I could to make things a little easier for her. She was always so tired. I hated that. When I was about fifteen, Mom got sick." Her voice shakes. "She began missing days at work and spent a lot of time in bed. It was a couple of months before she told us she had leukemia." Tears fill her eyes. Watching her stare down at the clenched hands on her lap, I almost tell her to stop, but I don't. I need to hear her story; I need to know her better.

"Mom quit her job when the treatments began, and she started receiving a disability check each month. I got myself a part time job after school, to help with the bills. Anna was always getting into trouble; she was hardly ever home. I covered for her when I could, but I hated lying to my mom almost as much as I hated how upset Anna was making her. We fought about it; all the time."

A tear escapes, sliding down her cheek. Her tears gut me. I've seen her cry so many tears since I met her. I want nothing more than to hold her and make it so she never needs to cry again. "Two years into Mom's treatment, we found that it wasn't working anymore. There was nothing more they could do. Chemo had killed her liver and her heart was failing. I took some time off school so I could stay home to take care of her. We didn't have the money to pay for private nursing, and there was no way I was letting my mom die alone in a hospital. I pulled my bed into her room and spent every second I could with her."

Life is so fucking unfair. Charlie had been through so much at such a young age.

"Mom died when I was seventeen. Anna may have been gone a lot growing up, but when Mom passed, she was there for me. She held my hand and helped me get through it. I was a wreck. After a couple weeks, I got a job working after school until midnight, five nights a week and another working weekends. I finished high school and went to college right after, to get my nursing degree. Anna went back to partying all the time and doing whatever she wanted. I never had a clue where she got her money, but I refused to give her any whenever she asked."

Another tear falls. "One night, she came home wasted and brought a bunch of friends with her. I got home from work and found they'd eaten every bit of food in the house. I didn't get paid for another week. I don't think I've ever been so angry." She swallows thickly. "Anna and I got into a huge fight and I kicked her out of the house. It was a couple of weeks later that she came back and we talked. She promised to straighten up and pull her own weight, and she did, for the most part. She got herself a job as a waitress in a bar, started helping me with bills. She never stopped living wild, but at least I had some help."

She shrugs then, looking up at me. "My sister and I haven't always had it easy. I love her; she's the only person I have left."

I swallow down the bowling ball that seems to be lodged in my throat. She's just as alone as I am. All her life, she's been taking care of everyone else but had nobody to take care of her. I wish more than anything that I could be the one to do that. Doesn't matter though – I may wish it, but I can't do it. I had made a decision and there's no going back. As much as it hurts, she needs better than me.

"Pretty heavy stuff. You're an amazing woman, Charlie. After everything you've been through, you've still managed to make something of yourself and take care of your sister at the same time." I tilt my lips up in a small smile. "You don't need to worry about Anna. My buddies will make sure she earns enough to pay back the Devils, and that she's safe while she does it."

She nods, looking reassured. "What about you? Do you have any brothers or sisters? Besides the ones that ride motorcycles?" She smirks at me and I realize then that we might just be ok. Maybe we can be friends after all.

"Nah. It's just me."

"What about Jase? You guys seem close." At her mention of my best friend, I remember back to the clubhouse that very night, when the two of them were standing close, his arm around her shoulder. I had watched them together until I'd seen her place her hand on his face. *Fucking Jase.* Jealousy washes over me.

"Not much of a story there. We've been buddies for as long as I can remember. Jase is a lot of fun, but I warn you now, stay away from him. He's been known to break more than a few hearts."

She looks surprised at first and then her eyes go blank. I've lost her. "Yeah. Wouldn't want my heart to get broken, would we?" She closes her eyes and a single tear rolls down her cheek. "I need to go to sleep now."

Fuck. I sigh, running my hands through my hair and stand. "Night, Charlotte."

She twists and turns out the lamp, blanketing the room in darkness before whispering, "Night."

Chapter Sixteen

Charlotte

I'm not surprised to find that Ryker's long gone when I wake up the next morning. My chest aches and my stomach is still roiling so I don't even bother trying to eat anything. My eyes are tight and puffy from crying myself to sleep, yet again. It feels like all I do is cry anymore.

I spend the day puttering around the house, doing laundry and sweeping floors. I take breakfast out to Tease and he gives me a small smile as he takes it. *A smile!*

When I'm ready to go, I step out of the house and am alarmed to see that Tease is gone and Reaper is standing there, arms folded across his chest, glaring at me.

"Um … hey." I haven't spent much time around Reaper, and he still scares the shit out of me. I can tell he doesn't like me which doesn't help my fear one bit. Offering him a small smile, I move towards his bike. He just snorts and shakes his head, clearly not happy with his chauffeur duties.

When we arrive at the nursing home, I hand Reaper his helmet and mutter a quick thanks before turning to hurry into the building. I don't even make it a full step before his hand clamps down on my upper arm with a firm grip.

"Not so fast, Princess." He whips me back around to face him, pulling me right into his space. He glares down at me. "You need to stop fuckin' with my boys head."

I'm confused. My heart hammers in my chest because he's looking at me like he wants to rip my head off. Reaper is already scary as hell, but with that look on his face, he is terrifying. *What is he talking about?* "I – I – I'm not sure I know what you mean?" I try taking a step back to gain some distance from him, but he maintains an iron clad grip on my arm.

He sneers at me. "I – I – I," he mocks. "I mean, you need to either fuck Ryker or leave him the fuck alone. Ever since you came along he's been fucked in the head and I know it's 'cause of you." He gives me a little shake and I yelp. "Stupid uppity bitch. You come along with your fuckin' golden pussy, and think you can lead him around by his fuckin' dick."

I just gape at him, mind racing. I haven't done anything to Ryker. He's the one fucking with *my* head. "I don't un –"

"Yeah. I'm gettin' that. Look, Ryker's our VP. He's soon going to be the president. A lot of guys are counting on him for a lot of things. He doesn't need a fuckin' princess like you comin' along, gettin' herself – or worse – him, killed."

I'm shocked. *Their VP? Ryker's the MC's vice president? Why didn't I know that?* Anger burns through me. I didn't know because Ryker didn't want me to know. *Fucking bastard.* Not only is he fucking me and fucking Lucy, along with God only knows who else, but he'd also really never told me one damn thing about himself. *How could I have been so stupid?* I don't know anything about him or his life and honestly, I'm not so sure I even want to anymore.

As for Reaper, fuck him. I'm so sick and tired of being scared all the damned time. I don't have anything to lose. *What's he going to do? Hit me?* Maybe, but even though I know Ryker doesn't want me for himself, he would tear Reaper's head off for laying a finger on me.

Ripping my arm from his grasp, I lean into *his* space. "You're an asshole."

Surprise flashes in his eyes before he hides it with a sneer. He chuckles. It's a menacing sound and I *almost* back off, but I'm so sick of this shit. "You just figurin' that out, Princess?"

I snort. "No. I knew." My voice shakes with anger. "Everybody knows. What you don't know is, I don't give a fuck what you have to say. You're a prick, and you know not one thing about me, or my golden pussy. I want nothing more than to be done with you, Ryker, and your stupid fucking club, but none of you will leave me the hell alone!"

I turn and storm into the building, leaving Reaper outside. I'm furious. I don't want to do this anymore. I just want my life to go back to normal. I need to find a way to get the MC to leave me alone and let me live my life. I know Ryker won't back off until he knows that Krueger's gone for sure, but there's been no news on him for several days. No news is good news. *Right?*

There's no way I can work my shift tonight – I'm a wreck. I approach my supervisor, telling her that I'm not feeling well. Never one to take time off, she gives me a sympathetic look before telling me to go on home. I call a cab, requesting they pick me up at the back entrance. Reaper will never even see me leave; if he's still out there.

I jump into the cab, and as it pulls out of the parking lot, I see Reaper sitting on his bike in a shaded area at the far end of the lot. He doesn't see me. *Dick.*

Entering my apartment alone for the first time since my attack is a little scary. I swallow down my fear and try to relax. Every sound I hear makes me jump. I'm nervous as hell, but I just try to ignore it and go about my business. I clean the apartment, tidying up the mess in my bedroom, have a bite to eat and then curl up in the tub with my book.

I'm just getting out of the tub when my cell phone goes off, alerting me to an incoming text.

Ryker: Where the fuck are you Charlie? Dr. Dickhead told Reaper you left hours ago. Wtf?

I swallow, feeling a little bad. I'd left Reaper to sit outside standing vigil over me while I'd snuck out the back. Jeremy must have seen him waiting and wondered why he was still there after I'd gone home. Maybe I don't feel bad. Reaper's an asshole. I'm actually kind of proud of myself for slipping past him.

Me: I went home. I can't stay with you anymore. Thanks for helping us, but I'm ok now. You don't need to worry about me.

I send the text, biting my lip in worry. I know Ryker is going to be pissed, and he might even show up at my door. If he does, I will have to tell him, yet again, that I'm ok and they don't need to watch over me anymore.

My phone alerts again.

Ryker: I'm coming over. DON'T LEAVE

My shoulders slump. Of course he is. I'm so tired of this; all of it. Being scared, Ryker's rejection, scary biker assholes, and most of all, not being able to live my life.

There's a pounding on the door. *That was quick.* I take a deep breath, readying myself for the battle ahead. I know Ryker won't leave easily, but I'm more than ready to fight him for my freedom. I walk to the door, phone in hand, and swing it open.

The air rushes from my chest; it's not Ryker. Krueger stands before me, an evil smile splitting his face. "Hey pretty lady. You and I have some unfinished business."

His fist swings out, catching me in the temple. Pain crashes through my head as I crumple to the floor. Through tear filled eyes, I watch Krueger step inside just before the darkness takes ahold of me.

***

Ryker

Anger and worry for Charlie's safety battle through me as I break every traffic law imaginable to get to her apartment. I'm pissed at her for giving Reaper the slip, and for trying to fuck me off with that text. *Thanks for helping her out, but she's ok now? Fuck that!* The problem is, I still haven't been able to get a lock on Krueger, and the Devils say he's gone rogue. This means that fucker's still out there somewhere. Charlie's not safe.

I'm pissed at Reaper too. Fucker had called to say Charlie was gone and he'd sounded almost bored; like he didn't give a shit that she could be in danger. I'd deal with that son of a bitch later.

Pulling up in front of Charlie's building, I park in a handicap space and run up the stairs. The security door opens with a couple of good yanks and I hurry up the stairs. Pausing for a second, I see the door to her apartment standing ajar.

I pull my gun from it's ankle holster, and quietly rush up to the door, opening it cautiously. Nothing. No sign of struggle, but also no Charlie. After a quick sweep of her apartment, I know she's gone. Stepping back into the living room, I see her phone lying on the floor near the front entrance. The screen is cracked. I turn it on, and through the spider web glass it shows the last thing she'd looked at; the last text from me. Did she throw the phone and leave? I can't see her doing that.

Looking around once more, I notice a dark spot, about the size of a quarter, on the hardwood floor. I crouch down for a closer look. Blood. Fear for Charlie causes the hair to stand up on the back of my neck and the blood to pound through my veins. I search the floor for more blood. Halfway down the hall, I see another spot. It's just a few drops, but I find more farther down. Every drop I find causes the fear and anger to claw at my gut. I follow the trail of blood down the back stairs until it ends completely at the back door.

Whipping my phone out, I call Jase.

He answers after the first ring. "Talk to me."

"Charlie's gone."

"Yeah. You told me. Right before you tore out of here like a bat outta hell."

"No. I mean gone. From her apartment. There's blood on the floor and her cell is broken right beside it."

"Fuuuuck. Ya think he's got her?"

"I *know* he does." Panic bubbles its way up my throat. I need to take a deep breath and figure out what to do. *Where would he take her? What does he plan to do with her?* I look down at the blood on the floor and I know in my gut that it's hers. He's got my baby girl and I don't know if I'll ever see her again. *What the fuck do I do?*

"What do you need me to do, Ryker?" Jase's voice brings me out of my panicked fog.

My mind scrambles for an answer. "Call the Devil's Prez. Last I heard, Krueger'd gone rogue. They may have an idea where he'd be now. Let Gunner know what's going on. If you have any other ideas, just go with it."

"On it. You cool?"

I can hear my own heartbeat pounding in my ears. "He's got her, Jase."

"I know, brother."

"She's bleedin'."

"We'll find her Ryk. Take a breath. You're not gonna be any help findin' her if you're freakin' out, so you need to lock it *down*."

I nod, swallowing down the bile in my throat. "I will. I'll lock it down."

"Alright. Text me that number." He hangs up. I flip through my contacts and text him the one for Deed, the President of the Devils. Deed wants to find Krueger almost as bad as I do; I know he'll help however he can.

I rack my brain, trying to figure out what to do next. Forcing down my emotions, I go back upstairs to lock Charlie's apartment before hurrying to my bike. We need a plan; and fast. I need to find her. I need to find that fucker, Krueger; he's gonna bleed tonight.

Chapter Seventeen

Charlotte

I slowly claw my way out of the darkness, my head pounding along with the beat of my heart. I move to touch my temple, where the worst of the pain is, but my arm doesn't co-operate. Slowly, I work to peel my eyelids open with a groan. Dazed, I take in my surroundings.

I'm lying on a bare and filthy single mattress that sits on a rusted metal bedframe. My hands and feet are tied to it, spread eagle, with a dirty nylon rope. The bed sits in the corner of a tiny, wooden, one room cabin. There's a little table with one rickety wooden chair, a small cupboard and a sink with no faucet. An old, beaten up love seat and coffee table sits directly across from me, the table holding several empty beer bottles and a small stack of magazines.

Lifting my head slightly, I try to get a good look at the bindings on my wrists. My head swims with pain as I tug and wiggle my arms, desperately looking for a way to get out of them. They don't budge. Tied tight, the rope cuts harshly into my skin, and with every tug my skin tears more and more. I can't stop though. I keep struggling with them, even as I cry out in pain when the blood starts trickling down my arms.

Fear overwhelms me, my breaths coming out in sobs and gasps. Lying my head back in defeat, my mind races for a solution. *I need to get out of here!* The door to the cabin opens, and there he is.

Krueger stalks into the room carrying a case of beer. Looking up, he smiles at me, baring his crooked yellow teeth.

"Well, rise and shine, sleeping beauty. I was startin' to wonder if you'd ever wake up." His friendly tone doesn't put me at ease – it only freaks me out more. *Is he delusional?*

He approaches me, reaching to his hip as he gets closer. My heart stutters as he pulls a knife out of the brown leather case on his belt. Standing at the side of the bed, he holds it up, showing me the tool he's used to end the lives of others. The smile on his face is wicked and cruel. I lose it. I scream, struggling and yanking on my bonds, not caring if I have to cut my own hands off with that filthy rope. I know beyond a shadow of a doubt that he doesn't intend to let me leave this bed alive.

My mind flashes to Anna. What will she do without me? Who will take care of her? And Ryker. He is going to feel so guilty. He tried his hardest to keep me safe, but I'd ruined that with my stupid broken heart and wounded pride.

Krueger silences my scream by thrusting the blade of his knife against my throat. I freeze. I'm afraid to breathe. If I move even a fraction, his blade will cut into my skin, possibly ending my life. Staring at him, eyes wide, I try to get control of my breathing so that my throat doesn't move. My chest burns from the effort.

With his free hand, Krueger reaches down and runs his finger along my body, daring me to squirm. "You know how I got my name?"

I don't answer. I can't move. I just continue to stare into his eyes. They scare me more than his knife does. They're cold and empty; dead. It's like staring into the eyes of a shark.

"With this knife? I do shit that makes Freddy Krueger look like a saint." He sneers down at me and grabs my breast, squeezing painfully. A squeak escapes but I manage to hold still, the knife still at my throat.

Releasing my breast, he moves the knife from my throat. Plucking the front of my shirt away from my body, he runs the knife along it, slicing it open from hem to neckline. He does the same with my shorts, leaving me in only my cotton thong panties and a see through, white lace bra. He hums his appreciation low in his throat, causing my stomach to churn.

"I've fucked your sister in every position you can imagine." I squeeze my eyes closed, trying to block the mental image from my mind. "She's a good lay, but every time I fucked her, I pictured it was you I was fuckin'." He runs the tip of his blade across my stomach, stopping to flick it across my belly button. I lay there, fear freezing my body solid, goosebumps racing along my skin.

"Hottest fuckin' bitch I ever laid eyes on. I almost had you last time. I woulda kept you too, but then you knocked me over the fuckin' head and kicked me in the balls." He growls in anger, bringing the knife up and placing the tip against my breast. "Then that fucker Ryker calls, and suddenly my Prez tells me to leave you alone. I'M NOT SUPPOSED TO HAVE YOU?" He's screaming at me now. His eyes wild, chest heaving as he glares down at me.

"I'm gonna have you though," he whispers. His face splits into a wide, crazy grin. "Just can't keep you." He brings the knife down to the right of my belly button. "They can't do shit if they can't find a body."

The pain overwhelms me when he plunges that knife deep into my soft belly.

***

Ryker

I'm clutching my phone, waiting to hear something, anything, when it rings. I don't even look at the caller I.D. to see who it is. Selecting the "Accept" option, I put the phone to my ear. "Yeah?" My voice sounds hoarse.

"Ryker? Deed." Deed and my old man had hated each other. The two clubs had never gotten along. Since I became vice president of the Kings, I'd worked hard to mend that relationship. Allies were always better than enemies. I considered Deed a friend; maybe not a close one, but a friend nonetheless.

What've you got?" It's five o'clock in the morning. Krueger had taken Charlie around ten o'clock the night before. He's had her for seven hours now. Each hour my hope of finding my girl alive dwindles just a little bit more.

"Well, it could be nothin'. Then again, it could be exactly what you're lookin' for."

"What the fuck've you got?" I don't have time for fucking riddles. My skin is crawling with dread, and I pray to whatever fucking God may be out there that he can tell me something useful.

"We managed to track down a cousin of Krueger's. They ain't close, but he wouldn't tell us shit. Had to rough him up a bit. Guy's a fuckin' pussy. Said Krueger had come to him for money. Mentioned he was in some hot water. Was goin' to stay at their Grandpa's old fishin' shack for a while."

I sit up in my seat. "Where?"

"About forty five minutes west of Ottawa. He showed us on a map. I'll text you the GPS co-ordinates." He pauses. "I don't know if he's there or not, but it's the best I've got for ya."

Hope floods me, replacing the despair I was feeling. This is the best lead we've had. This has to be it. Charlie's life depends on it. A remote fishing shack would be the perfect place to take a hostage. "Text me the details."

"On it. And Ryker?"

I'm already heading for my bike. "Yeah?"

"As much as you're gonna want to … don't kill him." *What the fuck?* "That sick fucker has a lot to answer for, and we need to talk to him first. You'll get your blood, but we need a chance to interrogate him."

Fair enough. "Done."

"Texting you now. Good luck, brother. I hope you find your girl."

I manage to bark out a quick "Thanks", adrenaline coursing through me. Disconnecting, I swing my leg over my bike and start it up. The text comes through with the location. Copying it, I send a mass text to all my brothers with the details, calling everyone to action. Then, I take off to find my baby girl.

Chapter Eighteen

Charlotte

So much pain. My body shakes violently, pain taking over, erasing my fear. I can't breathe. Krueger yanks his knife free and lifts it to his face. Grinning, he runs his tongue along the length of the blade, my blood collecting on the tip.

"Fuckin' delicious." Lowering the blade, he slices it through the center of my bra, leaving a deep cut directly between my breasts. The cups fall to the side, baring my breasts to the chilly air, and his hungry eyes. Those eyes drink the sight in with greed.

Fast as lightening, he darts down and wraps his lips around my nipple, sucking deep. Revulsion courses through my veins.

"You fucking cocksucker!" I scream at the top of my lungs. Rage dulls the pain in my belly. I struggle and flail, once again desperate to release the bindings on my wrists and ankles.

Pulling away, he licks his lips before sneering at me with cold, hate filled eyes. His blade comes down again, plunging deep into my side. I scream in pain, squeezing my eyes closed. Blood gushes from the two puncture wounds in my torso, sticking me to the mattress like cheap glue.

His teeth are on my nipple at the same time I feel his blade at the crotch of my panties. Slicing the tiny piece of fabric, he rips away the last bit of covering I have left. He bites down, hard enough to draw blood. I struggle with everything I have in me, pulling and straining, praying the blood from my wrists acts as a lubricant to make my hands slip free. I can't feel my hands and feet anymore, blood pouring from beneath the rope. Gasping, I can't get enough air to fill my lungs and my head swims.

I hear him doing something at the side of the bed. Looking over through blurry eyes, I see him undoing his pants. He climbs up onto the bed, fitting himself between my legs, dick in hand. I try to scream, but the sound is muted from my lack of oxygen. Blackness fills my vision. I'm fading.

Just as I give up, letting the darkness rescue me from the horror of this nightmare, a crash comes from the other side of the cabin. A roar of fury fills my ears as I drift away into the peacefulness of the dark, thanking God for the escape.

***

Ryker

I'd sent the message to all of my brothers, rounding up the troops from wherever they were, to come and meet me at the cabin. I arrive first, Reaper close on my tail. We pull to a stop at the entrance to the path. It's a three kilometer hike in and I can't wait for back up. I need to get to Charlie.

Without a word, Reaper and I climb off our bikes, check our guns and take off down the beaten trail. As we get closer, a scream breaks the silence. I break out in a run, Reaper right behind me. She sounds like she's in pain. Terror rips through me as I push myself to run faster.

We come to a clearing, seeing the cabin several hundred feet away. Slowing, we take in our surroundings, looking for any signs of danger. That's when I hear her scream again. The sound is quieter; weaker. *Fuck.*

As one, Reaper and I hurry to the door. I stand aside as he lifts a giant foot and boots the flimsy door in. When I look through the open door rage overwhelms me, a roar of fury escaping my throat. The scene before me is straight out of a horror movie.

Charlie lays tied to an old bed, spread eagle, blood covering her torso. Her eyes are closed, skin white as a sheet. Krueger kneels on the bed, right between her legs, his filthy cock in hand. His turns his head to the door, a look of surprise on his face.

Aiming my gun at his head, I place my finger on the trigger. Reaper clamps his hand down on my arm, a silent warning that we can't kill him. I don't care. One look at Charlie and I want nothing more than to rip his guts open with his own knife, then hang the son of a bitch with his own shit filled intestines.

"Stay back!" he roars, raising his knife high over his head, a clear threat that he won't hesitate to bring it down into her chest. I lower the gun slightly. His body relaxes just before I squeeze the trigger, shooting him in the shoulder.

The knife drops from his hand as he clutches it with shaking hands. His scream of pain fills the tiny cabin. I rush him, knocking him off the bed, away from Charlie. Climbing on top of him, I raise my fist and punch him in the face. Then I punch him again. And again. And again. I grunt with effort every time I land a blow. Blood coats his face and my knuckles. At first he tries to fight me. I don't even notice when he stops fighting back. I keep punching him, blinded by rage; all reason gone. I'm not aware of anything but my need to kill this motherfucker.

"Ryker!" Reaper's anxious voice roaring my name slows my fists. He's on the edge of the bed, untying the last of Charlie's bindings. My rage clears, panic taking its place. I jump to my feet.

"Charlie!" She's motionless. Her skin's so pale, I can see the blue of her veins beneath it. "Baby girl! You need to wake up!"

Helpless, I look to Reaper. He whips off his t-shirt, ripping it in half. Glancing at me quickly, he moves to put pressure on two large gashes on her torso. "Call 911. Give them the co-ordinates. We'll carry her out to the road to meet them."

In a daze, I make the call, giving them the address, only telling them a woman's been stabbed before hanging up.

"Put pressure on these." I move to press the ripped t-shirt over the two gaping holes. "She's alive, but barely." Reaper is anxious, but in control. "She's not good, brother. She needs a hospital, fast." Grabbing a ratty afghan off the loveseat, he throws it over her, covering her nudity. "We need to move her to the road without jostling her too much."

I nod, eyes locked on Charlie's lips. Those beautiful lips that have given me the most amazing kisses I've ever received; they're turning blue. Reaper looks quickly around the room, then hops off the bed. He moves to the center of the cabin and kicks over the coffee table. Picking up the edge of a ratty pea green area rug, he drags it over beside the bed.

"Help me lift her," he demands. I stop putting pressure on just long enough to grab her under the arms while Reaper grabs her feet. Together, we lift her down and place her in the center of the rug. "Give me your belt."

I yank my belt off, handing it to Reaper. He wraps it around her belly, using it to hold the wadded t-shirt in place. He takes off his own and does the same with the other wound before looking up at me. "You know the cops will show?"

I nod, heart hammering in my chest. I can't speak. The words choke me, stuck in my throat. Charlie may not make it. Deed may not get his interrogation right away, but I don't give a fuck. Charlie needs an ambulance, and an ambulance means the cops will get involved. I may go to jail for this. I don't even know if Krueger will live. He may be dead right now for all I know, and it was me that beat him. None of that matters though. Not my freedom. Not my club's shaky relationship with the Devils. Nothing matters but helping Charlie.

We each take an end of the rug, folding Charlie up in it, and hurry out the door. Jase is running up to the cabin just as we exit. He looks down at the rug, a question on his face.

I finally find the words to speak. "We're taking Charlie to the road to meet the ambulance. Stay with him 'til the cops show."

"Cops? We're lettin' the cops in on this shit?" He sounds surprised.

I look down at Charlie before answering. She's wrapped up in that filthy carpet, covered in blood. She may not live and I don't know if I can live with that. "Charlie's in rough shape, Jase. We *had* to call an ambulance. The cops will be right behind them. We didn't do this so we have nothin' to worry about. Krueger is the one that kidnapped her, likely raped her and stabbed her, not us; we stopped him. Just tell 'em the truth."

Anger fills his features when I describe what happened to my girl. He nods, then stalks into the cabin.

We make it to the road, arms aching from the long hike, carrying our precious parcel, just as the ambulance approaches. The cops come screaming along right behind them, sirens wailing through the woods.

In a flurry of activity, Charlie's loaded into the ambulance, tubes sticking out of her everywhere. In the commotion, I hear them mention a possible collapsed lung and internal bleeding. I barely manage to scramble in behind them just as they shut the door. The medic starts to protest, but I glare him down, grab my girls hand and squeeze.

Leaning into her, I kiss the tip of her perfect little nose, and press my forehead into hers. "Stay with me, Charlie. You hear me? You can't fuckin' leave me." Every beep of the machine gives me hope. *Fuck. I love her.* I didn't realize it before, but now that I face losing her, I can't deny it. I can't imagine a life without Charlie in it.

The beeping in the background becomes a long, steady buzz; her heart monitor. The medic flies into action, beginning CPR. "Sir! You need to sit back. I need to get at the patient." I blink up at him, my heart dying right along with hers. "Sir! Move!"

He elbows me back, bringing forward the pads of the AED. I slump back against the wall, defeated. Running my hands through my hair, I watch as he tries to shock life back into the only woman I've ever loved.

He places the pads on her chest and steps back. "Clear!"

Chapter Nineteen

Charlie

I wake up slowly to a steady beeping sound coming from somewhere beside me. My body aches, and before I even open my eyes, everything comes rushing back to me. Fear for my life. Krueger. I remember him stabbing me; about to rape me. I'd passed out before that; I'd thought I was dying.

My throat is dry, and it hurts to swallow. Opening my eyes, I know from the familiar sounds and smells that I'll find myself in a hospital. I look around the room, amazed I'm still alive. My sweeping gaze stops when I see Ryker slumped in a chair directly beside me. He's sound asleep, clothes rumpled, hair a mess and a full beard covers his face. Even in sleep, he holds my hand.

My heart clenches a little. *God.* I was so angry at him. Actually, I'm still angry at him, but here he sits, likely worried about me, wanting to be a good *friend.* I'd screwed up sneaking away from the protection of the club – I'd almost died because of it. Ryker had been trying to protect me, and I'd let my wounded heart get the better of me, putting myself in danger. So now, I'm angry at *me* too.

Just then, a nurse comes quietly into the room. She smiles when she sees me, approaching the bed with a glance over at Ryker. "You're awake," she whispers.

I try to answer but my throat feels like I've swallowed a handful of razor blades. She reaches over to the bedside table and pours me a cup of ice water from the pitcher that sits there. She places a straw in it and holds it up to my lips. I take a sip, finding the cool water does wonders to soothe my pain. I gulp it down, managing three swallows before she pulls it away. "Not too much, honey. You need to start out slow so you don't make yourself sick."

She pulls out a thermometer and places it under my tongue. While waiting for the results, she nods over to Ryker. "Your man over there hasn't left your side since you got here."

I glance over at him. He's so gorgeous. My gut clenches and I try to push back the swell of love I feel for him. *I can't love him. I hardly know him.* Not to mention, he used me for sex and then went and screwed Lucy only hours later.

"He's kinda scary." I look back at the nurse, seeing her stare at him. She looks back at me and winks. "You're a lucky girl."

Tears fill my eyes. If she only knew; I'm not lucky. Ryker's here because he cares about me, sure, but that's as far as it goes; as far as it will ever go. She finishes what she's doing and gives my arm a squeeze. "I'll send the doctor in."

Nodding, I smile weakly. The closing door clicks loudly when she exits the room, causing Ryker to jump. He sits right up, eyes darting around the room, sleep still heavy on his face. When they land on me, I hear his breath catch.

"Charlie?" I blink slowly, still trying to battle the first round of unshed tears. His voice hitches when he says my name. "Oh, baby girl. Thank fuck." His voice hitches again with emotion, and a single tear escapes my eye. He reaches his thumb out and swipes it away before it gets too far down my cheek. "I was so worried about you. I'm so fucking sorry, baby. So sorry." His own eyes glisten with unshed tears.

"Not your fault." My voice is scratchy, my words slow. It hurts to talk. Closing his eyes, he leans forward to rest his forehead on mine for a moment before pulling away, holding my eyes captive with his own.

"It is. I promised you he'd never hurt you again and I didn't keep that promise. I will never be able to tell you how sorry I am."

Another tear falls; he catches that one too. "My fault."

"No, baby. No it wasn't. I know why you left, and I get it. I just ..." I place my hand on his cheek. "God, Charlie." He catches another tear on my face. "I'm just so happy you're ok. When I walked into that cabin, I thought you were dead. And fuck me if I didn't want to die right along with you." Guilt. I know he's feeling so much guilt.

Emotions swirl through me, causing my sore throat to close up and the blood to rush between my ears. Tears fall freely from my eyes. Placing both hands on my cheeks, he wipes them away with his thumbs. "No more tears. That fucker gets no more of your tears."

God. Why does he have to be so damned sweet? I need to harden my heart to him or I'm never going to survive. I can't accept his friendship or his concern. He'd used me. I'd been falling in love with him, and he'd called us a "mistake."

I close my eyes and turn away from him, needing a minute to strategize. How can I deal with this guilt ridden, sweet as hell Ryker? I need to remember everything that went on before Krueger got ahold of me. I need to or I'm going to fall back under his spell, and he's going to crush what's left of my heart into dust.

"Sleep, baby girl. I'll be right here when you wake up." He misunderstands my closed eyes for fatigue and that's ok with me. The less I have to deal with him, the better. I want him to leave, but at the same time, I need him to stay. His presence helps keep my fear at bay. For me, Ryker equals safety.

I lay that way, my heart aching, eyes closed, face turned away for a few more minutes before sleep claims me, the darkness once again rescuing me from danger; even if that danger comes from my own heartache.

***

Ryker

Charlie's been in the hospital for eight days now. Three of those days were spent with her unconscious, and today they were finally releasing her. I haven't left this place once since arriving in the ambulance with my girl. They'd almost lost her a few times. Her lung had collapsed and she'd had a lot of internal bleeding, not to mention the huge amount of blood she'd lost. After a lengthy surgery, several blood transfusions and four days in the intensive care unit, then four more to recover, she was finally able to go home.

Jase and Tease had spent a lot of time here also, waiting out in the waiting room for news on how Charlie was doing. They'd been a huge help, bringing me food and a change of clothes when I needed them. They both knew there was no way in hell I'd ever leave her again.

That douche fucker Jeremy had been here too. He'd brought her flowers, and I have to admit, I was jealous as hell when she'd smiled at him and asked for some privacy. I left the room without complaint, standing out in the hall, but I heard them in there. She actually had a conversation with him, reassuring him that she was ok and trying to ease his worry. She rarely talked to me at all. That just about killed me.

Jase had dealt with the police. They'd come to question me and I'd told them everything. They considered my part in beating the hell out of Krueger self-defense. Krueger was in the hospital for a couple days before being moved to the local remand center, awaiting trial. He'll be in jail for a long, long time.

As for Deed and the Devils, they were pissed. Getting the cops involved went against biker code and I'd broken that by calling an ambulance. I couldn't bring myself to care though. Charlie would have died otherwise, and there was no way I'd have let that happen. I hadn't spoken to him myself, but I'm pretty sure I can smooth things over with Deed if Gunner can't. It's not like they can't get their information from Krueger in jail. They have plenty of brothers in custody right now, and they can get that dirty job done from the inside.

Charlie's been quiet and I have to admit, I'm worried. I've avoided bringing up Krueger, or that night, because I don't quite know where her head's at. What she went through is enough to fuck up anybody's mind and I want to protect her from any further pain.

Now we're just waiting for the doctor to sign her release papers. I watch Charlie sitting on her bed, eyes to the window, quiet. Too quiet. I'd give anything to know what's going on in that head of hers.

Just then, the door swings open and Charlie's doctor walks in. "Alright Ms. Daniels, your release papers are signed and you should be ready to go." He offers her a smile. She looks up at him, face blank and just nods. A small frown creases the doctor's face before he continues. "As I've mentioned to your boyfriend here, you –"

"He's not my boyfriend," Charlie rushes out, sounding annoyed. "Please forward all information to *me* regarding *my* care."

I notice the doctor glance over at me, but my eyes are glued to Charlie. This is the most emotion she's shown since that first night she woke up, but I'm not sure I like the way she's showing it. Is she pissed at *me*?

Her doctor clears his throat. "Ok, well, as I've shared with Mr. Cole, you will need to have someone stay with you for a couple of weeks. Your injuries are healing, but there is still danger of infection, and you have to be *sure* not to exert yourself. I want you on bedrest for at least another couple weeks, at which point, we will reassess your progress."

Tears shine in her eyes as Charlie listens to what I've already heard, her expression bordering on hopeless. "Ok. Um … ok. I will call a friend and see if –"

I jump out of my seat, moving to stand in front of her. Placing my hands on either side of her face, I lean in close. "Charlie. Look at me."

She hesitates, then raises her eyes to meet mine. *Fuck.* The light in her eyes is barely even there anymore. She looks so broken. *How can I fix this?* "Baby girl, do you really think I'm gonna let you go home and not take care of you?"

A tear slides down her cheek; I quickly swipe it away with my thumb.

"You don't have to come home with me, Ryker." She sighs. "I have friends." Her eyes harden and her jaw tightens. "Real friends. And they will be more than willing to come and help me out for a couple weeks."

"Fuck that, Charlie." Frustration slowly creeps its way in and I try to keep it from coloring my voice. "You're coming home with me. I'm going to take care of you. Not some girl from work. Not Dr. Douchebag. Me."

Her voice cracks and the tears flow faster now; too quickly for me to wipe away. "You don't have to do that, Ryker. Krueger is gone now. I'm not in danger anymore. You don't have to take care of me out of guilt. I'll be fi –"

Before I can stop myself, I reach out and grab her ponytail, sitting high at the back of her head. I wrap it around my fist, then tug her head back firmly so she has to look me right in the eyes. "Enough!" I'm so far past frustrated now, barreling my way right through to anger. *Guilt? She thinks I'm doing this out of guilt?* I see the doctor take a step towards me, but I ignore his ass and focus on my girl. I need to make her understand.

"This has nothing to do with guilt. Not one fucking thing." I'm breathing heavily, my breaths causing her hair to blow around her face. "I'm going to take care of you because your mine to fucking take care of. I should have done it from the beginning." I shake my head in frustration and groan. She's staring at me, eyes wide, lips parted in shock. I've finally gotten her attention. Using my fist in her hair, I bring her face closer.

Slanting my head, I place a gentle kiss on her lips. She kisses me back just as gently, and I hear her swallow back a sob as she brings her hand up, cupping the side of my neck. My lips still on hers, I whisper, "Baby, you've been taking care of everyone else your whole life. It's your turn to be taken care of. Let me take care of you."

A sob escapes her throat before she nods and looks up at me, tears streaming down her cheeks. We stare into each other's eyes for a moment before we hear someone clear their throat. *Shit. The doctor.*

We both turn to him and find him smiling wide at us both. "Now that we've got that settled, here are your prescriptions, after surgery care instructions and your next appointment date." He hands a small stack of papers to Charlie, then looks to me. "She's to stay in bed as much as possible. She only leaves it to use the washroom. It's very important that she maintains minimal physical activity."

I reach out and grab her hand, giving it a squeeze before answering. "Got it. She's in good hands, Doc. Thanks."

"Also," he continues, giving me a hard stare, "she needs to be kept calm. Getting her worked up is not good for her recovery. Try to keep her happy, ok?"

I look down at her and kiss the tip of her nose. "That's the plan."

Chapter Twenty

Charlotte

I'm going insane. Two weeks I've been in this stupid bed and stared at these same damned walls. Two weeks I've been staying at Ryker's house, waiting for the doctor to remove his bedrest order. That also means, it's been two weeks I've been sleeping in the same bed *with* Ryker, enduring his sweet and protective side; I need to get the hell out of here.

It turns out, Ryker is pretty amazing. He can be so gentle and kind. Both of these he has been in spades since I got out of the hospital. Each night I have nightmares. I wake up in the night screaming, still feeling Krueger's blade at my throat or teeth on my skin, his voice still ringing in my ears. Each time, Ryker holds me and soothes me, eventually helping me get back to sleep.

We don't talk ever about these nightmares. He knows what they are and I know they bother him. I can tell by the set of his jaw, and the look in his eyes when he asks if I'm ok. The truth is, I'm not ok. Though, other than the nightmares, Krueger never enters my thoughts. I don't cower from men or have vivid memories of that night while I'm awake. He's not the reason I'm not ok; the reason I'm not ok is Ryker.

He'd broken my heart. He'd used my body, and while I'd been falling in love with him, he'd pushed me away. Now, with him so near, it's extremely hard to hold him at arm's length. He's in my space all the time. He brings me food and drinks, helps me to and from the bathroom, then waits outside the door, prowling like a mother lion, until I finish what I need to do. Each day is filled with us, in his bed, watching endless Netflix marathons and playing video games. Sometimes, he tries to talk to me and I can't help but get sucked in.

He tells me about his past. His father was a monster and his mother's death was tragic. He'd been through so much at such a young age. I know what it's like to be alone after the death of a parent. He tells me funny stories about him and Jase, and growing up in the MC clubhouse. His childhood was so very different from mine. I answer his questions about my mother and sister, tell him about James and how I've never had many friends. He listens intently, as if soaking up every little piece of information about me he can.

During these talks, I realize that Ryker is funny and intelligent. He praises me over and over for being brave and strong. He also tells me that he wishes he had met my mother, because it's clear from my stories that I get my strength from her. Maybe he's right.

Through all of this, my heart keeps getting sucked farther and farther into a deep, irrevocable love for him. The heart that he'd broke slowly mends and it seems to forget what he'd done to break it in the first place. But my mind doesn't forget. I remind myself constantly that he played me for sex, then screwed that skank the very same night. He said that I wouldn't make a good old lady, and with the way he'd said it, I knew that he'd meant it. I know he cares about me, and it's clear he was scared for me, but now I just need to go home.

Ryker and I have just returned from a trip to my doctor, who had looked me over, asked me a million questions and then, finally, granted me my freedom. I still have to take it easy. He'd stated that I was healing nicely, but rigorous exercise or movements could impede my healing. As long as I promised to follow his orders, he said there was no reason why I had to stay in bed anymore. Needless to say, I'd made that promise.

Now we're back at Ryker's house. He hadn't said much as we left the office or when we got back to his house; he went right to the kitchen. I can hear him banging stuff around out there, and I have no clue what he's doing, but I couldn't care less. I have some packing to do.

Pulling out the small backpack I'd used the first night I'd come here, I start shoving my clothes into it. I search through every drawer and under the bed, wanting to make sure to leave nothing behind. That way, once I'm gone from here, I'll have no reason to return.

There's too much stuff to cram into my bag, so I start a large pile of clothing on the bed. I'll have to ask Ryker if he has one I could borrow. I'm just about to go into the bathroom for my toiletries, when Ryker comes stalking into the room, a bottle of beer in each hand.

He has a slight smile on his face, but when he sees my bag and pile of clothes, his face creases with a frown. "What are you doing?"

I try to keep my tone light. "Packing my stuff." He stiffens and places his hands on his hips. "You heard the doctor. I'm ok to be alone now, Ryker. I'm sure you must be itching to get your room back."

"You're not going," he declares.

Um ... what? I sigh. I don't want to fight with him. "I am, Ryker. My stuff is almost ready to go. If you aren't going to take me, I'll call a cab."

Ryker breaks from his stance and stalks over to me. I watch him come, gasping when he doesn't stop in front of me, like I expect. Instead, he sets both bottles on the dresser, grabs my arms firmly, using them to back me against the wall. His face lowers to mine until we're almost nose to nose.

"Don't go," he whispers.

My belly flutters. Looking into his eyes, I see tenderness swirling through them. I need to ignore that. I need to leave. "I have to. I can't stay here anymore."

His eyes search mine. I can only hold his stare, unable to breathe. His closeness is wreaking havoc on my heart. Finally, he moves impossibly closer, running his nose along mine. "You're still pissed at me."

My belly stops fluttering, anger taking its place deep in my gut. Standing up straight, I place my hands on his chest and attempt to push him back. He moves only a little while he takes in my glare.

"Yes, I'm still *pissed* at you!" I give him another shove. "Did you think if you were nice to me for a few weeks, I'd just forget?"

His eyes close and he rests his forehead on mine. He stays that way for several seconds before taking a deep breath and looking into my eyes once more. "I'm so fucking sorry, Charlie. I promised you that fucker would never hurt you and I fucked up. I'm mad at myself –"

"You think I'm mad at you because of Krueger?" I'm shocked. All this time, he's been blaming himself about that?

He frowns, nodding but not breaking eye contact as I lean forward. "Krueger was not your fault, Ryker. Anna started that whole fiasco. That psycho getting ahold of me is not on you. It was me who ran away from you. I made it easy for him to get to me." I pause, watching as he takes in my words. "And I ran, because I couldn't be around you anymore. I still can't."

He lifts a hand, placing it against my cheek. I grab his wrist and squeeze it, trying to pull it from my face. "I don't have a lot of experience with men." He stills. "What I do know is, a man that can fuck me in the morning, like I was someone special, and then fuck some whore in the evening, proving I'm not, isn't a man I want to be with."

He rears back as if I'd slapped him. His eyes narrow. "What the fuck?"

I plant my hands on my hips. "Lucy told me everything, Ryker. She told me that she fucked you the night we were together. She told me that you said you were getting rid of me.

And then you did. You said I was a mistake. You said I wasn't fit to be your old lady. You broke my heart, but then continued to keep me close. I couldn't handle it, so I left."

Throughout my speech his breaths come out more and more rapidly, his face turning red. He looks pissed. Well good for him. So am I! "After I woke up in the hospital, I kept waiting for you to leave, but you just wouldn't." A tear rolls down my cheek. "I need to get away. Every time I look at you, my heart bleeds."

"You done?" he growls.

Shocked, I just stare at him and nod, another tear escaping my eye.

"Good. 'Cause it's my turn to talk." He takes a step forward, boxing me in again. "You are special Charlie, so get that shit outta your head right now. That morning was fuckin' incredible. I haven't been able to stop thinking about it. I've never felt that shit for anyone before." My breath catches and my tears stop flowing. "I didn't fuck that bitch. I haven't been anywhere near her in months. She was fuckin' with you. She didn't know it then, but when she did that, she fucked with me too. I'll deal with her nasty ass later."

He didn't sleep with her? She'd lied? Well, I admit, that makes me feel better. It still doesn't erase the fact that he'd ended things with me after, what I'd thought, was the beginning of something special for us – after I'd already started falling in love with him. "You were never a mistake, baby." My eyes shoot to his and he places a hand on my cheek again. "I only told you that because I was convinced my life would put yours in danger." My forehead creases with a frown. "I told you about my mother. That shit happened to her because of my father and the club." His eyes close and he shakes his head slightly. "I wouldn't survive if it happened to you."

My heart clenches. His reason makes complete sense, but I have to protect what's left of my heart. There's no way I can trust him after the way he slam bam thank you ma'amed me. "I can see why you felt that way," I admit. "But that doesn't change anything. You made me feel terrible about myself. Like a slut. Nobody's ever made me feel that way before. I won't let you do it again."

He shakes his head. "I won't, baby girl. I am so goddamned sorry for cuttin' you loose. I convinced myself it was for your own good, but really it was for mine." My eyes widen in surprise at his admission. "I was afraid. I don't have a family. I don't have people in my life that I care about. I've never had feelings for anyone before, and the thought of losing you ..." He squeezes his eyes closed and shakes his head. "Fuck. I really thought I'd lost you. Forever. I can't lose you baby. You're the only good thing in my life."

It makes sense. Ryker's actions were to protect me. *What an ass.* "Ryker?" He opens his eyes and looks at me. "You're an ass." His eyes flash and he opens his mouth to speak, but I cut him off. "What happened to your mother had nothing to do with the MC. What happened to your mother happened because your dad was a slut who couldn't keep his dick in his pants."

One look at his face tells me that what I've said has penetrated. "What happened to me was because Anna is a needy brat. Danger comes in many forms, for many reasons. I've always lived my life on the safe side. I've never gotten into any trouble, and I spent a lot of years being afraid. Afraid of people, afraid of disease ... afraid of being alone. If nothing else, that night Krue ..." I can't even bring myself to say his name. "The night it happened, I realized I've always sheltered myself so much that I've never really lived. I'm so tired of being afraid, Ryker. I want to live."

He crushes me to him, nose in my neck. "I want to live too, baby."

The tone of his voice both breaks and mends my wounded heart. Ryker's past had broken him too. I don't know what to say so I just nod, my heart pounding wildly.

He stares at me for a moment, then his face splits into a wide, panty melting grin. *And there it is. The dimple.* "When did you get so fucking smart?"

I put my nose in the air. "I've always been smart. You were just too busy trying to get into my panties to pay attention."

He chuckles softly. "Yeah. You're right. They're very sexy panties." His smile fades as he brings his hand up, fisting my hair at the nape of my neck. "You were right about something else too." I look up at him, belly fluttering all over again. "I'm an ass." I can't help it. Hearing him say that makes my face break out in a grin.

He looks at me with such intensity, my heart flip flops in my chest. "Charlie, I love you." I suck in a breath. *Did he really just say that?* "I think I've loved you from the moment I first laid eyes on you. The way you handled Smokey; the way you were with me. Baby girl, you're the most amazing woman I've ever met. To be honest, it did scare me. Fuck, it still scares me. When Krueger had you, and I thought you were going to die ..." He squeezes my hair. "Fuckin' agony." He runs his nose along mine once again. "Don't leave baby," he whispers. "Let me fix us."

Oh. My. God. Everything he's said tumbles around and around in my mind. He loves me. He didn't sleep with that skank. I'm not a mistake. And it's worth mentioning again - he loves me. Looking back on everything he'd done since the first time Krueger had attacked me, I can see it. Everything he'd done was because he loved me. A man doesn't do any of that for a woman he doesn't love. My heart swells. Standing up on my tip toes, I place my lips softly on his. "I won't leave, baby."

And then he kisses me. A toe curling, earth shattering, need to get him out of those jeans kiss. I can feel everything in that kiss. All of his love, and his passion, and his fear that I'd almost died; I also feel his surrender, his acceptance and his relief. It takes my breath away. I tug his shirt out of his pants, hands shoving up inside to feel the smooth, hard flesh on his back.

Both of us are panting when he pulls away and smiles at me with pained eyes. "Over exertion, baby girl." He adjusts himself, the outline of his erection evident through his jeans. "Let's get you unpacked," he whispers before kissing the tip of my nose.

***

Ryker

I can't remember ever feeling completely happy. Content yes, but never happy. That night, laying in my bed, Charlie asleep on my shoulder, I am. We'd talked more over dinner and decided that she would stay with me for a while, at least until she goes back to work. That gives me at least four weeks to convince her to stay here permanently.

I want nothing more than to bury myself in her and let her feel what she does to me – how much I love her – but I can't. The doctor had said that physical activity wouldn't be possible for a few more weeks. That's ok though; I can wait. As long as she's in my bed, surrounding me with her smell, letting me kiss her when I want to, I'm ok with waiting.

Charlie's been asleep for a while, but I can't fucking sleep. She'll be awake soon. Every night, after about two hours, she wakes up screaming. Each of those nights, I hold her. I rock her and whisper to her and tell her that she's safe. I won't fall asleep until that happens because I don't want her going through that shit alone.

As if on cue, Charlie bolts upright in bed, eyes wide but unseeing, a scream ripping from her throat. Sitting up, I place my hand on her back, soothing her with my words. "It's ok baby. You're safe. I'm right here." Seeing her like this rips me to shreds. I hate knowing that she lives with these memories.

When her body relaxes, I pull her to my chest and lay back down, stroking her hair with one hand while the other squeezes her tightly to me. Usually, she lays like this for a while before sleep finds her again; tonight, she looks up at me with tears in her eyes.

"Ryker?" Her voice is small and full of uncertainty.

Yeah baby?"

"I need you to make love to me." My body freezes and she rushes on. "Please. I know that the doctor doesn't want me to exert a lot of energy, but I can't stop thinking about him." Anger churns in my gut. "Every night I wake up and remember him touching me. Getting ready to ..." she swallows. "Rape me. I want you to touch me. I need you to. Please just love me and wash it all away."

God. How can I say no to that? But I can't do it – she's not ready. "I can't do that, baby." I hear her frustrated and sad exhale before I continue. "But I'm sure I can come up with something."

I roll her to her back, placing my hand on her smooth, silky thigh. I love that when she's here, all she ever wears to bed is one of my tees and her panties. It's one of the sexiest fucking things I've ever seen. Leaning forward, I take her lips in a hard, frantic kiss, swallowing her gasp of surprise.

My dick is already hard. *Fucker.* He's gonna have to wait awhile. This is about Charlie. Slowly, I pull up her t-shirt, exposing her flat belly, and then her perfect tits. *Fuck.* This is going to be difficult. I'm going to need a cold shower afterwards.

The glow from the nightlight Charlie insisted on shines across her body, highlighting each and every one of her curves. I see the faded yellow shadow of bruises left by that monsters teeth, surrounding her nipple. *That son of a bitch. I want to kill him for touching her. For marking her.* I lean forward and lave my flattened tongue across her nipple. She squirms, letting out a low moan. Pulling back, I give her a stern look. "Stay still baby, or I stop." If she moves, I will lose what little fucking control I have.

She nods and grabs the back of my head, pushing it back down towards her tit. I can't help but chuckle. *My naughty girl.* I pull her nipple into my mouth, flicking it with my tongue. She doesn't move, but her moans get louder.

I focus all of my attention on those full, round tits. Worshipping them; worshipping her. I glide my hand across her belly, carefully avoiding the still healing wounds, and slowly reach down inside her panties. She tilts her hips just a little, causing my balls to ache with the need to release. I growl at her, nipple still in my mouth; she stops squirming.

Parting her flesh with the tip of my finger, I graze her clit lightly. *Fuck.* She's so wet. My dick screams at me, but I ignore it. I slide my finger deep inside her, hooking her in that perfect spot. Using the heel of my hand to rub her clit, I nip and lick at her swollen nipples, using my finger to drive her over the edge.

She moans from deep inside her throat. I know she's close when her body starts trembling. Watching Charlie come is fucking incredible. Her hair is wild, lips swollen and a deep shade of pink. The flush on her cheeks has spread down her neck and across the creamy white flesh of her breasts. She is magnificent. Her body tenses, calling out my name with her release.

Slowly, I withdraw my hand, looking into her eyes while I suck her pleasure from my fingers. "Fuckin' delicious, baby girl."

Seeing her staring up at me like that, eyes hooded, cheeks flushed even brighter, just about makes me come undone. *Fucking Christ.* I need to cool off.

I pull back, pausing to kiss the tip of her nose. "That'll have to do for now. As soon as the doctor clears you, I'm gonna bury myself deep inside that pretty little pussy of yours and I'm not comin' out for days." She grins at me then, her face lighting up in that way that never fails to knock me on my ass. That light she had lost is back in her eyes.

"Sounds like a plan to me," she whispers.

I grin back, then flop to my side, ignoring the raging hard on I'm sporting. Pulling her against me, I bury my nose in the crook of her neck. "Now sleep, baby."

Chapter Twenty One

Ryker

It's been a little over a month since Charlie and I found our way back to each other. It's been fucking incredible. We laugh, we joke, we argue, and then we fuck. A lot. We can't seem to get enough of each other. If I'm not seducing her in the kitchen, she's attacking me in the shower.

I've learned quickly that Charlie's not as meek as I'd first thought. The girl has attitude, and fuck me if I don't love it. When she gets angry, her cheeks flush and her little fists ball up at her sides. It's so fucking cute. To shut her up, all I have to do is kiss her and the next thing I know, she's climbing me like a goddamned tree. Like I said – fucking incredible.

I spend most of my days running around doing shit for the club, leaving Charlie on her own for most of the day. I always make sure to get home early though, so I can spend time with my girl. The couple of times I had been late, I'd found her asleep in my bed, looking completely fuckable, wearing nothing but my Kings of Korruption t-shirt. Both those times, I'd woken her with my tongue between her legs. I don't know which of us loves that more. My girl tastes fucking divine.

Today though, I got done with my shit early and headed into the city, stopping at a popular antiques store. A fucking antique store. The things I do for this woman.

Charlie had told me about the antique vase that had once been her grandmothers, and how she'd always kept it full of fresh flowers because they remind her of her mom. I know it had broken her heart to lose that vase, so I'd found her a new one. I know it's not the same; it's not a family heirloom, but it is old, and it is beautiful, and I know she's going to love it.

Pulling into the driveway, I climb off my bike and open the saddle bag, taking out the shiny white, ceramic vase. I've filled it with a fresh arrangement of summer flowers that the lady at the florist said any woman would love. *Fucking flowers. I can't believe I'm doing this shit.*

I climb the stairs, careful to keep the vase behind my back, just in case Charlie peeks out the window. Walking inside, I see that I shouldn't have worried; Charlie doesn't even know I'm home. I stand in the doorway watching her, grinning from ear to ear.

She's wearing a tiny pink tank top and a pair of cut off jean shorts, hair in a messy bun and earphones hanging from her ears. The mop in her hand is flying across the floor as she shakes her sexy little ass to the music, singing the lyrics to a Def Leppard song at the top of her lungs.

Still grinning, I take another step into the room. She catches the movement from the corner of her eye and screams, hand flying to her chest.

"Jesus Christ, Ryker! You scared the shit out of me!"

I chuckle. "I see that." Moving towards her, I grab her by the hip and pull her to me. "You've got some sexy moves, baby. You're gonna have to do a little strip tease for me later." I wink.

She laughs. Her laugh is incredible. I love hearing it and work hard to get it; often. "Yeah. Think you could handle it?"

I grin at her and lean in, placing my lips on hers. "We'll just have to find out, won't we?"

Wrapping her arms around my neck, she smiles widely at me. I straighten, still keeping the vase behind my back with one hand.

"I got something for you today."

She looks at me and tilts her head to the side. "You did?" She puts out her hand, wiggling her fingers. "Gimme."

I chuckle softly. Pulling my arm from behind my back, I present her with her vase of flowers. If her gasp is anything to go by, I think she likes it. She presses both hands over her mouth and just stares at it. *Ok. Maybe she doesn't like it.*

"I know it's not the same, but it's an antique like your other one. I just thought you might like something new to put your flowers in." I feel awkward; like I've done the wrong thing. She keeps staring at it, a few tears shining on her cheeks. "We can take it back and you can pick out one you like. It's no big deal."

She gasps again and snatches it right out of my hands, hugging it to her chest. "You will do no such thing, Ryker Cole. It's perfect."

I can't help but smile widely at her. *Ok. She likes it.* It didn't seem like it at first, but what the fuck do I know? Women confuse the shit out of me.

"Where did you get this?"

"I went to that antique store downtown."

"*You* went to an antique store?" Her tone is incredulous.

"Babe. You needed a vase."

She keeps the flowers clutched to her chest and tears fill her eyes. "Do you have any idea how much I love you?"

Her words cause my heart to drop right into my stomach. I'd told her I loved her well over a month ago but she has yet to say it back. I'd ignored it, wanting her to say it when she was ready, not just because I'd said it to her. That didn't mean I didn't wonder though.

Grabbing the vase from her hands, I set it on the hall table. I wind her ponytail around my fist and grip her waist tightly. I pull her to me, pressing her body into mine. "Say it again," I growl. I *need* to hear her say it again; to prove I hadn't imagined it.

She holds my eyes. Placing a hand on the side of my face, she uses her thumb to caress my cheek. "I love you, Ryker."

Fuck. I pull her face to mine and claim her mouth with my own, kissing her hard and deep. I pour all of my love for her into that kiss, *feeling* all of her love for me when she kisses me back.

I need her. I need to fuck her. I need to bury myself inside her, mark her somehow. *Fuck. She loves me.*

Breaking the kiss only long enough to whip her shirt over her head, I rub my hand across her stomach. Feeling the scars on her belly, my gut twists a little. I need to find a way to get rid of those fucking things. Every time I see them or feel them, I think of what that crazy fuck did to her. I hate that he can invade our bedroom, even if it is only in my thoughts.

I pull my lips away, reach for the button on her shorts and slide them, and her panties off her hips. Turning her away from me, I press her front into the wall. "I can't wait, Charlie. I need to fuck you."

She grabs my hand and slides it down her belly. Using her finger, she presses mine over her clit. "Then shut up and fuck me, baby."

Jesus. Nobody has ever turned me on like Charlie. I need to hear her say it again.

Sliding two fingers deep inside her pussy, I rub the heel of my hand on her clit. Wanting to hear her voice, I pinch her nipple, causing her to cry out. "Say it again."

She pants heavily, her breaths ragged and stuttered. "I —" Moaning, she grinds her hips down onto my hand.

"Fucking say it!"

"I love you, Ryker," she gasps out.

I yank my fingers out and drive myself inside of her, pinning her to the wall with nothing but my dick in her pussy and my hands on her hips. *Fucking Christ, she feels magnificent.*

Crying out, she places her hands flat on the wall and uses them to help her drive her hips back onto my cock. She is so fucking tight. We'd both been tested for STD's and Charlie had been on the pill for a full month now. To be safe, we'd been using condoms as well, until her birth control was in full effect but I couldn't wait any longer. She is so silky and wet. Feeling my baby with nothing in between us makes my eyes roll back in my head. She needs to come soon; I'm not going to last.

"Come for me, baby," I growl into her ear.

She gasps and pants, still driving her hips back into mine. Her body shakes and her pussy clenches me like a vice, milking every ounce of pleasure from my cock, pushing me over the edge. We come together, our bodies totally in sync.

Still buried deep inside of her, I reach up, gripping one of her tits in each hand. I pinch her nipples hard, causing her pussy to squeeze me once again. "I fuckin' love you too, baby girl. So fuckin' much."

She moans but turns her head to mine, capturing my mouth in a hot, claiming kiss. I pull away and catch her eyes. "Move in with me."

A laugh bubbles up from her throat. "What? Ryker? You can't be serious."

I just continue to stare at her, my face showing her just how serious I am.

"Ryker!" She turns in my arms, disconnecting us and faces me. The look on her face is serious and grave. "Baby, we've barely known each other for two months."

Grasping her face in my hands, I stroke her cheeks with my thumbs. "Charlie, I love you. I want to be with you. You're my whole fucking world. That's not going to change. You said you wanted to live. Let's live, baby. Move in with me."

Her face softens and her eyes search mine. She tilts her head into my hand, nuzzling her cheek against it. "Ok, honey. Let's live."

I wrap my arms around her waist and pull her to me, lifting her feet up off the floor before kissing her hard and fast. "I fucking love you."

She smiles widely. "And I love you."

Fuck yeah. She loves me.

***

Charlotte

I'm just putting the final touches on my makeup when the doorbell rings. Ryker pops his head out of the shower and looks from me to the open door of the bathroom.

"It's ok, honey. I'll get it."

He looks at me for a moment before nodding. "I'll be out in a minute."

I head out of the bathroom, hurrying down the hall towards the door when the doorbell rings again. The prospects are coming to help Ryker move my stuff from my apartment to his house while I'm at work. I'd protested that I wanted to do it myself, but Ryker had insisted I shouldn't be doing any lifting. He wouldn't budge so I'd reluctantly agreed. It wasn't like I had much of a choice. Besides, I was busy today anyways. This is my first shift back at the nursing home since my attack. I'm looking forward to it; to getting back to life.

Pulling the door open, I pause when I see that it's not the prospects. Reaper stands in the doorway, jaw tight, his eyes on me.

"Uh … hey. Ryker will be right out." I pull the door open wider and gesture to the inside of the house. "Come on in."

He doesn't take my invitation. He stares at me, intensity burning in his eyes. "Actually, I wanted a word with you. If that's cool."

Shocked, I nod, unease swirling in my belly.

"I was a dick. That night ..." He spears his fingers through his hair and lets out a deep breath. "I shouldn't have said the shit I said to you. I'm glad my boy has you, and I'm glad you're ok." His words are growled but I know this is his way of apologizing. I also know this isn't something he normally does.

I owe this man my life, so I don't make him work for it. I forgave him long ago. Smiling up at him, I place my hand on his arm. His eyes follow my movements before flicking up to me, surprise evident on his face. "Thank you, Reaper." I hold his stare. "For everything. I wouldn't be here if it weren't for you." I give his arm a gentle squeeze.

He nods his head and noticeably swallows. Knowing that he's not comfortable with this whole conversation, I pull away and step aside so he can come in. "You want a beer?"

He follows me in slowly. "No." He pauses, clearly uncomfortable. "Thanks though. We gotta be goin' soon."

I nod, at a loss for what else to say. Just then, Ryker comes out of the bathroom. He looks from me to Reaper, eyes assessing the situation. Looking back to me, he asks, "Everything cool?"

"Yeah, honey. I was just offering Reaper a beer. You want one?" I smile at him, showing him that everything is completely fine, and he has no need to worry.

He shakes his head. "Nah. We gotta get you to work, and I got shit to do today." I smile up at him and he winks. "Go get your shit. We gotta go."

The smile still on my face, I head off to the kitchen to grab my "shit". I can hear Ryker and Reaper talking in the other room.

"What's up, Reap?" Things had been strained between the two of them for a while. I don't know what had happened, but I have a feeling it's because of me. I know the tension has bothered Ryker though. He doesn't have many close friends, and Reaper is important to him.

"Just thought I'd come by and help you guys get Charlotte's shit moved."

"Yeah?" I stand in the kitchen, holding my breath, waiting to hear what he says next.

But it's not Ryker who speaks. It's Reaper. "Yeah. You should know, I had a word with Charlotte."

This is followed by silence. I peek around the corner and see Ryker staring at him; assessing. Reaper stares back. Ryker seems to find what he's looking for because he lifts his hand and claps it down hard on Reaper's shoulder.

"Glad to have your help, fucker. You can ride with the prospects."

Reaper's face contorts. "Fuck that. I take my bike. I'll meet you at her place." He turns, stalking out of the house.

Entering the room, I approach Ryker as he chuckles after his friend. "Everything ok, honey?"

He pulls me into his arms, smiling down at me before sliding his nose along mine. "Yeah, baby girl. Everything's great."

He leads me out of the house and down the driveway to his motorcycle. I love riding on it now. The fear I used to feel about bikes is long gone. Ryker and I take leisurely drives on it all the time, and now, even though he thinks I'm joking when I say it, I want one of my own.

I wrap my arms around him, taking in his scent and let the feeling of flying carry me away. I've never been so content with my life. I'm moving in with a man I love, who loves me back just as fiercely. I'm going back to a job that makes me happy. My sister is almost done paying back her debt, and apparently has found her own motorcycle man to take care of her. I'd met him, and although he's a little scary, he really does seem to care about her. For the first time ever, I feel free. I am living.

Ryker pulls up to the entrance of the nursing home and I swing my leg over, climbing off the bike like a pro. He grabs my waist, pulling me up against his side and smiles at me.

"Have a good night, Charlie."

I smile back and lean in to kiss him. "You too, honey."

When I pull back slightly, his eyes are narrowed on something behind me. His jaw clenches, but before I can turn around to see what he's looking at, he pulls me into him once again. His lips capture mine with a burning intensity. Even now, I'm amazed at how one kiss from Ryker can cause my heart to race.

I part my lips in a gasp and he takes full advantage, sliding his tongue along mine; tasting me. I tilt my head, swept away by the love I feel for this crazy man. He reaches down, gripping my ass and pressing me against his thigh. He continues tangling his tongue with mine and I grab onto his leather cut, oblivious of my surroundings and enjoy the ride.

My heart is pounding, my head swimming, when he finally pulls back. He grins at me, eyes crinkling at the corners. I try to catch my breath and lean in, giving him one final peck on the lips. He grabs the back of my head, keeping his lips on mine and rumbles, "See you tonight, baby girl."

I smile against his lips. "See you tonight."

Slowly, he releases me and I take a step back. He winks as I turn towards the building – and then it makes sense. He was staring at Jeremy. Jeremy stands by the entrance, face pale, a bouquet of flowers clenched in his fist.

I whip back around and glare at Ryker. "You –"

"Now he knows." The matter of fact way that he states it causes anger to burn low in my belly.

"Why don't you just pee all over me? Mark your territory."

He chuckles. "Not into that shit babe, but I'm willing to try it if you are."

I narrow my eyes at him causing him to burst out laughing. *He is so infuriating sometimes.*

"He needed to know, Charlie. Now he knows." I roll my eyes, making his smile wider. "Have a good night, baby girl. I'll be here at eleven to take you home."

Forgetting my anger, my belly flip flops when he reminds me of "home". Our home – together. I can't hide my smile. "See you tonight."

I turn again, noting that Jeremy is gone, and without a backward glance, hurry into work.

Epilogue

Charlotte

Accepting a beer from the prospect behind the bar, I turn and let my eyes sweep over the clubhouse. There are a few old ladies and several club whores, who like me, are all waiting for the guys to get finished with their meeting.

They're all here for the same reason I am. Tonight is a celebration. Tease is finally getting his patch. I'm beyond happy for him. He may not be the friendliest person I know, but I'd seen a small glimpse of the man he really is, buried beneath his scary exterior. I know he doesn't seem to have anyone in his life but the club, and he had done a lot for them with absolute loyalty. If anyone deserves a patch, it's Tease.

Lucy's here too. Ryker had told me he'd "dealt with her." Since then, anytime I was around, she stayed far away from me. She still gifted me with dirty looks on occasion, and I saw her watching Ryker and I when we were together, but she never spoke to me. Ryker had said the guys liked her, and as long as she left me alone, we shouldn't have any more problems from her. I wasn't so sure.

Just then, the guys come filing into the room. Tease is in the center of it all, looking uncomfortable with the attention, but wearing his new patch proudly. I catch his eye and shoot him a small smile. He gives me a small chin lift in return. It's better than nothing.

Ryker approaches me, bright blue eyes burning into mine. He leans into me, pressing against my side before whispering in my ear. "Hey, baby girl."

His breath blows across my cheek and down my neck, causing me to shiver. I can't help but smile when I look at him. It just comes naturally now. "Hey."

He glances over at Lucy. Her eyes dart away instantly, face flushed from being caught watching us. "Any problems while I was gone?"

I smirk. "Nope."

He scowls, then nods. "Good." Grabbing my left hand, he brings it to his lips, and rubs his thumb over the sparkling new engagement ring and wedding band that sit on my ring finger.

Last weekend, Ryker and I had taken living to the next level. With Jase tagging along, we rode to Montreal and picked up Anna. The four of us then went on to Quebec City, where Ryker and I were married at a Justice of the Peace in a private ceremony. I hadn't wanted a big wedding and I knew without a doubt that I'd never get Ryker into a tux even if I did. Anna was my only family, and though not related, Jase was Ryker's family. The whole thing had been perfect.

Ryker grabs a fresh beer from the prospect, then turns to watch the party with me. One of the brothers, who I'd learned was

Mouse, is across the room, comically instructing a couple of the whores how to do a proper strip tease. Everyone else is watching and laughing, a couple of the brothers cheering him on.

"Crazy fuckers." Ryker smirks at me and shakes his head.

I just laugh, continuing to watch them all for a minute before it dawns on me. "You know, a while ago, you told me that you didn't have a family."

He turns towards me again, eyebrow raised, holding my gaze but saying nothing.

"Looks to me like you have a pretty big one."

His eyes widen in surprise. "Who? This bunch of jokers?"

I laugh at the look on his face. "Well ... yeah. You grew up with most of these guys, right? You have a relationship with almost all of them. They take your back when you need it, and you return the favor. They're all loyal to the club and it's members. You all get together to celebrate and unwind. Those are things you do with your family. Seems to me like you have a pretty great one."

His smile kept growing wider as I spoke. When I finish, he dives in and takes my mouth in a hard, swift kiss. "Fuck, you're sexy when you get all wise on me."

I manage to keep a straight face. "I'm always wise."

He nods and buries his face in the crook of my neck, placing soft kisses all along the side. "And you're always sexy." He pulls his face free, looking me in the eye, suddenly serious. "You're right. They are my family, but you are my most *important* family. And if I'm stuck with these assholes, then so are you."

We stare at each other, his grin mirroring my own. "I can live with that."

He growls and pulls me off the stool, putting his shoulder to my belly to lift me up. I squeal in surprise. "Ryker! Put me down!"

He brings his palm down on my ass in a sharp slap. "Not happenin', baby girl. I'm gonna show you just how sexy you are."

Oh! I like the sound of that! I stop squirming and grin. Looking up just before Ryker turns from the room, I see Reaper smirking at us from under his beer bottle. He sends me a wink and shakes his head. Tease is watching too, lips twitching slightly. He raises his bottle in the universal "cheers" motion, then moves to take a sip, but his cell phone rings before he can.

Down the hall, Ryker turns into his room. It's much cleaner now that I'm the only one cleaning it. It doesn't hurt that Ryker has no use for it anymore. He lowers me to the ground, my front rubbing along his as I go down.

"Alright, Mrs. Cole." He runs his hands along the sides of my body, then takes a step back. "Take off your clothes."

I hold his stare as I slowly undo the buttons on my shirt and peel it off. Standing before my husband in nothing but a pair of tight jeans and a demi cup bra makes my heart flutter and my breaths to come out in hot, shallow pants.

I reach for the button on my jeans but his hand stops me. "No. Not yet." His gaze is moving along my body, his eyes dark and hungry. "Fuck. You're gorgeous."

My skin grows hot as he watches me but I stand still, waiting for his next instruction.

"Take off those jeans, baby girl; panties too. I need to taste you."

My hands shake as I unbutton my jeans and pull them, along with my panties, down over my hips. Ryker lowers me to the bed, and then my husband tastes me.

Tease

I pull out my cell phone, looking at the screen. *Who the fuck is calling me?* Everyone I care to know is right here, in this fucking room.

The screen shows an unknown number, but it's local.

I lift the phone to my ear, pressing the accept button. "Yeah?"

A feminine giggle fills my ear. "Yeah? That's how you answer your phone?"

I freeze, instantly recognizing that voice. "Laynie?"

"Uh – hunh." She giggles again. She sounds strange.

"Are you drunk?"

"Yeppers. Wasted." Her words are slurred, and she giggles at her own declaration.

"Where are you?" The thought of her out, alone and drunk puts me immediately on edge.

"At home. Me and Dexter are cuddled up on the couch, drinking a few bottles of wine." I relax. If she's at home and her dog is with her, she's safe. "Well, Dexter's not drinking wine. I am."

I smirk. This woman's crazy. "How is Dexter anyways?"

She sighs. "He's ok. Just needs a couple days of rest." I hear her pause and take another gulp of wine.

"I nearly killed that fuckin' kid that hit him." And I had. When that kid had come flying down the sidewalk, he'd paid no attention to what was going on around him. I'd seen him coming, and seen the dog shuffle Laynie out of the way, but he'd taken the bike on himself in the process. Good fucking dog.

"I remember. It was kind of hot." My eyes widen in shock as she giggles again. "Anyways, I was thinking, as a thank you, do you maybe want to – " I hear a crash in the background and what sounds like glass breaking, followed by a thump. "Ow! Shit!" Her voice sounds distant now.

"Laynie? What the fuck was that?"

"Hello? Travis?" I hear movement in the background. "Shit! I dropped the phone," she calls out. "Dexter! Get your drunk ass over here and help Mommy find her phone."

"Laynie?"

I hear more movement. "That's it, baby. Find Mommy's phone." There's more movement in the background before the phone fills with the sound of breathing. I hear, "That's my good boy. Thank you, baby." Her voice fills the receiver again. "Ugh! Gross! Now there's slobber all over it." I shake my head. Again, crazy. "Travis? You there?"

"I'm here."

"Sorry. I dropped my phone." Another girly giggle follows a small hiccup.

"What was that crash?"

"Just the table." She hiccups again.

"What broke?"

"Something on the table?"

"You don't know what that something was?"

"Travis, I'm blind. I've got no clue what the hell it was."

I can't help the chuckle that escapes me. Such a smartass.

"Fuck me. Did Tease just fuckin' chuckle?" My eyes cut to Jase, remembering instantly where I am. Everyone is staring at me, wide eyed. Jase continues, ignoring my glare. He elbows Reaper. "Did you know he could do that?"

Mouse leans around Reaper and looks at Jase, eyes wide and stage whispers, "I didn't even know the dude could fuckin' talk!"

Everyone around me start laughing. I'm just about to lay into them when I hear Laynie yelp in pain. "Laynie? You ok?"

"Um. Yeah?" She hiccups and then slurs out, "I'll be fine."

"You don't sound fine." She'd sounded like she was hurt.

"I just stepped on glass or something. I'll be fine." She pauses. "Anyways, I won't keep you. I just wanted to invite you for dinner tomorrow. Or this week. Or whenever."

Dinner? Nobody'd ever invited me to dinner before – especially not a gorgeous blonde with a smart mouth. I can't think about that right now. If she's hurt, I need to know. "You bleedin'?"

"What?"

"Your foot. You bleedin'?"

"Uh. Yeah. I think so." There's another pause. "Ahh! Yep. Definitely bleeding." Her voice is tight and laced with pain.

"Be there in ten." I turn and head towards the exit of the clubhouse. I can hear everyone murmuring as I leave, but I ignore each and every one of those nosey fuckers, and move toward my bike.

"No! Travis, I'm fine. I'll just – "

"I said I'll be there in ten. Sit your ass down and don't move."

"Travis! Don't you dare talk to me li – "

"Can't talk to you and drive my bike, babe."

"Travis – "

"Say what you gotta say in ten minutes. Sit tight." With that, I hit the end button. All I can think of is her being hurt, bleeding all over the place, and not able to clean it up herself. I don't know why I even care, but I do. Ever since I first saw her, I haven't been able to stop thinking about her.

And then I met her. Fuck me. Her smart mouth makes me hard.

My phone rings again. I don't even bother checking. I know it's Laynie. She's pissed I hung up on her. I can't fight the grin that takes over my face as I roar out of the parking lot on my bike.

Watch Out For

Tease

Book Two in the Kings of Korruption MC series

Coming November 2015

Acknowledgements

I don't even know where to start! So many people had a hand in helping me with this project and I never could have done it without them.

To Mike – Thank you for putting up with me ignoring you while I had my head wrapped up in this story. And for taking care of the kids, making supper, cleaning the house and just being generally supportive throughout all of this. This book is finally done but it's time to do it all over again!

To Robin from Wicked By Design – Thank you for an amazing cover. You were so easy to work with and you designed a kickass MC logo! I don't know if anyone would have even looked at this book if it weren't for your sexy as hell design! I can't wait to see what you come up with for the rest of the books in this series!

To Christina – This story is partially your baby too. Thank you for all of your ideas, opinions, thoughts and encouragement. You are an amazing sounding board and I love that you treat characters like real people just like I do. Looking forward to doing book tours with you as my sexy entourage!

To Jacqueline M Sinclair – I thank God that you messaged me on Goodreads, looking for a beta swap partner. You helped me hammer out so many details and your suggestions were like gold to me. You stroked my ego when I needed it and were completely honest when I needed that too. I could never have finished this book without you. I'm still waiting on you to put forth the one I read for you. It was a kickass book and the world will love it!

To all of my beta readers – Each of you provided helpful comments and suggestions that, to a new author, helped keep me headed in the right direction. I appreciate you taking the time to look at all the different rough versions of my story and still manage to read them more than once.

To all of the bloggers that shared my posts and made posts of their own – You're support has been overwhelming. An indie author would never make it in this world without people like you holding them up and helping them along the way.

To my readers – Thank you for taking a chance on me and reading my debut novel. Without you, my dream would never come true. It has been an incredible journey and I hope you will continue to follow me and watch me grow!

About The Author

Geri has been an avid reader for as long as she can remember. She can usually be found curled up in a comfy chair, reading on her iPad both day and night. Geri is an incurable night owl, and it's not uncommon for her to still be awake reading at 4 am just because she can't put the book down!

Geri loves all genres of fiction, but her passion is anything romantic or terrifying; basically anything that can get her heart pumping. This passion has bled out onto her laptop, and became the Kings of Korruption.

Writing this first book in the series knocked off the #1 thing on Geri's bucket list, and publishing it has been an absolute dream come true. She hopes you love the Kings as much as she does.

Visit Geri's website:

http://geriglenn.weebly.com

Follow Geri on Facebook:
https://www.facebook.com/geriglennauthor

Follow Geri on Twitter: https://twitter.com/authorgeriglenn

Follow Geri on Instagram:
https://instagram.com/authorgeriglenn/

Follow Geri on Pinterest:
https://www.pinterest.com/authorgeriglenn

CPSIA information can be obtained
at www.ICGtesting.com
Printed in the USA
BVOW11s2159170316

440807BV00014B/78/P

Ordinary

HEROES

John Gardam OMM CD BA

Foreword: George Hees - Former Minister,
Veteran Affairs Canada

GSPH

Published by

GENERAL STORE
PUBLISHING HOUSE

1 Main Street Burnstown, Ontario, Canada K0J 1G0
Telephone 1-800-465-6072 Fax (613)432-7184

ISBN 0-919431-58-5
Printed and bound in Canada

Layout Design by Leanne Enright
Cover Design by Hugh Malcolm

Copyright ©1995
The General Store Publishing House
Burnstown, Ontario, Canada

General Store Publishing House gratefully acknowledges the assistance of the
Ontario Arts Council.

Canadian Cataloguing in Publication Data
Gardam, John 1931-
  Ordinary heroes
Includes Index.
ISBN 0-919431-58-5

  1. World War, 1939-1945--Personal narratives, Canadian.
2. Heroes--Canada--Biography. I. Title.

D811.A2G38 1992   940.54'8171   C92-090399-1

First Printing July 1992
Second Printing April 1995

Dedication

I dedicate this book to all those veterans who gave me their wartime stories. May their contribution to Canada never be forgotten.

FACES FROM THE COVER

Henrie Tellier	Ross and Archie Anderson	Marjory Hall
Verne Barr	Joe Wood (right)	Fred Williams
Kay Christie		Whitney Carr
Jacques Dextraze	Bill Carr	Bill Crysler

Contents

All profits received by the author from the sale of this book will be donated to the Canadian Forces Personnel Assistance Fund to aid sailors, soldiers, air personnel, and other men and women of the Canadian Forces who are in financial distress.

Back cover photograph: Author holding a copy of **50 Years After.** (Ottawa Citizen photo by John Major)

By the same author:

The National War Memorial
(Veterans Affairs Canada, 1982)

Seventy Years After 1914 - 1984
(Canada Wings Inc., 1983)

The Legacy
(Department of National Defence, 1988)

Fifty Years After
(General Store Publishing House, 1990)

The Canadian Peacekeeper
(General Store Publishing House, 1992)

The Honourable George Hees, PC. OC.

Foreword

When I was Minister of Veterans Affairs in the Government of Canada, someone once asked me to define a *veteran*. I guess I could have used such glorifying words as *fearless, intrepid, unafraid, courageous, gallant* or *heroic*. But I didn't.

The word that came to my mind was *friend*.

Those men and women who wore the uniform of Canada, and who put their lives on the line to protect our country and the people of the free world, were truly our friends. They were friends to their families and neighbours who were helpless against aggression; friends to their buddies who shared a slit trench, a mess deck or a cockpit seat; friends to their provinces from coast to coast; friends to Canada.

The shoulder flash read, "CANADA". It didn't read Manitoba, Quebec, Nova Scotia or Alberta. It meant what it said—Canada.

My friend, Colonel John Gardam, has assembled another collection of stories about a number of friends of Canada, told by those people themselves. The stories are not boastful. They are not self-serving. They are the truth.

When I read these first-hand accounts, I thought again of another expression I have used many times since my days in the Canadian Army: "It's not too often things like this come up with the rations."

Congratulations, John. Your readers are in for a real treat.

George Hees

Preface

Ordinary Heroes was written at the urging of Tim Gordon and his staff of General Store Publishing House. The positive reader reaction to **Fifty Years After,** which was published in 1990, caused Tim to implore me "to gather up more Second World War stories of sailors, soldiers and airmen, as there must be a lot of stories left untold."

I have followed the same sequence and style used in my earlier books but have added a few new concepts. Family stories where three or more members served have been included. I have also taken the liberty of writing about the ordinary men and women who did great things long after the war ended. All of these personalities had that same shyness about telling me "their story". The same numbers refused to describe their experiences, be they as a prisoner-of-war in Hong Kong or serving at sea in a Royal Navy submarine or as a civilian in post-war Germany.

Sources of historical reference have continued to pour forth from publishing houses. **The D-Day Dodgers** by Daniel Dancocks, **The Sea Is at Our Gates** by Tony German and many other recent books have captured my interest and increased my knowledge. I have also read several unpublished manuscripts by former air force members; these eyewitness accounts from the boys in light blue have a special, hands-on quality about them. I hope to see those stories in print.

My five years with the Canadian Agency of the Commonwealth War Graves Commission have had a significant impact on me. One cannot come that close to the awesome reality of 110,000 Canadian war dead and not gain an indelible imprint on one's very soul.

Once again, my twelve-year contact with the Royal Canadian Legion has influenced me. In his book, **Service,** Clifford H. Bowering wrote of the members of the Legion:

> In a world where materialistic considerations play a
> large part, it is well for a nation to have in its midst a
> group of men and women who place SERVICE high
> among the virtues ... and sense of duty to their country
> and countrymen.

The men and women in this book all had that sense of duty.

In Victory at Sea, Hal Lawrence told of an event in 1986 in Victoria, British Columbia. At this reunion of sailors from the Korean War, Rear Admiral William M. Landymore, Royal Canadian Navy, said, "Do we then glorify war when we remember the exploits of our fighting men? No, not at all. We remember those who did their duty to their country."

As my two previous books have been, so is this a tribute to veterans. It is also a tribute to their families, who, in their family tree, have one or more who had the courage and feeling for Canada to stand up and be counted when the call to arms came.

The title for this book came from a newspaper article written by Ruth Latta for the **Ottawa Citizen** in June 1991. Every person in this book was a volunteer; when they signed up to fight for Canada, they did not know where their future would lead them. All of them were ordinary citizens before they joined, and they were all heroes in the fight to defend the ideals of their home country. I am sure that you, too, will see them as heroes.

This may well be my last book of oral history on the people of the Second World War. If I have caused someone to take a greater interest in Canada's military history or to gain a better understanding of people at war, my goal will have been accomplished.

Chapter One

The Royal Canadian Navy

It took months to build a ship but years to build a fighting naval tradition.

Admiral of the Fleet Cunningham

The Royal Canadian Navy (RCN) was created from virtually nothing, and it had returned to virtually nothing by the end of the war. But during those war years, the RCN had a powerful impact. Tony German wrote of the achievement in **The Sea Is at Our Gates:**

> Twenty-four ships went down and nearly 1,800 gave their lives. All but four of the ships were lost in the U-boat war. In return the navy sank thirty-one of the U-boats and disposed of forty-two surface ships. In the give and take the little ships [escorts] saw 25,000 merchant voyages across the Atlantic. ... [This] was Canada's most decisive contribution, not just to the war at sea, but to the war itself.

Actually, the RCN accounted for twenty-two U-boats by itself, and another twelve in conjunction with aircraft and ships of other nations.

Until April 1943, 100 per cent of the direction of the RCN came from the Royal Navy (RN). Canada provided ships and individuals aboard RN ships as required. Yet, Canada's sailors were as dedicated during those years as they would have been under a Canadian admiral. A sailor's loyalty to his current ship was the tie that bound the crew together as a ship's company. The importance of the competence of the officers and senior hands was never taken lightly, nor should it have been.

The Battle of the Atlantic forged a tight link between the allied navies and air forces. Aircraft sank "twenty of the fifty-two U-boats sunk ... between Newfoundland and Ireland in the first five months of 1943" (Milner, **North Atlantic Run**). The close cooperation between surface ships and the Royal Air Force's Coastal Command is still in evidence in the Canadian Forces Maritime Command today.

For the average wartime sailor, memories of the navy are a series of firsts—joining his first ship, being part of a convoy escort group, that first Force Seven storm, the clammy feeling of being soaked through, warship food and rum rations, a first encounter with an enemy U-boat or aircraft, foreign ports, the horrible sight of merchant ships on fire or sinking, air raids on a city while the sailor's ship was tied up helpless at dockside, meeting shipmates both good and bad and, above all, that glorious, unprecedented feeling when the war was all over. The stories I collected—not enough, but a good sampling—describe some of those firsts in the words of those who went "down to the sea in ships".

An Army Dentist with the Navy

A new wartime service in the Second World War was the Royal Canadian Dental Corps (RCDC), which was authorized on 31 August 1939. Although the RCDC was an army corps, its members were used by the other services, as well.

Charles Cornish joined the RCDC in April 1942. "We graduated from the Faculty of Dentistry at the University of Toronto and were the first class to go right into the army." Because Charles had been a member of the Canadian Officer Training Corps (COTC) throughout his university years, he was fully trained and could begin his military dentistry practice at once. The Dental Company in Victoria assigned Charles first to the large camp in Vernon, British Columbia. Two years later, in 1944, Captain Charles Cornish was posted to the RCN Dental Company:

> The idea of a naval Dental Company was new. We were sent overseas as individuals and concentrated at Aldershot in England. I was sent to Londonderry, Northern Ireland, with five other dental officers and some dental assistants and technicians. Londonderry was the overseas terminal for the Newfoundland Escort Force. This "Newfie to 'derry" arrangement had been going on since 1942. We set up our Canadian clinic, including a laboratory section, in a quonset hut left vacant by the United States Navy. The patients were all Canadian. Some of the dental officers went to sea in the English Channel, but I was not one of them.

Caring for patients was made difficult by the often long delays between appointments. The sailor might well have sailed from 'derry to Newfoundland and back before he could be seen a second time. But the clinic staff managed. If it was a case of fitting dentures, for example, "our technicians were excellent and had them made quickly."

Charles remembers vividly the day the war ended in May 1945, because "the ships all sounded their whistles". Joseph Schull described the scene in **Far Distant Ships:**

"Make Noise" was the signal of the British Commodore commanding at Londonderry as one of the last of the Canadian mid ocean groups departed under a lowering dawn sky. Readily complying, the ships let loose with guns pointed at the clouds and sirens blowing until the last ounce of steam died down.

The Dental Detachment was sent to HMCS *Niobe* in Scotland. Charles volunteered for the Pacific Force, so he was sent to Farnborough in England to rejoin his army cohorts. The Pacific Force RCDC element was concentrated in Camp Borden, Ontario, but it disbanded in August 1945 as the war came to a close.

Charles Cornish, Ingersoll, Ontario, April 1942.

Charles Cornish remained in the army and served in Manitoba and British Columbia. He was again posted to the RCN in 1953, serving aboard the cruiser HMCS *Ontario* when she sailed to England for the coronation of Queen Elizabeth the Second. From England, HMCS *Ontario* went to Australia. Charles returned to the army in 1954, and over the next sixteen years he had postings in Calgary, Germany, Quebec and Ottawa. He retired from the Forces as a colonel in 1970, but Charles continued to practice dentistry, in Ottawa, until he retired in 1985.

Above and Below the Deck

Gerry Juneau served in only one ship during the Second World War, HMCS *Rimouski*, which from 2 December 1942 to 9 September 1944 was captained by John Pickford. Here are their stories.

Gerry was born and raised in Ottawa's Lowertown, and was just sixteen when he joined the Regiment de Hull soon after war broke out. He was too young to go active, but as soon as he was of age in 1942 he tried to enlist in the Royal Canadian Air Force (RCAF) as an air frame mechanic. Told that there was a six-month waiting period, Gerry decided, "I couldn't wait that long so went and joined the navy."

After a couple of months in HMCS *Hochelaga* in Montreal, Gerry went on to Cornwallis, Nova Scotia, the major RCN Basic Training Centre. It was there that he learned all the seamanship skills, gunnery, boat drill and communications he needed to perform as part of a ship's crew. Instead of getting intensified trades training, which would have narrowed his employability, Gerry became part of the "deck group" of general purpose able seamen. In December 1942, Gerry joined his first and, as it turned out, only ship: K121 HMCS *Rimouski*. Launched in 1941, *Rimouski* was one of the sixty corvettes that were the mainstay of Canada's escort fleet.

A young officer, Lieutenant John Pickford, also joined HMCS *Rimouski* in December 1942. Says Pickford, "I assumed command of K121, known at that time (in fun) as the Polish Corvette" (all Pickford quotations taken from **Salty Dips**). He was the ship's captain for the next two years.

A 1943 duty for these two sailors—one commanding, the other an able seaman—was filled with all the ingredients for a James Bond novel. In John Pickford's words,

> It seemed that some U-boat officers had escaped from a prisoner-of-war camp in Northern Ontario. They had made arrangements to be picked up by a U-boat in Baie Chaleur some time in the next few days. Our security people, the RCMP and so on, knew all about this, and plans were afoot not only to recapture the prisoners but,

more importantly, to get the U-boat. [The plan was to let the U-boat in, screen the opening of the bay with six other ships, use *Rimouski* as a decoy small coastal vessel to get close to the U-boat, and seize or sink the German vessel.] So in we went, and, to make a long story short, nothing came of it. We didn't get the submarine and I didn't become a hero.

The *Rimouski* was on the Triangle Run in 1942—a series of Halifax-to-Boston convoy escorts. Although the visits were short and the places not far from home, Gerry remembers that the U.S. ports seemed a world apart from wartime Canada.

A refit in Liverpool, Nova Scotia, extended *Rimouski's* fo'c'sle, improved the radar and re-arranged the compass platform, asdic hut and chart room. (Asdic, a term derived from the acronym of the Anti-Submarine Detection Investigation Committee, was a type of sonar.) Said John Pickford, "She came out a vastly better ship than when she went in." At the same time, the ship's company above deck increased by two officers, and fifteen more men crowded into the lower deck area.

The next assignment was the run from Newfoundland to Northern Ireland (Newfie to 'derry). *Rimouski* spent seven months on the North Atlantic run, and the convoy "didn't lose one ship due to enemy action".

John Pickford left *Rimouski* in September 1944. He was replaced by Lieutenant C.D. Chivers, who was to be the commanding officer until the end of 1944.

Rimouski spent April 1944 in the English Channel, with little time spent in port as the pre-invasion activity increased daily. One of the first actions leading up to D-Day—6 June 1944—was the passage of the original blockships from Oban in Scotland to the Omaha Beach, where the Americans landed. Gerry recalls that everyone was "keyed up, as we kept having asdic contacts with the many wrecks on the bottom." The captain recalled, "My only problem getting to Omaha Beach was navigational. It was essential to find the dimly lit buoys marking the swept channels through the minefields off the French coast. ... But we arrived at the right place at the right time."

For the next three months there was steady work escorting Mulberry blockships from the Thames Estuary to the beaches. Then *Rimouski* was slated for refit, so in August 1944 they sailed from 'derry in a westbound convoy for Halifax. Gerry came ashore there, becoming an RCN messenger in Halifax and later at headquarters in Ottawa, where he was working at war's end.

Gerry Juneau aboard HMCS *Rimouski*, 1944.

What are Gerry's memories of wartime service? Picking up survivors in the North Atlantic and the English Channel; watching a merchant ship sink and an oil tanker burn; the spirit of the sailors of the Merchant Navy as they were saved; the long, tedious hours; the cold; the food; the constant motion. He will never forget the patrols against German E-boats in the English Channel, the excitement of making contact with a U-boat and the disappointment of not sinking one.

Gerry worked for the Royal Canadian Mint in Ottawa from 1945 to 1979, when he turned 55. He then joined the Canadian Corps of Commissionaires, and for the past 12 years he has been at either entrance of National Defence Headquarters. He is now retired.

I met Rear Admiral Pickford when he was the Commander Maritime Command Pacific in Esquimalt, British Columbia.

Serving in the Trail

Cal Krauter joined the RCN in April 1942 at HMCS *Prevost* in London, Ontario. He was a qualified plumber and sheet metal worker, so his future was decided without too much discussion: it was the engine room for this young sailor. On arrival in Halifax he was assigned to Shore Patrol (naval police who ensured that sailors kept out of trouble). Cal's words typify his spirited attitude: "I asked to be transferred out of that duty, for I did not want to spend the war fighting the battle of Barrington Street!"

When reassignment came in November, Cal was given just two hours to join his first ship, HMCS *Trail*. The commanding officer was Lieutenant Commander George Hall, "a fine man, who wasn't one for getting his ship into trouble. But how he insisted on cleanliness—and that meant the whole ship!" *Trail* was on the Triangle Run, and Cal remembers well the problem of ice on the superstructure, which had to be removed by hand and steam pipe; "but as we moved into the Gulf Stream, the ice fell off in huge chunks."

On one occasion, HMCS *Trail* and *Shawinigan* were escorting a convoy to Goose Bay. A U.S. convoy was ahead of them, and U-517 had just sunk an army transport, *Chatham*, loaded with construction workers. The incident is well described by James Lamb, then the executive officer of *Trail*, in his book **On the Triangle Run:**

> We came upon *Chatham's* survivors. Most of them, jammed tightly into the ship's big lifeboats, were chilled and stiff after a night afloat in Northern waters ... but for those who had been forced to take to the water before managing to pull themselves on a life raft, the night had been a cruel ordeal. Many were covered in oil. ... Others had been injured in trying to get clear of the ship, which had sunk in just three minutes. Some were dead, others would die, but we pulled them over our low bulwarks, our fellows lining the waist and hanging in the scramble nets overside to help the survivors aboard and hustle them forward into the mess decks and the warm blankets that awaited them there.

The Engine Room Crew. Cal Krauter is first from the left in the third row, 1943.

Cal Krauter was on duty in the engine room throughout the rescue, and he remembers the event distinctly.

HMCS *Trail* was on the Halifax/St John's/New York/Boston run most of the time Cal was a crew member. On a couple of trips they went as far south as Cuba and Jamaica. "Another time we were to be relieved off Halifax by an Atlantic escort, but because of German U-boat activity we took the convoy right across to 'derry in Northern Ireland." On another occasion, "we sailed from Londonderry to Gibralter and then back to New York."

Little did Cal realize that his days as a stoker were drawing to an end, for he was developing ulcers, which started to bleed while he was at sea off the coast of Iceland. He was in the RCN Hospital in Newfoundland in March 1944 when the survivors from HMCS *Valleyfield* were brought in. Cal recalls, "They were in bad shape from the exposure to the sea and the oil. It was a wonder any of them lived."

In late June Cal came out of hospital and was promoted to engine room artificer (ERA). Unfortunately, the diet aboard ship was not suitable for an ulcer case, and Cal was back in hospital before July was out. In August he was admitted to hospital in Halifax, boarded as medically unfit and discharged from the navy.

A year later Cal married Marguerite, a nurse he had met in Hamilton. For many years Cal ran a thriving plumbing and heating business in Brussels, Ontario. He went into municipal politics as a reeve, moved on to country warden and finally worked with the Public Utilities Commission. In 1985, Cal retired.

A Newfoundlander in the Royal Navy

When war broke out in September 1939, the young men and women of Newfoundland automatically turned to the British forces. Many young Newfoundlanders did join the Canadian forces, but in the main their ties were to the "Imperials".

Fred Williams, just out of high school in St John's, waited impatiently for his eighteenth birthday in February 1940, when he eagerly joined the RN. Although Fred had no experience with the sea and his three brothers had joined the army, the RN was Fred's unhesitating choice.

Two months later, Fred left St John's with a draft of Newfoundlanders—all dressed in civilian clothes—and in due course they joined a convoy out of Halifax. They arrived in Liverpool after twenty-two days at sea, and went immediately to Chatham Barracks—HMS *Pembroke*—for basic training. After seamanship training, including gunnery, Fred qualified as an ordinary seaman. He joined his first ship in the autumn of 1940:

> HMS *Diamede* was a six-inch [gun calibre] light cruiser, which had just been refitted in Bermuda. Our first task was to assist in hunting for the German battleship *Bismarck*. Luckily for us, our engines failed after just a day and a half. We wouldn't have stood a chance against such an opponent.
>
> *Diamede* was next employed on contraband control in the South Atlantic and the Pacific. We went through the Panama Canal eight times. Our task was to stop German and Italian ships coming out of neutral ports such as Boston and New York and, on the other coast, San Francisco and San Diego. We sailed 186,000 miles [300,000 kilometres] while I was in that cruiser, before I left her in August 1942.

One of the port visits made by HMS *Diamede* was to Vancouver, where Fred was asked if he wanted to transfer to the RCN. His answer was no, for he was "in a happy ship with a real good skipper".

Fred Williams aboard one of His Majesty's Ships.

Fred's memories of shore leave are the good times he and his mates had in London. Their fun was interrupted by the bombing, but "I made a lot of good friends". Once, Fred managed to see his brothers Cecil and Harold, who were serving with the British Army, and Len, who was in the Canadian Armoured Corps. Len did not survive the war; he was killed while serving with the Sherbrooke Fusiliers and is buried in Belgium. Fred's mother had insisted Fred make the effort to see his brothers, and, says Fred, "I am glad I did, for that was the last time I saw Len."

Fred's next ship was HMS *Tracker* a "Woolworth" carrier [so-called because they were cheap, but effective]. We picked her up in Portland, Oregon. Lots of action: we were attacked from the air and our aircraft made lots of U-boat sightings. The weather on North Atlantic patrol was not the best. I suppose you could sum it all up as "nothing spectacular".

Fred managed to get back to St John's three times. Twice he served in Canadian-built ship—one a minesweeper, the other a landing ship tank. Fred is quick to say, "All four ships I sailed in were happy ships."

Fred was on a minesweeper in St John's in May 1945 for V-E Day, and on V-J Day he was in Quebec City, so he has "very fond memories of that city and that day."

Since 1946, Fred and his wife Elizabeth have been constant members and supporters of the Royal Canadian Legion, at all levels. In 1990, Fred was elected president of Dominion Command. He would have become past-president at the convention held in Quebec City in June 1992 had he not died of cancer eight months earlier.

One Torpedo, One War

Jack Jolleys tried to bluff his way into the navy in 1941, but the recruiting officer recognized the ploy of an enthusiastic sixteen-year-old. Undiscouraged, Jack returned to his trade of moulder's helper at Mainland Foundry, where they were casting parts for merchant ships. With another year and a lot of physical labour under his belt, Jack tried again after his seventeenth birthday in November 1942. This time he got in, and after five months at HMCS *Discovery* in Vancouver, he was on route to Sydney, Nova Scotia, for basic training.

For trades training in gunnery, Jack went on to HMCS *Cornwallis* near Digby, Nova Scotia. After graduating as an anti-aircraft gunner, he took his final sea training aboard HMCS *Hamilton* in local waters.

Jack's one and only wartime ship was the aircraft carrier HMS *Nabob*, which is described in **Far Distant Ships** as

> the largest ship operated by the Canadian Navy...
> 15,000 tons, a length of 492 feet [150 metres] and
> accommodation for twenty planes. Her ship's company
> of over 1,000 men was mainly Canadian but, since there
> was as yet no Canadian air arm, her flying personnel
> was British.

The captain was Horatio Nelson Lay, RCN. Captain Lay began the initial shakedown cruise in local waters. Jack recalls,

> We were landing aircraft on the flight deck for the first
> time. As we turned into the wind we ran aground in the
> mouth of the Fraser River. Two ships tried to pull us
> free at high tide, but to no avail. We sat there for three
> days; the Vancouver papers referred to us as HMS
> *Standstill.*

In **The Sea Is at Our Gates,** Tony German mentions that things did not go well for Lay. "*Nabob* picked up the RN's 852 Squadron with their Avenger torpedo-bombers in San Francisco in January 1944." The engine room was manned by British Merchant seamen, and it was difficult to get all three groups to work together, particularly as pay and rations differed between the groups. As German put it, "This ship's company was a real dog's breakfast." There might have been a mutiny in the Caribbean had they not had to go to action stations in those dangerous waters. But when *Nabob* docked at Norfolk, Virginia, several "young new entries" jumped ship and deserted. Lay flew to Ottawa, spoke to the Naval Board and arranged that all men were to be paid and fed according to the more generous RCN scales, rather than the RN ones.

Jack's memories are not of these problems, however. Instead, he recalls the brief but unforgettably exciting port visit in New York just before *Nabob* sailed for Liverpool. The convoy—Escort Force 18—included nineteen ships from New York and seven from Boston.

On 2 August 1944, HMS *Nabob* sailed into Scapa Flow, where she joined up with a naval task force. Seven days later, the force was off to mine the waters off the coast of Norway. "A squadron of twelve Avengers, each carrying a single mine, took off from *Nabob*" (Schull, **Far Distant Ships**). The operation went smoothly, and after stopping in again at Scapa Flow, the fleet went back to the Norway area. *Nabob* and *Trumpeter* (another carrier) were ordered to fuel three destroyers. But this operation would not go as well.

It was late afternoon. The aircraft had been lowered into the hangar, and lengths of hose were being readied for the refuelling. Suddenly, "a torpedo from an undetected U-boat [U-345] struck *Nabob* in the starboard side." Schull's account describes how nearly that torpedo came to causing a disaster:

> All electrical power failed... The temperature in the engine room [shot up] to 150 degrees, making it necessary to shut down the main engines and boilers. [Through] a hole fifty feet [fifteen metres] long by forty feet deep [twelve metres], water flooded in. ... The stern sank eighteen feet [five or six metres], and a list to starboard developed.

Jack's memories of this event stand sharp in his mind:

> I had just stood down from "action stations" and was in the forward ammunition locker loading Oerlikon magazines when the torpedo hit us. I was flung against the bulkhead. The ship seemed to lift out of the water

Jack Jolleys, 1943.

from the explosion. The noise was like a massive car crash.

A second torpedo intended for *Nabob* struck the destroyer escort *Bickerton,* instead. *Bickerton* was damaged so heavily that she sank later that night, with a large loss of life.

Nabob managed to launch two Avengers from her twisted deck to go after the U-boat, but the wily sub escaped. And for the listing *Nabob,* with twenty-one killed and six injured, a voyage of 1,100 miles (1,800 kilometres) to Scapa lay ahead.

Two hundred fourteen of *Nabob's* men were transferred immediately to the destroyer *Kemphorne*. Later, another 200 men were transferred from *Nabob* to HMCS *Algonquin*. Both times, Jack stayed on duty. With the remainder of the ship's company, he worked almost around the clock for three days and three nights to keep *Nabob* afloat. Thanks to the dedication of men like Jack, *Nabob* survived the high seas to pass the gate into Scapa Flow on 27 August. But *Nabob* would not sail again.

Jack was next stationed in Saint John, New Brunswick. Having asked for a sea draft, he was in Halifax waiting for a ship on V-E Day, 8 May 1945. The infamous riots that occurred then in Halifax get just a cryptic "that was something to remember" from Jack.

But the war was not over. Volunteers for Pacific Force lined up, and Jack was one of them. On V-J Day, when the war finally ended, Jack was aboard HMCS *Cornwallis* taking a gunnery refresher course and learning Japanese aircraft recognition. He was discharged from the navy at HMCS *Discovery* in October 1945.

Jack joined the Royal Canadian Legion in 1947, becoming the first vice-president of Branch 83. In 1968 he transferred to Branch 6 and became the president. Positions at Zone, Pacific Command and Dominion Command followed. In 1991, with the death of Fred Williams, Jack Jolleys became Dominion President.

Of Ciphers and Signals

For a long time, W.E. (Sandy) Sanders refused to tell me his story, for he thought it uninteresting. Poppycock! Sandy's feelings for the RCN and what it did for him are meaningful and highly interesting, to me and, I'm sure, all my readers.

Sandy graduated from high school in Saskatoon in June 1941 and promptly enlisted in the Royal Canadian Navy Voluntary Reserve (RCNVR). After basic training in Saskatoon, he went to St Hyacinth, Quebec, for four months of signals training. Training then continued in Halifax.

> We learned all the various codes, how to use cipher and all the skills required by a signalman aboard ship. Much of what we covered we later learned was of value during major fleet operations, something I never got involved with. We did learn to use the coding machine, something I used a lot.

In January 1944, Sandy was assigned to his first ship, HMS *Woldegrove,* destroyer escort built in Boston. Work ups (training of the crew) were done off Boston and then the ship sailed for Ireland. Recalls Sandy, "The crew was all Canadian except for the officers, who were all RN!"

In the United Kingdom, Sandy was sent first to Manning Depot, HMCS *Niobe* in Scotland, and then to HMCS *Kincardine*, "a Castle class corvette built in Middleborough, England, for the RCN." *Kincardine* was not commissioned until 19 June 1944, and by then the German U-boat threat had become minimal. Although Sandy was taking part in a major war effort—the mid-ocean escort force in the Atlantic—he found life aboard ship "boring, with the state of the sea our major enemy". Because he spent so many hours in the coding shack, he had little opportunity for sightseeing, even during "action stations". The frigate HMCS *Stonetown* was Sandy's final ship, and on 2 September 1945, Sandy was released from the RCNVR.

In 1948, Sandy graduated with a degree in Commerce from the University of Saskatchewan. For a year he worked for Revenue Canada as an auditor, but in 1949 he joined the Department of

National Defence. Sandy progressed to the position of Assistant-Director of Audit, and in 1977 he became Director General Audit in the Deputy Minister's organization. Now retired, Sandy Sanders lives in Victoria, British Columbia.

Sandy Sanders, 1944.

Chapter Two

The Canadian Army

The Canadian Army had over 730,000 in uniform: 22,917 were killed and 52,699 were wounded.
(Goodspeed, **The Armed Forces of Canada 1867-1967)**

When war broke out in September 1939, there were two groups of Canadians getting ready to go to battle. The first group included the men in the Permanent Force and the Militia, and the second, that enormous number who wanted to enlist. "In September alone, 58,337 men and women joined the army" (Goodspeed, **The Armed Forces of Canada 1867-1967)**. Many of the people in this book were in that second group. The determination to join regardless of hurdles was magnificent. If one branch of the service would not take them, they lined up for another branch, and kept lining up until they got in.

Those who joined a local regiment found themselves with friends from school or from the local area. The significance of close association came forth time and time again. Father and son, brother and brother—it was common to see them fighting together in the same unit.

The soldiers shared the discomfort of British winters, the dust and scorching sun in Sicily and Italy, and mud. One of the worst things they had to share was a shortage of reinforcements, a dilemma caused by foolish General Staff acceptance of British casualty ratios (from the desert), General Ken Stuart's reluctance to reveal the blunder, and poor formation leadership. The war effort could not keep up with the attrition on the battlefield caused by a skillful and determined enemy.

The Canadian Army was able to maintain its national identity and, for the most part, its distinct Canadian leadership. It suffered the years of inaction in England from 1939 to 1943 (except for Hong Kong and Dieppe), when the largest threat was from training exercises and boredom. Direction came from Winston Churchill sooner than from Mackenzie King, but the Canadian Army managed to succeed despite this factor.

The soldiers remember basic training, the lack of time to learn those essential life-saving skills, the voyages on troop ships, life in England and invasions of Sicily and France. They saw friends die beside them, people they had known for years, played poker with, watched rise in rank and responsibility.

When the war came to an end in Europe, some soldiers wanted to stay in the army of occupation, some wanted to fight in the Pacific, and some just wanted to go home. None of these veterans would ever look at life the same way. The coming of age had been dramatic for this generation of Canadians.

> Living amongst us are many Canadian widows of infantrymen killed on the Italian battlefields. ... If for no other reason than this, we should as a nation honour the Canadians who fought, bled and died in that far-off land. To do otherwise is totally unconscionable.
> (Dancocks, **The D-Day Dodgers**)

From Cavalry Stables to City Hall

Bill Law joined Lord Strathcona's Horse (Royal Canadians) on April 7, 1933, after having already spent some time in the Calgary Highlanders as a drummer and piper. It was not his musical prowess that enabled him to get a coveted position in a Regular Army cavalry regiment, but rather his skill as a soccer player. In Bill's words, he was "a far better soccer player than a horseman".

When war broke out in 1939, Bill was a sergeant and a small arms instructor, first at Sarcee Camp and then at Lethbridge, Alberta. In early February 1941, Sergeant Law was told to report to Mewata Armouries in Calgary to see Lieutenant Colonel Bradbrooke, the commanding officer (CO) of the Calgary Tank Regiment. Bill had known him as his squadron commander in the Strathcona's, but was not prepared for what followed. The CO asked the slightly built sergeant for the names of big, well-trained men in the Strathcona's and the Princess Patricia's Canadian Light Infantry (PPCLI) who would make "good regimental sergeant majors [RSMs], ones who would put the fear of God into the young soldiers joining the regiment." Bill gave him some names, and the CO went back into his office. A while later he called Bill in and said to the assembled officers, "Gentlemen, I would like you to meet our RSM."

The Calgary Tanks were sent to Camp Borden in March 1941 for kitting out and training, and then despatched to England in June of that year. In May 1942, Bill was selected for officer training. Until that time, officer training had been done in England, but Bill was to be part of the group who returned to Brockville, Ontario, for a "ninety-day wonder" course that qualified him as a lieutenant. Bill recalls, "It was a mixed blessing, for I got to see my son who had been born two months after I had gone overseas, but I did not want to leave the regiment." Bill was in Brockville just long enough to teach the other candidates some drill; as an ex-RSM, it was obvious that he did not require basic training! Nonetheless, Bill was still in Canada in August 1942 when news of the Dieppe raid was released; he was saddened to hear how many men had been lost from his regiment on those ill-fated beaches.

RSM Bill Law (right) in England, 1941.

In January 1943, Bill rejoined the Calgary Tanks in England. For a few months he was a troop leader, but he was made the regimental quartermaster before the invasion of Sicily in July. Bill's comment, "We did very little in Sicily," is confirmed by G.W.H. Nicholson in **Canadians in Italy**: "The Calgarys had only eight wounded in Sicily."

Bill left the quartermaster job when the regiment arrived in Italy. There, he joined C Squadron under Major Amy, first as a troop leader and later as battle captain. In January 1944 he left the Calgary Tanks near Vairano and reported to the Royal Armoured Corps tactics course in England.

Once the course ended in June 1944, Brigadier Bradbrooke called Bill back to London. Once again a change in career was to be made. Bill recalls, "The plan was very hush-hush at the time, but ten or twelve Canadian officers were to be sent to India for jungle fighting experience. I was the only armoured officer." Bill was sent to the 3rd Carabineers (Prince of Wales Dragoon Guards), who were in action in the Kabaw Valley trying to force back the Japanese Army on the Manipur River on the Burma/India border.

Bill arrived as a captain but very quickly became a troop leader in C Squadron—it was at that level where battle experience was to be found. What a difference from Italy! The jungle reduced visual contact with the enemy; the front line was hard to distinguish from the rest of the battle area; the terrain was composed of steep hills, a dense foliage canopy and fast rivers; and bridges could take only foot and light vehicle traffic.

Bill's initial action was in an area near Tiddim:

> Beyond Tiddim, we found that the whole side of a mountain wall had been rebuilt by the Japanese. They had rebuilt approximately 100 yards [90 metres] with the aid of bamboo—a complete section of road. The question was, Would it take the weight of the Squadron's tanks? ... It was decided a vehicle would test it. Trooper Palmer volunteered to drive the first tank across and did so without any crew. He made it to the other side. [The others followed.]
>
> **(The Reminiscences of Four Members of "C" Squadron, Burma Campaign, 1943-45)**

Battles were usually fought on a one-tank frontage, using machine guns to shoot snipers out of the trees and now and then getting a shot away into a Japanese bunker from the 75 mm General Grant tank gun.

In October 1944, Bill's tank was knocked out of action by Japanese anti-tank weapons, which smashed off the left track. Bill bailed out, and asked the squadron commander about the two forward tanks, which had also been knocked out. The wounded crews of the tanks had returned, but the drivers had remained with their tanks. Bill was detailed to find out what was happening.

Malcolm Connolly, the driver of the first tank, was sitting quiet and alone in his damaged tank, when "I heard the sounds of someone coming up, following the tracks that had been made by us earlier in the day. This turned out to be Bill Law, the Canadian officer who had been sent up to find out what had happened to me. ... 'You are going to wait and take your tank back after dark? I will report this back to the Squadron!' he said, and then he went off, leaving me on my own once again" **(The Reminiscences of Four Members of "C" Squadron, Burma Campaign, 1943-45)**.

Bill was still searching for the second tank when he felt something hard press into his spine. He called out in English, but to no avail: two Japanese soldiers with rifles had taken him prisoner.

> They marched me down this trail toward their positions. Suddenly, shells started falling from the British artillery. The one in the front took off down the trail,

and the one behind me moved into the ditch. At a good time I swung out and kicked him; he rolled down the ravine with his rifle and I turned and ran back toward our lines. After a long night of hiding in the jungle and moving cautiously back toward our forward troops, I took off my shirt so that they might see I wasn't Japanese. A British soldier challenged me with "Who are you?"

I replied, "Carabineers." He was a West Kent. I said, "Do you have a major with you from Canada?"

He replied, "Yes, I do."

I said, "Take me to him," and soon I was talking to Pat Tighe of the Loyal Edmonton Regiment.

When Bill returned to Canada in the spring of 1945, he went to Vernon, British Columbia, where the Canadian 6th Division was to be formed to go to the Far East. Before that could happen, however, the war ended, and Bill left for Fort Frontenac, Kingston, to attend Staff College.

Bill served in various staff positions in Canada and was Officer Commanding Troops when the first contingent of the United Nations Emergency Force sailed aboard HMCS *Magnificent* for the Middle East in December 1956. He retired as Deputy Director of the Armoured Corps in 1964 after 31 years of service. In civilian life he became the Director of the Ottawa and District Retarded Children's Association for four years. He was subsequently elected to Ottawa City Council as an alderman and Controller, serving a total of six terms in office. In the four years before his final retirement in 1988, Bill was a trustee on the Ottawa Board of Education and a part-time teacher at Algonquin College. He still lives in Ottawa today, escaping to Florida when the temperatures drop.

First in the Canadian Armoured Corps

Every now and then you get to meet someone who was "first". As explained in **Worthy,** Jack Wallace of Ottawa has the distinction of being the first "other rank" to have been sworn in (number B4400) as a member of the Canadian Armoured Fighting Vehicles School in Camp Borden right after war was declared on 10 September 1939. As a civilian, Jack had been the driver of a Carden Lloyd machine gun carrier during the 1938 summer exercises under Major Frank Worthington.

Jack's progress in the Canadian Armoured Corps was swift. He was commissioned from the rank of sergeant and sent to the Royal Canadian Dragoons, an armoured car regiment, which sailed for England in 1943. Then Jack's father, an officer with the Three Rivers Regiment in the United Kingdom, "claimed" his son; claiming was a system whereby a father or older brother could request that the younger member join his unit.

The Three Rivers Regiment was one of three regiments in the First Canadian Armoured Brigade. When the decision was made to send Canadians to Sicily, the Three Rivers Regiment soon made a name for themselves. They "played so vigorous a part in the advance of the 1st Canadian Division" and "they played an important role within the British Eighth Army." Their losses in Sicily were twenty-one killed and sixty-two wounded.

Jack's memories of Sicily were quoted in the **Toronto Sun** of 30 November 1980, in the article "Our Unknown War Heroes":

As the tanks groaned across the dusty terrain, the crews sweated as the temperature inside climbed to over 100 degrees. Guys who had been with the 8th Army in North Africa said it was hotter in Sicily than in the desert because of the humidity.

Jack also recalls that it was their first encounter with anti-tank mines, which "tore the tracks off ten of the eighteen tanks in the advance, including mine."

During the interview I had with Jack in November 1990, he remarked that the one action he remembered best was the Salso River operation—4 August 1943, just north of Highway 121 in the area of Agira and Regalbuto. This operation was of particular interest to me because my wife and I had seen the countryside and the Canadian graves when we visited the Commonwealth War Graves Cemetery at Agira in November 1984. We had read Nicholson's account in **Canadians in Italy:** Brigadier General Chris Vokes, using the Edmonton Regiment, Princess Patricia's Canadian Light Infantry (PPCLI) and the Seaforth Highlanders of Canada, and supported by C Squadron of the Three Rivers Regiment, was to advance down the Salso River Valley and take control of the high ground. Jack's story begins:

> I had never been to a brigade orders group before. The other troop leader and I stood in the background and heard Vokes tell Major Mills, "I don't care if I lose all your tanks, you have to get forward and support the Seaforths." We knew where we had to go so did a foot reconnaissance to pick our route through the PPCLI. We walked a mile to the river bed and found a railway bridge that crossed it; this was to be our start line. We walked back six miles [ten kilometres] to our tanks. It was now 2300 hours. Three hours sleep and then, mounted, we drove in darkness to Salso River and the bridge which I decided we would cross. [They didn't know if it would carry them, but they made it.] The route turned out to be clear and the hills they were to support the Seaforths onto were visible. We could hear the Seaforths' Bren guns and the enemy's faster Spandau MGs. I saw one lone figure in the distance. It was Bert Hoffmeister, their commanding officer. He said to me, "I want you to get onto the top of the hill, take up a fire position and take on any targets you can see. You'll also fire on anything that holds us up." So far so good. The hill was a mass of boulders and it took a long time to get to the top. What a view! We could see the main road, the traffic, a wonderful chance for the tank gunners. We fired until 1000 hours and then were ordered to send two tanks down the hill. I took my

troop back and supported the Seaforths' attack toward Adrano.

Jack said the reason he remembered this action was that, although they could have been slaughtered out in the open, everything went according to plan. Jack finished by saying, "This is the type of action you can get thrown at you when you are sent to help the infantry. It is not spectacular, but the morale boost they get from tank support is so obvious." Nicholson's final sentence says it all: "Before dark the road was firmly held, and the first phase of the Brigade's operation against Adrano had been completed."

When the campaign in Sicily ended, the Italian mainland was invaded. The Three Rivers Regiment arrived at Taranto on 25

Lt. Governor Mathews pins Military Cross on Jack Wallace in Toronto, Ontario, June 17, 1945.

September 1943 and in due course came under command of the British 78th Division. They went into action at Termoli on 5 October, a day that Jack would remember forever:

> We were directed to move off at first light along Highway 16 and speed forward to the beleaguered bridgehead [a British force that had landed from the sea into an area near Termoli and was now being attacked by the German 16th Panzer Division]. ... At 1500 hours both squadrons swept across the bridge and made straight toward the battlefront. ... The Start Line was

crossed at 0725 hour. ... No 5 Troop [Jack's] on the left moved forward in the two up formation [two tanks forward supported by the third tank]. Enemy infantry, dug-in, were engaged. ...

The first part of the advance went well but [Jack's] troop was in a fully exposed position. ... The troop was not able to do much except fire on everything which moved. Around mid morning tank 5B (Cpl Campbell) on the extreme left was hit five times. [The British had incorrectly reported that there were no German tanks in a nearby wood.] Campbell managed to destroy one enemy vehicle before evacuating his tank. ... At about 1500 hours the Squadron Commander gave the order to move further forward. ... The lead tank [Jack's] had not moved more than a hundred yards [ninety metres] when it was hit several times in the rear [which had lighter armour], the enemy anti tank coming from the same area as the shots which hit Cpl Campbell. (**Armour Bulletin**, Volume 2, 1987)

The tank's driver and gunner were killed, and Jack's left leg was smashed. Jack sent one more radio transmission to his squadron commander saying, "The fire seems to be coming from the small wood." Much to his disgust, the British came on the air and said, once again, "The wood has been cleared." As it turned out, three more German tanks were destroyed in that "cleared" wood.

Jack was evacuated on the rear of his troop sergeant's tank. Jack remembers how the brigade commander, Bob Wyman, stopped the tank and gave him some words of encouragement, "You did a hell of a good job today, Jack." Jack went on to the forward dressing station, ultimately arriving in Algiers, where his left leg was amputated. The action of 5 October resulted in a Military Cross for Jack.

When Jack came home to Canada, he continued to serve in the army for a while before going to work for the Emergency Measures College in Arnprior, Ontario. Now retired, Jack spends his summers in Ottawa and his winters in the sunny south.

Signaller with the 3rd Division

Verne Barr joined H Section, 3rd Divisional Signals on 20 June 1940 at the age of eighteen in Saint John, New Brunswick. As soon as the unit was up to strength they were sent to Barriefield Camp at Kingston, Ontario, where, for the rest of that year, he learned foot drill, Morse code and radio telegraph (RT) procedures. All the hours spent learning Morse were to be of use only when Verne spent two months at Corps Headquarters; the remainder of the time, Verne used voice over the wireless (radio).

In July 1941, 3rd Division Headquarters (HQ) sailed for England. The Signals Section was well trained; it was not until June 1944 when one solder was killed and three wounded that this close-knit group required reinforcements.

Verne recalls being visited by royalty on two occasions, the first by Her Majesty the Queen accompanied by the two princesses (Elizabeth, our present monarch, was serving as an ATS officer at the time). His Majesty the King came to see the troops before D-Day. Verne recalls, "I was so close to him I could see the freckles on his face."

Training went on without pause. Signals was a big part of the Divisional HQ. The exercises—with names such as Bumper, Tiger and Spartan—were more tiring than the real thing; no one got any sleep! When not at the HQ Verne was sent out to the various infantry units: "They were in such good shape that they could not be worn down."

Brigadier P.A.S. Todd was the Commander Royal Artillery under the command of Major General R.F.L. Keller. The 3rd Division was chosen to cross the beaches on D-Day—6 June 1944—so their training was top priority. Verne remembers one run-in with Brigadier Todd after he returned from a six-week assault course conducted by the British Commandos at Seaford. All webbing (pouches, straps, etc.) had been discarded except for the waist belt and a small pack. When Todd's morning inspection caught Verne unprepared, the brigadier curtly remarked, "I don't care what they do at Seaford. I run this HQ and you get all your webbing on!"

On D-Day Verne was with F Section attached to 13 Field Regiment supporting the Eight Infantry Brigade. In command was Lieutenant

Verne Barr, 1940.

Colonel Clifford, "So good that there was a rivalry between him and Brigadier Todd." Just before the invasion, General Montgomery gathered all the gunners of the 3rd Division together. He said, "Don't tell this to the infantry, but the artillery have won all my battles." Verne explained that the 3rd Divisional Artillery, firing from their landing craft, did support the infantry right before the landing on the beach. "The four Canadian field regiments, while still seaborne, were to fire heavy concentrations ... beginning half an hour before H Hour" (Stacey, **The Victory Campaign**).

Verne recalls that day clearly: "The most impressive sight was the rockets: They hit the beach with such force. I don't know what it did to the Germans, but it sure scared me."

Throughout that month of June 1944 there was no rest for anyone in the artillery. The routine in 13 Field Regiment was that the signaller spent three days forward at the observation post and then three days at the gun positions. The battle was so intense that the regiment wore out the barrels of their self-propelled guns (105 mm), which were then replaced with the twenty-five pounders.

When Verne reached Carpiquet airfield he saw a mural on a hangar wall. A quote from Hitler read, "Whenever this German soldier stands, no one else can come." Verne said it was almost true: the fighting at Carpiquet was some of the fiercest encountered in Normandy.

In August, just before the 2nd Division assaulted Dieppe, Verne was wounded in the chest and shoulder. The policy at that time was to hold all wounded, unless severe, in the forward area so that they could rejoin their units. Reinforcement shortages were already a problem. If a wounded man was sent back to England he would end up in the reinforcement stream with no assurance he would rejoin his former unit. Verne's wounds meant that he missed the tragic Allied bombing of 3rd Divisional HQ. He says, "I think we would have closed the Falaise Gap sooner had it not been for that disastrous bombing raid."

Verne next remembers the Scheldt and the Leopold Canal, where he was wounded again. "A machine gun bullet went through both sides of the wireless truck, smashed a bag of earphones and ricocheted into my leg. The medical officer pulled it out with a pair of forceps." Verne also recalls the flooding in that area: "Farm houses were surrounded by water." Two of Verne's friends drowned when "their amphibious vehicle sank like a stone".

When the war ended Verne was "near Emden and no one seemed very excited; it seemed like an anticlimax." The orders were strict about not fraternizing with the Germans, but it was tempting when "it got warm and the German girls started to enjoy the sun". Then came the best part of Verne's experience as a signaller: all the wireless communications shut down and signallers just had to run the telephone exchange.

Verne went back to England with lots of money in his paybook. He went repeatedly on leave until there was space aboard a ship going home. He finally sailed for Halifax on the *Duchess of Bedford*, then immediately went on to Ottawa. Verne married Ruth Sawyer in Hull, Quebec, on 13 October 1945. Ruth had served in the Royal Canadian Air Force (RCAF) for three years. After they were both discharged it was home to New Brunswick. Verne's last comment, "That was the end of the army for me," was a phrase used by thousands in those months right after the war.

Verne Barr's brother Frank served with the Royal Canadian Engineers (see **50 Years After**). On just two occasions they saw each other on the Continent. The first time was by chance when Frank's jeep caught up to Verne's vehicle in France. The second time was months later in the war just before the crossing over the Rhine River.

In 1955, Verne went to work for Citzenship and Immigration. He retired in 1988 and now divides his time between Florida and St Stephens, New Brunswick.

Gunner-Surveyor with the First Canadian Survey Regiment

During the Second World War, I recall meeting only one Canadian in our home in Conington, England. He was my cousin Clive from Westlock, Alberta, serving with the First Canadian Survey Regiment, Royal Canadian Artillery (1CSR RCA). Clive had completed two years of engineering at the University of Alberta in Edmonton before he became a gunner-surveyor in 1CSR.

When the decision was reached to send the First Canadian Corps to Italy to join the 1st Canadian Division in October 1943, 1CSR left the United Kingdom. The convoy of ships passed through the Strait of Gibraltar on 4 November. 1CSR did not go directly to Sicily, but first docked in Algiers, where they set up camp at Blida. A week later another ship took 1CSR to Sicily, where they docked at Catania. It was not until after New Year's Day, 1944, that 1CSR crossed the Messina Strait and, 36 hours later, arrived at Altamura near Bari.

Clive explained how 1CSR's role was unique:

> There were three main tasks carried out by the regiment. First, a surveying group to provide the surveying services for our artillery batteries; second, a flash-spotting group for visual spotting of enemy guns, either by the gun flashes during the night or the smoke from the discharge during daylight hours; third, a sound-ranging group to pick up the sound of enemy guns using sensitive microphones deployed along a five or more mile [eight or nine kilometre] front and analyzing the wave shapes of the gun blasts recorded on a multi-track recorder or oscillograph. (Each artillery gun had a distinctive "fingerprint" wave shape that provided identification.) Enemy gun locations could then be determined by triangulation of line of sight (flash spotting) or speed of sound (sound ranging). The latter group included a meteorological section to make necessary corrections for wind, fog and barometric

pressure, which could affect the speed of sound or the apparent direction from which the sound came.

A fourth duty of the Survey Regiment was to carry out calibration of the artillery guns to determine the accuracy of the gun sights. This had to be done for newly issued guns and as a check for guns that had been in service for some time and whose perfor-mance might be affected by wear in the barrel.

Clive Gardam, Nutfield Surrey, England, 1943.

These specially trained artillerymen had worked together in the United Kingdom for over two years:

> Although a number of reorganizational changes were made during our stay in England, including Operation Split, which broke up the regiment into two regiments, the final make-up of 1CSR when we left for Italy included two batteries, each containing one survey troop, one flash-spotting troop and one sound-ranging troop. In addition, there was one survey troop, G Troop (of which I was a member) attached to regimental headquarters to provide surveying services for medium and heavy artillery batteries and calibration services for all sizes of guns. This arrangement remained essentially constant during the war.

On 25 February 1945, 1CSR left Italy by sea. After two days they landed at Marseilles, France, then drove in convoy to join the 2nd Canadian Corps in Kuurne, Belgium.

The following account could come under the heading of "If things can go wrong, they will go wrong":

On March 18th, right half section of G Troop was sent to Wenduine on the north coast of Belgium near Ostende to calibrate guns for various regiments. After check-out of the base and its communication system, mostly telephone, calibration started on March 20th and continued almost daily until April 4th. Many regiments had their guns calibrated. An incident with the Royal Navy occurred on March 21st while we were warming up two new guns for the 17th Field. (In the 1940s, a new artillery gun, like a new car, had to be broken in before an accurate calibration could be done.) This warm-up was accomplished by firing 50 to 100 rounds from each gun before starting observation of fall-of-shot for calibration. These two guns were firing out to sea from a position a couple of miles [three kilometres] inland from the coast. During this period we were observing the fall-of-shot occasionally but not taking readings and we failed to notice that a fog was closing in over the target area. Warm-up of the guns continued. Suddenly, a Land Rover came racing along the road and stopped at our plotting centre. The driver, in a naval uniform, quite upset, reported that an MTB [motor torpedo boat] submarine chaser had sent word that an artillery battery near Blankenburg (a town about five or six miles [eight or nine kilometres] east of our location) had fired on them, causing them to lose contact with a U-boat they were chasing. We were the guilty party.

Procedures were changed at once. Never again were shells fired if the fall-of-shot could not be seen.

After war's end, Clive came back to Alberta and continued his university education, graduating in 1948. He and his family were living in St Catharines, Ontario, in 1951 when I visited his home as a recruit at Camp Borden. Clive moved to the United States in 1954 and worked in Toledo, Ohio, until he retired.

Canadian Forestry Corps Overseas

Whitney Carr was one Canadian soldier who took his peacetime occupation to the war overseas and then continued after war's end. Whitney was a lumberman in Cochrane, Ontario, cutting logs on his own property and hauling them to the pulp mill nearby, when he decided to enlist in 1940. He signed up at Kirkland Lake, Ontario, where he joined the Canadian Forestry Corps. This branch of the Canadian Army had produced at least ten companies for service in England and France during the First World War. The skills of a lumberman could quickly be transported to any forested area, and the lumbermen's output in timber could be used at once for the war effort.

After a short period in Kirkland Lake, Whitney and his fellow forestry workers were sent to Valcartier, Quebec, where they were given basic training and brought up to full unit strength. After eight months they were ready to sail for Scotland. A nine-day voyage in convoy brought them to Greenock: "We landed in the morning and that night the Germans bombed the Clyde Bank shipyards, causing heavy damage; we were on our way to Loch Rannoch so were not affected."

It had been decided to build a sawmill at Carrbridge near Granton-on-Spey. "All the machinery had been shipped over from Canada, the mill was built, and we got down to doing what we had done at home—felling trees, hauling them to the mill and making rough lumber and timbers." At first, most of their products were used as pit props in the coal mines, or for rebuilding bomb-damaged buildings in the United Kingdom. After June 1944, the majority of their output went directly to France to be used in bridging.

A Department of National Defence publication, **The Canadians in Britain 1939-1944**, gives a good account of the size and significance of the war effort by people like Whitney Carr:

> Canada had agreed to provide twenty companies of the Canadian Forestry Corps. Because Britain had asked for these specialized soldiers they paid for all aspects of their employment except "for pay and transportation to and from Great Britain". The work of the Forestry

Whitney Carr, 1940.

Corps became so critical that "finally a total of 30 companies were engaged in lumbering operations". The operational unit of the Corps was the company—6 officers and 188 other ranks [Whitney served in 11, 12 and 22 companies]. By June 1943 the Corps overseas "totalled 224 officers and 6385 other ranks". From Monday to Friday "the men felled, sawed and transported lumber. On Saturdays they donned battle dress and ... engaged in drill, musketry and tactical exercises". This was done to ensure the Canadians would be available for "an operational role in the defence of Scotland". During October 1943 ten companies received refresher training to be ready for employment on the continent once the invasion took place.

During one leave in Glasgow, Whitney met Jeanie Clark, and on the day before Christmas, 1942, the young couple was married in Perth.

In the spring of 1945, Whitney's company was told to make ready for a move to France, but V-E Day came before the move. Whitney left for Canada on a troopship, sad to leave his wife and baby, who would follow with the war bride contingent.

Back home in Canada, Whitney sold his property in Cochrane and bought a property in West Guildford, Haliburton, Ontario. It was to West Guildford that he brought Jeanie when she arrived. Jeanie remembers that "things were remote and rather wild, but the people made me welcome." Of the original twenty war brides in the area, the twelve remaining still keep in touch.

Whitney and Jean visited Scotland in 1975, and he "was thrilled to see one of the lumber mills still in operation." Retirement from lumber mill work came in 1966. In 1990, Whitney celebrated his eightieth birthday and his forty-eighth wedding anniversary.

Serving as a Sapper

When I asked Joe Wood why he joined the Canadian Army in 1939, his reply was to the point, "As a bricklayer I had tried to keep working all through the Great Depression. Trying to bring up a family was very hard. The army was steady work and wages." Joe was sent first to Camp Borden, Ontario, and then, in late September, to Camp Petawawa. Petawawa is about 100 miles [160 kilometres] northwest of Ottawa on the banks of the Ottawa River. Joe's account begins:

> Our first connection with the name Petawawa was the railway station. We marched through the tiny village and into the sandy wasteland where we were to build H-huts. We erected tents that would be our "home" until well into winter. Truckloads of green lumber arrived along with cement for the footings. It was daylight-to-dark work and as soon as each H-hut had a roof and walls troops moved in. There were no windows or doors and it was some time before electrical wiring and plumbing were installed.
>
> It was late October before we got our hut and we slept on the wooden floor on straw mattresses. The mosquitoes and black flies did not leave us alone until the snow came. Once we had the huts built it was time to build rifle ranges and other training areas. Troops were coming into camp from all over Canada, they were given training and then left for overseas staging camps such as Debert, Nova Scotia.

Joe's skill as a mason was required for the concrete footings, but anytime there was a pause it was "route marches to places like Pembroke and back; the officers were trying to toughen us up." As units were brought up to strength, they were assigned to divisions and sent overseas. Eventually it was Joe's turn, but on his final medical he failed to meet the standard. In his words, "I had broken my back just two years before the war began, and the long route marches with full kit were just too much for me."

In such cases as this the soldier was often released, but qualified masons were hard to come by. Nevertheless, Joe said that he had a long wait to get back to his trade; in the meantime, "it was guard duty, kitchen help and other odd jobs". As it was obvious he was not going to leave Petawawa, Joe found an apartment on the upper floor of a house in nearby Pembroke for his family (the owners of the house were the family of Angus Campbell, who would later become mayor of Pembroke). Joe's wife Edythe and their two daughters arrived in Pembroke in 1943, and Joe was able to visit them on his odd weekend off. "I took the bus in from camp, and in order to get back in time for roll call in the morning I would go back to Petawawa with the milkman."

Sapper Joe Wood (right) at Camp Petawawa, Ontario, October 1939

In 1945, the government decided to put military inspectors in charge of supervising the building of Sunnybrook Hospital in Toronto. Joe was promoted to corporal and sent to Toronto, but "after two or three days the civilian foreman told me that the men didn't want to be supervised by someone in uniform." After the contractor made one or two phone calls to Camp Petawawa and Ottawa, he called Joe in and said, "Joe, you now wear civilian clothes; your release will be here very soon." Joe stayed on the job until released.

Joe Wood worked at Dominion Magnesium Limited in Haley Station, Ontario, until he was close to seventy years of age. He died in 1988. I married the youngest of his two daughters, Elaine, in 1955.

From Hockey to Hero

Cliff Chadderton is one of the better known Canadians in this book, not for his wartime experiences with the Royal Winnipeg Rifles but for his postwar work.

When the war began, Cliff was wearing two uniforms: one as a hockey player with his regimental team in the Manitoba Senior Hockey League; the other on nights and weekends as a rifleman. His civilian job was that of news editor with the Canadian Press in Winnipeg. Cliff signed up in the Active Force on 5 July 1940 and the regiment moved to Camp Shilo, Manitoba. By August Cliff was a corporal and by October he was a sergeant in 7 Platoon A Company. The unit was in Debert, Nova Scotia, for almost a year and then sailed for Britain in August 1941.

The usual method of becoming an officer was to join as one or be commissioned from the ranks from within the unit. Sergeants Mitchell and Chadderton were the first two men commissioned from the ranks in the Royal Winnipeg Rifles; they returned to Gordon Head, Victoria, British Columbia, and Camp Shilo, Manitoba, for training. Training took over a year, for it was November 1943 on the Isle of Wight in the south of England before Cliff took command of a platoon in the Rifles.

Says Cliff, "I landed in France on June 15. Immediately upon joining the battalion I was promoted to the rank of captain and made second-in-command of D Company." A violent storm hit the coast on 19 June, and unloading over the beaches had to almost cease for over three days.

Life in an infantry battalion at this time was one of great stress, sudden and violent close combat with the enemy, and the ever-increasing "fog of war", which resulted in infantry and tanks not attacking together, artillery fire plans not happening as ordered and higher headquarters constantly urging on the forward troops. Picture the confusion, with soldiers who had left the security of Britain two weeks before now facing casualties, missing in action and the grim task of burying comrades. In **Canada's Battle in Normandy**, the statistics speak graphically:

Casualties during June totalled 226 officers and 3,066 other ranks—somewhat more than one-fifth of the Canadian assault strength [of these, 53 officers and 698 other ranks were killed or died of wounds. The Royal Winnipeg Rifles had 256 casualties on 8 June, 105 fatal].

The soldier's desire to remain with his regiment even though wounded comes out in this account by Cliff of an action on 4 July, when the Rifles were attached to the 8th Infantry Brigade:

The company objective was the village of Carpiquet on the outskirts of Caen. We were on a road beside a high stone wall and we came under machine gun fire. As we jumped into a ditch all I remember is dropping my Sten gun. Then I felt the blood running down my pinkie finger. Somebody wrapped a field dressing around it and we went on to clear the village. When things quieted down I went looking for the regimental aid post. Doc John Caldwell wrote out an evacuation tag and ordered me to jump on one of the ambulance jeeps, carrying back the wounded. I was worried. I figured a week at the Casualty Clearing Station and then I would get posted to another battalion. Anyway, I went back to Doc and got him to tear up the evac slip and put some sulpha on the wound, and he let me go back to my company. (When my pension slip came through after I left the Army, there was no mention of the gunshot wound in the hand, although the scar is still plainly visible and on x-ray there is still some shrapnel. The Pension Commission said something along the lines of "Are you sure this isn't pre-enlistment disability?")

One of the important factors of war is to get the enemy to surrender and thus save a large number of casualties, and that's what Cliff tried to do on 2 September 1944. The Canadians were clearing the various channel ports and neutralizing cross-channel guns, which could fire over the English Channel to Dover. At Cape Gris Nez there were three main batteries, one of which was Battery Todt at Haringzelles with four 380 mm guns. The commanding officer of the Rifles realized he

Cliff Chadderton as a hockey player (back row, third from right).

would lose a lot of men if he assaulted the battery, so he held an Orders Group, and Cliff volunteered to take an offer of surrender to the German commanding officer.

> We commandeered a jeep. I dug out my dress "wedge cap" and we rigged up a huge bed sheet. Al Ferrier volunteered as the driver, as he could speak French. My company sergeant major, Jim Sharpe, agreed to go along. We followed a trail up the slope and noted that the Germans had constructed a huge defensive line with barb wire entanglement and cement pillboxes. The road was blocked by an ingenious system of anti-tank obstacles, with just enough room for a command vehicle to zig zag through. After a hasty telephone conversation, the guards let us through and we proceeded to the top and into a vehicle compound. We

were grabbed and placed against a wall, and a sinister-looking German SS officer began shouting orders. Eventually I was escorted down at least three levels of steps and paraded before a commandant, who, fortunately, spoke English. I remember mumbling something about "would you like to surrender" and "the Geneva convention that would be accorded to his troops." As is stated, accurately, in our regimental history: "His retort deserves a place of honour in the Rifle Archives. 'Come and get me,' he said."

I had no inclination to extend the discussion and raced up the stairs and headed for the jeep. It must have occurred to the German commander, when we were half-way down the hill, that we had got a pretty good look at his defensive positions. Anyway, his troops commenced firing at us, but we made it back to the safety of the village.

The episode did have one positive effect. Later it was decided that the 9th Brigade (3rd Div) would put in a major assault. I was able to brief Brigadier Rockingham about what I had seen and he immediately asked the Division for more artillery and air support from the Typhoon low-level bombers.

According to C.P. Stacey in **The Victory Campaign,** "That night for the first time in four years, Dover was safe."

Many actions took place as the Canadians cleared France and moved into the Low Countries. Cliff's final action took place on the Netherlands/Belgium border on the Leopold Canal:

We crossed Leopold Canal sometime in the very early morning on October 6th, 1944. We withstood eight or nine counterattacks in four days. On the 10th, about noon, the CO told me to take a recce into Graf Jan, a small village, to see if the Germans were still there. There was only one road as the Germans had flooded the fields. We got about 100 yards [90 metres] off the dike—which was, in fact, the north side of Leopold Canal. It had been strongly fortified with bunkers by the Germans. On the patrol we came under heavy mortar fire and I lost two men. We zipped back to the log and cement bunkers and I got hit by a a German 88 anti-tank gun shell just as I was diving for cover. Just lucky that I was not the first to reach the bunker. That fellow, a rifleman named Bob Bell, was killed by the concussion. I regained consciousness in about an hour. It was dangerous to move along the top of the dike but the nearest kapok bridge was about 200 yards [180 metres] away. I started out on my own but had to stop. I remember trying to tie a tourniquet around my right leg. The left foot and knee were badly shot up and I had a splinter in the gut. But it was what was left of the right leg that was bleeding.

I recall only vaguely what happened next—the stretcher bearer (not from our unit) who crossed the bridge and, with a buddy, got me out. [In September 1989, Cliff learned that the stretcher bearer was Leo Ryan of Dartmouth, Nova Scotia, then with the 17th Duke of York's 7th Recce.] The stretcher bearers took me back to our own regimental aid post. It was now dark, and my mind kept drifting off, partly from the morphine and partly from the rum which Doc Caldwell was giving me. The regimental stretcher jeep could not take me out as the tiny roadways couldn't be seen due to darkness—so I was evacuated the following morning to the Casualty Clearing Station. I remember the MO [medical officer] put on some surgical dressings and then [I went] by ambulance to a Field Ambulance Unit in Bruges, Belgium. By now it was midnight, the 11th; when they amputated the leg below the knee, they told me this was essential.

The doctor said there was only a slight hope they could save the left leg and they were evacuating me on a priority basis to England. They loaded me with morphine and I vaguely remember an ambulance ride to a large hangar and a trip across the Channel on a DC-3 loaded with stretchers and Canadian and British casualties. I ended up at a Canadian General Hospital somewhere in the south of England, in and out of surgery for a few weeks. I eventually came home on the hospital ship—the *Lady Nelson*— arriving in my home town of Winnipeg the day before Christmas in 1944.

Clifford Chadderton, chief executive officer of War Amputations of Canada and recipient of the 1988 Royal Bank Award, plays with two-year-old Lindsay Anne Hilton of Halifax, N.S., who is a participant in the CHAMP program for child amputees.

I stayed in Deer Lodge Hospital in Winnipeg until May, but could not be fitted with an artificial leg. Fortunately, they managed to salvage the remaining leg, but when they told me there would be more surgery on my stump I said no dice. I had a job waiting for me in Ottawa so I took off on crutches. The Minister of Labour, name of Humphrey Mitchell, was looking for a wounded veteran for his staff. I got the job and had two titles. The first was Director of the Reinstatement in Civil Employment Act and the second was Secretary of the Interdepartmental Committee on Rehabilitation. Later I

was made Director of Rehabilitation. My discharge
from the army finally caught up with me when I
received my first government paycheque in Ottawa.

Cliff had gone from being a hockey player, through the ranks to acting major, and was now a civilian and a war amputee.

I first met Cliff in 1952 when he was Secretary of the Army Benevolent Fund—bailing out soldiers who were in financial distress through the Canadian Army Welfare fund. Cliff has been the chairman of the National Council of Veterans Associations since 1984. His work with the War Amputations of Canada has spanned more than a quarter of a century; since 1965 he has been their chief executive officer. When asked what was his greatest achievement after being a member and officer of the Order of Canada since 1977, he replies, "Working with amputee kids. There is nothing like it. They challenge you every day."

A German Surrender

This story concerns a soldier who rose from the rank of private to that of lieutenant colonel during a few short years. Jacques Dextraze [JA Dex] joined the Fusiliers Mont-Royal in Montreal in 1940. "Many of the soldiers of the unit had gone to school together, we were a family." The originals had gone to Iceland and it was now time (after Dieppe) for yet another battalion to be formed. Many of these men would go overseas as reinforcements.

JA Dex was training one or two nights a week and still working for Dominion Rubber Company. When he decided to "go active", he left for the training camp at Farnham, then Sorel. He quickly went from private to corporal to sergeant and began training recruits. By January 1942 he had taken all the courses offered, including small arms and physical training, and had trained four platoons. Sergeant Dextraze was proud of his work and ensured that his trainees "came top" each time. The men worked well for him, for he did everything he asked of his recruits.

One day the company officers decided that JA Dex should go before the Officer Selection Board. In their wisdom, the Board concluded that Segeant Dextraze did not "show enough leadership qualities" and he was turned down. In a word, JA Dex was chastened—after all, he was running the platoon! The officers were more interested in the social aspects of soldiering; it was JA Dex who was teaching the men. A few months later, another selection board decided the young sergeant should go to Brockville, Ontario, for officer training. He came second in his class and, on graduation in early 1942, he was held as a bilingual platoon commander on the school staff. The course was three months in length and his platoon graduated in July 1942.

The Dieppe Raid on 19 August changed everything for Lieutenant Dextraze. The Fusiliers Mont-Royal had suffered heavily at Dieppe, and JA Dex was warned for overseas draft. JA Dex contacted his fiancee, Frances Paré, and they decided to get married before he left; just ten days later, 2 September 1942, the wedding took place. Then it was overseas to Whitley Camp, England.

Jacques Dextraze in 1944 as a L. Col. Written on the photo is this plea to his former workers at Dominion Rubber Co., Ltd., "Let us not be English Canadians. Let us not be French Canadians. Let us be CANADIANS."

Lieutenant Colonel Guy Gauvreau, the commanding officer of the Fusiliers, came to see the reinforcements. He chose Lieutenant Dextraze as his intelligence officer; later he was the transport officer and then the adjutant. In the late autumn of 1943 the unit left for Wales for more training, and on 30 December Captain Dextraze was appointed second-in-command of D Company. Very shortly thereafter he was promoted to major as a company commander.

As the time for the invasion drew close, the Fusiliers were moved near Dover as part of the 6th Brigade in the 2nd Division. On 6 June 1944, the brigade was ready to follow the invasion force. JA Dex remembers "standing on the cliff in the early morning as the sun came up and seeing a sea filled with ships of all sorts."

The 2nd Canadian Division landed in France in the first week of July. On the 20th, the 6th Brigade was ready for its first battle, in the area of Verrieres Ridge. Stacey's **The Victory Campaign** explains the plan: "The 6th Brigade crossed its start line at 3:00 p.m. ... The Cameron Highlanders of Canada were on the right ... the South Saskatchewan Regiment in the centre and the Fusiliers Mont-Royal on the left." The plan looked good on paper, for it followed all the rules learned in training in England. But battles don't follow rules, and the Germans had other ideas for these young men. JA Dex explained:

> The first battle was to capture the village of Ifs. B Company was on the right and C Company was on the left. D Company was to follow B Company. Once B Company seized their objective then D Company was to take the village of Verrieres.

When JA Dex visited the old battlefield in the summer of 1990, he concluded that the battle plan was illogical. "No one really understood how hard the Germans would fight," JA Dex reflects today. "The FMR were ambitious and brave, but we didn't have experience."

B Company was stopped short of its objective, and as JA Dex led his D Company forward, they were "caught in a German mortar barrage". Most of D Company were casualties—all the officers and most of the non-commissioned officers (NCOs). After dark the commanding officer was told that D Company was only twenty strong, so they were withdrawn to the start line. Reinforcements came forward along with the Left Out of Battle (LOBs). (LOBs were composed of a percentage of the unit who did not fight that day. They formed the nucleus for reforming the unit after heavy losses.) JA Dex reformed his company, and the following evening moved off to seize the original objective of C Company on the left—Troteval Farm. Apart from three German tanks that he could not destroy, the attack was successful.

An entire brigade finally took the objective that had been assigned to D Company. The advance continued village by village, church by church. In one action against a church, JA Dex saw his lead platoon commander cut down by German machine- gun fire. He rushed forward, "took over the platoon, moved across the road, through a break in a stone wall, the second platoon following, and seized the church, driving out the Germans." This sort of "take charge and push on" attitude resulted in achievement against odds, time and time again.

Paul Sauvé (later the Premier of Quebec) was the commanding officer on the Fusiliers' return to Dieppe. He planned the action in detail, getting everyone to contribute to the plan. The Germans had evacuated, so there was no fight. And even though there was "not a single veteran of Dieppe in the unit when we returned", the French civilians were overjoyed to see the badge of the Fusiliers.

Paul Sauvé, already a member of his provincial legislature, returned home when he was re-elected. JA Dex was then promoted (25 December 1944) to lieutenant colonel and named Commanding Officer. He was just twenty-five. JA Dex remembers Paul Sauvé as

> broadminded, a man of vision, one with the ability to get the very best out of everyone. Paul's great desire, which we often discussed in the dugout at night, was to get the French and English elements of Canada fully united. He often told me that one day he would do it. Unfortunately he died before he could make his dream a reality. Paul's ambition was to eventually go into federal politics. We never discussed in what capacity; he would have been a great Prime Minister, acceptable to both the English and the French. He was bright and a great leader.

In April 1945, the Fusiliers were in action at Groningen, Holland. In **The Victory Campaign,** C.P. Stacey says simply, "The German commander and his staff surrendered on the 16th." JA Dex tells the full story.

Ordered into Groningen, the Fusiliers crossed the Ems Canal by a bridge that had been seized two days before. House by house, the infantry moved toward the centre of the city to the market square. JA Dex says, "This type of fighting is the most nervewracking that one can be engaged in." In the early morning of 16 April, the left-hand company captured a number of German officers (two colonels, plus staff officers and others from divisional headquarters). The prisoners were kept under guard while JA Dex moved forward to see what lay ahead for his battalion. Suddenly, two German captains ran up to the commanding officer with their hands held high. Through the interpreter (Willie, a Dutchman) JA Dex learned

> that if I would go with them to their divisional HQ, they were sure their general would surrender to the Canadians.

I suddenly saw the chance to shorten the war, to cut down on casualties. So without further adieu I said, "Okay, we'll go to your HQ." I called Brigadier Allard and told him I wanted all artillery gunfire stopped while I went into the town. I sat the two German captains on the front of my Bren gun carrier with a large white flag. Gabbie, my driver, Willie the interpreter and my two signallers and I drove to the German HQ; it was quite a distance. The HQ was in a large monastery. I was wearing a pair of corduroy pants, battle dress tunic and my officer's peaked hat—no pistol, but I had my map case. I went inside with Willie; my soldiers remained with the vehicle. On the top floor we were met by the German general. He had on an immaculate uniform, high shiny boots, very smart looking indeed. Suddenly I said to myself, "What the hell am I doing here?" I turned to Willie and told him to tell the general "that I've come here to ask him to surrender".

The general shouted out, "Nein!" and said that I should surrender to him.

I told Willie to explain the battle situation from my map board. I then said, "Tell the general I will allow him to go to my HQ and speak to the captured German officers held there and that I will wait here until he came back." In doing this the general could see for himself that he was up against a strong force.

The general looked at me, then said to Willie, "While I go there, he [meaning JA Dex] will remain here until I come back?"

Willie said, "Yes."

The general then left and, what seemed like hours later, he returned in my Bren gun carrier. I had told my unit and brigade what was happening over the radio. The general came back and spoke to me in perfect French!

He said that he agreed to surrender as long as his troops were well treated. They formed up and, with me in my carrier leading, they marched to the POW cage. The general came to my HQ, gave me his pistol and camera and then was taken to brigade HQ.

The official history caps this amazing story by stating, "The four-day battle cost the 2nd Division 209 infantry casualties ... and 2,400 prisoners were captured."[This action resulted in a second DSO for JA Dex.]

The war was coming to a close. The Fusiliers Mont Royal saw V-E Day at an airfield in Germany. JA Dex volunteered for the Pacific Force, leaving his regiment behind. There was a plan to make him commanding officer of the 48th Highlanders, but, as JA Dex says, "Can you see me in a kilt?" He finally was named commanding officer of the Hastings and Prince Edward Regiment, which was to form up in Kingston, Ontario.

When V-J Day ended the war, JA Dex started the staff course at Fort Frontenac, Kingston. Ottawa finally told him he could remain in the Regular Force if he reverted to the rank of captain, but he would be junior in rank to all Permanent Force captains. He told Ottawa what they could do with their offer and took his release. Back home to Montreal, he started work as the Woodlands Manager for Singer Sewing Machine Company.

In 1950, Lieutenant Colonel Dextraze was asked to form and train an infantry battalion for Korea. He served in the Congo; as Commandant, Royal Canadian School of Infantry; as Brigade Commander in Petawawa; as Deputy Commander of Mobile Command; and as Chief of Personnel in Ottawa. In September 1972, JA Dex was appointed Chief of the Defence Staff. He retired on 1 September 1977 and was appointed Chairman of the Board of Canadian National Railways on the same day. He is now retired and lives in Ottawa.

A Doctor and a Nurse

This story is unique in that it contains the war experiences of two members of the Royal Canadian Army Medical Corps (RCAMC), Major John Barr and Captain (Matron) Marion Crawford, who became husband and wife just two days after the war ended in Europe.

John Barr began his six years of undergraduate training in 1934 at Queen's University Faculty of Medicine. In his freshman year he was a member of the Canadian Officer Training Corps, so at the outbreak of war in 1939, he resumed his military training. That same year, John met Marion Crawford while both were working at the Ontario Hospital at Kingston.

When he graduated in 1940, John went to the Civic Hospital in Ottawa until that September:

> On Labour Day weekend I was in charge of my own wards (paediatrics and "soldiers' surgery") at the hospital, I was on call in the operating room, in charge of admissions and I was the intern in Emergency—I was run off my feet. For this I received my "keep" and $25 a month, of which the hospital kept $10, so I netted 50 cents a day, and the meals were awful! Meanwhile some of my university friends were with 23rd Field Ambulance on Porter's Island, where they were making $5 a day and eating like kings. On 14 September I applied for admission to 23rd Field Ambulance and was accepted as a lieutenant in the RCAMC.

Marion trained in the Victoria Hospital in London, Ontario, where she received her RN on graduation. Her first job was with the Victorian Order of Nurses. Later she went to the University of Toronto where she was awarded a certificate in Public Health Nursing. Marion then specialized in psychiatric nursing at Whitby, Ontario. These qualifications led to a position at the Ontario Hospital in Kingston as an instructor. Marion recalls,

> I had never taught psychiatric nursing to anybody in my life before. I had no notes to teach from. The class came in a day ahead of me! For the first year I had to

work twenty hours a day. I prepared my lessons, taught them and then started the whole cycle again for the next day. Finally, when the Superintendent of Nurses left I was promoted to her position in the hospital. I joined the army in Kingston, Ontario, in June 1942 and after serving in Kingston went to Ottawa to Porter's Island. It was here that I was assigned to 12 Canadian General Hospital [CGH]. We concentrated at Sussex, New Brunswick, from all over Canada. When we were up to strength we sailed from Halifax on the *Queen Elizabeth* for Scotland in September 1943 with a large number of troops aboard.

Marion served with 10 CGH in England until 12 CGH was set up near Horley, Sussex, as a 1,200-bed hospital in wartime buildings. Marion remembers proudly that the unit worked well together; the lack of previous affiliations meant there were no petty jealousies or personality clashes.

In recalling the personalities of 12 CGH, Marion says, "We had a wonderful commanding officer, Colonel W.A. Fraser from Victoria. He was a marvellous person. Our matron was Miss Sara Miles from Rothesay, New Brunswick—a jewel." Marion remembers a German V1 bomb landing near the hospital and a dogfight overhead between an Allied and a German aircraft. A lot of surgery was done in the hospital, and there were wards for medical and other specialized forms of treatment.

John's unit moved to Debert, Nova Scotia, in October 1940, into an uncompleted camp where, in some cases, windows and doors were still to be installed on the buildings. Red mud was everywhere.

Each field ambulance cared for the minor sick of their brigade and, before leaving for Britain, the medical staffs spent a lot of time "boarding" the men to ensure they were fit for overseas duty. John recalls the foul-up when "our unit of 10 officers and 170 men, all RCAMC, arrived and the camp expected 1 officer and 17 men from the Postal Corps!" Parts of 7th and 9th brigades were in the camp. The 22nd Field Ambulance was in Debert in support of the 7th Brigade, while the 23rd Field Ambulance supported 9th Brigade.

In the summer of 1941, John Barr sailed for Scotland from Halifax. He became suddenly popular when, as the ship sailed up the Clyde, they passed a large building with "Barr's Distillery" on the hoarding. "That popularity lasted only until it was realized that my family did not own the distillery."

The first place 23rd Field Ambulance set up was at Crookham Crossroads, near Fleet, where they shared Queen Elizabeth Barracks with the 17th Duke of York's Royal Canadian Hussars from Montreal. One of John's strong memories of those days is that "I had never been hungry before, but the British rations kept me starving all the time." John recalls,

> At this time a pattern began for my employment. Because I was the youngest doctor in 23rd Field Ambulance and single, I became the temporary regimental medical officer (RMO) for any 9th Brigade unit that needed one. I started off with the North Nova Scotia Highlanders in Aldershot. Simply marvellous men, the adjutant was Don Forbes (who postwar became Director of Infantry). It was on field exercises that I learned how to run a regimental aid post and how to keep up with these very fit men.
>
> In the spring of 1942 I was sent on a platoon commanders' course; I thought I was going to take the daily sick parade but I found I was a candidate. I stayed and qualified as a platoon commander. In June I was the RMO for another course run by the 3rd Canadian Division in assault landings. For three weeks we learned how to use toggle ropes, climb cliffs and cross obstacles, and we toughened up. I believed the doctor must be able to keep up with the men he is supporting. One day I was just getting out of bed when a German aircraft started bombing an airfield near us. As the plane was leaving, it fired its machine guns into our accommodation. There were several casualties among the staff of the course headquarters, including the

engineer officer and a nursing orderly. Both were
mortally wounded and died en route to hospital.

John remembers a brave NCO, C.C. Chambers, who went after
Royal Air Force personnel who had strayed into a minefield.
Chambers rescued seven men from injury. "One poor fellow was
blown to pieces. I wrote up a citation for Chambers, and he got the
British Empire Medal."

John was posted to the Highland Light Infantry in 1943 as the
RMO, "the best job in the world". The unit was in Scotland on assault
landing exercises when John saw the *Queen Elizabeth* sailing towards
the Clyde; he did not realize that Marion was aboard. Soon after
returning to England, John was moved to the headquarters of the 3rd
Canadian Division as a "staff learner, medical". Once again it was
time for "reboarding", as all the unfit men were removed from the
combat units that were to be in the assault force on 6 June 1944.

John was also involved in research to determine means to control
seasickness. The day of the trial aboard a landing craft, "the sea was
like glass, not a wave". Based on other trials, preventative measures
were developed, and hundreds of tablets were issued for the troops
who were to make the crossing. On D+5 (11 June), John crossed to
Normandy. "After many exercises when we got all wet, this time we
drove ashore onto the dry beach. The only enemy we saw or heard
was the occasional German aircraft."

After a month John asked to go back to a field ambulance company,
and he became the company commander of 22 Field Ambulance in
support of the 8th Brigade. As the advance to Caen progressed, John's
company set up near Colembelles. All the bridges over the Orne were
one-way, so there was no way to get the wounded back to the rear:
"We had to hold the casualties." On the second day, John was with the
unit when they were moved into a position on top of a hill at night.

Hardly had we arrived when the enemy artillery shells
began to land and gradually crept closer. I tried to dig a
slit trench in the shale. I managed to scrape out a trench
in which I could lie all except my feet. There was an
ungodly bang and the whole earth shook. I heard
something go "drip, drip" and I thought I'd been hit in

my feet. I wasn't hit, it was the radiator of the jeep behind me that was the casualty! The shell fragments had blown over me in my shallow trench.

In the fight for Quesnay Woods, John remembers that the units of the 8th Brigade suffered very severe casualties. On 10 August "between 10 o'clock at night and 4 in the morning, over 160 patients passed through our company, where there were just two MOs." Many of the wounded were very badly hurt, and all had been through the regimental aid posts already. "One lad from the Queen's Own died as I tried to treat his chest wound. I felt so badly, as he was a husky young fellow and I could not resuscitate him."

In describing casualty evacuation during the long advance through France, John mentions the importance of stabilizing the patient so that he could withstand the two- to three-hour ambulance ride, sometimes over tank tracks. On one occasion he had room for only one more stretcher in an ambulance, but he had two cases with head wounds. He chose to evacuate the German prisoner rather than the Canadian patient because he believed that the Canadian would not survive. The next morning, the Canadian had rallied and was in better shape to make the trip; "his life may have been saved because I had to keep him for the night." When the 8th Brigade reached the south bank of the Scheldt, John's patients began being sent back to St Andre near Bruges, Belgium, where 12 CGH was in operation.

To make room for another hospital to care for casualties from Normandy, Marion's unit was cleared of almost all patients just before D-Day. 12 CGH was then concentrated in Whitby, Yorkshire, "where we marched with full pack for ten miles [sixteen kilometres]! Some of the packs were [surreptiously] lightened, much to the delight of the people of Yorkshire who got the discarded kit." On completing their field training, the unit went to Southhampton and then by ship to France in August 1944. On arrival, with "full gear, we climbed down the side of the ship on scramble nets into a landing craft." The unit stayed with 10 CGH at Bayeux, where it was "life under canvas" for over a month. In mid September, 12 CGH moved near Bruges to set up in "a home for wayward girls run by a religious order". Facilities were very primitive. The unit opened on 5 October 1944 and by the 9th they had 1,200 patients. Marion recalls,

The patient load was pretty constant until after Christmas. At the time of the battle for the south bank of the Scheldt, casualties came to us directly from the field ambulance companies. The patients came by ambulance, were assessed, had major surgery done when needed and when they were fit to travel they were sent to Britain by air. There was a constant flow of casualties in one door and out another, all of which was made possible by the soldiers from the British Pioneer Corps who carried the stretchers from the ambulances between the floors and within the hospital. In the hospital itself, the "up patients" assisted in the care of bed patients. With only two nursing sisters on duty on a ward of seventy-five patients, they needed all the help they could get.

Casualties passed through very quickly. I remember one patient, seventeen years of age, with a bad chest wound; his name was Struthers. He was very popular with the nursing staff because he was so young and such a good patient. One afternoon he suddenly died. It was an awful shock because he had been doing so well post-operatively. The memory of that young soldier is still with me after these forty-seven years.

As 1945 began, John had problems with a skin infection that resisted common treatment, so he was sent back to 12 CGH for five days. It was then that John and Marion made plans to be married; they did not want to marry until after the war ended, because the policy was that married nursing sisters were sent back to England. They set the 10th of May as their wedding day, sure the war would be over by then.

In February, John was promoted to major and appointed second-in-command of 23 Field Ambulance, the unit he had joined in Ottawa. The weeks passed too quickly, with the war dragging on. V-E Day finally came on 8 May 1945, just two days before the planned wedding day. Unfortunately, John's unit was in Leer, Germany, a long way from Bruges. With help from his friends at the

The wedding of John and Marion Barr, May, 1945

headquarters of the 3rd Canadian Division and a quick trip in a "liberated German staff car", John arrived in Bruges on 9 May.

On 10 May, the wedding ceremony began as planned at the town hall, where the Burgomeister read their vows in Flemish. After a short delay caused by a breakdown in the staff car, the couple finished with a religious ceremony in the local Anglican church. Then followed a five-day honeymoon in Paris, France, after which Marion and John rejoined their respective units.

John and Marion joined the Canadian Army Occupation Force in the late summer of 1945. Marion was the matron of 16 CGH and John was the commanding officer of 6 Canadian Field Dressing Station. They returned to Canada together in April 1946. John continued his post-war RCAMC career as a student at the Canadian Army Staff College in Kingston, Ontario. Marion began her new career as a homemaker.

The following years brought postings in Canada, in England and with the North Atlantic Treaty Organization (NATO). In 1970, John was promoted to major-general and appointed Surgeon General. He retired from that post in 1973 and became the Registrar of the Medical Council of Canada, a position he held until he retired in 1981. In 1976 the appointment of Colonel Commandant of the Medical Branch was accorded to John Barr, a post he still holds today.

A Sapper's View of D-Day

When one reads about 6 June 1944—D-Day—one is impressed with the size and scope of the invasion forces. This story of Sapper Bill Crysler recounts one man's memories of that day in history from the point of view of a Royal Canadian Engineer section of ten men.

D-Day will be long remembered for the night attack of the Royal Air Force (RAF) Bomber Command on the ten German artillery emplacements that could fire upon the beaches, the bombing attack of the American 8th Army Air Force on the beaches and the naval bombardment from "some 250 vessels, ranging from battleships to corvettes". There were three airborne divisions and five infantry divisions who would drop from the sky or land on the beaches from assault craft that day. One division, the 3rd Canadian Infantry, was assigned the lodgement area known as Juno Beach. 7th Brigade was on the right and 8th Brigade on the left. Supporting the Canadian invasion force were 5th, 6th, 16th and 18 field companies. Bill Crysler was with 6th Field Company.

The field companies had the task of "helping the Division get ahead once it had landed". Helping could be anything—blasting holes into concrete bunkers, lifting mines, cutting railway lines with explosives, removing booby traps or filling craters that impeded wheeled vehicle movement. The breadth of their duties makes a section of ten assault engineers seem to be men of great prowess. They carried all their warlike stores on their backs, including the standard .303 rifle and grenades.

Bill landed just after H Hour in support of 7th Brigade, on the extreme right of the Canadian sector.

> We arrived at the beach in our small landing craft and the sailor dropped a gangplank over the side. The corporal went first, the water came up to his chest. [Each section included one corporal and nine men.] I followed, and only my head was clear. It was just as well, for I could not swim. I was carrying full "fighting order" plus about 125 pounds of demolition stores. The noise was really something. Those huge naval shells

going overhead sounded like freight trains. There was a bluff about twelve feet [three and a half metres] high in front of us, and we went through a gap and were off the beach. Our engineer reconnaissance [recce] section had gone in with the first wave of the infantry assault. They were inland when we landed. We were to await orders from them or do what ever the infantry wanted us to do.

Sapper Bill Crysler in London, 1944.

As Bill went forward he realized that it was essential to work together to ensure that the enemy would not kill or wound them. They used the buddy system to watch each other's back. Nonetheless, 6th Field Company had twenty-six casualties that day, and very quickly Bill was to hear that one of his section had died, "Johnson or Johnston, a twin—there were the three brothers in our company." Johnson had gone forward in a British vehicle; they were shot at, the vehicle went off the road, and the Canadian was killed. A member of their recce section came back and told the other twin, "Your brother has been killed up forward."

The advance inland continued, and they came to a small settlement of buildings. A German tank, bypassed in the advance, was causing them problems: it would move forward, fire at the advancing Canadians and then move back out of sight. "We had no armour and so I did not see the German tank destroyed. We were moved to another area and I was to look for mines with a mine detector." Later that day Bill's section came upon a group of "older" German soldiers. They did not put up a fight but "just gave us their rifles". Bill took the bolts out of the rifles and threw them into a nearby well. The Germans then left unescorted, heading for the beach.

Looking back to that day, Bill recalls how few orders they received. Simply put, "if the infantry wanted us to do something to help them, we did it." When asked if better equipment would have helped his answer said it all: "We were better equipped than the Germans."

Bill had followed a traditional route from enlistment to Normandy. He had joined at seventeen in Cornwall, Ontario, taken his basic training with the Stormont Dundas and Glengarry Highlanders and then moved to Camp Petawawa. In just three months, March to May 1943, he was considered trained as a field engineer and was on route to Scotland by ship. Bill was assigned to 6th Field Engineer Company, 4 Section, 4 Platoon, on the Isle of Wight where assault landing training was taking place.

In early 1944, Bill began training for the invasion, "most of it consisting of long route marches to toughen us up". On 4 June 1944 he embarked for the trip across the Channel. Two days later he was in action. An interesting sidelight is that Bill's father was a petty officer in the Royal Canadian Navy (RCN). The records are not complete, but it appears as if Neil Crysler may have been serving aboard HMCS *Prince David* on D-Day.

Bill was wounded at Emmerich in Germany when the sapper ahead of him hit a Schu mine. Some of the fragments cut Bill's face, but he was not hospitalized. By then, there were "only two men left in the section," where there were supposed to be ten.

Bill Crysler returned to Ontario on 26 December 1945. After his discharge he repaired the family home with his release pay. He is now fully retired, lives in Fenwick, Ontario and spends his summers at a cottage near Golden Lake, Ontario.

A Strathcona's Story

Bill Milroy was attending the University of Alberta (commerce) when war broke out in 1939. As a member of the Canadian Officer Training Corps (COTC), Bill had already begun military training, and it was to continue both on and off campus throughout his student years. He had spent the summer of 1939 taking a small arms course, and that fall was commissioned as a second lieutenant in the COTC.

The summer of 1940 saw Bill running courses at the Small Arms School in Sarcee, Alberta. He then was assigned a company of the Veterans Guard—First War veterans who were to be the guards at the prisoner-of-war (POW) camps. "In that first group," recalls Bill, "were two veterans with the Victoria Cross." Bill returned to the university in the fall of 1940 to give military instruction to the 700 male students who did not belong to the COTC. (This was the Command Contingent.)

In the summer of 1941, Colonel Cunnington helped Bill write a letter to explain why he should become a Strathcona. The letter was successful, for on 13 August 1941, Bill reported to Lord Strathcona's Horse Regiment in Camp Borden, Ontario. He became troop leader of 2nd Troop, A Squadron. The regiment went overseas in November in a convoy accompanied by U.S. Navy battleships and cruisers, "which seemed to be going the same way we were going". (The United States was still officially neutral at that time.)

An Aldershot cavalry barrack was home for that first Christmas away from Canada. The first tanks issued to the regiment were General Lees, followed by General Grants and finally Canadian Ram Is and Ram IIs. In the summer of 1942, Bill was promoted to captain. He remembers the excellent tank training they had when they exercised on the South Downs.

In early 1943, some Canadian Army officers were sent to North Africa to serve with the British Army. One was Major Jack Turnley, Commander of B Squadron, Strathcona's Horse. As the second-in-command under Turnley, Bill assumed command of the squadron. On 1 December 1943, the day the regiment landed in Italy, Bill was still commanding B Squadron and was given a field promotion to major.

Early in January 1944, the regiment was equipped with Sherman tanks and finally went into action. The official history (McAvity, **A Record of Achievement**) recounts what happened when the first shots were fired at the enemy in January 1944:

> 1st Troop B Squadron opened up on an enemy observation post located in a tower in Orsogna. Some infantrymen are passing and we see haggard faces illuminated by the gun flashes, faces which should be young but are not; these "poor bloody infantry" look as though they have been in slit trenches for weeks; ... boots with inches of mud clinging to the soles and heels ... perhaps the Armoured Corps is the place to be.

Five months later the regiment and the reconnaissance troop in particular did a wonderful job at the Melfa River crossing. At the crossing, however, Major George Wattsford, the regiment's second-in-command, was seriously wounded. Bill took over for him, and was still second-in-command during the tense events of the next day.

While the regiment was in "harbour" (an administrative area out of direct enemy fire) heavy German artillery pounded the regiment "just before two in the afternoon—all hell broke loose!" The regiment was in serious trouble, trucks and tanks ablaze, ammunition exploding, "men lay dead, dying and wounded, others diving into slit trenches or under tanks." Twelve men were killed and thirty-five wounded, six mortally. The official history describes Bill's part: "He was everywhere as spasmodic shelling continued. Thirteen out of thirty-seven officers had been lost in the two days [not all killed], so the head as well as the body of the unit had suffered severely." Reorganization had to be done at once, and when reinforcements arrived, Bill returned to B Squadron.

In late August the unit approached the Gothic Line in the area of the Foglia River. The Strathconas could actually watch the British Columbia Dragoons (BCD) fighting hard against the German 4th Parachute Regiment. (Jack Turnley was commanding one of the

Bill Milroy, 1942.

Dragoon's squadrons.) At "12:30 in the afternoon the BCD had reached their objective, albeit at a heavy cost." Then B Squadron, under Bill's command, moved forward to relieve the Dragoons, and during the evening the Perth Regiment (infantry) joined them. Early on 1 September things started to heat up. Bill heard all kinds of gunfire, the enemy were "infiltrating the position. Vicious in-fighting developed." Bill spoke to all his troop leaders on the radio, and then,

I stuck my head out of my tank and somebody shot at it. ... I ducked down again and got the Thompson submachine gun out and fired back at the area of a shack where the bullets were coming from. I then tossed out hand grenades as all of our people were supposed to be in their tank or taking cover. The tank gunner was the only person in the tank with me. He fired the machine gun at the track. This went on for some time. [Later Bill was to learn that a German company was all over their position.] Bullets were going everywhere. It finally quieted down. [Bill was to learn later that he had been reported as having been killed.] The CO of the Perths joined me and two of my officers in front of my tank. Orders then came over my radio to "Advance!" We couldn't see two inches in front of our faces. I got out of the tank and told the others that we were to advance.

All of a sudden there was an loud bang. When I came to I was the only one of the four still there. One of my tank crew was patching up wounds to my head and back. The other officers had not been killed; I saw them after the war ended. I handed over to Lieutenant Vic Gar [who was killed by a shell that same day—1 September 1944]. I was evacuated and didn't get back for a couple of months.

Always a Strathcona sums up the events described by Bill Milroy: "For the Germans this was a critical failure. The Strathcona tanks and the Perth(s)... were the deepest wedge driven into the Gothic Line on the Canadian Corps Front."

Bill returned to the unit and the command of B Squadron before the three-month "rule" could see him removed from the unit organization. His next major operation was the drive from Arnhem to the Zeider Zee in the Netherlands in April 1945. (All the Canadian formations had transferred from Italy to Northwest Europe in January 1945.) The advance was no simple matter: German resistance was strong, and anti-tank fire caused losses to the Strathconas. In one action, a race developed to see who could get to Nunspeet first:

1st Brigade managed to get one truck into town before the Regimental speedsters (B Squadron). Major Milroy's lads covered the distance in exactly nineteen minutes....

Because the Infantry Brigade continued on through, however, the Strathconas were credited with being the first Allied troops in Nunspeet.

This last action of the war had been costly: "fourteen killed, died of wounds, and missing, as well as twenty-eight all ranks wounded." Enemy losses were higher, however, with fifty-eight dead and 318 taken prisoner. The Distinguished Service Order (DSO) was awarded to Major Milroy for all of the successes he and B Squadron had achieved together since those early days in Italy.

Bill volunteered for the Pacific Force, but while waiting to be called he transferred to the Army of Occupation and was named second-in-command of the North Nova Scotia Highlanders, 3rd Battalion. In May 1946, Bill left to attend the Canadian Army Staff College in Kingston, Ontario, before joining the Regular Force. He served as Canadian Liaison Officer at Fortress Monroe, Virginia, United States, and as Canadian member of the Directing Staff at the British Army Staff College, Camberley. He was Director of Public Relations (Army) for two years and Director of Training (Army) for over three. His commands included the Canadian Armoured Corps School, Third Infantry Brigade Group, Canadian Army Staff College, Canadian Defence Education Establishments, Training Command and Mobile Command. His final appointment was as Assistant Deputy Minister (Personnel) in the rank of Lieutenant General.

On retiring, Bill stayed in Ottawa. He managed the firm of E.A.C. Amy and Sons, becoming president and chairman. Bill is a Life Governor of Ashbury College and the Dominion of Canada Rifle Association. He is chairman of the Ottawa Advisory Board of the Salvation Army, the first vice-chairman of the National Board of the Canadian Corps of Commissionaires and a member of the Board of Management of the Ottawa Grace Hospital.

The Andersons' War

This story concerns three brothers, sons of Colonel Ross Anderson formerly of the 45th Victoria and Haliburton Regiment, Ontario. All three brothers served overseas, but one did not return. Jack, the eldest, served in the Argyle and Sutherland Highlanders; four years his junior was Archie, Royal Canadian Artillery and the Queen's Own Rifles; seven years younger still was Ross (Buster), a driver, postal clerk and cook.

In 1939, Buster first tried to join the RCAF, but they were not recruiting. His next attempt was the Midland Regiment in Bowmanville, Ontario, where he "stood in line from 5:00 a.m., and when I was just three from the door they closed it with the statement, 'That's all for now!" Undaunted, Buster went on to the Royal Canadian Army Service Corps, where he was finally accepted in May 1941. In just five short months his training as a driver was complete and Buster was on route to England in the ship *Orcades*.

After a rough crossing, the troops disembarked in Liverpool and were sent to Aldershot. Buster's first unit was the Dental Corps, but "as we had no vehicles, I did not have much to do". Even after the vehicles arrived, Buster found the driving job boring, so he requested a transfer to the Canadian Postal Corps (CPC). His request was granted, and he was posted first to the Base Postal Unit at Manchester, then to Glasgow and finally to London. London was undoubtedly his favourite posting, for it was here that Buster met Kathleen, who later became his war bride.

A month after D-Day (D+30), Buster's postal detachment crossed the channel and began the long advance through France and on into the Low Countries. As a friendship developed between Buster and the unit cooks, he began helping out now and then with some of the food preparation. Soon he was asked to "temporarily" take on cooking full time. Buster recounts,

> One fellow we had was from the Catering Corps
> [British]. He was smoking when the orderly officer
> walked in to inspect the cleanliness of the field kitchen.
> The long ash from the cook's cigarette fell into the

Brothers, Ross (left) and Archie (right) in 1945.

food. He just stirred it in! The cook was fired and I was asked if I would take over for awhile.

It was a long temporary job, for Buster never did return to sorting the mail: he cooked until war's end. He was in Nijmegen in May 1945 when V-E Day came. Buster was accepted into the Army of Occupation, but when he learned that Kathleen was expecting their first child he requested his release and returned to Canada. Buster took off his uniform on 7 March 1946. Only once did Buster see his brother Jack in England, but Archie was his best man at the wedding in England and once visited Buster in Nijmegen where, says Archie, "We ate steaks in the officers' mess kitchen."

Archie's involvement with the war began in 1940 when he went to work at the Defence Industries Limited plant in Ajax, Ontario. During the war years, this one plant "produced 40 million shells and employed more than 9,000 people". As foreman, Archie supervised a shift of people mixing amatol, "a dangerous job, for one spark and everything would go sky high".

Archie tried to join the RCAF in 1941, but, like his younger brother, he could not get in. On 21 July 1942, July he was accepted as a gunner in 10 Light Anti-Aircraft Regiment, Royal Canadian Artillery, and went to Camp Petawawa, Ontario. He was sure he was "going overseas, so Jean and I got married at the end of August 1942." A month later, he found out that 10 Light Anti-Aircraft was to be disbanded and he was to become a field gunner on twenty-five-pounders with the 1st Field Training Regiment in Debert, Nova Scotia.

Archie completed his artillery training and made it to "bombardier with pay [corporal] by 1943". It looked as if "we were not going overseas, so Jean joined me—we lived in a farmhouse with other couples". During the next year Archie took a mechanical course and continued training on every small arms weapon in the Army. Evenings, he would often play poker with the other men in the farmhouse, and his winnings often "paid for our rent and food". After Archie and Jean spent a leave back home in Ontario, Jean stayed on with family for a while, comfortable in the belief that Archie would be staying in Canada. But the day after Jean returned to Debert, says Archie, "I was told I was leaving for England on the *Monarch of Bermuda.*"

On arrival in Liverpool, Archie saw England in style, "from the front seat, upper level of a doubledecker bus". He spent Christmas Day 1944 in this rather novel way on route to Aldershot. Despite all of Archie's specialized training, the army apparently had no requirement for artillery reinforcements at this late date in the war. He and the other men newly arrived from Canada were told they were being transferred to the infantry, but none of this group made it to the Continent before the war ended.

Seventeen days after the war came to a close, Archie Anderson was flown to Brussels in a bomber "with no seats, so we sat on the floor". During the subsequent train ride to join the Queen's Own Rifles of Canada, Archie "took down his gunner badge and put up the silver maple leaf of the QOR of C." The Queen's Own Rifles remained in Germany until November 1945 before returning to Canada via England. On 20 December 1945 the Regiment arrived in Toronto, and Archie was released on 4 February 1946.

Jack Anderson joined the Prince of Wales Rangers in Peterborough, Ontario, on 7 May 1942. He had been working for the Massey Harris Company in Woodstock and living in Brantford with his wife Thelda. Jack was posted to Prince George, British Columbia, and a year later took a leadership course in Calgary. His course report read, in part,

A bright lad whose father was a LCol [Lieutenant Colonel] in the last war. He aspires to follow in his father's footsteps. He has no special trade in mind—above average intelligence—bright and ambitious, pleasant personality—sound, suitable for overseas draft.

Jack sailed for Britain on 13 May 1943, arriving nine days later. He, along with hundreds of others, went to Number 5 Canadian Infantry Reinforcement Unit. Although Jack had been both a lance corporal and a corporal in Canada, he was reverted to the rank of private while waiting to be sent to a regiment.

Eventually, Jack was sent to the Argyle and Sutherland Highlanders of Canada, which was part of the 10th Canadian Infantry Brigade. Jack's date of joining the Highlanders is missing from his wartime records, although it may have been on 11 September 1944, when, according to the regimental history, "80 reinforcements arrived to fill the depleted ranks".

Jack had joined his new regiment after a terrible battle in which the battalion lost sixty-three men. When Jack arrived, the Highlanders were fighting alongside the Algonquin Regiment to establish a bridgehead over the Ghent Canal four miles [six and a half kilometres] south of Bruges. The official history explains what took place on 14 September 1944:

All parts of the bridgehead were under intense fire from all kinds of German weapons. ... Ammunition was running low. ... About noon, Capt. J.L. Johnston ... was killed by a shell which landed directly where he was standing. ... The position across the canal deteriorated steadily, too quickly to be saved by any reinforcement, and at 1300 hours the sad decision was made to withdraw our [Canadian] troops from the further bank. ... Some wounded men had to be left behind. ... Not a round of any kind of ammunition remained when the decision was made to withdraw.

Jack Anderson was killed in battle that day, along with Captain Johnston and Corporal N. Russell. Jack was buried by his fellow soldiers in an orchard nearby. His body was later moved to Adegem War Cemetery in Belgium, where I visited the gravesite in November 1984.

Jack's story is but one example of the reinforcement system of that time. He never had a chance to develop the close bond that was a characteristic of Canadian wartime regiments. Nonetheless, Jack made the supreme sacrifice for his country.

Jack's headstone in Adegem War Cemetery. Photo by Commonwealth War Graves Commission.

Jack Anderson had $11.50 in his pocket at the time he died. A small box held his entire estate, sent to his grieving widow.

This story of three brothers is typical of many where all the eligible sons joined up and served their country. Archie and Buster are now retired, Archie in Nepean, Ontario, and his brother Ross in Tory Hill, Ontario.

The Glow Worm Who Had to Stay Home

Ken Major began the war as a member of the Royal Canadian Artillery (RCA) at Ford Rodd Hill, Victoria, British Columbia. Like so many others, Ken's first attempt to enlist was in the RCAF. Colour blindness ruled him out, and Ken finally enlisted in the army on 12 November 1940.

In 1940, the Sperry searchlight was being used along with the fixed coastal guns. The fixed beam for target illumination and harbour flood lighting was powered by a diesel electric generator. As a searchlight operator, or *glow worm,* Ken waited anxiously to be sent overseas.

Ken soon learned that the "army promise" to be allowed to serve overseas would be broken not once, but many times. Time and time again, Ken tried to get on an overseas draft. In February 1943, he thought he had finally succeeded when he was put on a train heading for Halifax, but it was not to be. When the train made its stop at Petawawa, Ontario, just west of Ottawa, Ken was one of the hundred or more gunners taken off and put into the 6th Anti-Tank Regiment.

At last orders came for 6 Anti-Tank to go to Debert, Nova Scotia, to await a ship overseas. This time, Ken was sure the promise would be kept, for the commanding officer said, "Even if the paperwork is not here before we sail, I will list you on the manifest as a batman [officer's orderly] and take you with us." But on final inspection for overseas, Ken was taken off the draft. His civilian qualification of draughtsman made Ken more valuable to the army in Canada. As 6 Anti Tank went on to Halifax and England, Ken was heading west back to British Columbia.

With a new career as a topographical draughtsman, Ken was posted to Prince Rupert, British Columbia, to draw charts for harbour defence. Soon afterward he was promoted to sergeant and moved back to the Directorate of Artillery in Ottawa. It was in Ottawa that Ken met his future wife, Iris, who was serving with the RCAF.

At war's end, Ken applied for his release but was told that "he was deemed necessary" so could not leave the service. It was several months before Ken finally gained his release.

Ken Major (he once told a major that the only difference between them was that he [Ken] was "born to the name") returned to Langley, British Columbia, where he worked for the town office for over thirty years. He is now retired and living in that city. All these fifty or more years after the war, he still feels regret that the promise to send him overseas was not kept.

Ken Major and his wife Iris in Fort Langley, B.C., 1946.

From Special Services Force to the Senate

Stan Waters was born in Winnipeg, Manitoba, on 14 June 1920. Raised in Alberta, he was attending university there when war broke out in 1939. Stan joined the Calgary Tank Regiment as a trooper (soldier, rank of private), and had made it to the rank of sergeant by March 1942 when he was selected for officer training. Then in England, Stan was sent back to Canada on the SS *Batory,* a Polish ship:

> There was a group of NCOs aboard ship, and in the steerage compartment were the toughest German prisoners of the war. They were mainly survivors from U-boats that had been sunk or forced to the surface. Cliff Chadderton and Jack Mitchell from the Royal Winnipeg Rifles, John Sims from the 8th New Brunswick Hussars and I would sit on this platform above the prisoners with a machine gun across our knees. What a hardened group we guarded, not a great way to take an ocean voyage.

Stan completed his officer training at Brockville, Ontario, in August 1942 and was sent to Shilo, Manitoba. It was at this time that Operation Plough was envisaged. In **Six Years of War,** C.P. Stacey explains the philosophy behind this novel idea:

> The First Special Service Force [was] a unique international organization whose personnel was drawn partly from the Canadian and partly from the United States Army. ... The original scheme for the raiding force contemplated a unit composed of Canadians, Americans and Norwegians [the latter did not provide troops]. ... On 14 July the Minister of National Defence authorized the movement of 47 officers and 650 other ranks to the United States. ... A Combat Force of three small "regiments" [was formed]. ... The Canadian component usually amounted to a little more than one-third of the Combat Force. ... It wore U.S. uniforms with special badges and [reluctantly] U.S. badges of rank.

In the summer of 1942 the Special Service Force organized at Fort William in Montana. Training was hard and included parachute training, proficiency with U.S. small arms, mountaineering, winter warfare (under Norwegian instructors), night fighting, hand-to-hand combat and the use of captured weapons (German and Japanese). In 1943, after amphibious training, the Special Service Force took part in the invasion of Kiska. On 19 November 1943, the Force was moved to Italy.

Daniel Dancock's **The D-Day Dodgers** gives extensive coverage to the Special Service Force, including several interviews that were held with Stan Waters. The initial action for the Force in Italy was Hill 960, a part of the mountain range at Cassino. Dancock's account is as follows:

> The task of taking the mountain was given to the 2nd Regiment. The assault battalion was commanded by LCol Tommy MacWilliam [a Canadian; Capt Waters was a company commander]. ... The operation was divided in two parts: the first night, a seven hour climb part-way up the mountain; ... the final ascent the next night. ... They took the Germans by surprise on DIFENSA. At dawn on Friday, 3 December [the] assault battalion, climbing ropes and masked by fog, scaled the final cliffs and swarmed across the mountain top.

This was the start of a costly battle, which lasted for six days, One hundred seventy-three men were killed, including Lieutenant Colonel MacWilliam and two senior company commanders. As a result, "Stan Waters went into action as a junior company commander; by the time it ended, he was commanding a battalion."

The next major action for the Special Service Force was at Anzio on 22 January 1944, when "one American and one British division landed". The Force arrived on the beachhead on 1 February. The 2nd Regiment was at half strength, but the Canadian Army was not sending reinforcements. The Special Service Force took over "one-quarter of Anzio's thirty-mile-long [forty-eight-kilometre] front." Anzio confirmed the Germans' fear of the Special Service Force, which they called the Black Devils. A captured diary read, "The Black Devils are all around

Lieut. Col. Fraser Eadie and Major Stan Waters (right) at Kolkhagen, Germany, April 24, 1945.

us every time we come into the line." (The book and movie entitled **Devil's Brigade** are about the Special Service Force.)

Anzio was a battle of attrition, with casualties mounting. John Sims, a platoon commander in Stan Water's company, recalled,

> As night fell we carried our wounded back down to the rear area. We then loaded up with ammunition, food and water and replenished our platoons. At times the

small streams were tinged with blood. I swore I would do something to help the sick if I survived. [John graduated as a doctor from McGill University and became a well-known general practitioner in Ottawa.]

After Anzio, Canadian reinforcements arrived in the form of 15 officers and 240 other ranks. The reinforcements had not had the training of the originals, but some had battle experience and all were a welcome relief. Stan recalled one embarrassing moment: "Four of the newcomers were black, and Jack Akehurst, the senior Canadian, had to sit these guys down and say that the Special Service Force could not take them." Someone on the Canadian side had forgotten that U.S. forces were segregated.

Operation Dragoon (7 to 28 November 1944) brought the Allied invasion of the southern coast of France. Once again, the Special Service Force was in the lead, but "the final days of the Force were at hand". The official history, **The First Special Service Force**, by Lieutenant Colonel R. Burhans, described the end of this unique force:

The end came quickly on December 5. At 2:00 pm the Force gathered on the Loup River flats under a warm sun. ... The chaplains read a prayer for the dead. ... Then the colors moved forward—United States, Canadian and Force—to remain a minute whipping in the breeze while the Adjutant read the inactivation order. ... The Canadians withdrew from ranks and formed their own battalion to march past behind their own colors. [Thirty-seven officers and 583 other ranks left for Naples. Major Waters left to join 1st Canadian Parachute Battalion, 3rd Parachute Brigade, 6th Airborne Division, in the United Kingdom.]

The closing lines chosen by Burhans are from a quote from Watt of the **Montreal Standard:** "Their legend is a feat of arms which will remain celebrated in military history which should be remembered even longer—an example of international brotherhood which deserves enduring honour."

When Stan arrived at 1st Canadian Parachute Battalion, he found a situation that was a mix of *esprit de corps* and humour:

The company I was to command was ready to engage in Operation Varsity, a parachute assault with 18th U.S. Airborne Corps. 1 Canadian Para was to capture an area near the Issel River. The incumbent company commander was about to leave for Canada for repatriation; he had been overseas for five years but he convinced the CO he should stay. On 31 March 1945 at Ladvergen I was told to take over the company. I was now commanding B Company.

Stan returned to Canada in June 1945 as the second-in-command of 1st Canadian Parachute Battalion. He served at Niagara on the Lake until the unit was disbanded. He rebadged to the Princess Patricia's Canadian Light Infantry (PPCLI). He held various command and staff appointments over the years, culminating with Mobile Command in 1973. He retired from the Forces in 1975.

In civilian life Stan worked for Calgary construction magnate Fred Mannix. In 1987 he helped form the Reform Party of Canada and became Canada's first elected Senator. Senator Stan Waters died on 25 September 1991. At his funeral, Ross Harvey of the New Democratic Party said, "Stan was one of those giants who occasionally Alberta seems to throw up; a person of monumental integrity and dedication to what he conceived to be the right thing to do."

(Special Note: Senator Stan Waters died before I could complete my interviews with him. Two of his wartime friends, Tom Gilday and Fraser Eadie, assisted with my research.)

A Van Doo Remembers

Henri Tellier's military career began on 5 September 1939, when he and some of his friends tried to join the Royal Canadian Navy Volunteer Reserve (RCNVR) at HMCS *Donnacona* in Montreal. They were drawn to the navy because of their interest in sailing. There were no vacancies, so Henri joined the Canadian Officer Training Corps at the University of Montreal, where he was studying. After being commissioned as a second lieutenant, Henri transferred to le Regiment de Joliette. On 8 September 1940, he went with his regiment to summer camp, where over 1,000 recruits a month were being trained. Henri then became a full-time militia officer, taking leave of absence from his civilian job in Montreal.

In July 1941, le Regiment de la Chaudiere was being readied for overseas at Sussex, New Brunswick; they sent out a call for three volunteers, and Henri was one of them. After training in different places in England, Henri was selected in October to be a liaison officer at 8th Canadian Infantry Brigade Headquarters. Three months later, "Lieutenant General H.C.G. (Harry) Crerar, the Corps Commander, chose me as one of his aides de camp" (ADC). Henri recalls Lieutenant General Crerar as

> a very demanding but fair person and I learned a great
> deal from him. He said that an officer should lead
> always, drive seldom, but when you drive, drive hard.
> He also said of the staff that the staff officer is the
> servant of the troops, not the master.

When recalling his service as a platoon commander in le Regiment de la Chaudiere, Henri remembers how the soldiers first looked him over to see "how this city boy was going to measure up". The best infantry soldiers, in Henri's view and apparently in the view of those men, were "farmers, fishermen, woodsmen and miners, not city folk". These ideal men were tough, used to working with their hands. As most came from large families, they knew how to "get along with others; they were a great bunch". Recalls Henri, "I reckon I passed the test, but just."

As ADC to the corps commander, Henri got to know the general and his staff, Guy Simonds and, later, Church Mann, first hand:

In planning field exercises in England the general would stand in front of a large map and think out loud with me standing by in silence. Once he said, "Henri, I think out loud for three reasons. First it helps me to think clearly and to recall better, second you will learn from this process and third if I become a casualty and you do not, you will know what was in the mind of the Corps Commander at the time and you will be able to tell others."

It was during those months when Henri was ADC that the Dieppe Raid was planned. As C.P. Stacey wrote in **Six Years of War,** "Although McNaughton and Crerar ... endorsed the plan ... they had nothing to do with making it. Montgomery had not delegated the responsibility ... but had kept it in his own hands." Montgomery and Crerar met weekly in the office or car while visiting units. Henri was thus privy to many of their conversations.

In August 1942, Captain Henri Tellier was recommended by General Crerar for the Canadian War Staff College Course No. 5 in Kingston, Ontario. After graduation, Henri was promoted to acting major and posted to Ottawa as a staff officer in the Directorate of Military Training.

In July 1943, Henri's request to be posted overseas was granted, first to Army Headquarters, and then to 1st Corps Headquarters the day before it sailed for Italy. He held a few "minor" staff jobs at Eighth Army Headquarters, Corps Headquarters and 1st Canadian Division. In was during this last job that he made a hospital visit to Major Jean Allard, who was having a leg wound treated. Allard had been his teacher at Staff College and was now the commanding officer of the Royal 22nd Regiment—the Van Doos. He suggested that Henri join his regiment. Says Henri,

When I arrived at the Royal 22nd, the unit was in the line in a defensive position just North of Ortona, having recently fought at Casa Berardi where Paul Triquet had won the Victoria Cross.

As a company commander for about twelve months, first as a captain and then as a major, I served under

Jean Allard from January 1944 to March 1945 when he left to command a brigade in Northwest Europe. During these months the R22eR was in the winter line north of Ortona, then they participated in the attacks on the Gustav and Hitler Lines, i.e., Cassino, May 1944. Then came the Gothic Line, Aug-Sept '44, followed by the series of river crossings in the Po Valley, late '44 early '45. At most, there were in combat a hundred soldiers in an infantry company at the start of an operation. In my time A Company suffered 242 casualties, killed or wounded. Four platoon commanders were killed and I had no less than six company sergeant-majors. [In the Canadian Army only ten per cent of all troops were infantry, but they suffered seventy-six per cent of the casualties.] Only about one to two per cent of an army corps actually fight face to face with the enemy. It seems to me that it is here with the assaulting infantrymen that you will find your "ordinary heroes", in particular among the lieutenants, sergeants, corporals and privates.

The success of the R22eR was largely due to high morale and the superb quality of leadership it enjoyed. The R22eR was "family", each person looking out for the other and gaining their inspiration from officers like Benatchez and Allard. The former has been described as the heart and soul of the regiment and was much loved by all; Jean Allard as the brain and respected by all. They were both respected and loved, but with different emphasis.

Remembering some fifteen major actions, mostly attacks, Henri says,
My most difficult action by far was the crossing of the Marano River in the early hours of 14 September 1944. My company was the leading company. That day was the bloodiest of WW11 for the R22eR, i.e., the day we suffered the most casualties. I only achieved partial

Henri Tellier, 1945.

success. We got across the river on foot, established a shallow bridgehead, dug in and hung on. Tanks and other designated troops were not able to make it to support us for hours. We were not able to secure the dirt road parallel to and slightly beyond the river, i.e., I was short of it, my final objective, by a couple of hundred yards, but we dominated it—we repulsed the counter-attack. My officers, NCOs and soldiers— their names and faces are in my head and heart—were dying and wounded left and right. No less than forty of them that day. Two days later on the 16th, after receiving a draft of reinforcements, we attacked and captured the Palazzo des Vergers about one mile north—another tough one. In the Chateau itself some two miles [three kilometres] south of Monte Fortunato, there were some ninety rooms. Even while fighting was still going on in one wing of it, there were dead Germans, dead Canadians, wounded Germans, wounded Canadians and German POWs. Very messy. It was about 1700 hours as I recall when we finally mopped up the place.

Stretcher bearers Dagenais and Tremblay saved most of the thirty wounded Van Doos.

We now come to 19 September 1944, 1940 hours: Monte Fortunato was the objective of the R22eR. Two other units had tried that day and failed. From start line to consolidation, all uphill, about one mile, took less than one hour—we were on time. My company captured about sixty-five POWs and we lost two men wounded. For these actions from 14 September to 19 September—the crossing of the Marano on the 14th, Palazzo des Vergers on the 16th and Monte Fortunato on the 19th—one Military Cross and three DSOs were awarded to officers of the R22eR, an MC to Simard. Allard, Trudeau and Tellier were awarded DSOs.

Henri remembers, too, the bravery of his soldiers:

For soldiers, especially in bad weather and over protracted periods when one loses a close buddy, or a corporal has a whole section wiped out, the temptation to become a straggler or even a deserter is great. In a very real sense the infantry corporals, who stuck it out day in and night out, are the stuff of which heroes are made—we had quite a few.

Once the Canadians moved from Italy to Northwest Europe, Henri was appointed second-in-command. He was acting commanding officer of the regiment for the last weeks of the war, as the commanding officer was on leave:

From about mid April 1945 all Canadian combat unit commanders received instructions not to press home attacks on the enemy. The Germans had threatened to blow the dykes and flood a large portion of Holland. This created quite a dilemma for the CO who was trying to preserve his soldiers' lives. Negotiations were going on to bring about a ceasefire and surrender of the enemy. In spite of this the Van Doos suffered some fifty casualties during this period. After the ceasefire was ordered on 5 May 1945, some 4,000 Germans surrendered to the Van Doos.

On his return to Canada, Henri was posted to the office of the Minister of National Defence. The offer to remain in the army came with the proviso of dropping a rank. He refused, so the army kept him on as a major.

Over the many years until retirement in November 1973, Henri Tellier served in Viet Nam, Cyprus, Europe and the United States. His final posting was as the Canadian Military Representative to NATO in Brussels. A stalwart worker for the Canadian Red Cross, Henri served as National Commissioner and Secretary-General from 1973 to 1983. He is now retired and resides in Stittsville, Ontario.

To War and Back without Basic Training

Doug Fisher, political columnist, television commentator and ex-politician, was an unusual soldier in the Second World War in that he was in a fighting squadron of the 12th Manitoba Dragoons, the Second Corps' armoured car regiment, without having basic training.

The day Neville Chamberlain declared war in 1939, Doug heard him on the radio of a gull-winged Stinson Reliant flying into Swain's Lake (between the Red Lake and Pickle Lake gold camps) in Northern Ontario. Doug had worked as a miner in the region and that summer had been a fire ranger with the Ontario Forestry Branch, largely giving prospectors burn permits and erecting a few timbered watch towers. At the latter chore he gashed his foot with an axe and was flown to his hometown in Sioux Lookout for stitches.

It was in Sioux Lookout that he spent August days listening to the build-up to the attack coming to the world via Poland's short-wave radio. Like many his age, he wondered if the coming war would affect him. Many of his school friends in Fort William were already in the Royal Canadian Navy Volunteer Reserve, and even more were thinking RCAF. Doug was interested in the army, but he was told he was unfit for active service because he wore glasses.

Shortly after Canada joined Britain at war, Doug was heading a crew of civilian lads sent to guard a big railway bridge in the remote bush north of Lake Nipigon. When fears of German sabotage dissipated, he went back to Fort William. He found work in early 1940 at the Canada Car Company plant, then beginning to produce Hawker Hurricanes.

The factory mushroomed, and Doug soon found himself head chaser; about forty female chasers moved the different parts between departments, and Doug was their supervisor. He also joined a militia battery in Port Arthur and spent a fortnight at Shilo, some of it helping to keep the peace between two feisty infantry battalions, the Calgary Highlanders and Winnipeg's Queen's Own Cameron Highlanders. When the battery went active, he was again rejected because of his eyes, and was rejected a third time in mid-summer of 1941 when the Lake Superior Regiment was recruiting. A druggist friend in the

Medical Corps at Brandon then promised to slip him through the medical and into his hospital unit, and it worked. The hospital at the A4 Artillery Training Centre was crammed with patients so Fisher was immediately put to work, partly in the office, partly in the kitchen.

When a serious epidemic of sleeping sickness struck the centre, the medically trained staff, all male, were focused on these dangerous cases and Doug found himself the orderly in charge of the "mumpers and clappers" ward, a rowdy chore that led the commanding officer, a Captain Findlay, to say kindly: "Fisher, a guy your size and disposition is not for a hospital." He promised a transfer and suggested the Winnipeg Grenadiers, then adding strength in Winnipeg. Fisher wanted the Manitoba reconnaissance (recce) regiment—the Dragoons—and hung out for it. It was fortunate for him that he did, for the Grenadiers soon left for Hong Kong and a cruel destiny.

The Dragoons (then the 18th Armoured Car Regiment) were training at Camp Borden when the Japanese hit Pearl Harbor, and the regiment was rushed to Vancouver Island to meet "the threat". A few days after the unit got to Esquimalt and observation posts at Otter Point and Jordan River, Fisher joined it, and was put in B Squadron. Thus, less than a week from the "clappers" ward, he was in a trench on a point on the Straits of Juan de Fuca, peering seaward for Japanese with a partner showing him how a Ross rifle and a Bren gun were loaded and fired.

Bruce Tascona writes in **XII Manitoba Dragoons: A Tribute,**
> The regiment received word on December 13 [1941] that it was going to the West Coast. ... It was one of the few Canadian regiments at hand which had some level of training. ... By 0800 hrs, Dec. 15, they left Camp Borden for the West Coast and possibly for an uncertain fate. ... On Dec. 21 a 24-hour watch was established and patrols were sent out along the coastline between Milne's Landing and the Jordan River.

Fisher recalls that, as he joined the regiment that Christmas time,
> The country's focus on the war was changing remarkably with the Pacific menace. There was more surge in the civilian economy. Jobs became very

plentiful, and this went against the call for recruits for the military. Certainly we thought the Japanese would arrive and apprehensions were high, especially among the civilians on the B.C. coast. Watching the straits we saw battered battleships and cruisers limping toward the Bremerton yards, in from Hawaii for repairs.

One day a captain asked at morning parade if anyone could type. When Doug said he could, he was immediately transferred into the squadron orderly room as a clerk. Doug said, "I leaped into the core of the regiment's operations, never having shouldered arms or done a route march."

It was as a clerk that Doug went with the regiment to Debert, Nova Scotia, in May 1942, where the 4th Division was gathering. In August Major-General Frank Worthington reviewed his division and everybody packed for the Atlantic trip, including Doug. On the dawn of the day to entrain for Halifax he was suddenly given a train ticket to Camp Borden. The reason: He couldn't embark without a respirator, and at that stage the quartermaster hadn't been able to find him one large enough. So his comrades went east, and he went to Borden.

Doug's lack of training was again ignored and he was put on his choice, a despatch riders' course. Before completing the course, however, he smashed one of his toes during a hill climb and was sent home for two weeks in a leg cast. Blood poisoning ensued, and when he finally returned, weeks late, to Borden there was a special respirator for him and a place on an armoured corps draft destined for Aldershot in the United Kingdom. They crossed on the *Queen Elizabeth* through vicious storms. (Years later, Doug learned through naval books that this was one of the worst Atlantic storms in mariners' memories.)

At the Aldershot depot they took one look at Doug and said, "He's for here; he's Provost Corps size." It was either that or go to the Calgary Tanks as a reinforcement after Dieppe; since Fisher aimed to get "home" to his Manitoba outfit eventually, he stayed with the Provost Corps. Thus he became an NCO for the first and last time, an acting lance-corporal provost.

On one day it was dicey. A tunnelling unit was just back to Aldershot from Gibraltar, and one of the men went berserk in a drinking spree, driving everyone from the top barracks floor by firing a rifle at those who tried to contain him.

Doug remembers that the senior provost told Doug,

"Ask his comrades about the guy—where was he from; what was he?" The sketch was a young, hardrock miner from the Kirkland Lake camp. My leader knew I'd mined and came from the bush, so he ordered me to climb the stairs and talk the lad into surrendering. It took a difficult hour of persuading but down he came, handing over the gun. I was "made" as a provost. The next week, however, my pleas to my old sergeant-major worked. Out of the blue a jeep came, and an order for my transfer. So, early in 1943, I was back home with the Dragoons.

In the field, everything was pitched to advance training and filling in the skills required by the regiment. Doug took two courses, one as a radio operator, the other as "water duties" man, ensuring that the water truck had a tank-load of drinking water. In this latter role he went to Normandy with the regiment (now titled the XII Manitoba Dragoons and under Lieutenant Colonel Jim Roberts). He and his driver served A Echelon (wheeled support vehicles), and in early July he also went out on night relief chores to work a mobile radio watch.

The sergeant major, a friend, had warned him to cease ribbing the echelon commander. Doug ignored the warning, and one morning after some heavy ironies with this captain Doug was told to throw his gear in a truck. He was off to A Squadron as a replacement for a departed loader operator. He went, fearing the worst, though shortly afterward and ever since he thought it the best move ever forced on him—and out of his own misjudgement! Among other reasons for liking the move, Doug's first and second successors on the water-truck were killed in action.

Doug joined A Squadron, under the command of Major Ken Farmer, just after the regiment crossed the Seine near Elboeuf. Although the troop officer lacked an operator, he refused to take

Doug: "Too big for the turret." And so Doug became Farmer's operator in head-quarters. It was a lucky break, because Farmer, once the captain of Canada's hockey team at the Berchtesgarden Olympics of 1936, was an exceptional personality. Fisher remembers, "He was a truly shrewd commander and he was then and remains today a fine, fun-loving gentleman."

The most taut, exciting day for A Squadron began outside St Omer before a September dawn—a race to the environs of Dunkerque, over the Belgium border to the edge of Ostend by 11:00 a.m., then suspended there alone for hours, waiting for

Trooper Doug Fisher in 1942.

the tanks and trying to get radio permission from 4 Division to go into the port. A Squadron then had a long drive, retreating back as dusk fell on a very jumpy night in France.

We were told to run as far as we could toward Ostend. When we hit Berques, an old outpost fort of Dunkerque, we looped, our troops running on two routes. As we ourselves made the turn, Farmer spotted a German gun-position but no one fired at us. We rolled at speed toward our limit, thinking the 10th Brigade were not far behind. When the first tanks (The South Albertas) got to our loop point, two Dragoons we'd left behind as radio bridge warned the tankers of the Jerries. Instead of taking the loop they ploughed toward Berques and were hit hard. That afternoon as we wasted time near Ostend, the brigade skirmished against what turned out to be the durable Nazi "Fortress Dunkerque". Had they looped and been with us with carriers and tanks, I think we'd have had Ostend before the Jerries blew the quays. Some "underground" men were offering to take us into the harbour where the Germans were placing demolitions. If only we'd forced our way in and sent some other troops through to Blankenburg and to the Scheldt Estuary, a lesser distance than we'd gone that morning! It was surely possible, for a few hours that very day, to force through the western side of what became the Breskens pocket and which denied us the use of Antwerp port for so long.

The next morning, A Squadron raced not to Ostend but to Bruges, with orders not to fight into it because of its medieval treasures. A sister squadron went to Ostend and found the harbour blown. And to the right of Bruges, they came full stop at blown canal bridges. Later, the infantry arrived, and soon they were into the battle of the Leopold Canal.

Doug describes an un- usual, though perhaps not unique quality of the Dragoons as a community of squadrons:

Partly because so many were plain prairie boys from farms and small towns, partly because a large proportion of the men were talented and very easy with their junior officers and NCOs, there was little gulf between other ranks and those in immediate command. A lot of the men were not interested in promotion. The regiment was "home" for the duration, and being a mere trooper was fine with most. It was a troopers' regiment, particularly after Jim Roberts came and literally inspired everyone.

After the war, when Doug made it through university with honours, studying under and with so many of Canada's brainiest, he realized how loaded with abilities the regiment had been. One buddy, Dunc Blewitt, became a psychology expert, pioneering drug addiction studies; his brother became number two man in Saskatchewan Power

Corps; three of the regiment became members of Parliament; two became members of their provincial legislatures; two became provincial deputy ministers; another set up the first gambling casino and hotel in Las Vegas; another took a Rhodes Scholarship; another became a merchandising tycoon. Says Doug, "As a consequence of such talents and attitudes, ours was an outfit whose discipline grew out of an *esprit de corps* of fellowship, rather than from fear of punishment and tough applications of military law."

Doug particularly remembers two of his crewmates:

They were the smartest young men I knew in my army years. It was long after the war I learned that in the summer of '44 they pulled strings in high places in order to give up their commissions and get overseas to be troopers with the Dragoons. One, David Wanklyn, was a linguist—French, German, and Russian—and a superb gunner. I saw him knock off enemy at 1,800 yards [1,600 metres] with the 37 mm; and the other, Charlie Woodward, was a good bow-gunner, the ablest scrounger in the outfit and a fine short-order cook. Later David became a nuclear physicist, then head of a big corporation, and Charlie ran Woodwards in B.C. Of course, our crew commander [Farmer] went on to be a luminary in the accounting field, head of the Canadian Olympic Association, first leader of the National Sports Council and a member of Canada's Sports Hall of Fame.

In June 1945, Doug took a chance and volunteered for the Pacific. That's why he was home landing on Quebec docks, V-J Day. He had been sent home for the basic training he had never received, but which he would have needed before going against the Japanese.

Doug went on to university, allowed as a veteran to do so without having completed high school. He took degrees in history and librarianship at Toronto, studied archives work at the University of London, then reorganized documents at Queen's University Library before going to the Lakehead to establish what has grown into Lakehead University Library. This experience drew him into politics with the Co-operative Commonwealth Federation, and in 1957 he ran in Port Arthur against the incumbent member of Parliament, "the minister of everything", C.D. Howe, and won. After eight years in the House, Doug left politics to become a full-time columnist (**Toronto Telegram**) and television commentator.

Since the mid 1970s, Doug Fisher has written the column "Between Ourselves" in **Legion Magazine.** In 1992, at age seventy-three, he continues from his base in the National Press Building across from Parliament Hill as the country's longest-running regular political columnist (thirty years) and the host of the longest-lasting weekly interview half-hour on Canadian television (twenty-nine years). Through such roles, he has often been back to Britain and through Europe, visiting, when he can, the graves of acquaintances from Brookwood to Bernieres to Bergen Op Zoom. "The war's experiences," he says, "have not dominated my life since, but they've made me appreciate how good it's been to be of my generation, and how fortunate I was in my country, regiment and squadron."

From Horses to Staghounds

John (Spike) Malone's army career spanned the years from pre-war (1938) to post-war (1968). When the war began he was a trooper with A Squadron, Royal Canadian Dragoons, serving in St Jean, Quebec (B Squadron and Regimental Headquarters were in Stanley Barracks, Toronto, Ontario). The day war was declared, Spike was on stable piquet when the Orderly Officer, Lieutenant A.P. (Doc) Ardagh, came to the stables and ordered the men to get their rifles and a bandolier of ammunition. He also put two additional men on guard duty at the ammunition magazine. The Dragoons were housed in what is now Le College Militaire Royal.

Spike was part of the Royal Escort for King George VI in May 1939 and, as were all the cavalry soldiers, was very attached to his "long-faced pal", his mount. In early 1940, the death knell of the cavalry was sounded by Army Headquarters, and all mounts with more than ten years' service were ridden to a local abattoir in St Jean and shot in the forehead. The edict was made on the assumption that a cavalry mount of that age would not "adjust to civilian life".

The French Embassy in Ottawa heard of the situation and sent a buyer to purchase horses for the French Army. Thus, at dockside in Montreal, Spike and his cohorts said farewell to another group of their horses. After the ship sailed, France fell; the ship was rerouted, and the horses ended up in Scotland. The remainder of the mounts were sold at public auction in St Jean and were taken away. (Seven of the horses escaped from their new owners in the night and found their way back to the squadron stables in St Jean.)

The Dragoons came together as a regiment at Camp Borden where Spike Malone, now a sergeant, became a Vickers machine gun instructor. The training conducted by the Dragoons was limited to driving and operating the Renault tank, wireless procedure and, the bane of Spike and others, learning Morse code.

Spike was part of the advance party that sailed for Liverpool, England, aboard the *Monarch of Bermuda*: "She had just come from being a cruise ship in the Caribbean and was beautiful. The main ballroom was the mess hall, but the food was awful. Codfish and English sausage for breakfast."

When the ship docked, the advance party, under the command of Major H.I.T. McLeod, went by train to Brookwood and then marched to Dettinger Barracks near Aldershot. The regiment joined them later, and the years of training and equipping began. Spike recalls going to Wales for a gun camp and then a major reconnaissance exercise. The exercise was described in **Dragoon—The Centennial History of The Royal Canadian Dragoons, 1883- 1983** as follows:

The last week of May [1943] brought Exercise Bear, a tactical move of the whole Regiment, to Kirkby Stephen, in the far north of England, where the troops lived in tents and went out each day to shoot at Warcop ranges.

It was at this time that the regiment was equipped with the Staghound armoured car. Spike remembers this vehicle as "very fast, both ahead and in reverse, but a real problem in mud." The gun was a 37 mm cannon, which, being useless against German armour, was nicknamed "the paint chipper".

The Royal Canadian Dragoons were sent to Italy and arrived "off Augusta [Sicily] on November 8, [1943] ... and after a short rail journey to Syracusa, [were] deposited in a one-time Italian police barracks." It was here that the men waited to be moved to Italy and war. They felt "marooned on a desert island, without equipment and with only the dimmest of prospects in the role for which they were prepared."

Spike recalls an incident in Sicily that resulted in a severe loss to the regiment:

Two officers—Lt Jarvis and Craven—and forty other ranks ... on a route march ... stopped to explore an abandoned coastal defence battery, and the two officers descended a shaft leading down to the magazine. ... [It] had been booby-trapped and an explosion ... killed Craven and badly burned Jarvis. (Greenhous, **Dragoon**)

The flames also burned a group of other ranks, and one of them, Lance-Corporal Eckhardt, with all of his clothes burnt off except for his boots, ran for help from a British unit half a mile away. When the entire matter was over, two officers and three other ranks (including Eckhardt) had died and four others were so badly burned that they never returned to the Dragoons. Eckhardt was awarded a posthumous British Empire medal and, in Spike's words, "it should have been a Victoria Cross".

Dragoon recalls another disastrous event for the Royal Canadian Dragoons:

Malone mounted on Mike in St. Jean, Quebec, 1937.

"C" Squadron's mission on the 3rd was to advance along Highway 16 (the Via Adriatica) as a flank guard for an infantry-tank attack by 1CIB [1st Canadian Infantry Brigade] ... aimed at clearing German positions between Conca and Riccione ... The Germans had a near-perfect ambush and made the most of it.

In Spike's own words the advance began in dense fog and when the wind from the Adriatic blew the fog away, C Squadron was lined up on the highway, nose to tail. The ambushing German guns in dug-in positions just cut them to pieces. Spike was the leader of fourth troop and another sergeant had fifth troop. The three other troops were commanded by lieutenants, who were all killed. The acting squadron commander, Captain A.J.H. La Vigne, and the battle captain were also wounded. Spike extricated first, second and third troops and brought the squadron out of the line. Sergeant Major Taffy Deeming did a

Major Malone in 1968.

great job getting the wounded out and was awarded the DCM. The toll was three officers and four other ranks killed, and three wounded.

Spike, his gunner and his driver were wounded in another action, and he spent from 18 October to 7 December 1944 in hospital. Spike was promoted to warrant officer second class and shortly thereafter was selected to attend officer training back in England beginning in March 1945.

When Spike arrived at Sandhurst, he took down his wreath-and-crown rank badges and "put up the white tapes" of an officer cadet. Spike was the "granddaddy" of the course and was nicknamed "the colonial". For both V-E an V-J Days, Spike was still a student at Sandhurst. He remembers V-E Day for the "pandemonium in London where you could not get near a pub" while he spent a quiet V-J Day at Gravesend sleeping in a cemetery waiting for the pubs to open at 6:00 p.m.

Lieutenant John Malone came home to Canada in 1946 and was posted to London, Ontario, responsible for 57 School Cadet Corps.

In 1954 he was posted to Indo-China. Five years later, as a major, he commanded a squadron with the United Nations Emergency Force in Egypt. In 1968 Spike Malone retired. He now lives in Owen Sound, Ontario.

A Tanker's War

Robert Hunter Dunn was a member of the McGill University COTC programme in 1940. After summer camp he was commissioned and sent to the Small Arms Training Centre at Connaught Ranges near Ottawa. Then it was on to Farnham and later Huntington, Quebec, as an instructor in basic training. In August of 1941 he applied and was accepted for training at Brockville and Camp Borden as an armoured corps officer. In April 1942 he sailed for England as a reinforcement officer, and in June he became a member of the 8th New Brunswick Hussars (8NBH).

In October 1943, the 8NBH was part of the 5th Armoured Division enroute to Italy. The ship Hunter was in went to Algiers, whereas others went directly on to Naples. It was this second group that was bombed. (See the story of Jack Dohan.) In early January 1944, the regiment's Sherman tanks were issued. Hunter was the troop leader of regimental headquarters troop with four Sherman tanks—one for the commanding officer, one for the second-in-command and one for a sergeant. The commanding officer's tank had a dummy gun made of wood to make room for a map table in the turret for the adjutant, who was in radio contact with brigade headquarters. The commanding officer was able to speak to the commanders of his three fighting squadrons and to the regimental reconnaissance troop.

On 29 January the move toward the front began. The regiment would start to see action on 9 February, in a muddy olive grove south of Ortona where it was snowing. At first, small groups went forward to the 1st Canadian Division to get an idea of what real action was like. Hunter took part in amphibious training and one day tried firing tank guns from landing craft. The naval officer suddenly shouted, "Cease fire!" When Hunter asked what the trouble was, he was told, "The excessive vibration from the tank guns has split open the landing ship's seams. We are sinking!" Full speed toward shore saved the day and the six tanks.

Hunter was always devising new ways of using tank guns for indirect fire (gunners not able to see the target). When the 8NBH was issued six tanks with 105 mm guns in August 1944, Hunter came into his own and very quickly adapted his novel methods. These guns were

Hunter Dunn in England, 1943.

often used to support the 8th Hussars in local actions, such as crossing the Lamone River just north of Ravenna.

The Gothic Line battle was one that Hunter and many others will never forget. Hunter wrote of the event, in part,

The line consisted of tank turrets welded into concrete emplacements of reinforced dug-outs and slit trenches carefully sited on the high ground overlooking the valley of the Foglia [River]. ... Mine fields intended to slow the progress of tanks and infantry were laid on the ground, dominated by the hills.

The sector in which the 8NBH supported the 11th Infantry Brigade was about 1,000 yards (900 metres) wide on the extreme left of the 5th Armoured Division front. A Squadron supported the Perth Regiment, B Squadron the Cape Breton Highlanders (CBH) and C Squadron the Irish Regiment of Canada. The attack began at 1730 hours on the 30 August. The flat ground of the valley, 1,500 to 2,000 yards (1,300 to 1,800 metres) wide, had been cleared of all buildings and vegetation so that the German defenders had a clear field of fire as they tried to stop the Canadians. They had also dug an anti-tank ditch some fourteen feet (four metres) across. Many lives would be lost and a large number of 8NBH tanks would go up in flames before this line was broken.

Reading Hunter's account of the battle, I was struck by the degree of the "fog of war"—so many things went wrong. For instance, a

Provost Corps pointsman would not let the tanks move forward to support the Cape Breton Highlanders; tanks were immobilized by anti-tank mines; the troop leader walked into a position filled with live angry Germans and escaped back to his tank; an 8NBH sergeant charged Germans with nothing but his bare hands after his tank was knocked out, and was killed in the process; and during the critical stage, the tank crews were short of fuel, water and ammunition. Into this disorder came one man who saved the day, Captain John Boyer. One does not often get to read a unit's war diary recording the minute-to-minute action, but Hunter provided a copy of the one from the 8NBH. From 31 August, I copied these words from the pages typed almost fifty years ago:

> Captain J.S. Boyer, A1Ech [wheeled vehicles carrying supplies] Commander had formed a forward dump and Honey tanks [light American tanks with the turret removed] from the Recce Troop carried the supplies forward to the tanks. Captain Boyer distinguished himself by his complete disregard for personal safety as he maintained liaison with the squadron which was under heavy shell and mortar fire.

In the regimental history **The 8th Hussars**, Douglas How explained how Jack Boyer

> roared across the Foglia River in his jeep [then] he made his way forward on foot ... and located a position for a forward dump. I really mean "forward". It was about 400 yards [360 metres] in rear of the fighting tanks [who were to] drop back a troop at a time. ... It was a good example of decisive action and it had a mighty important bearing on the outcome of the battle.

John Boyer was awarded the Military Cross for his actions. Many years later I met John Boyer, but before I could record his wartime story first-hand, he died of cancer.

In September, Hunter was promoted to captain, and in due course came the major attack on Coriano Ridge. Hunter had been moved to A Squadron as battle captain. Afterward Hunter went on a course and learned about the seventeen-pounder gun that was now being mounted in the Sherman. The Firefly, as it was known, was a welcome addition and far more effective than the 75 mm gun. While on the course, Hunter came down with jaundice and did not return to the regiment for some time. Before leaving Italy, he provided excellent service with the 105 mm guns in various actions, using them as a six-gun battery.

In Belgium the regiment refitted and then moved to the Nijmegen area, going on into Arnhem and on 14 and 15 April. Arnhem had just been cleared by the British Army. The regiment was advancing twenty-five miles (forty kilometres) a day; opposition was light, and the town of Putten fell to them easily. The 8NBH ended the war at Delfzijl—"the last time I used the 105s," recalls Hunter. The day before the war ended Hunter was sent to London; he was to be promoted to major to train armoured reinforcements. He arrived in London on V-E Day.

Hunter returned to the regiment in Northwest Europe and attended university upgrading classes. He was discharged in 1946 and commenced a four-year civil engineering programme at McGill University. He worked in private industry and for the National Research Council. He retired in 1983, but still does consulting work.

Off to War with a Dentist's Drill

Jack Dohan was born and educated in Swift Current, Saskatchewan. He went to McGill University in Montreal where he studied dentistry, graduating in 1940. With the war then in full swing, "I had no intention of starting a civilian practice, but wanted to join up as soon as possible." The Canadian Army Dental Corps (CADC) was short of equipment, so there was a wait to get in, but by late September Jack was enrolled at Work Point Barracks, Victoria, British Columbia.

Instead of receiving military training, Jack was told "that for one dollar he could buy the book **Corporal to Field Officer**, and that was all he needed." His first military post was the Nanaimo Military Camp where, under canvas, he had the British Columbia Dragoons and South Alberta Regiment as patients. Jack remembers many hockey games that winter; the prairie soldiers had the clear advantage.

The dental clinic had one 100-watt bulb and whatever light came through the tent opening. All the equipment for the clinic came in two trunks. The dentist's chair was poor, hard to adjust and uncomfortable. The drill was treadle-powered, and the dentist could "pump it, standing on one foot, or have the dental sergeant pump, or, better still, the next patient waiting his turn for treatment. "The steel burs were hard on the patient, and the whole process was not easy on the dentist."

The brigade camp was built, but Jack was posted to Camp Borden, Ontario, where he joined 13th Field Ambulance Company, who were also "under canvas". An arrangement was made for Lieutenant Dohan to take the officers' course at Brockville, Ontario, but fate interceded. Jack was chosen as part of the 5th Armoured Division advance party. He never did receive his military training. Jack recalls,

> I asked the CO if he would have the RSM [regimental sergeant major] take me on to the parade square so that I would know how to get the men to go forwards, backwards and sideways so that I could get them on board the ship, and, more important, get them off when we reached England. That was done. There were ten of us, medical and dental soldiers. I was given the dental

Jack Dohan at the Nanaimo Brigade Camp, 1941.

records of the unit and I placed them in my suitcase with my Sam Browne belt and a bottle of rye. The bottle leaked, and when I got to England the records were saturated with whiskey and brown shoe polish. They all had to be replaced from Canada.

The *Monarch of Bermuda* was the ship (see Spike Malone's story), and the trip went well. When the unit came together at Aldershot, Jack took leave and celebrated New Year's Day in Scotland. There were twenty-four dentists in the unit; thus, two could be on leave at any one time. Some time later Jack was sent to the Lord Strathcona's Horse as their dentist. In November 1942, Jack met a local doctor in Glasgow, whom he married in 1943. (They divorced many years after the war.)

The 5th Canadian Armoured Divison was sent to Italy. Jack's dental unit embarked on the U.S. troopship *Santa Elena*. A Montreal **Gazette** article dated 6 November 1988 describes what the Canadians discovered:

> good food for the first time in years. Instead of tinned mutton ... we had white bread, real eggs, real meat. The German air and U-boat attack began [after passing though the Straits of Gibraltar on 6 November]. A squadron of Nazi planes swarmed over the convoy. Two ships were hit: the *Santa Elena* and a small Dutch vessel. In return, the convoy shot down about seven German planes. [A torpedo hit the *Santa Elena*.] ... It

tore a hole six metres in diameter in the ship's side.
[The only casualties were in the engine room.]

The Canadian nursing sisters from 14 General Hospital, who were also aboard, got into the ship's lifeboats and pulled away from the sinking ship. The rest of the passengers "were on their own for two hours in the water and in rafts which had been tossed into the sea. At about midnight the *Monteray,* another American troopship, came alongside." They got aboard and next day they were off Phillipeville (now called Skikda), Algeria, where some went ashore. (Jack was not one of them.)

Jack finally arrived at Naples, Italy, and was sent to a camp at Casenta where "there was nothing to do but sit and wait, 2,000 of us castaways". When the dentists reviewed the situation, they realized that all their stores, records, vehicles and dental equipment had been lost. Twenty-four dentists for the division—unable to do a thing! The Strathcona's advance party was nearby, so Jack renewed old friendships and spent some memorable days sightseeing with the regimental doctor.

Jack spent Christmas 1943 in hospital in Naples. It was decided he would be a reinforcement dentist in Algiers, then go back to England in March 1944 aboard the *Strathmore.* He was posted to 1 Special Hospital, a venereal disease centre north of Winchester. Jack recalls, "there was not a lot of dentistry. There were fifteen patients from Basingstoke, number 1 Plastic Hospital. These men had broken jaws that were wired, and my job was to maintain the wiring until the bones healed". Jack said this was his happiest time, for he could get to Sussex to be with his wife. He was in Sussex when the war ended on V-E Day. Jack sailed home to Canada in September 1945 aboard the *Louis Pasteur,* but it was December before he was released.

Jack's memories of his days as an army dentist include treating Major General Chris Vokes, divisional commander in Italy; rush jobs to replace dentures lost during bouts of seasickness on route to England; and, above all, the inferior equipment that made dentistry difficult and painful. Jack retired from civilian practice in Victoria in 1982 at age sixty-five. He is now the Honorary Colonel of 13 Field Ambulance Company, Militia—his career has come full circle. He and his wife live in Victoria, British Columbia.

Nursing Sister at Hong Kong

Kay Christie began her nursing training at the Toronto Western Hospital in 1930. After graduating three years later, she became a staff nurse for a year, then a private duty nurse in Toronto, and for the summer of 1940 was the nurse at a camp for crippled children. Recalls Kay, "The polio scare in 1938 is still clear in my memory, and many of the children at the camp were polio victims."

On 27 November 1940 Kay enroled in the Royal Canadian Army Medical Corps; six months later, after being commissioned, she held the rank of lieutenant. Soon, she was sent to Hong Kong.

In 1992, the CBC television special, **The Valour and the Horror** once again created a Canadian interest in Hong Kong, 1941 and all it entailed. Kay Christie's story was told in part, and an actress spoke the lines written for her, although in a distorted setting. Her story is now told through the medium of **The Voice of the Pioneer,** by Bill McNeil. **No Reason Why** by Carl Vincent is used as I paint the bigger picture.

Just before the attack on Hong Kong, the British Government, wanting to strengthen the garrison in Hong Kong, "asked Canada to send two battalions. Canada agreed and these troops arrived shortly before the Japanese attack" (Vincent, **No Reason Why**). The two battalions chosen were The Winnipeg Grenadiers and The Royal Rifles of Canada. This force of 1,975 left Vancouver for Hong Kong on 27 October 1941 aboard the *Awatea.* "Two nursing sisters accompanied the force, despite the fact that the General Officer Commanding (GOC) at Hong Kong had stated that medical orderlies were what were really needed." Kay one of those nurses, and the other was May Waters of Winnipeg, Manitoba.

Once on the island, Kay and May were sent to the British Military Hospital on Bowen Road. As could be expected, "the two nursing sisters proved themselves of incalculable worth." The actual war lasted three weeks. For Kay, it began when she was "on duty at Bowen Road Hospital and the shells and bombs started to hit the hospital," (one hundred and eleven hits in all). The shelling forced the nurses to evacuate the third floor, and then Japanese snipers did the same to the second floor. With the Allied surrender on Christmas Day, the full force of Japanese brutality hit home. Rapes, decapitations and the burning of bodies all created a horror never to be forgotten.

The grim statistics of this fatal action are described in **No Reason Why:**

Kay Christie, 1941.

> By the time the last Royal Rifleman had passed into Japanese hands, 290 Canadians had already died in Hong Kong. A further 267 were to die in the course of an incredibly brutal captivity. Of the 1,418 remaining members of the force who lived to return to Canada there were few who had not suffered physically and mentally from their ordeal.

Kay was transferred to the Stanley Civilian Internment Camp with all the female staff on 10 August 1942. At the camp were a total of 2,400 men, women and children. Kay was assigned to Room 11 in Block 10 of what had been the residence of St Stephen's Chinese boys school. It was approximately nine feet wide and twelve feet long (two and a half by three and a half metres) and completely without furnishings; three nurses were to live there. "Three weeks later we got our trunks, two of which placed end to end served as my bed; the other two had canvas camp cots." Kay remembered that in her earlier days of nursing in Toronto, even the poorest homes she had visited on public health duties were palatial compared to Room 11. Kay laughed as she recalled the room, for they had been told that "the nurses would receive preferential treatment". Unbeknownst to Kay, their quarters were much superior to the squalor the Canadian soldiers were to endure.

This prison was to be "home" for thirteen months; a total of twenty-two months in all were spent as a POW and civilian internee. Weight loss due to the poor food, and the lack even of that, began. Kay mentioned that the people with excess weight began to show the ravages first, and then it eventually hit even the slender ones like Kay. "Our constant but unwelcome companions were large flying cockroaches, which sailed in through the windows, where there was very little glass; bedbugs that came out of the walls where the plaster had been damaged during the fighting; and large centipedes that seemed to fall from nowhere." Boredom and hunger were the greatest problems as "one endless day rolled into another".

As 1942 came to an end the future looked very bleak. In 1990 Kay wrote to me of that New Year's Eve:

All year we had obeyed the rules laid down by our Japanese captors. Today we women internees in Block 10 suddenly decided that New Year's Eve was the time to be reckless and do something devilish—reminiscent of the good old days of freedom. As I write this, almost forty-eight years later, how very innocent our plan seems.

With our limited worldly goods, we decided to have a masquerade in the entrance hall of our building—no fancy theme or costumes and a singsong to go along with it. May Waters, the other Canadian nursing sister, and I used our camouflage capes to cover us to form what we thought would be a camel, but the singing switched to "Waltzing Matilda".

Rules demanded that all internees be in their own rooms by 10 p.m. and all lights out—when we had any lights—by 10:30 p.m. Our fun came to a nasty halt when the Japanese guard burst in on our celebration, screaming and brandishing his rifle with bayonet blade in place. Unable to understand what he was saying, his demands were made clear to us by his wild gesturing. As we made our way upstairs to our rooms, word was spread among us to come out into the hallway at midnight.

Needless to say, none of us went to sleep and, as planned, at midnight we assembled in the dark, lining the staircase, and as we crossed arms in traditional fashion and sang "Auld Lang Syne", it seemed that the curved bannister was a continuous wave of arms. The guard must have been out of earshot because we were able to complete our singing. There were tears in the eyes of each individual as we returned to our rooms, with a silent prayer for "home next year".

However, May Waters and I were the only two from that group for whom those words came true. The following September we were included in the group of Canadian civilian internees who were repatriated with the remaining American civilian internees from the Far East, and after a ten-week sea voyage we were at home for the next Christmas and New Year's.

But it was not the joyous time for us that everyone expected it to be, as we remembered our colleagues still in Stanley Camp and our Canadian troops in the POW camps. In fact, that sad memory of our group standing with clasped arms while we sang "Auld Lang Syne" is still very much with me and is the reason this episode has never been related. (Oops, here come the tears again.)

Throughout their incarceration, rumours abounded, usually of their imminent release by some means. However, in July 1943 a rumour of repatriation of internees spread around; this would be between the United States and Japan, under the auspices of the International Red Cross. "We had difficulty believing it, but it did become fact."

On 23 September 1943, Kay, May and the other Canadian internees left Hong Kong on the Japanese ship *Teia Maru*. Four weeks later, after stops at the Philippines, Vietnam and Singapore for additional internees, they arrived at Goa, a small Portuguese territory (neutral) near Bombay, India. There they were officially exchanged and transferred to the Swedish-American liner MS *Gripsholm*. Six weeks later they arrived in New York, then went by overnight train to Montreal and finally home to Toronto.

> Kay recalls that after being home for several months, she thought, Canadians should know and feel the effects of bombing, shelling and real food shortages. People in general were much too complacent and had no idea of what our service people in the various theatres of war were going through.

After a short time, Kay was posted to a military hospital in Toronto, where she served until 30 October 1945. On returning to civilian life she became a medical secretary to a medical specialist for several years and then to a neuropsychiatrist until 1980, when she retired. Kay still lives in Toronto. Her nursing sister companion May Waters died on 18 December 1987, the forty-sixth anniversary of the initial attack on Hong Kong.

A Corporal in the Princess Patricia's

If ever there was a man born into a regiment, it is Gault Donaldson of Ottawa. His father served in Princess Patricia's Canadian Light Infantry (PPCLI) from 1915 to 1919, naming his son Gault after Hamilton Gault, the regiment's founder.

Gault was born on a farm near Kinburn, Ontario, on 25 January 1920. In 1939, Gault wanted to enlist in the PPCLI and his father wrote to Colonel Broeke at the PPCLI Depot in Winnipeg, Manitoba. Arrangements were made for nineteen-year-old Gault to have a medical in Ottawa, and on 1 April 1940 he paid twenty-two dollars for a rail ticket from Smiths Falls, Ontario to Winnipeg, Manitoba. Thirty days later he was sworn in at Fort Osborne Barracks, and a month later he was on route to Halifax, and then overseas.

The voyage to Scotland aboard the *Smaria* was uneventful. It was not until January 1941 that Private Gault Donaldson (by this time known as Don) became a member of 9 Platoon. His platoon commander was Lieutenant R. Coleman, who later commanded the Edmonton Regiment in Italy.

In 1943 Don was a section commander in 8 Platoon under the command of Lieutenant "Willy" Mulherin, who went on to become aide de camp to Major General Chris Vokes (and many years later, after the war, was the commanding officer of 1st Canadian Guards). Don recalls,

> By the spring of 1943 it was obvious that something big was about to happen. The regiment went to Inverary twice at the Combined Training Centre. Our transport was being waterproofed. I still managed to get a short leave to Brighton to see Joyce Chandler, who was to become my war bride.

In **From Pachino to Ortona,** the training is described as "hardening training, hill climbing, practice with 'scrambling nets', assault landings, fast marches and sniper training."

The 1st Canadian Division was ready for action, and the invasion of Sicily was to be the place. "We embarked on the *Lamgibby Castle,* and on 1 July 1943 we sailed down the Clyde. We did not know our destination." Later, when summer kit was issued they were told of Operation Husky, the invasion of Sicily.

> The day before we were to land the weather got worse, high winds and high seas. As nightfall came the weather got better and we loaded our equipment into the landing craft, which was slung from stanchions on the side of the ship.

From Pachino to Ortona contains the details of 10 July 1943:

> The attack was to be made in darkness in the early hours of 10 July. ... The Canadian Division formed the left wing of the Eighth Army. ... The Canadians were to land on the beaches at the base of the west side of the Pachino Peninsular. ... In war, however, events have a habit of taking leave of the scenario.

In Don's case, all went well at first. His platoon was called forward to get into their landing craft, with Don, now a corporal, was leading his section. As the small craft left the ship, it spun and hit the side of the ship, bending its ramp. Don recalls, "We couldn't go forward at any speed without shipping water, so we went in reverse." In no time it was obvious that the landing craft would not reach the beach, so they returned to the ship. 8 Platoon was to stay aboard for the rest of the night. That morning at day light the platoon went ashore from a larger landing craft. Don said, "I looked out to sea and saw this vast array of ships in all directions." The platoon moved off the beach and came under enemy fire for the first time in their lives. Said Don, "We were well spread out so no one was injured, but it was still terrifying." Once clear of the bridgehead the long marches under an unbelievable sun started. In **Canadians in Italy**, the PPCLI war diary said of the battalion's march to Modica, "every time they stopped they fell asleep". The officers and men marched mile after mile in clouds of "fine white dust". Another unit recorded that in the three days since landing "they had only had eight hours sleep".

Don's story continues: "On 21 July we were outside the town of Leonforte. The Edmontons got into the town but a German counterattack forced them to halt their advance." **Canadians in Italy** explains how the Edmontons were saved by this action:

> "C" Company of the Patricias, a troop of four tanks
> from the Three Rivers Regiment and a troop of the 90th
> Battery's antitank guns ... thundered down the road to
> the ravine, the infantrymen riding on the tanks and in
> the tractors and clinging to the guns. ... The column
> swept ... into Leonforte. ... It fell like a whirlwind upon
> the German posts ... and won their immediate
> surrender. [Don was in A Company.]

Don mentions that as the final clearing of Leonforte took place, he led "his section over a low stone wall and Lance-Corporal Currie rushed forward with the Bren gun." Don was then to witness an event that is as clear today as it was forty-nine years ago: "A German machine gun opened up and Currie got two bullets in his forehead." Don's fellow section commander, Corporal C.J. Lord, saw the German gun and "took it out". Don hesitated for a moment and then took the Bren gun from Currie's hands. This was the first, but not the last time he would see a friend die in battle. Things did not improve that night as "our own artillery fire fell on our position; one of our signallers got back the word to stop the fire." One of those killed was "Jacky Cousins, who had been so brave that very morning". In **Canadians in Italy** it is mentioned that Private Cousins "with complete disregard for his own life, rose to his feet in full view of the enemy and carrying his Bren gun ... charged the enemy posts." Don says, "Jacky should have had the Victoria Cross, but all he got was a posthumous Mentioned in Despatches."

The next serious battle for A Company was the "attack at Agira, a town built on the top of a hill." The enemy was supposed to be clear of area, but "we soon found out differently". The streets were so narrow that a small German rear guard slowed their progress. The advance progressed house by house and Don led his section "through a deserted enemy machine-gun post complete with empty ammo boxes—it was a very dark night."

Don's section cleared the far side of the town when "Moaning Minnie" rockets fell upon the platoon. The next day it was German 88 mms. The Germans knew the range to every part of Agira, having just left it. The PPCLI finally got to a rest area at Militello, but Don came down with malaria and was evacuated to hospital at Catania. In short

Corporal Don Donaldson in England, 1942.

order he contracted jaundice and was evacuated to North Africa and a British Military hospital at Philipville.

After some months Don went back to the PPCLI as a reinforcement, joining the same platoon he had left in Sicily. On 30 November 1943, the PPCLI crossed the Sangro River and by 5 December were facing the Moro River at Villa Rogatti. Don's platoon had no officer, but "with a man like Sergeant Moore, everything would be okay." Lt-Col Ware [the CO] decided to cross the river on a one-company front. At midnight "B" Company forded the river. ... Assaulting from the left, the Patricias rushed and silenced two machine gun posts. ... The Panzer Grenadiers ... were taken by surprise. ... Slowly "B" Company forced its way into the central square [of Villa Rogatti]. ... "A" Company [Don's] ... swung to the right towards the northern part of the village and began clearing houses and caves. (Stacey, **Canadians in Italy**)

Don recalls, "As we got into the town a German motorcyclist arrived in our midst and fell of his bike, firing his weapon. One of the platoon was hit in the hand." The Germans reacted to the PPCLI's success, and 7 Platoon was soon overrun when they ran out of ammunition. Don recalls, "It looked like it was over for us in 8 Platoon, but the British tanks arrived and saved the day." A mule train loaded with ammunition and food also arrived. Another counterattack came; "we held on, but Sergeant Moore was wounded. When things eased up he handed over command to me," says Don. The next day the

PPCLI were relieved by a British battalion and "the British lieutenant I handed over to was a bit taken back by my rank."

2nd Brigade was on the move again. This time the objective was San Leonardo, south of Vino Ridge, which overlooked Ortona. By 12 December the PPCLI were holding positions along one side of the ridge with the Germans close by on the other side. The PPCLI was under strength, and on 14 December a Royal Canadian Regiment officer was killed whilst commanding a PPCLI company. Don finally handed over the command of 8 Platoon to Lieutenant A.G. Robertson, but very soon after Robertson became the company commander, Don had the platoon once more. On 18 December 1943, Don was not to know it, but his war was about to end:

> About noon I got out of my slit trench to check on the platoon cook of the day, Private J. Joss. He was heating up some food on a small stove. He was protected from view by the reverse slope of a small gully. I had only gone a few steps when a German mortar bomb landed behind me. A piece of steel went through my right hand at the base of the thumb. It felt like someone had hit me with a baseball bat. Private Joss and Corporal Lord from another platoon bandaged my right hand. [Sgt Lord was killed at the Hitler Line 23 May 1944.]

Don walked back to the regimental aid post where the doctor examined his hand and sent him back by ambulance. There were many other wounded men, and the Germans were shelling the roads. Don arrived at "a British advanced dressing station where a Scottish doctor operated on my hand." The next day Don could see the end of his right thumb protruding from the cast so he "knew he had not lost it".

At the end of January 1944 Don was evacuated to England aboard the hospital ship *Lady Nelson,* arriving at Liverpool. Under the medical category system Don was slated to be sent back to Canada. He convinced the doctor to delay his medical board long enough to marry Joyce in Brighton.

Colonel Ware was now commanding 2nd Brigade Holding Unit. Don saw him, explained his situation and just one week later was sent to the Non-Effective Transit Depot and home to Canada. It was

January 1945 when Corporal Gault (Don) Donaldson arrived at Lansdowne Park, Ottawa. He was released on 2 June 1945.

Don was employed by Veterans Land Act, Department of Veterans Affairs, from 1945 to 1947 and then he went to the Department of Agriculture. Don worked in plant pathology at the Central Experimental Farm until December 1978. He and his war bride are retired and live in Ottawa.

The Story of Two Royals

Two members of The Royal Canadian Regiment, or "Royals", are joined together in this final story in the Canadian Army chapter. They never served together during the war, but now live just miles apart in Kingston and Mallorytown, Ontario. Bert Hovey was a pre-war Royal, and Ron Barkley joined as a reinforcement at Campobasso, Italy, in October 1943. The two stories have been joined to portray the fortunes of war and how a twist of fate could result in totally different war experiences. Bert recommended the Barkley story as a typical "ordinary hero".

Bert Hovey, now eighty years old, joined The RCR in August 1931. As Bert said, "I got the second last vacancy in the regiment, maybe because I had been a cadet lieutenant in the Sussex Cadet Corps and a sergeant in the signal platoon of the New Brunswick Rangers." Basic training was conducted in the Halifax Citadel, the recruits being instructed in "drill, small arms, grenades, fieldcraft as well as receiving a lot of physical training." When the trained soldier platoon marched out of the Citadel, the mayor of Halifax accepted the key, for "no longer would we be accommodated there, and we moved into Wellington Barracks." In his own time Bert qualified as a wireless operator for ships; he was about to leave the army for the sea when "the company commander sent me on an infantry signaller course to learn the signal lamp, Morse code, semaphore, heliograph, telephones and field exchanges." There was no leaving The RCR, Bert was in for a career.

In December 1937 Bert was married to his Sussex girl-friend—without permission, because no marriage could be sanctioned until the soldier was twenty-six. When that birthday arrived they married again just to keep the records straight! Bert was a keen athlete, involved in soccer, track, hard ball and badminton, and he could run the mile in five minutes.

By 1939, Corporal Hovey was qualified to be a sergeant and along came the war. The RCR were placed on their war establishment, and recruiting began to fill out the ranks with private soldiers from civilian street. Lance Sergeant Hovey was now in the signal platoon, but in no

Lt. Hovey with admiring Dutch children, Ijmuiden, 1945.

time he was promoted to platoon sergeant major (WOIII) and was given command of 8 Platoon in A Company.

The RCR was designated as part of the 1st Canadian Division, and on 18 December 1939 embarked on the *Almanzora,* a Royal Mail Liner. "It was our second wedding anniversary, and my young wife stood back in the crowd like the rest, waving us goodbye."

The winter of 1940 was awful. It was one of the coldest on record, and the accommodation was not up to the standard of Canadian warmth. "Eating breakfast in the sergeants' mess, fully dressed including greatcoat" was the norm. During the summer months The RCR suffered their first war casualties when the "Luftwaffe dropped bombs on the company next to ours during the night. Some of their men never knew what hit them." Bert was made the acting company sergeant major of A Company, where he had started out as a private in 1931.

As part of 1st Brigade, The RCR was sent to France "to help the French defend Paris". They landed at Brest and got as far inland as Chartres, but the French Army collapsed. Bert says, "We had to get out the best way we knew how." Most of the French railwaymen left the train, and Canadian soldiers took over as firemen and train engineers. The regiment got back to Brest, destroyed their transport and under enemy aerial attack got aboard the last ship that made it back to England. Later WOII Hovey hoped to be named regimental sergeant major (RSM) but a junior WOII was given the post. Bert went before the commanding officer, who told him "he wanted me to apply for officer training because he could see me as a trainer of officers." This meant a three-month course in England and promotion to lieutenant. But it was not to be, for a course to train officers had been set up in Canada at Brockville, Ontario. Three and a half years after leaving Halifax, Bert was back again, but this time as an officer cadet. The RCR was on its way to Sicily, but Bert was on route to Ontario.

The story now turns to the second Royal. Ron Barkley joined the Canadian Army on 30 November 1942 in Brockville, Ontario, at the age of eighteen. He was trained as an infantry soldier and sent to England as a reinforcement. After spending some time in Aldershot, Private Barkley was sent to Italy via North Africa and he became a member of The RCR at Campobasso in October 1943, where he became a member of D Company, 16 Platoon, commanded by Lieutenant Mitch Sterlin. It is interesting to note that up until this time "the Regiment had advanced nearly 450 miles [724 kilometres] in 63 days and had executed the tasks entrusted to it" (Stevens, **The Royal Canadian Regiment**). Ron was to understand a statement made by another regiment's historian. "It had been manoeuvres with live ammunition rather than a war." From here on, every foot of land was to be fought for against a most determined enemy.

Captain D. P. Schleihauf was D Company commander as the reinforcements settled into The RCR routine. At the end of November, action was about to commence.

The rest of Ron's story comes from a 1992 interview he gave to Ian Hodson and Bert Hovey as part of The RCR Historical Research Project conducted in Kingston, Ontario. Ron recalled his first time in action:

> As we moved forward the Germans shelled us really heavy. We got down into the mud and just stayed there with our heads down. It was wet and cold and I was scared and hungry. We moved through the Hastings and Prince Edward Regiment west and north of San Leonardo up against the enemy infantry. 16 Platoon was out in front all by ourselves. There were 20 of us when we started out, half of what there should have been.

Private Barkley was about to be a part of what The RCR now refer to as the forty-eight hour battle of Sterlin castle. The RCR had been ordered to move up on the right flank of 2nd Brigade who were holding San Leonardo. The RCR attack failed, and in the pull-back the message did not get through to Lieutenant Mitch Sterlin and his 16 Platoon. Stevens recorded the action as follows:

> Only 16 Platoon stood in the path of the enemy advance
> and it gave the Regiment one of its finest hours. When
> the enemy struck [the Italian farm house) the riflemen
> held all doors and windows and the platoon Bren
> gunners were in weapon pits outside.

At the door of the house with a Thompson submachine gun was Ron Barkley. Lieutenant Sterlin was everywhere, organizing the defence, looking after wounded and watching the expenditure of ammunition.

> Eleven men were left in the farmhouse which had
> become the target of six German machine guns. About
> mid afternoon the enemy assaulted the house. ... An
> Oberleutnant was shot in the act of forcing a stick
> grenade [potato masher] through the bars of one
> window.

At last relief came to The RCR in Sterlin Castle when the artillery fired a concentration of shells around the house. It was just in time, for "the platoon's ammunition was running low". There were about thirty Germans killed or wounded trying to capture the farmhouse. Lieutenant Sterlin withdrew the remainder of his platoon after nightfall. Ron mentions that Sterlin should have "got a medal, but he was killed on December 19th and got nothing". Ron was asked to comment on Mitch Sterlin as a leader: "He was a man that looked after his men and tried to get the best for them that he could." When 16 Platoon left the farmhouse, "we ran like hell, over and across the Moro River."

Ron became a stretcher bearer late in the Italian Campaign and then, three months before the Canadians left for Northwest Europe, he came down with amoebic dysentery, so badly that he was hospitalized for three months and lost fifty pounds. Private Barkley was finally sent back to England to Number 3 Repatriation Depot, where he waited to go back to the Regiment. The reinforcement system seems to have

Ron Barkley in Italy, 1945. Note the Red Cross badge on left sleeve worn by Stretcher bearers.

missed him, for he saw The RCR come back to England and Aldershot in September 1945 but he was not allowed to rejoin his unit. The RCR sailed for Canada on the *Nieuw Amsterdam*. Lance-Corporal Barkley did not get on a Canada-bound draft until February 1946. The story now rejoins Bert Hovey.

2nd Lieutenant Hovey graduated and then took a one-month course and was given his "second pip as a lieutenant". In that rank Bert was kept at Brockville as a platoon instructor, a job which was to last three months. Platoon after platoon came and went and Bert did not get back to England as a reinforcement officer for a year. He had qualified at the Canadian Battle Drill course in Vernon, British Columbia, and commanded a half company of two platoons, but still he remained in Canada until he finally he got on an overseas draft.

Back in England, Bert was placed in command of a platoon of conscripts, known as *zombies*. Bert recalls an incident on the anti-tank range when a projectile did not explode. Bert and the sergeant went to the live round and blew it up. The platoon seemed to think that Bert had "saved their lives, and from that time on they would do anything I told them—they were good soldiers."

One day Bert was placed on a draft to go to Italy, but as the Canadians were about to leave for the continent he was held until The RCR were in Northwest Europe. Bert went to Belgium, was put on a draft to The RCR and joined them in the Reichwald Forest (Siegfried Line) where he became battalion transport officer for the final stage of the war in Holland.

Lieutenant Hovey was to ride a motorcycle in his new job, and he recalls "crossing the Rhine River on a pontoon bridge with no guard rails. As a non-swimmer, this was an unpleasant experience."

When the war came to an end, Bert quickly volunteered for the Pacific Force. Soon he was on his way back to Canada and disembarkation leave of thirty days. The day before his leave ended, the atomic bomb was dropped on Hiroshima, and the war in the Pacific soon ended. As a senior lieutenant, Bert was sent to Aldershot, Nova Scotia, to be the company second-in-command in the Carleton and York Regiment and later to The RCR Interim Force Battalion in Brockville, Ontario. Bert now had fifteen years in the army but as there were "fifteen officers for each vacancy" he was offered his release or a reversion back to the rank of WOII. Bert chose the latter.

Bert Hovey was recommissioned during the Korean War. He served in Camp Borden, Canadian Army Staff College and, as a captain, served in Cambodia with the Truce Commission. Nine years later Captain Hovey retired from the Canadian Army and became the COTC, Queen's University Contingent, training officer. He was the commanding officer when the Contingent was disbanded.

Bert Hovey is retired and lives in Kingston, Ontario. Ron Barkley lives in Mallorytown, Ontario, where for years he was a transport driver for British American Oil.

Chapter Three

The Royal Canadian Air Force

The crew that flies together, fights together and drinks together, survives together.

(aircrew saying)

The Royal Canadian Air Force (RCAF) covered more theatres of war than either the Royal Canadian Navy or the Canadian Army. By war's end, the dead from the RCAF could be found everywhere the war had been fought. Only Great Britain, the United States and Russia had larger air forces. In addition, no part of Canada's wartime force had such a large percentage of personnel serving with non-Canadian units. In bomber squadrons alone, almost 6,000 Canadians served with other Commonwealth air forces.

Often overlooked was the part played by the RCAF in the British Commonwealth Air Training Plan (BCATP). This plan made it possible for young men from Britain, Australia and New Zealand, as well as Canada, to man the aircraft that took the air battle into the heart of Germany and Italy. From October 1940 to March 1945, over 130,000 aircrew graduated from the BCATP, close to 50,000 of them as pilots. Those same air forces also flew against the Japanese. Canadian airmen were everywhere that planes were flown, radars were scanned and clandestine landings were made.

The desire to fly seemed to be in the hearts of young men in 1939. The visions of air battles from the Great War drew the young into the air forces. Although the large transfer of soldiers and sailors into the RCAF, as in 1914 to 1918, was not repeated, it is safe to say that the RCAF never lacked for recruits.

The statistics of graduates do not tell us of those who died in training. The Hurricane pilot whose wingman cut off his aircraft tail with his propeller; the instructor (DFC, DFM) who died at Calgary airport when his student banked an Anson too steeply; those who died over the Great Lakes, lost when out of sight of land; and the crew who died on a mountaintop near Quesnel, British Columbia, when they tried to fly without instruments, are just a few examples of many.

The first solo flight; the conversion to operational flying; that raid over occupied France; seeing a fellow member of the squadron fall from the sky in flames; bailing out of a burning aircraft over enemy territory—these were the experiences shared by the members of the RCAF. Sadly, the numbers lost in the RCAF passed the 17,000 mark. Almost one third of those men and boys have no known grave.

Shot Down on His Very First Mission

Harold Brennan's story is unique in that his exposure to the war in the air lasted just long enough for him to be shot down. And after three months in hiding with the French Patriots, Harold would see war no more.

Born in Lindsay, Ontario, in 1922, Harold was a station installer with Bell Canada when he turned eighteen in 1940. A year later, in Toronto at Christmas, he and a friend decided to join the RCAF. Harold waited but days to be called up in January 1942, just before his twentieth birthday. Like so many other young men, Harold longed to be a pilot. He was disappointed to learn that he did not have the required education, but disappointment turned to delight when the recruiting officer (a former boyfriend of Harold's sister) told him he would fix it so that Harold could be a pilot.

> I did my initial training at 6 ITS [Initial Training School] at what is now Ryerson in Toronto and did my elementary flying [Elementary Flying Training School—EFTS] on Tiger Moths at Sky Harbour in Goderich, Ontario. I took my service flying on Harvards at Uplands in Ottawa and got my pilot wings and my commission on February 19, 1943. I then attended a general reconnaissance course in Charlottetown, Prince Edward Island, and studied such things as celestial navigation, ship recognition and harbour identification.

All that training took Harold to June 1943. Having been in uniform for eighteen months, he finally went overseas, arriving just in time to see his first German air raid. Harold's training as a pilot continued, first on the Miles Master and then the Oxford, which qualified him to fly a twin-engine aircraft. He then converted onto the Wellington bomber and "picked" his crew. "All the aircrews were assembled in one place, and we simply got together; none of us knew the others."

Harold's crew consisted of R. Dickson from Vernon, British Columbia; A. Houston, Toronto, Ontario; J. Kempson, a Royal Air Force (RAF) radio operator; E. Trottier, Cornwall, Ontario; and

Harold Brennan in Lindsay, Ontario, 1943.

A. Elder, Vancouver. As their final test before being posted to active duty, the crew was to fly together on 20 April 1944. Their mission was to fly over France dropping "nickels" (leaflets advising the French what to do in the event of an invasion) and "window" (strips of foil to disrupt the German radar). Two other aircraft went with Harold's.

We reached our target in the wee small hours and dropped our load. We were soon attacked by a Ju-88 [Junkers-88, a German night fighter] and were required to take violent evasive action. We, of course, lost the other two aircraft and wound up way off our course for home. When the Ju-88 left us we resumed our way to England but were sufficiently off course that we flew too close to Guernsey Island. We were immediately hit by anti-aircraft fire and a shell burst below and sprayed up like a fountain, taking out both our wing fuel tanks. This left us with only our emergency tank [half an hour of flying time]. As we were bucking a head wind, I decided to head south in the hope of reaching land in France.

After about 20 minutes I saw a long fire on the surface that looked like a ship burning, so I decided to ditch beside it; we might then be picked up by air-sea rescue. When I got quite low I saw it was not a ship but a long building. I immediately climbed and started to circle, instructing my crew to bail out. They all left, including my bombardier, who had snapped on my chest parachute for me. I then found that I had a hell of a time getting our from behind the "wheel" with no one to help me. I fought the aircraft back into the sky, but the engines started to cough. I was out of gas. I raced down the stairway to the escape hatch. It was 3:00 a.m. and pitch black. As soon as I was out of the aircraft, I pulled the ring of my 'chute. It straightened me out with a real bang. I must have been lying on my side as my strap came up and hit my right ear, leaving me deaf on the right side. Although I could see very little, I heard the aircraft hit the ground just as I saw the branches of a tree. I landed very hard in a vegetable garden. A small dog barked at me but no one came. I rushed out of the yard, hid my parachute and only then did I realize I had the ring from my rip cord in my hand so tightly, I could not let go of it. (I still have that ring all these years later.)

It took just days for the French underground (Patriots) to round up the whole crew. Flying Officer Alfred Houston, Harold's navigator, was the first to be found. He gave the Patriots a description of the others. The one casualty was RAF Sergeant John Kempson, who had been hit by the flak. A Patriot doctor treated him, the but the wounds were too severe. Six days after bailing out, Kempson died. He was buried by his crewmates.

The next three months were passed in hiding. (Flying Officer Houston wrote an article for **Maclean's,** from which many of the following points were taken.) The Patriots decided to pass the crew from group to group until they could be smuggled into Spain. The French were glad to help the men. "It is part of our duty ... to help Allied airmen escape from the Germans." For the frightened young

Canadians, their next words were comforting: "We will lead you ... be your guides and your guard. We'll fight for you."

At first, travel was easy, but then the Gestapo closed in. There were some close calls as they hid in fields and barns across the French countryside. Houston wrote of one:

> We sighted a German patrol of twenty men. They saw us too. Immediately they started after us across the fields. The Germans gained on us. ... Their bullets were coming close. Soon we'd have to stand and fight. ... One of the Patriots suddenly said, "I demand permission to stay here and fight—I can hold them for half an hour while the rest of you get away." For a while we heard him firing at the Germans, then he stopped. We heard a man screaming. Later we heard that he had been wounded, captured—and promptly tortured to death.

Whenever the Germans caught a Patriot, it was the same horrible story: torture, then death.

Not long after the crew began their dangerous journey, the route to Spain became closed, so the crew was taken north into Brittany. Finally, it became too risky to continue. For six weeks the crew hid out in a small room in a mill. June 6th—D-Day—happened during their fifth week in hiding. "Les Anglais have landed!" shouted the mill owner's nephew gleefully the next morning, but soon afterward the miller ran in, screaming, "Allez, allez! Les Boches!" The crew rushed out to hide in a nearby swamp for two days.

Their new guide was a "beautiful blonde girl of about nineteen. She was one of the bravest and sweetest kids I've ever seen, and she performed especially difficult missions." For the next few weeks, Paulette led the crew right under the noses of the Germans! Her job was to get them safely to the coast. The last night was perhaps the most dangerous. With mine detector in hand, Paulette led the crew through a mine field. "As she found a mine, she dropped a handkerchief on it." The moon picked out the white marker clearly for the Canadians. "The last crew member picked up all the markers." Paulette had completed her special mission.

At the coast, a gunboat arrived to take the crew members off. An officer and two seamen, all French Canadians, came ashore in a row boat, but a German patrol came too close for safety. The gunboat was forced to leave, and the three French Canadian sailors stayed to hide with the Wellington crew. It was a week before the German patrols moved far enough off for the gunboat to return. Under cover of darkness, Harold and his crew were taken out to the gunboat, and soon were sailing back to England, safe at last.

On 11 August 1944, Harold was sent home to Canada on survivor's leave, travelling, appropriately enough, on the *Ile de France*. Back home, he wasted no time in marrying his long-time sweetheart, Rita, on 7 September 1944. After a two-month posting in Hagersville, Harold was sent to Rockcliffe in November to return to operational flying. He arrived to be told that there was a surplus of aircrew, and he could have his discharge if he wanted it. He did, and on 28 February 1945, Harold left the RCAF and returned to Bell Canada.

Harold worked for the Bell until 1984, when he retired to Peterborough after forty-three years with the same company.

Bombs Gone

Doug Scanlan, originally from Kirkland Lake, Northern Ontario (but now living in Toronto), clearly remembers the first time he put on that distinctive blue uniform of the RCAF aircrew. He felt like he was "walking six inches above the ground", and admits to a love affair with the air force that has gone on ever since.

The young pilot officer went through an Overseas Advanced Flying Unit (OAFU) in Cumberland, England, and an Operational Training Unit (OTU) in Nottingham before finishing up at a Heavy Conversion Unit (HCU) in Yorkshire, where he was familiarized with the four-engine Halifax Bomber. Doug would be a bombardier, the crew member who aims and releases the bombs. He recalls fondly his first reaction to the sight of a Halifax:

> From where I stood on the ground, it was twenty-three feet [seven metres] to the top of the nose of the aircraft (nearly three storeys high), and I was overwhelmed by the massive size of the oleo legs and wheels. I had difficulty believing that this mighty metal monster could actually get airborne with, or without, six and a half tons of bombs on board.

It was broadly believed in wartime Bomber Command that the group of officers and senior non-commissioned officers (NCOs) who made up the crew of a heavy bomber aircraft became, by the very nature of their operational duties, a "survival unit". This gave rise to such florid wartime phrases as "the crew that flew together, fought together and drank together would also survive together." The fact that the great majority of them died together only intensified the feelings of closeness and survivalism. Not surprisingly, Doug Scanlan thought then and still thinks now that he belonged to the best crew in 415 Squadron and 6 Bomber Group.

Doug speaks with great warmth and appreciation of the crew companions with whom he survived a tour of thirty-two operations against enemy targets over a period of seven months. Timmy, Roy, Skully, Ray and Bobby—the "baby" of the crew, who hadn't yet reached the age of eighteen by the time his tour was finished—are still large in his heart.

Doug can still vividly recall his first night operation over a German target and the mix of emotions that flooded him on that occasion:

> I was almost trembling with excitement—turned on and keyed up by an adventure and experience that I had never had in my life before. I was dazzled by the awesome array of brilliant searchlights, like a daylight forest all the way to the target. With course, height and airspeed of the bomber force already determined, the black night on the way to and over the target was already a sea of orange-red flak shells bursting from the German anti-aircraft guns almost four miles [six kilometres] below. I recall the shaking experience of seeing, for the first time in the blackness ahead of me from my prone position in the nose of the aircraft, a sudden and brilliant light in the night sky as one of our aircraft suffered a direct flak hit and exploded in a great ball of fire. It reminded me of the last words at the briefing before take off: "Remember, gentlemen: if you should have the misfortune to be shot down, you are to give only your rank, name and serial number. If taken prisoner of war [POW] you are under obligation from then until the cessation of hostilities to make every attempt to effect your escape."

It is ironic that all the detailed planning and preparation that goes into a massive air raid of a thousand bomber aircraft or more culminate in only a few (albeit critical) moments over a target. Although most area-bombing targets were German cities, there was always a specific aiming point within the target complex. To help the main bomber force find and destroy the aiming point, Bomber Command's pathfinding force flew slightly in advance of the main force to mark the target. Using sophisticated navigational aids, the pathfinders dropped target indicators according to a prescribed pattern of colour. The target indicators were brilliantly coloured, pyrotechnical aerial markers that lit up the whole sky over the aiming point; their release was timed to the split second in advance of the first wave of the bombing force. Weather and visibility permitting, bombing

Doug Scanlan in England, 1942.

strategy called for all bombardiers to bomb the target indicators, which were cascading slowly down over the aiming point on the ground below.

In the high drama that was a bombing run, the bombardier called, "Bomb doors open," and from that point on it was his responsibility to lead the aircraft to the aiming point so he could drop his bombs. During this brief run-up to the target, the bombardier did a last-minute double-check that all bombs were armed and that the camera was activated. The camera automatically took a rapid series of line-overlap photographs, thus documenting the entire bombing sequence from bomb release to target response. Such photography over a night bombing target was made possible by the simultaneous release of a 7.5 million candlepower photoflash, which dropped out of its armour-plated chute on the aircraft timed to burst into brilliant light as the camera shutter opened to record the accuracy of the exploding bombs on the target.

Doug continues his narrative of that first raid:

> There was a feeling of isolation and aloneness—all by myself in the nose of the aircraft. There were four main sounds on operations which I shall always remember. First, the reassuring roar of the four powerful Bristol Hercules engines as a constant noise from start up to shut-down. The second sound was the voices on the intercom of crew members speaking to one another. The third sound was the barely heard crump of flak shells bursting near the aircraft. Lastly, the terrifying noise of German flak striking and penetrating the aircraft. This

sounded much like gravel striking a car speeding down
a loose gravel road—only much louder and far more
deadly. My only company in the dense darkness was the
dim red lights of the bombing panel on my right, the
soft lights of the bombing camera on my left and,
mounted on the floor in the perspex nose of the aircraft,
the centrepiece of the bombing compartment—the
Mark XIV bombsight.

The bombsight was a highly accurate, yet simple to operate device.
The *bombing wind* determined by Bomber Command was usually fed
into the instrument in advance of the run by the bombardier. The fore
and aft axis line of the bombsight could be tilted forward to project the
hot night wire of the sight miles ahead in the dark night sky; this
allowed the bombardier to determine the accuracy of the approach to
the aiming point. The release point of the combined load of bombs,
incendiaries and photoflash was marked by a transverse hairline. When
it was time for the drop, the bombardier pressed a small black pair
switch, which set in motion the complex circuitry to drop the load of
bombs, incendiaries and photoflash simultaneously. Doug Scanlan still
has the pair switch he used on his thirty-two bombing operations to
drop almost 200 tons of bombs on German targets.

I have to admit there were feelings of elation and power
when I pressed that little black switch and all that action
took place. I was doing the job I had been trained to do;
I took satisfaction in what I was doing, and I never then
and haven't since felt the slightest bit of compunction
for what I was ordered to do and, let it be said, what I
enjoyed doing.

Bombing accuracy was largely determined by the accuracy of the
winds fed into the bombsight; course corrections to a target are usually
minor. As he sighted the target approaching him along the hot wire of
the bombsight, the bombardier called for course alteration to port by
saying "Left, left," or course alteration to starboard by saying "Right."
This ruling ensured that if voice transmission was faulty, the
instruction was not in doubt since two sounds were heard to change to
port and only one heard to change to starboard.

At this high point of the bomber attack, all searchlights on the ground were concentrating on *coning* the attacking aircraft. German anti-aircraft batteries were equipped with blue, high-intensity, master lights. When one of these settled on an attacking aircraft, four or five additional lights would join in to produce a brilliant *cone* from the batteries on the ground to the hapless aircraft, whose survival was now in question. In addition, the elite German night fighter force released parachute flares above the bomber force. The flares burst into daylight brilliance and filtered slowly down, backlighting the bomber force to the anti-aircraft batteries below and setting them up for attack by night fighter aircraft from above.

One significant offensive in which Doug was involved was Operation Hurricane. Sir Arthur Harris, Air Chief Marshal of the RAF, Chief of Bomber Command, had been handed a Directive from the British government. This directive was to "demonstrate to the German people the overwhelming superiority of the Allied Air Forces in the European theatre and the futility of continuing the war." Accordingly, on 14 October 1944, the German city of Duisburg experienced a daylight raid in the morning and a repeat raid that same night. During the course of this mighty "bomb and burn" air battle, 21 bomber aircraft (the equivalent of a full bomber squadron) were lost along with almost 150 crewmen.

The success of the double attack was brought home to Doug more than thirty years later, in 1975, when he stuck up a conversation with a German woman seated next to him on a flight to Canada. The woman had been a twelve-year-old girl in Duisburg during that eventful double raid; both her mother and her father had been killed. Remembering the event, she said to Doug, "You will never be able to understand how frightening, demoralizing and terrible it was to have been on the receiving end of a bombing raid." As tactfully as he could, Doug reminded the German woman that Hitler's Luftwaffe had indiscriminately bombed women and children in Rotterdam, Warsaw, Liverpool, Coventry and London before the same treatment was meted out to Germany.

During the six-year Bomber War (1939 to 1945), a number of traditions developed. For example, no bomber man was ever killed— h e *went for the chop—bought it* o r *didn't make it.* And whenever someone bought it, fellow officers or NCOs in his squadron would carefully go through his effects, pay off any mess bills, divide among themselves any sweets and cigarettes and then parcel up his clothing and personal effects to be sent home to his next of kin.

When I ask what had been his most terrifying experience of the war, Doug answers,

> The night of August 18-19, 1944, on a bombing raid on Bremen, Germany, when our crew repelled three successive fighter attacks and finally succeeded in shooting down an Me 109 [Messerschmitt 109] night fighter. It was the most frightening and gut-churning ordeal I ever faced.

His saddest experience?

> Being a pallbearer in the mass burial of twelve bomber men in the RCAF cemetery in Harrogate, which resulted from the loss of the "top of 415 Squadron", that is, the squadron leader, the bombing leader, the navigation leader, the signals leader, the gunnery leader and five others, in the fatal crash of two Halifax aircraft in Yorkshire. I recall carrying casket after casket from the chapel to a long open grave, then, in a final gesture of respect, coming to attention at the foot of each individual casket and silently saluting each. That memory will forever live in my mind.

The most amusing experience?

> It was the custom to post the names of crewmen detailed for bombing operations each night on a bulletin board at the entrance to the mess dining room. Since no one was ever killed in Bomber Command—he "got the chop"—this list quite naturally became known in time as the "chop list". On one particular occasion about ten days before Christmas, as a group was huddled around the bulletin board to see who was detailed for operations that night, a bright young gunner with a gallows sense of humour said, "I just thought of something—there are only seven

more chopping days until Christmas!" I confess I didn't know whether to laugh or cry.

Doug recalls an unusual story related to his home town of Kirkland Lake. By odd coincidence, that small town spawned another volunteer airman whose name was also Douglas Scanlon. The only difference was the spelling of the surname. The other Doug was killed, but on the war memorial in Kirkland Lake his name is misspelled Scanlan. The finally irony of this mischance was that Doug Scanlan, who had chaired the Legion committee, had corrected the error before it was cast in bronze, but his correction was somehow ignored. To this day, on visits back to his home town his small grandsons always insist on visiting the memorial, so they can see where their very much alive and loved grandfather "died for King and Country".

Doug unabashedly admits that when he landed at the end of his thirty-second bombing raid and left the Halifax aircraft for the last time, he knelt and kissed the runway. Along the way, Doug had managed to earn the Distinguished Flying Cross (DFC) "for the utmost courage and devotion to duty" and the gold operations wings of the RCAF for "a tour of gallant service in operational action against the enemy".

Soon after the war ended Doug was talked into transferring to the Canadian Army Reserve as a Provisional Second Lieutenant. He did his army training as a 48th Highlander and ended his army career as a confirmed lieutenant colonel and Commanding Officer of 106 Manning Depot in Toronto. Shortly thereafter, he accepted an invitation to return to the light blue uniform. In quick succession he served as the Honorary Lieutenant Colonel of 411 Squadron, the Honorary Lieutenant Colonel of 2 Tactical Aviation Wing and—where he still serves—the Honorary Colonel of 411 Tactical Helicopter Squadron, Canadian Forces Base Toronto. In addition, Doug is Chairman of the National Association of Air Force Honoraries, a trustee of the Canadian Warplane Heritage Museum and a special advisor to the Commander of Air Command. As well as the charitable work of the orders to which he belongs, his whirlwind life of activity includes fiction writing (**The Surly Bonds of Earth**, 1992). Doug is also the vice-president and executive assistant to the president and chief executive officer of Royal Lepage Limited, Canada's largest realty firm.

Photos from a Spitfire

Bill Carr left Grand Bank, Newfoundland, at the age of fifteen to attend Mount Allison University in Sackville, New Brunswick. At university, he joined the Canadian Officers Training Corps (COTC) and was assigned to the Royal Canadian Engineers.

Bill graduated in 1941, the same year he turned eighteen. He quickly enlisted in the RCAF, and that summer he was sent to RCAF Manning Depot in Valcartier, Quebec. "When they found I had been a second lieutenant in the COTC, I was put in charge of teaching drill and all that business. All of this as an aircraftman second class [AC2, the lowest rank in the air force]. I didn't even have a uniform." After Manning Depot, Bill was sent to Debert, Nova Scotia, where he "did guard duty at the camp entrance in front of a greasy spoon. All night I listened to the jukebox playing such songs as Elmer's Tune." To this day, Bill remembers all the words to some of those tunes.

After six weeks of guard duty Bill went to Victoriaville, Quebec, for Initial Aircrew Ground School and then to Ancienne Lorette, for elementary flying on the Fleet Finch on skis. Uplands (Ottawa) followed, and the aircraft was the Harvard. Because Arthur Bishop was a member of Bill's class, Arthur's father, Billy Bishop, VC, presented the pilot wings to the class on graduation.

Bill's request for the future was "to fly fighters". No attention was paid to the request, and, much to his chagrin, Bill went to Summerside, Prince Edward Island, to fly an Anson aircraft on general reconnaissance. Bill remembers how he and the three or four others sent from Uplands felt:

> We just knew that if we did well we would end up as instructors. We decided we would not do well. We thought that if we failed at Summerside we would get sent to fighters. Squadron Leader Frank Miller [later the first Chief of Defence Staff] was the commanding officer of the station. He called us in and said, "I'm wise to you fellows; you are going to stay here until you pass." We did and got out of there and were sent to England in the autumn of 1941.

Bill in Malta, 1943.

In England, Pilot Officer Carr still did not get the fighter assignment he wanted. One day a request was made for volunteers to go to Farnborough, Hampshire, to be involved in high-altitude test work. Bill went and was soon "in a pressure chamber at 40,000 feet and then at 50,000 feet" (12,000 to 15,000 metres). After a week of this, the men were checked for physical effects. At the end of the testing they were told, "Anything you want [to fly], you can have, as long as it is within Coastal Command." Bill's quick reply was, "Spitfires." The only part of the Command that had Spitfires was photo reconnaissance (PR).

To put PR into perspective compared to other means of warfare from the air, consider the words of General Werner Von Fritsch, of the German High Command: "The military organization with the best aerial photo reconnaissance will win the next war." General Von Fritsch said those words in 1938. To the side that could see into their enemy's back yard would go the advantage. In 1944, a German report said, "Enemy aerial reconnaissance detects our every movement ... [and] smashes every one of these objectives."

Bill Carr was not to fly and fight over England and the European continent, but rather the Mediterranean. Bill recalls his journey to Malta:

I was called in and told to ferry a Spitfire to Malta. This was to be my longest journey—from England to Gibraltar, Algiers in North Africa and on to Luqa airfield, Malta. I flew over Tunis, which was still in enemy hands. The plane, a Mark XI, had excellent range, and some of the "legs" were six hours in length.

In **Warburton's War**, Tony Spooner explains what happened to the young Canadian pilot. There was far more interest in the new Spitfire than there was in its Canadian pilot:

The adjutant said that "he doubted he [Carr] would be staying long." Bill was advised to see the CO of 683 PR Squadron Royal Air Force if he wanted to remain in Malta. He met a "person without rank badges ... drinking tea. ... He asked me about the Spit [I had flown in]." ... In due course he said Bill "could stay."

The tea-drinking Commanding Officer (CO) was Wing Commander Adrian Warburton, DSO and Bar, DFC and two Bars and DFC USA, once described as the "pilot who knew no fear and the most valuable pilot in the RAF". What a man to have as a CO.

Bill had arrived in Malta just in time for the invasion of Italy. He had missed Operation Husky, the invasion of Sicily. In no time there were twenty-two Spitfire squadrons, as well as squadrons of Mosquitos and Beaufighters. PR consisted of visual and photo coverage of both tactical and strategic targets in enemy-held territory (used for planning); pinpoint coverage (used to determine preplanned bombing targets and for bomb damage assessment); and post-operation coverage (to determine the accuracy of all of the weapons used). PR was a place for accurate flying and nerves of steel to take the photos and get them back to base for detailed analysis. Bill told me that, most of the time, he was scared stiff!

On one occasion Bill had completed a high-altitude mission in the Po Valley and was heading south back to his airfield at Foggia. Bill recalls,

They came up on the radio in clear and told me to fly over Anzio southwest of Rome. When I got there I could see a huge amphibious landing [two Divisions]

going in. I dodged flak, ran away from friendly fighters and took all kinds of pictures. [The PR Spitfire had no guns, but carried extra fuel in wing tanks. The purpose of these Spits was to gather intelligence, *not* to get into air fights.] Just before landing, after almost seven hours in the cockpit, the pressure to urinate was intolerable. In a PR Spitfire there was no relief tube, you either "held it" or, at altitude, you "let go" and the liquid evaporated quickly. As the airfield came in sight, for some psychological reason I could hold it no longer, so let it go and wet my pants just before the wheels touched down. The Press, waiting in large numbers to get the report from me on how things looked at Anzio, surrounded the aircraft. There was a rush to get the film out of the cameras. There I sat on my parachute seat pack in my wet pants. When I finally did get out my mechanic reached in, grabbed my 'chute, swung it onto his shoulder and, in front of everyone, got the full shower. What an image for a hero!

Bill was employed as close air support to the Eighth Army. "Once we had the photos we landed, and the film was processed as close to the front as possible. It didn't make sense to take them back to Malta and then fly the pictures back to Italy." Very casually Bill says, "The first time I went missing was in Sicily. In fact, all that happened was that I had a problem, so I landed at Syracuse, got some repairs and coolant and next day continued back to Malta." No one had passed on this fact to the squadron. When Bill got to his quarters he found that "all my stuff was gone". The drill was that when someone went missing, his fellow pilots helped themselves to what they needed.

During the Battle of Cassino, Bill was stationed just south of the infamous monastery and mountain. They were so close to the front that the German artillery could hit the landing strip. The aircrew lived in tents close by, and whenever the shelling started everyone rolled into slit trenches at the side of the tent. One night Bill rolled out and "landed in three feet of snow and water". Bill says, "If I was ever mad at the Germans, it was that time."

Bill was wounded on one occasion. He explained,

A 20 mm shell exploded in my seat. The parachute absorbed most of the blast. I thought I was finished, but the aircraft was still flying okay. I put my hand under my seat, felt shreds of metal, trousers and parachute hanging down. I thought it was my insides. Looking at my hand I saw blood. Luckily it was only a superficial wound.

Bill was awarded the DFC when he was commanding the PR unit supporting the Eighth Army in Italy in 1944. One operation he recalls involved the Pescara dams near Italy's eastern coast. The plan was to bomb the dams and flood the area north of Ortona to cut off the Germans. A PR sortie had to be flown to record what damage had been done. Says Bill, "Someone had to do it, and as I was running the outfit, I had no choice". The photos were taken, a few holes were made in the plane and the mission was a success. Field Marshal Alexander pinned on the medal.

Bill came home to Canada in December 1944 after 143 sorties—400 hours over enemy territory. He went by ship to England and was home in time for Christmas. He then volunteered to go to the Pacific, and while he was waiting to go and operate against Japan he was "put on Northern Survey flying a Mark VI Norseman whilst mapping the Canadian North." The day the war ended, Bill was on what is now called Victory Lake, in the Northwest Territories.

Bill Carr remained in the RCAF for more than thirty more years. In that time, he flew over a hundred different types of aircraft, including the Comet, Canso and Boeing 707. He flew over 1,000 hours in both the C130 and Canada's one and only C5. He commanded the United Nations Air Force in the Congo, he commanded Training Command, and he was Deputy Chief of the Defence Staff when he created and then commanded Air Command, which was his final posting before retirement as a lieutenant general in 1978. As Canada's Chief Scout, he was awarded the Silver Wolf. Until 1988, Bill Carr was a senior executive with Canadair. He is now the president of Carr Associates, an aircraft marketing consulting firm. He and his wife Elaine live in Stittsville, Ontario.

Pilot, POW, "Professor"

Don Morrison's story was a difficult one to capture on the printed page. Although I have known Don for some years, his story eluded me until I came upon a video produced by Lieutenant Commander Ron MacDonald for the RCAF Museum, Trenton, in March 1989. This video, with other material provided by Ron, has resulted in this story of a fighter pilot.

Don joined the RCAF in Toronto in October 1940, and began his initiation at Brandon, Manitoba. At the Manning Pool, issue of uniforms, inoculations and aircrew selection took place. Guard duty followed in Prince Albert, Saskatchewan (one time at -64°F), and then came Regina and Initial Training School, ground school and yet another aircrew medical. It was here that Don was selected to be a pilot, and he "was pleased as punch". Back he went to Prince Albert to learn to fly the Tiger Moth. The Tiger Moth was equipped with skis; "when it came time to do aerobatics, slow rolls and so on, it was a complicated procedure." After six hours of dual flight, Don soloed. In Dauphin, Manitoba, Don became familiar with the Harvard, "a wonderful airplane to fly".

Don arrived in Glasgow, Scotland, on the MS *Mosdale,* a Norwegian freighter. He went on to Bournemouth, England, the holding area for Canadian aircrew, but after just three days Don was on his way back to Scotland to 58 OTU. This "is where we saw our first Spitfires, Mark IIs, relics from the Battle of Britain—manual pump undercarriage and very poor radios." Don flew fifty to sixty hours at the OTU before it was finally time to join a squadron.

Sergeant Pilot Don Morrison's first operational unit was 122 Squadron, RAF, at Scorton, Yorkshire. For a month Don flew convoy patrols, scrambles and formation practice "nothing very exciting, just getting used to the routine". The one thing that Don found different from Canadian units was the "caste system". The officer pilots did not associate with the NCOs. "We flew with them, but never met them." Don flew on operations for the better part of a year before he was commissioned.

On 13 November 1941, Don was moved to Biggin Hill, southeast of London, to 401 Squadron, RCAF. He was told the news with these words: "Are you lucky! They just lost eight fellows in one sweep" (armed reconnaissance over enemy territory). Still, Don was thrilled to be going to a Canadian squadron.

Don's new squadron was engaged in sweeps over France and escorting bombers. The aim was to get the Germans to rise to the bait and give the Commonwealth air forces a chance to destroy them in the air or on their airfields. The squadron was flying the Mark VB Spitfire with four .303 machine guns, two 20 mm cannons and an engine bigger than the Mark II. Compared to the Germans' Focke-Wulf 190 fighter, the Spitfire was at a disadvantage with its small fuel capacity (eighty-seven gallons) and slower rate of climb. Nonetheless, two days after joining 401 Squadron, Don, now twenty, shot down his first enemy aircraft. In the next twenty days he shot down four more.

One of the big operations 401 Squadron was involved in was against the German navy. In **Victory at Sea**, Hal Lawrence describes the event of February 1942. This was the Germans'

> famous dash up the Channel from Brest [to Norway]
> with *Scharnhorst, Gneisneau* and *Prinz Eugen.* [The
> Germans] caught us with our pants down and were
> through the Straits of Dover before we sounded the
> Tocsin. ... The RAF flew off Spitfires, Swordfish ...
> and just about anything else that would fly.

Don remembers the occasion. "We were the first squadron scrambled out and we flew alongside this large convoy." With still-felt rancour, Don explained that the RAF would not accept the first sighting report because "it came from only a flight lieutenant". It cost the Allies a "good hour and a half to get a more senior RAF officer to confirm Bobby Oxspring's report."

On the first run, Don called on the radio to his leader and asked, "Don't you think we're flying a bit close?"

The reply was, "Don't worry, they're ours." Don and his flight were soon shown otherwise! On the second run, while they were escorting Swordfish torpedo bombers, Don's flight

Don Morrison in a Spitfire cockpit in England, 1942.

broke out of the cloud between the *Scharnhorst* and *Gneisneau*. It was just like the fireworks display at the Toronto Ex, but they didn't hit us. This whole event was a coup for the Germans and a black eye for the air force and the Royal Navy.

The next major event for Don was the Dieppe Raid, 19 August 1942. 401 Squadron, by then flying Spitfire IXs, was moved to Lympne airfield, the one closest to Dieppe. The night before the raid they were briefed that "it was Canadian troops. We were thrilled to be protecting our own." The first mission was to fly escort for U.S. Flying Fortresses, who were to bomb the aerodrome at Abbeville, "the main German fighter station for that part of France". No German fighters were in evidence, for they were busy over Dieppe. The Americans "did a magnificent job hitting dispersals and buildings, and they put the station out of action." After the 401 Squadron pilots had escorted the Americans part way back to England, the order was given to head for Dieppe. It was 10:30 a.m. when they arrived, and the pilots could see fires, shell bursts, sinking ships and troops on the beaches. German aircraft were everywhere, and 401 Squadron split into sections of two to take on the enemy. Don recalls,

> I spotted a single FW 190 about 1,500 feet [460 metres] below me. I just rolled down behind him; he never saw me coming. I fired, but I was too close: twenty-five to fifty yards [twenty-three to forty-five metres] away, he blew up, damaging my aircraft. A big glob of his oil hit my windshield and immediately spread over my whole coupe top. I couldn't see, so I put the nose down and

headed for home right on the deck. The engine started to act up and then stopped. I climbed as high as I could. I was unable to jettison the canopy, as my seat pack parachute got caught in it. I could not get free of the cockpit. I was hanging there looking down over the nose of the aircraft. The Channel was fast approaching. I gave one huge kick, spun around, and finally broke free. I cut my eye on the radio mast, but managed to pull the parachute rip cord. Seconds later I hit the water. Two of my buddies, Jimmy Whitman and Bobby Reesor, circled me and guided an RAF air-sea aircraft to me, and I was pulled out of the water. What a treat to see the bow of that speedboat coming toward me at full tilt!

The rescue craft did not take Don straight back to England. Instead, they sped toward Dieppe, were attacked by Focke-Wulf 190s and rescued the crew of two other rescue launches, before finally sailing back to Newhaven. Don was in the air again the next day.

On 8 November 1942, during an escort mission, Don's fighter pilot career came to a fiery end. At about 25,000 feet (7,620 metres), while 401 Squadron was escorting Fortresses home from a bombing run to Lille, France, Don's problems began:

Although I did not realize it, I was starting to have oxygen trouble. Just before we reached the French coast on the way home the controllers called us on the radio and told us that there were fifty-plus enemy fighters coming up behind the Fortresses. I made the big mistake of taking my section back to intercept them. At this point, I believe I ran into oxygen problems.

The early stage of oxygen starvation is just like being drunk. You have all kinds of confidence but your discretion is very much impaired. We dove down on two Focke-Wulf 190s. One of our fellows told me a few years later that there were two 190s, two Spitfires and four more 190s all diving in line astern. One of the 190s went on fire and then the two Spitfires, flown by Doug Manley and myself, went down in flames. I don't really know what happened. I do not remember my plane being hit or exploding. Somehow I managed to get out, pull the ripcord and parachute to earth. My leg was blown off above the knee and left in the cockpit. The only reason I did not bleed to death was that the cold at that altitude, approximately 25,000 feet [7,620 metres], congealed the blood.

I landed on a small French farm across the canal from some German soldiers, who were shooting at me with rifles as I came down. I am lucky they were poor shots. The French farmer and his helper were forced to put me in a boat and take me across the canal to the German soldiers. After putting a tourniquet on my leg, the soldiers took me to the Luftwaffe hospital in St Omer, where I was unconscious for about ten days. I think the German doctors and nurses did a great job of pulling me through. Following interrogation at Dulag Luft [Frankfurt], I was moved to a hospital in Obermasfeld, which was completely staffed by British Army doctors and orderlies who had been captured at Dunkirk, North Africa, Greece, Crete, etc. It was a real treat to be with other wounded British prisoners as well as many of the Canadian survivors from Dieppe. After convalescence at another British-staffed hospital at Kloster Haina, I was moved to Stalag Luft III at Sagan, where my friends Bob Tuck, Wally Floody and Aubrey Ferguson were at the gate to meet me.

A little known humanitarian action then happened that saw Don Morrison repatriated to England by way of Sweden under the auspices of the International Red Cross.

The exchange was for badly wounded and for noncombatants such as padres, doctors and medical orderlies. Most of them, however, elected to stay in the prison camps and hospitals where they continued to carry on their good work. In late 1943 they took us by train to Berlin. Just after we arrived the air raid siren sounded, and flares lit up the sky. I thought to myself, "What a place to be killed when I am on my way home!" Fortunately, the RAF was just taking photographs that night. We travelled on to a small German naval station on the Baltic, then by ferry to Sweden. No luxury cruise will ever be as great as that short trip! Just after we arrived, the Swedish Army band greeted us with nine verses of "God Save the King". That was a long stand for a group of badly wounded prisoners.

Half-way across Sweden we passed a train with the repatriated German prisoners of war on their way home. They didn't look nearly as happy as we did. After all, they were heading home to receive heavy bombing raids for the rest of the war.

Before Don left the POW camp, he was briefed by the senior air force officer on German air defences, secret German weapons such as the V1 and V2 and other information gathered from various sources. Don passed on all that information to the RCAF and RAF Intelligence Staff when he arrived back in England.

One of the conditions of repatriation was that Don was not allowed to go back into action. After he returned to Canada, he was employed as a flying instructor at both Oshawa and Trenton. He also did many speaking tours for the Canadian Red Cross and war bond drives.

Don retired from the RCAF on 14 March 1945 and eventually joined Trans Canada Airlines (later Air Canada) where he worked in the sales department for thirty-seven years. He retired in January 1985, but remains highly active through his involvement with many air force associations and his family. He lives in Don Mills, Ontario.

Driving for the Cross

Marjory Bratton's story has been placed in the RCAF chapter for one very good reason: Her story might not have happened had it not been for the tragedy of losing her RCAF husband to the war.

Marjory married Murray Minard, an Ottawa boy, on 18 May 1940. Murray became an observer in the RCAF and was sent to England. In March 1944, he was shot down and killed while flying in a training aircraft. Despite, or perhaps because of, her grief over the loss of her young husband, Marjory decided that she had take active part in the war. Within a month she had joined the Canadian Red Cross.

Marjory's first goal was to train as a medical secretary at the Rockcliffe Airport Hospital, but learning that drivers were urgently needed, she changed her path. She took a mechanic's course—"We were taught to change tires and oil, check spark plugs, etc."—then worked in a garage for a couple of weeks to qualify as an ambulance driver. "We met incoming trains with wounded from overseas, mainly acting as stretcher bearers."

In November 1944, Marjory was told she was needed in England. After a train trip to New York City in early January 1945, she boarded the *Rangitiki*—"an old passenger/cargo ship recruited from the Vancouver/New Zealand run. She had seen better days" (Day, **Memoirs—Women in War**). A large number of English children, evacuees, were on board, heading home after being cared for in Canada and the United States. "They got into the tuck shop and filled up on candies. When we sailed they all got sick." After twenty-one days the *Rangitiki* arrived in Liverpool, where the Red Cross workers parted company from the English children and went on to London.

Today's readers might be interested in some of the rules that the young women of the Red Cross had to follow:

- It is expected that Corps members will, on all occasions, conduct themselves as gentlewomen.
- Members will remember that when in uniform, they represent the Corps, the Red Cross Society and Canada.
- Members will not give information or interviews to the press.

Marjory, 1944.

- Alcohol will not be consumed during duty hours except under exceptional circumstances. (Mitchell and Deacon, **641: A Story of the Canadian Red Cross Corps Overseas**)

Marjory's first duty was to learn how to drive the four-stretcher "box" ambulance at Charlton Park. Casualties and POWs were being flown from the Continent to England, and Marjory's job was to pick up the casualties at the aerodromes and get them back to the hospital. Conditions at one aerodrome, Broadwell, were typical:

The station consisted of numerous Nissen huts, dispersed around the air strips. ... It rained almost every day. ... The ground was a sea of mud.

Marjory remembers driving back from her first visit to Broadwell—in the dark with only blackout lights, no map and four patients in the back, all on stretchers. Another time when Marjory's ambulance was loaded with four stretcher cases, one of the patients in the upper stretcher asked for a bedpan and an orderly gave him one. Not wanting to start over the bumpy road until the man had done his business and returned the bedpan to the orderly, Marjory

said to bang on the side of the ambulance when ready. A loud bang came and away I went. Ten miles [sixteen kilometres] later I stopped to discharge my patients, and this poor fellow was still sitting on the bedpan. I still don't know who hit the side of the vehicle.

When V-E Day came in May 1945, Marjory followed the rule on alcohol consumption and drank a bottle of champagne with two young officers. It was most surely "under exceptional circumstances"! It was November 1945 before Marjory came home on the *Queen Elizabeth*. With her war over, she left the Red Cross.

Marjory later married an ex-member of the RCAF by the name of Hall, but their marriage ended in divorce and Marjory returned to Ottawa. She worked for three years in the Senate as a secretary and typist. Today, Marjory is an active member of the Ottawa Red Cross Blood Transfusion service.

A DFC in Hollywood

Ron Emberg's story almost escaped me. He died in 1991, but a friend of his, Bruce Beatty, provided me with a videotape and Ron's log book. With these two items I was able to put together the story of this remarkable Ottawa veteran.

Ron began his RCAF career at Number 2 ITS in Regina in July 1940. Two months later he was at Windsor Mills, Quebec, learning to fly the Fleet Finch, and upon graduation he went to Uplands (Ottawa) to fly the Yale. Ron went through the training system quickly. With less than a year in uniform, he went to England in March 1941. On 21 April he first flew a Hurricane, which would be his aircraft for the next seventeen months. In June Ron trained at 56 OTU, Sutton Bridge, and one month later he was a qualified pilot in the rank of sergeant. His first of many squadrons was 402 Squadron, RCAF. Just twenty days after his arrival at the squadron, he carried out his first sweep over occupied France.

Reading Ron's log book leaves one breathless. This young Canadian went on mission after dangerous mission, often escorting bombers to Lille, France. On 15 October 1941, he flew his "height test to 33,500 feet" (10,200 metres). Later in the month he was to change the course of his career, for on 17 October he "flew with a 500 lb bomb" slung under the Hurricane fuselage. It was the start of his conversion to the Hurri-bomber, and he would soon be attacking shipping and targets in France. On 4 November he was "put into A Flight and flew to France to bomb a German airfield."

The names of friends killed, missing or wounded start to appear in rapid succession. At the end of 1941, the log book notes "367 flying hours", and in January 1942 Ron was promoted to flight sergeant. The next month contains this entry:

16 Feb 1942. Squadron attacked—6 destroyers near
Brest. Sunk 1, damaged 3 others. Met 3 109Fs [German
Messerschmitt fighters] on way. Shot one down in sea.
Two got on my tail, shook them, but plane damaged.
Crash landed near Plymouth, [England].

WO2 Ron Emberg in England, May 1942.

Four weeks later Ron was promoted to warrant officer second class (WO2) and posted to 175 Squadron, RAF, at Warnwell. April proved to be an eventful month for WO2 Ron Emberg. On the 6th, his log book notes, "22 years old today." Just days later, 175 Squadron put on a demonstration for the army; tragically, one of the pilots added to the team at the last moment "mistook spectators for target and killed 20 and wounded 60". At the inquiry, several senior RAF officers were fired for not allowing all pilots to take part in the rehearsal. On 30 April, Ron was leading B Flight on a shipping attack. The log book entry is cryptic:

Squad attacked 3 destroyers and 1 merchant cruiser. Blue and Green Sections set largest destroyer on fire and it is probably sunk. My section put all Ack-Ack guns out of action before dropping bombs—24 Spitfires escorted us—8 Hurris. Net result—1 destroyer on fire. ... Only plane damaged was mine. Rudder controls shot away, flaps shot practically off and large hole in starboard wing beside cockpit.

Despite the damage, Ron managed to get his aircraft back to England, though not to Warnwell. Undaunted, he hitched a ride back to his station in an Anson, as it "was going my way".

May 1942 was equally busy, with the only respite eight days leave near the end of the month. On 30 May, Ron was told he had been awarded the DFC. The video provides a detailed account of how he earned the medal:

We were scrambled to find some German ships that had been sighted in the Channel. We crossed about 200 feet [60 metres] above the water to stay below their radar. The sun was shining so we were in luck. As soon as we sighted them we flew toward the sun, then turned with the sun behind us; this would make it harder for the Germans to shoot at us. We commenced a shallow dive from 1,500 feet [460 metres]. I was leading the squadron in the attack. The destroyer put itself between us and the merchantman. I called on the radio and said that I and my number two would attack the destroyer. The rest of the squadron took on the rest of the ships simultaneously, thus keeping all the German gunners occupied. By the time I had reached the target I was at deck level right amidships. At the last second I released my bombs and pulled up and turned sideways to go between the ship's masts. The belly of my aircraft was in plain view of one of the merchant ships and I saw the tracer coming toward me. I heard a bang, one hell of a crash, then I started to climb, and as I looked back the destroyer blew up, I must have hit the magazine. My number two saw the bombs hit the deck right by the bridge. He pulled up to avoid the blast from my bombs.

I was heading back to England when I realized the wind was coming in on me. The side of the cockpit had been destroyed, there was a large hole in my starboard wing. My right leg was numb and I was sure it had been blown off. I reached for my scarf and put it around the calf and tied it tight. I dared not look down for fear of fainting if I saw the stump all bleeding. As I came in to land in England my number two called me on the radio and said not to use my flaps, for the starboard one had gone. When I landed I checked my leg: nothing missing, just numb from the crack I had taken from the explosion that tore away the right side of my aircraft.

Ron was involved in two attacks on shipping in June, with good results. Losses of friends continued with "F/L H gone west" and PO H killed" entered in the log book. Ron was commissioned on 29 July to the rank of pilot officer.

On 19 August, Ron flew three sorties over Dieppe during the infamous raid. He was shot down, but managed to parachute into the bridgehead. Along with many Canadian soldiers, he was swimming away from the carnage on shore when he was picked up by a Polish destroyer, which took him back to England. Ron got back to Warnwell the next day. Seven nights later, the indefatigable Canadian "attacked 4 merchantmen, 1 sunk, 1 probably, 2 damaged".

In September Ron was posted to another RAF Squadron—276 at Harrowbeer. He was now flying the Lysander and the Walrus on rescue missions. One of his last missions was on 17 October 1942, when he found a downed Wellington bomber: "The whole crew was dead except for the observer."

As the year ended, the powers that be decided that Ron was to return to Canada as a flying instructor. His first tour was at 1 OTU Bagotville. By March, he was signing his log book as a flying officer; he was also flying Ansons at the Bombing and Gunnery School at Mountain View, Ontario.

Ron's military career then took on a strange twist: He was sent to Hollywood as a technical advisor for the movies. In one—whose stars included Bing Crosby, Bob Hope, Frank Sinatra, Betty Gable and Harpo Marx—Ron "found himself in a mock-up of a cockpit with a filmed backdrop of sky, a smudge pot and a fan to simulate exhaust smoke." As part of the movie's promotion, Ron was Linda Darnell's escort. As Ron remarked, "War, at times, was hell."

With eighty missions behind him, a DFC and the war coming to an end, Ron closed his career flying various aircraft at 3 Communications Flight, St Hubert, Quebec. He had flown thirty-seven different aircraft types, including five marks of Hurricane. Ron left the air force at war's end and worked at various jobs in Ottawa until his death from cancer in 1991.

Tank Destroyer in North Africa

Unlike many of the others in these stories, Allan Simpson was already a military man before the war began. He served in the cavalry—the Strathconas—from 1935 to 1938. After a short break, he left Canada to join the RAF as a pilot.

In December 1939, Allan was flying the Lysander reconnaissance aircraft in 13 Squadron, RAF, supporting the British Army. During the German advance through the Low Countries and into France, Allan's squadron was part of the steady withdrawal to Dunkirk. One time, he was chased by two German fighters and had to dive right down "to the deck [sea level] to avoid being shot down".

By May 1940, it was obvious that the British Expeditionary Force was going to be driven into the English Channel. Allan found a battered Lysander and, with the help of some groundcrew, managed to con his flight commander into letting him fly it back to England. Allan recalls his sadness at having to leave the French behind on 22 May 1940 when he left French soil.

In 1941, Allan accepted a transfer to the Middle East in the place of a married pilot who did not want to leave England. He sailed from Liverpool to Freetown, South Africa, by troopship and then went by sea and air through the Congo to Cairo. Allan's story with 6 Squadron, RAF, is recounted in Lloyd Hunt's **We Happy Few.**

In Egypt, 6 Squadron was converting to the Hurricane II-D. "It was armed with two .303 machine guns and a pair of 40 mm Vickers guns. ... The 40 mm shells could penetrate the 20 mm armour plate on a German Mark 3 tank." Allan explained how their training had to be rushed, but in the end he and one other pilot got to a ninety per cent accuracy level on the target.

Allan's first mission with 6 Squadron was on 8 June 1942:
> Our targets were in the area of Bir Hacheim, where the
> Free French under General Koenig were surrounded. ...
> As we neared the target, we dove to pick up speed and
> attacked from about 1,000 yards [900 metres] at ten feet
> [three metres] off the deck. (Hunt, **We Happy Few**)

The Germans fired at the attacking Hurricanes and an explosive bullet came through Allan's windshield. "It burst a few inches in front of my chest." Allan was hit in his right arm, plus splinters entered his chest and lodged in his back. As Allan recalls, "I was hit and saw blood on my shirt; I assumed I was mortally wounded." Nonetheless, Allan managed to take on another Mark 3 tank and a truck. He then decided to get back over no-man's land. He barely made it, as the plane's engine started to run rough and "hot glycol sprayed into the cockpit". Bailing out was just a matter of time. In Allan's words,

> I started at about 1,000 feet [305 metres] ... [and] jettisoned the side panel. I had already let the canopy go at Bir Hacheim. Then I attempted to get out onto the wing, but the slipstream was too strong. I throttled back and trimmed the nose up, and got out on the starboard side. I was standing facing the tail, holding on to the back corner of the cockpit with my right hand and grasping the ripcord handle [parachute release] with my left. ... By this time I was at about 500 feet [150 metres]. ... I jumped sideways ... as the tailplane passed me. ... I pulled the cord. ... I was on the ground [in seconds] and lay there on the sand looking up at the sky.

Allan stripped off his shirt and could see metal pieces half buried in his chest. "Then, while I was examining myself, I must have run out of adrenalin. The pain hit me."

Within a very short time a British Army truck came to his rescue, and then an ambulance arrived "driven by E.T. Williams of the Royal Army Service Corps". Allan was taken to the Field Dressing Station at El Adem, given first aid and taken back to Tobruk by ambulance. After five days he was flown out in a Royal Australian Air Force plane, arriving in Cairo on 14 June. Four months later Allan was flying again with the 6 Squadron Training Flight at Shandur, north of Suez on the Canal.

Allan next went to Rhodesia and became a flying instructor on Oxfords. He returned to England in 1944 to serve as a staff pilot on Ansons. Later, while he was converting to Mosquitos, he requested a transfer to the RCAF. The request was approved, and in light of his long time away from Canada he was repatriated in 1945.

After the war, Allan remained in the RCAF. He worked variously in Public Relations, Intelligence and, in 1951 in Japan and Korea, Photo Interpretation. Allan flew his last sortie in Korea with the United States Air Force. After eight years on the Pinetree line (a radar line in northern Canada), Allan retired from the air force in 1964.

Since his "retirement", Allan has worked as a life insurance and investments

F/L Allan Simpson with 6 Squadron RAF in Egypt, 1942.

agent, a supervisor of programs at Ottawa City Hall and a management analyst with the Department of Supply and Services. He is currently employed with Midland Walwyn in Ottawa.

Allan has been a prolific writer since his military retirement. He is the author of **We Few,** fighter pilot stories from the Second World War and Korea, and has contributed to Les Allison's **Canadians in the Royal Air Force,** Bruce Barrymore Halpenny's **Fight for the Sky** and Lloyd Hunt's **We Happy Few.** He has also written for the **Financial Post** and **Reader's Digest.** Allan Simpson was president of the Canadian Fighter Pilots Association from 1985 to 1987.

Master Tunneller in The Great Escape

Wally Floody of Toronto had a very short career as a fighter pilot, but his experiences as a POW truly deserve to be told.

Wally joined the RCAF in 1940 and received his wings at Dunnville, Ontario. In due course he became a member of 401 RCAF Fighter Squadron at Biggin Hill on the outskirts of London. On 27 October 1941, "a very bad day for 401 Squadron, when six pilots were shot down," Wally bailed out of his Spitfire and became a POW.

After interrogation at Dulag Luft in Frankfurt, Wally was sent to Stalag Luft I at Barth, on the Baltic Sea coast, and finally to Stalag Luft III in East Germany, the scene of the Great Escape. Over 2,500 RCAF POWs were held at Stalag Luft III, but they were incarcerated in several different camps and mixed with airmen of all Allied air forces except Russia's. Three and a half years would pass before Wally would finally see freedom, which came at the end of the war in 1945.

When he was asked if it was his duty to try to escape, Wally replied, "It wasn't just your duty; you did your very best to get out." Those sentiments were felt by many at Stalag Luft III, as author Arthur Durand describes:

> Paul Brickhill's book **The Great Escape** and the movie based on his book have made the name Stalag Luft III synonymous with escape. ... No other camp activity so exhibited the prisoners' ingenuity, dedication, and sense of community spirit and purpose. ... By the time the prisoners were transferred from Barth to Stalag Luft III in April 1942, they had adopted escape as an operational mission. (Durand, **Stalag Luft III**)

Into this situation appeared this six-foot-four Canadian who did not want to remain behind the wire. Wally had already established himself at Barth as a proven tunneller, so the Escape Committee, or X Organization as it was called, soon chose Wally to plan and execute the Stalag Luft III escape. X Organization planned to dig three tunnels—Tom, Dick and Harry—so they could organize a mass escape. Only Harry would be completed. Because Wally had worked for a while in a gold mine at Kirkland Lake, Ontario, he became the master tunneller.

The problems faced by Wally and his fellow inmates would have daunted lesser men. The camp had been built by the Luftwaffe, and the guards were also from the German air force, thus airmen were looking after their own prisoners. The barbed wire, watch towers, roving patrols and ferrets (guards detailed to look constantly for signs of escape) were effective deterrents. The huts were built on pillars so that the only part that touched the ground was the chimney base, which was well secured in an excavation to withstand the weight of the bricks and mortar. To make escape more difficult, all the trees surrounding the camp had been cleared, and frequent calls for *appell* made all prisoners line up and be counted (a POW's time was never his own). To counter these interruptions when serious escape plans were in progress, the X Organization produced stooges, whose continuous moving about during the *appell* made a proper count impossible.

The escape plans needed a host of auxiliary skill groups. Besides lookouts and tunnellers, the operation needed carpenters, air circulation operators in the tunnels, document forgers, tailors to make civilian style clothing from dyed uniforms, people to gather and hoard food from the Red Cross parcels, and on and on. Still, of the 1,500 prisoners in the compound, only a small proportion knew about or worked on the tunnel. The fewer that knew, the lower the chance of a security breach.

Perhaps the most treacherous job was that of the *penguins,* a job that had to be carried out in the open under the watchful eyes of the guards. The soil excavated had to be moved to the tunnel start point and brought to the surface. There, it was hidden between walls, above ceilings—anywhere it could be. The penguins took part in this dirt spreading. Dirt-filled bags were fastened inside the men's trouser legs, and as they walked around the camp—especially in the countless gardens cared for by the prisoners—they loosened the necks of the bags, so the dirt was discreetly spread about above ground.

Tom, Dick and Harry all led from beneath the living quarters out toward the perimeter wire. In the case of Harry, the tunnel was over 350 feet (107 metres) in length, twenty-eight inches in diameter and at a depth of over 30 feet (9 metres). It took about fifteen months to

Wally Floody, 23 years old, May 24, 1941.

complete the tunnel. Naturally, the tunnellers ran into different types of earth and rocks as they worked. Says Wally, "The soft sandy red soil was better and it was worse." On the negative side, the soft soil meant a higher chance of a tunnel cave-in and the different colour was harder to conceal on the surface. On the positive, it was easier to dig, which meant the men could go faster, reducing the time when discovery was possible.

When a tunnel crew went down, they stayed there all day, digging at the face, moving the sand back in the small carts, transferring loads every 100 feet (30 metres) to the enlarged areas (named Piccadilly and Leicester Square as in London's subway system), bagging the sand and moving the bags to the surface. Every foot of the tunnel had to be shored up using bed boards from the 1,500 bunks. To throw the Germans off the scent and keep up the supply of shoring, the men also burned bed boards in their stoves; new boards were brought in and the tunnel progressed. Wally knew first-hand the importance of that shoring: when he ignored the lack of it, he was almost the victim of a cave-in. "I got too far ahead of the shoring and my helper had to pull me out from under the sand. It was a close call."

The entrance was under the stove in hut 104. As Wally explained, "The chimney flu drew the stale air out of the tunnel and fresh air went into the tunnel." The method used to lift the stove, remove the tile, expose the tunnel shaft and cover it again could be done in seconds.

What is essential to understand is the logistical difficulty of digging a tunnel under the very noses of the vigilant German guards. In Durand's excellent account, he gives the details:

> One ton of sand was excavated for every three and a half feet [one metre] of forward progress. Approximately eighteen thousand individual trips were made by the penguins ... from the traps to the dispersal areas ... for each day's work was sixty pounds per minute for a period of one hour. ... Fifty bed boards were supplied daily for shoring, Harry took over two thousand. ... Thirty Klim [dried milk] cans were needed each day for the air lines. ... Each week the parcels officer had to acquire three hundred feet [ninety metres] of string, which was braided into rope for hauling trolleys. ... Eight hundred feet [245 metres] of single-strand, insulated, damp-proof electric wire was stolen from German workmen ... to power tunnel lights [before this, margarine lamps with string wicks were used].

Spring was coming, and with it the time for the escape. Escapees would be able to survive living off the land and travelling on rail cars—"riding the rods". Wally explained the different groups in the 200 men who were chosen to break out using Harry:

> The first group would be in civilian clothing, have full documentation and have the ability to get by in a language other than English. The next group (called the hard-assers) would be in uniform and would try to live by their wits to escape. The final destination was England, but routes were to Spain, Switzerland or even Russia to link up with the advancing Red Army. Lots were drawn to determine the order in which one would go into the tunnel. The very first men had to dig through the final few feet of frozen ground and the roots from the nearby trees. The day chosen was 24 March 1944.

With everything almost ready, the tension, apprehension and fear grew. Two weeks before the break-out, Wally, George Harsh (the main security person), Peter Fanshawe (who directed sand disposal) and seventeen others were moved to another Stalag twenty miles [thirty-two kilometres] away at Bellaria. Wally says later, "We never did find out [if we had been detected], but they did have a pretty good shot at getting rid of key people on the escape committee."

The escape itself is a full story in its own right, but, in brief, things went from bad to worse. In Wally's own words,

> The first thing to go wrong was that it took longer to dig out those final few feet. In the tunnel were dozens of escapees and a few got claustrophobia. When the opening was made it was thirty feet [nine metres] short of the woods: the exit hole was in plain sight. The escape began and then at about number eighty-one a German guard discovered what was happening and sounded the alarm. The rest crawled back into hut 104 with their spirits very low. Four were captured at the mouth of the tunnel.

Of the seventy-six men who escaped, only three got back to England. Hitler was so furious that he ordered a *Grossfahndung*, the highest priority search order in the land. Wally recalls, "They even called everyone back from leave." The confusion created by those seventy-six prisoners at large was, in Wally's words, "as great as if two Allied parachute divisions had landed on German soil." Hitler then issued the infamous Sagan Order, which ordered more than half of the escapees, when caught, to be shot—or, as Wally says, murdered. Among this gallant group of fifty men were twenty Britishers, six Canadians, five Australians, five Polish, four South Africans, two New Zealanders, two Norwegians, one Argentinian, one Belgian, one Czech, one Frenchman, one Greek and one Lithuanian. The Canadians were

> F/Lt Henry Birkland a pilot, age 25 from Calgary, Alberta. F/Lt Gordon Kidder a navigator, age 29 from St Catharines, Ontario. F/Lt Patrick Langford an air observer, age 24 from Victoria, B.C. F/Lt George

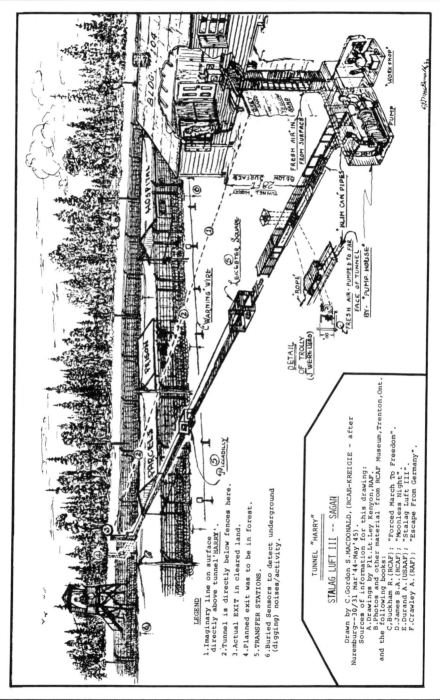

LEGEND

1. Imaginary line on surface directly above tunnel 'HARRY'.
2. Tunnel is directly below fences here.
3. Actual EXIT in cleared land.
4. Planned exit was to be in forest.
5. TRANSFER STATIONS.
6. Buried Sensors to detect underground (digging) noises/activity.

TUNNEL "HARRY"

STALAG LUFT III -- SAGAN

Drawn by C.Gordon S.MACDONALD,(RCAF-KREIGIE - after Nuremburg--30/31 Mar'44-May'45).
Sources of information for this drawing:
  A.Drawings by Flt.Lt.Ley Kenyon,RAF.
  B.Photos and other material from RCAF Museum,Trenton,Ont.
and the following books:
  C.Buckham R.(RCAF); "Forced March To Freedom".
  D.James B.A.(RCAF); "Moonless Night".
  E.Durand A.(USAAF); "Stalag Luft III".
  F.Crawley A.(RAF); "Escape From Germany".

McGill an air observer, age 24 from Toronto. F/Lt James Wernham an air observer, age 27, from Winnipeg, Manitoba. F/Lt George Wiley a pilot, age 22 from Windsor, Ontario. (Commonwealth War Graves Commission Register)

All six have their ashes buried in Poznan Old Garrison Cemetery, Commonwealth Section, Poland.

In 1989, when asked about missing the two chances in three of being caught and then shot, Wally said, "Every day of living is a bonus."

Wally was not released until July 1945. His long three and one half years out of circulation was over at last. From 1947 to 1950 he was in business in England, after which he moved back to Toronto, where he and radio announcer Herb May operated a two-plane air service out of Toronto Island Airport. In the summer of 1962, Wally was the technical advisor for the film, **The Great Escape**, with Steve McQueen and James Garner.

Wally always felt a great deal of compassion for his POW friends. For two years in their Scarborough Bluffs home, he and his wife Betty looked after George Harsh, who was in a wheelchair. Wally and his friend Don Morrison spent many hours with other incapacitated ex-POWs of the Germans. In 1989, Wally died suddenly after attending a reunion of POWs in Ottawa.

Tail Gunner in a Halifax

Tony Little's first encounter with the military lasted just one day. He joined the Canadian Army on 5 May 1941, and one day later was released when it was discovered that he was under age. In due course he was allowed to join the Royal Canadian Ordnance Corps as a boy-soldier (reduced pay and no overseas service).

Tony trained as an armament technician, but one day "while walking down Queen Street in Ottawa, I saw a .50-calibre machine gun in the window of the RCAF recruiting office." Drawn by the weapon, he went in and asked to transfer from the army to air force. Eventually, his request was granted.

Tony did not mind having to repeat the basic training, "but worse than that I had to have all the needles again". The army had given him a complete armful of needles when they released him the week before, but because his documents were lost, the RCAF repeated the pleasure.

At RCAF Manning Depot, Tony went down a long hall passing countless young men all trying to become pilots and navigators. He couldn't see the attraction. When his turn came, Tony said, "I want to be an air gunner and nothing else." The RCAF sent him to a ground school for air gunners at the University of Montreal for an upgrading in mathematics and physics, plus aircraft recognition. The next phase was in Prince Edward Island at 10 Bombing and Gunnery School, flying in the Bollinbroke aircraft. By 10 March 1944, after fourteen hours and forty minutes in the air, Tony was qualified on the .303 machine gun and gained his air gunner half-wing. His training continued at Three Rivers, Quebec, where the aircrew was put through a six-week commando course in which escape and evasion were emphasized. Finally, they were considered ready to go overseas. The British Commonwealth Air Training Plan qualified 25,611 RCAF air gunners, most of them to serve in Bomber Command.

Tony sailed aboard the *Empress of Scotland,* and on arrival was sent to Gloucester instead of Bournemouth (the usual manning pool, which was in the south of England and was one huge armed camp ready for D-Day). Some of the air gunners went directly to squadrons, but Tony went to 22 OTU near Stratford-on-Avon for three more months of training. Then the crews formed: "We were all in a room together and we picked out each other until we had the right numbers and skills." Tony ended up in an all-Canadian crew as the tail gunner in a Halifax heavy bomber.

The first Halifax Tony went up in had problems right from the start. As Tony recalls,

> We took off one day in a Halifax II, and as we got airborne I called up the skipper [pilot] and said from my seat in the rear turret I could see there was a lot of smoke coming from one of the starboard engines. The flight engineer said that it wasn't smoke but high octane gasoline. One of the groundcrew had not replaced the filler cap. We did a circuit and the pilot cut the engine closest to the spewing gasoline then cut the other starboard engine. At that point one of the port engines cut out. We were in deep trouble. The bombardier called out directions to the pilot to line us up with the runway. The second port engine cut back in and we made one of the most frightening landings I ever was party to. After a quick refuelling and the cap made secure, we took off for a cross-country trip.

Four days in January 1945 were to produce events that would mature Flight Sergeant Tony Little, then age nineteen, in a hurry. On the 13th was Tony's first air raid on Saarbrucken, and his first sight of German night fighters deep into German territory. The next night was another raid, and on the 15th there was a training trip over the United Kingdom. Tony's squadron, 420 RCAF, was keeping the crews busy and training them as fast as possible.

The third raid, on 16 January 1945, was to be Tony's last. The raid was to be a deep penetration to Magdeburg near Berlin, but things did not go as planned. After crossing the North Sea, they did not hit landfall at the correct place, and the navigator realized they were off track. A few rapid checks showed that the compass was inaccurate.

The navigator managed to get them back on track quickly. They knew they would be late over the target, but as this was a large raid, they would fit in with one of the last waves of bombers. By the time they arrived, the target was in flames. The bombardier decided they should fly a diversion before making the final run in, and, despite all the problems, they dropped the bombs only seven minutes late from the time ordered. Then things went very wrong:

We had company. The bombardier looked out of the perspex in the nose and I agreed with him, what we could see were all Ju-88s, night fighters. We left the target area, nose down, going as fast as we could. Just south of Hanover they had flak and fighters. For about an hour, myself and the upper gunner tried to beat off the fighters, but the Halifax was hit on the port side and the port wing was on fire. There were three or four fighters attacking us and dropping flares. We could not get away. The upper gunner and I were firing at an attacker when the skipper ordered us to bail out, because the fire was spreading. I was now in real trouble, for my parachute chest pack was in the fuselage, not on me. I got myself turned around, got my 'chute on and then opened the rear gunner's hatch. I tried to leave, but my feet in fleece-lined flying boots got caught. The plane was getting lower and lower. Those "one-hour seconds" were clicking off—a decision had to be made. I wasn't scared: I was too numb to be scared. I yanked the ripcord as my torso cleared the hatch, and the pull of the chute ripped me out of the aircraft. The soles of my boots were torn off and left in the turret. I came down into a frozen ploughed field, lying on my back. I can still see the stars—there were millions of them, as I had the wind knocked out of me. I crawled into a nearby pig sty. The next thing I remember was waking up in a farmer's kitchen with two German soldiers hovering over me. One soldier helped me walk some distance, and I ended up in a prison cell.

The days went by, and Tony passed through one camp after another. Every trick was used to get the young flight sergeant to divulge information. In the second camp, who was there but the upper gunner

Sgt. Tony Little on graduation, Mt. Pleasant, P.E.I., March 10, 1944.

from Tony's Halifax, Ken Reid. Ken had two very black eyes, and Tony thought their captors had beaten him. Ken thought much the same when he saw his friend Tony with dried blood all over his face. For both men, however, the wounds had been caused by their exits from the doomed Halifax. Then, "in came our navigator, the old man of thirty-three," still carrying his Mae West and wearing the brown "teddy bear" flying suit. The three crew members were taken to Frankfurt by train and then by streetcar to Dulag Luft, where they remained for ten days in solitary confinement.

The prison that was to be "home" for Tony was Stalag 13D near Nuremburg. Run by the German army, Stalag 13D contained as many nationalities as there were Allies. Many of the POWs were "a lot of U.S. Army taken at Bastogne. They had been marched for miles in their bare feet, with hands frozen onto their helmets. They were in bad shape." Tony was in a barrack block built for sixty-five, but it contained over 200 POWs. Among the 200 were all of Tony's crew mates except for the pilot and flight engineer. (It was not until Tony was back in England that he learned that the pilot and flight engineer must have been killed in the crash.) The food situation was grim, too: "Eight to fourteen would share a small loaf of black bread. On one occasion we were given cheese; when it didn't kill us we saw no more—it was given to the German civilians."

More and more prisoners were brought in, and with one of them a hidden radio (Sammy) got past the guards. The advance of the Allies could now be tracked. Tony and his fellow airmen had been told not to plan to escape, as the risk of being killed by their own side as friendly troops advanced was too high.

Tony and many others were moved by train to Stalag 7A at Mooseburg. It was there, on 29 April 1945, that General George Patton drove up in his jeep, followed by an American tank, and liberated Stalag 7A. [He was searching for his captured son-in-law.]

In due course, the ex-POWs were moved to Ingolstadt airfield for a flight back to England. Tony remembers dropping to the tarmac there when the U.S. Army anti-aircraft gunners suddenly started firing over their heads. The trigger-happy gunners thought they had sighted an enemy aircraft, but what they shot down was a Mosquito bomber; fortunately, the crew survived.

Tony sailed for Canada on the *Ile de France*, landing in Halifax on 13 July 1945. When he arrived home in Ottawa he was broke, without even enough money for the streetcar. But Tony's uniform was money enough for the motorman, and Tony was soon home.

Tony left the RCAF on 30 October 1945, but in a very short time he was back in the air as an air gunner for the RAF. After three years he returned to Canada, where he joined the Department of Supply and Services in the armament section. He retired from the Government of Canada in 1980. He is now a consultant and lives in Nepean, Ontario. Tony Little is the president of the Ottawa chapter of the RCAF Prisoner of War Association.

Chapter Four

The Rushtons and the War

The population of Canada between 1939 and 1945 varied between eleven and twelve million. Well over two million made a direct contribution to the war in uniform and by working in industry, government, or on associated tasks. This amounted to total mobilization for war on the Home Front because virtually everyone else in the population was a dependent or unavailable for "essential" war work.

(Douglas and Greenhous, **Out of the Shadows***)*

As this book unfolded and each interview ended, I had the feeling that the family story in each case was being overlooked. The chance to tell a family story came from a casual conversation with a neighbour in Nepean. The Rushton family had four sons and two sons-in-law who amongst them served in all three arms of the service: Royal Canadian Navy (RCN), the Canadian Army and the Royal Canadian Air Force (RCAF). What is remarkable is that all six

Louis Rushton. Queen's Own 4th Hussars, Dublin, Ireland in 1899 prior to his departure for South Africa as a corporal.

Paul Rushton, England, 1942.

saw action, all six returned at the end of the war, none of the six had been wounded and none had been made a prisoner of war.

In 1939, sixty-seven-year-old widower Louis Rushton was living at 24 Chatham Avenue in Toronto with his five sons and two daughters. His wife, Edna, had died two years earlier. A staunch supporter of all things British, Louis had served in the Boer War as a corporal in the Queen's Own 4th Hussars. One of his regimental officers had been Winston Churchill, and Louis named his youngest son after the man who would later become Britain's wartime prime minister.

Winston (Wint), Louis's youngest boy, was ten years old when Canada declared war on 10 September 1939. He remembers the day clearly:

> That afternoon when I came home from school I went through the front door and I could hear a lot of voices in the kitchen. My father was there and so was Paul, who was in his army uniform, as was my sister Margaret's boyfriend Les Bentley. There was an army rifle in the corner. Paul, who was a corporal, was helping Les with his uniform and his webbing. I asked Dad what was happening, and he said Les had signed up and Paul was showing him what to do. Dad also said my brother Wilfred had phoned to say that he was leaving the Canadian National Railways for the Royal Canadian Navy Voluntary Reserve [RCNVR]. Mary's boyfriend Ed Smith had decided to join up with Wilfred.

Within the next two weeks, Wint's eldest brother Lou had joined the RCAF. This only left brother Harold and Wint out of uniform, and Harold soon changed that by joining the RCNVR.

Life at 24 Chatham changed in a big way. Only Wint, Mary and Margaret were at home with their father. The others came home between training courses and before going overseas. Mary married Ed in Toronto on 13 October 1939, before he left to go overseas with the RCN. Margaret and Les were married on 9 December 1939, two weeks

Harold Rushton, 1943.

before Les left for England with the Royal Canadian Army Service Corps. Paul was selected for officer training at Brockville from the rank of sergeant, and then he also left for England. Lou completed his navigator training at Chatham, New Brunswick; as a sergeant, he also left for England. Wilfred, training in naval gunnery, became part of a ship's company on North Atlantic convoy patrol.

Determined to do their bit for the war effort, Mary and Margaret found jobs in munition plants—Mary at John Inglis, Colt Browning Division; Margaret at GECO Munitions filling bombs. Wint continued impatiently with his schoolwork.

By the time he was thirteen and in grade eight, Wint was almost fully grown. He asked his teacher to sign the appropriate form so that he could enlist, for he knew his father would not sign. Looking at Wint's eager but childish face, the teacher refused, saying, "You should stay home with your Dad." Wint had to accept this blow, although he badly wanted to be in uniform like his four brothers and two brothers-in-law.

Company Sergeant Major Les Bentley, RCASC, England, 1943.

How was it for Wint's young relatives overseas? Wilfred was aboard HMCS *Teme* when she was torpedoed on 29 March 1945 in the English Channel. One of his shipmates was killed by the blast, and Wilfred was part of the burial party at Falmouth where HMCS *Teme* was towed, never to sail again. Paul served as a captain with the Royal Canadian Army Service Corps as part of Canadian Armoured Divisions in Italy and Northwest Europe. Lou was commissioned in the RCAF in November 1942; much to his father's joy, Lou was spoken to by King George VI while he was inspecting Lou's squadron in May 1943. Harold's career took him to HMCS *Carleton* and *Cornwallis*; as a stoker in HM*CS Meon*, he saw action in the English Channel. Les Bentley served overseas with the Royal Canadian Army Service Corps, and Ed Smith saw service in the North Atlantic.

When the war ended, the young men came home to a different Canada:

> Home to what? A new Canada, certainly, with new ideas, morals, perceptions formed while they were away, a different way of life into which they had had no input. These millions in uniform, whether serving in war zones or in Canada, had

Lou Rushton and his wife Eileen leaving for their honeymoon on March 28, 1943, England.

existed apart from the nation. Now it was their turn to make their voices heard. (Broadfoot, **The Veterans' Years**)

Lou, the eldest, managed a grocery store for a while and then rejoined the RCAF, serving overseas and at various radar stations such as Edgar and Foymount. Now retired, he lives in Pickering, Ontario, with his English war bride, Eileen. Paul went into business in the Toronto area and now he and his wife live in Dorset, Ontario. Wilfred did well as a trucker; he died in Toronto on 10 January 1989, and his widow Mary lives in

Ed Smith (left) Wilfred Rushton (right) in Toronto—home on leave.

Scarborough, Ontario. Harold went into the printing trade and he now lives in Mississauga, Ontario. Ed Smith was in the trucking business until he died in Toronto on 10 July 1982; Mary (Rushton) Smith lives in Newmarket, Ontario. Les Bentley became an ironworker in both Canada and the United States; he died on 6 April 1988, and his widow Margaret (Rushton) Bentley lives in Scarborough. Wint Rushton has his own contracting business in Nepean, Ontario; his wife Velma died in 1990.

Louis Rushton died in 1960 at eighty-eight years of age, the proud father and father-in-law of all these ordinary heroes.

Epilogue: The Veteran

And now that to-morrow had come—a to-morrow called peace. ...
Perhaps in the months to come will that fabulous "to-morrow" really
be to-day—a day when all the bells and voices of our great memories
shall ring out, cry out, peal, and shout, in one wild tumultuous song of
thanksgiving ... and it shall swell and reverberate through our beings
in unforgettable strength and beauty so that we shall know that to-day
has come, and all those black yesterdays are forever left behind.
(Patterson, A Short History of the Tenth Canadian Infantry Brigade)

As I interviewed the people in this book, I became engrossed in that special breed of people who are our veterans. Most of these people were heartbreakingly young when they went off to war, and they lived a lifetime of memories in just months. For some, the memories are so indelible that their voices changed and tears glistened in their tired eyes as they recalled wartime events. For so many the war was their most exciting time of life. Peacetime has seemed tame in comparison.

The authors of **Champagne Navy** wrote, "War has been said to breed but one virtue: a spirit of comradeship and community rarely seen in saner times." That statement was confirmed for me in the words of one soldier I interviewed, who said, "Each month I read 'Last Post' in **Legion Magazine** to see who has passed away from that special group I served with in the war."

I often sit and watch people in shopping centres, airports, bus terminals or just walking along the sidewalks of Ottawa. I can pick out our veterans, walking erect, moustache trimmed, service button in lapel and, in November, in Legion dress selling poppies. All of them have a tale to tell, but many would sooner forget the war. When I am in uniform they may open up and say a little more, but many secrets will remain locked forever in older hearts and minds.

The one group of veterans who display their vintage ribbons every day are the members of the Corps of Commissionaires, who serve until their own Last Post sounds. Three years ago a veteran of the First World War rode the bus with me many times; he died on the job with "the Corps". They are a noble group of veterans, whose close ties with the uniform make them unique.

Why did I stop writing and not include more "ordinary heroes" in my book? I felt I had pushed my cause as far as I could. There were other stories that I would have liked to have included, but many veterans simply wanted to forget, and I had to respect their wishes. Also, sadly but not surprisingly, some of the veterans I wanted to interview passed away before I could meet with them. It is difficult to read a book, a war diary, an airman's log book or a wartime personal file and try to reach out to someone who is no long alive. I have tried, and many wartime friends have given me personal accounts so that an ordinary hero's story has appeared in print. May my minute sample of stories serve to tell of some of those ordinary heroes who stood tall for Canada at a time when personal sacrifice for country was a way of life.

The November 1991 issue of Reader's Digest included an article called "War and Peace". In it were these moving words:

> Within a generation, we will encounter a Remembrance Day devoid of personal recollections of the [war]. ... Is there any point in singling out November 11? ... A society with any sense of its own history must carry forward the memory ... or condemn itself to learn nothing from history and thus repeat old mistakes.

These final pages are my tribute to the men and women of Canada who, in the years 1939 to 1945, put aside their own aspirations and gave their time and energy to their country, Canada. In these times of national unrest and uncertainty, human sacrifice in war for Canada is being forgotten. Every Canadian, every one of us, must ask ourselves this vital question:

> To save this world you asked this man to die. Would this man, could he see you now, ask why?

(Kohima war memorial, India)

Acknowledgements

The research for this book was done in less than two years. I used my own extensive military library for most of my research. People also loaned me books that had a direct bearing on their story. Each of the quotations I used from published sources is credited, but not footnoted. Instead, I have listed the bibliographic information in these acknowledgements. Personal quotations have been reproduced as written or as I taped them. I have resisted condensing or editing personal accounts, for this book is oral history; however, where there was a variance between memory and a published historical record, I used the latter.

As an amateur historian, I sought the help of three professionals from the Directorate of History, Department of National Defence: Michael Whitby read the chapter on the Royal Canadian Navy; Bill McAndrew, the Canadian Army; and Michael Bitten, the Royal Canadian Air Force. The final book is my responsibility; any errors rest entirely with me.

Some of the books I used deserve special mention and they are listed below, chapter by chapter.

Chapter One: The Royal Canadian Navy

Tony German, **The Sea Is at our Gates** (McLelland & Stewart, 1990). James Lamb, **On the Triangle Run** (Macmillan, 1986). Hal Lawrence, Victory at Sea (McLelland & Stewart, 1989). Marc Milner, **North Atlantic Run** (University of Toronto Press, 1985). Brian Nolan and Brian Street, **Champagne Navy** (Random House, 1991). Joseph Schull, **Far Distant Ships** (Stoddart, 1987, reprinted from 1950 version). Frederick Watt, **In All Respects Ready** (Prentice Hall, 1985). Once again I relied upon all three volumes of **Salty Dips** (Naval Officers' Associations of Canada, Ottawa Branch) for story leads and for personal accounts.

Chapter Two: The Canadian Army

The most helpful source is still the three-volume work on Canada's military history: C.P. Stacey, **Six Years of War**; G.W.H. Nicholson, **Canadians in Italy**; C.P. Stacey, **The Victory Campaign** (Queen's Printer, 1955, 1956 and 1960). Other books I used include the following titles: Robert Burhans, **The First Special Service Force** (Washington Infantry Journal Press, 1947). Daniel Dancock, **The D-Day Dodgers** (McLelland & Stewart, 1991). Department of National Defence, **The Canadians in Britain 1939-1944** (King's Printer, 1944). Department of National Defence, **From Pachino to Ortona** (King's Printer, 1944). John English, **The Canadian Army and the Normandy Campaign** (Praeger, 1991). W.B. Fraser, **Always a Strathcona** (Comprint, 1976). D.J. Goodspeed, **The Armed Forces of Canada 1867-1967** (Directorate of History, Department of National Defence, 1967). Howard Graham, **Citizen and Soldier** (McClelland and Stewart, 1987). Brereton Greenhous, **Centennial History of The Royal Canadian Dragoons-Dragoon** (Campbell Corp, 1983). Douglas How, **The 8th Hussars** (Maritime Publishing, 1964). George Kitching, **Mud and Green Fields** (Battleline Books, 1985). Lieutenant Colonel J.M. McAvity, **A Record of Achievement**, the official history of Lord Strathcona's Horse. Bill McNeil, **Voices of a War Remembered** (Doubleday, 1991). Jim Roberts, **The Canadian Summer** (University of Toronto Bookroom, 1981). Reg Roy, **The Canadians in Normandy** (Macmillan, 1984). C.P. Stacey, **Canada's Battle in Normandy** (King's Printer, 1946). "Our Unknown War Heroes", **Toronto Sun**, 30 November 1980. Bruce Tascona, **XII Manitoba Dragoons: A Tribute** (Friesen Printers, 1991). Carl Vincent, **No Reason Why** (Canada's Wings, 1981). Jeffery Williams, **Princess Patricia's Canadian Light Infantry** (Leo Cooper/Secker & Warburg, 1972). Larry Worthington, **The Spur and Sprocket** (Reeve Press, 1968). Larry Worthington, **Worthy** (T.H. Best, 1961). Colonel Mike Houghton loaned me three books on the Royal Canadian Regiment, and Colonel Strome Galloway provided input into "The Story of Two Royals". The classic on memoirs: C.P.Stacey, **A Date with History** (Deneau, 1982). Last but not least, an absolute treasure, John Marteinson, **We Stand on Guard: An illustrated history of the Canadian Army**, (Ovale [Tormont] Publications, 1992).

Chapter Three: The Royal Canadian Air Force

The wartime log books of aircrew members were of great help for they not only recorded dates and events but also other remarks, which added to the accounts. Bill Carr loaned me a book by Tony Spooner, **Warburton's War** (William Kimber, 1987), and it provided insight into photo reconnaissance in the Mediterranean. Jean Ellis, **Facepowder and Gunpowder** (S.J.R. Saunders, 1947). Hal Lawrence, **Victory at Sea** (McLelland & Stewart, 1989). M. Mitchell and F. Deacon, **641: A Story of the Canadian Red Cross Corps Overseas** provided good background for M. Hall's story. Alfred Houston, "Escape", **Maclean's**, 15 December 1944. Arthur Durand, **Stalag Luft III** and Paul Brickhill, **The Great Escape** assisted in the Wally Floody story. The details of the six RCAF members killed in the Great Escape were provided by Marlene Moffatt of the Canadian Agency, Commonwealth War Graves Commission.

Chapter Four: The Rushtons and the War

Barry Broadfoot, **The Veterans' Years** (Douglas & McIntyre, 1985). W.A.B. Douglas and Brereton Greenhous, **Out of the Shadows** (Oxford University Press, 1977).

Epilogue

Frances Day, **Memoirs—Women in War.** Brian Nolan and Brian Street, **Champagne Navy** (Random House, 1991). The quotes from "War and Peace", **Reader's Digest,** November 1991, and Major R.A. Patterson, **A Short History of the Tenth Canadian Infantry Brigade,** along with the epitaph from the Kohima Indian memorial, gave greater power to the final part of the book.

... and thanks to ...

My final acknowledgements go to George Hees, former Minister of Veterans Affairs Canada, for the foreword; Verne Murphy of Veterans Affairs Canada; Gordon MacDonald for the drawing of Tunnel Harry; Heather Ebbs, my editor, past president of the Freelance Editors' Association of Canada; Tim Gordon of General Store Publishing House Inc., of Burnstown, and all his staff past and present; and all those veterans who shared their stories with me.

I could not have produced the book without the patience, skill and understanding of my wife, Elaine, who suffered the results of my handwriting and the countless rewrites for this, my fifth book.

Index

About the Author

John Gardam was born in England in 1931, emigrated to Canada in 1946 and graduated from high school in British Columbia. He is a graduate of the University of Manitoba in history. Today, he is the Project Director for the Peacekeeping Monument, which is to be dedicated in October 1992 in Ottawa. A former officer in the Regular Force and present Reserve Officer in the Military, he is an avid amateur historian, with his interests being primarily in the First and Second World War.

John Gardam served overseas with the United Nations Emergency Force in Egypt in 1960 and 1961. After retiring from the Regular Force in 1984, he spent five years with the Canadian Agency Commonwealth War Graves Commission, returning to the Department of National Defence in 1989 to his current position. He has the distinction of being one of the few military persons to have received his third clasp for forty-two years of service. Colonel Gardam was made an officer of the Order of Military Merit in 1980.

Colonel Gardam lives with his wife, Elaine, in Nepean, Ontario. They have four sons and seven grandchildren.

For more copies of

ORDINARY HEROES

send $17.95 plus $3.00 for GST,
shipping and handling to:

GENERAL STORE PUBLISHING HOUSE
1 Main Street, Burnstown, Ontario, Canada, K0J 1G0

Telephone 1-800-465-6072
Facsimile (613) 432-7184

Korea Volunteer $17.95
Choco to A.I.F. $14.95
Valour On Juno Beach.................................... $14.95
Black Crosses Off My Wingtip $14.95
The Ridge.. $14.95
Trepid Aviator $17.95
The Wing and The Arrow $17.95
In The Line Of Duty (softcover)....................... $39.95
     hardcover.. $59.95
Dragons Of Steel $17.95
Charlie's Story... $14.95
One Of The Many... $14.95
Fifty Years After $14.95
The Canadian Peacekeeper $12.95
The Surly Bonds of Earth............................... $12.95
The Memory Of All That $14.95
No Time Off For Good Behaviour $14.95
To The Green Fields Beyond............................ $14.95
Time Remembered $14.95

For each copy, include $3.00 to cover GST, shipping and handling.
Make cheque or money order payable to:

GENERAL STORE PUBLISHING HOUSE

1 Main Steet, Burnstown, Ontario, Canada K0J 1G0